"Probably no theological challen͜g ͜ recover a worldview in which faith and science can relate constructively, informing and critiquing each other in the interest of helping humans find their place in God's universe. In writing *Trinity in Relation: Creation, Incarnation, and Grace in an Evolving Cosmos*, Gloria Schaab has done the theological community a great service. The text is comprehensive and informed by the very best science and theology available to us. Schaab demonstrates a masterful grasp of the theological and philosophical sources that have shaped Christianity. She is able to bring forth the deep value of that tradition while also pointing to insights and challenges from the natural and social sciences that can further the development of the Christian tradition and enhance its relevance today. This superbly written text is an excellent choice for upper-level undergraduate and graduate courses that explore the Trinity, the theology of God, Revelation, or the relationship between faith and science. I highly recommend this text."

—Dave Gentry-Akin, professor of Roman Catholic theology
Saint Mary's College of California

TRINITY
In Relation

Creation, Incarnation, and Grace in an Evolving Cosmos

GLORIA L. SCHAAB

Created by the publishing team of Anselm Academic.

Cover and interior art: *Strange Attractor*, by Margie Thompson

The scriptural quotations in this book are from the New American Bible with Revised New Testament and Revised Psalms. Copyright © 1991, 1986, and 1970 by the Confraternity of Christian Doctrine, Washington, D.C. Used by permission of the copyright owner. All rights reserved. No part of the New American Bible may be reproduced in any form without permission in writing from the copyright owner.

The excerpts on page 164, 224, 253, 263, 299, and 300 are from the English translation of the *Catechism of the Catholic Church* for use in the United States of America, second edition (*CCC*). Copyright © 1994 by the United States Catholic Conference, Inc.—Libreria Editrice Vaticana. English translation of the *Catechism of the Catholic Church*: Modifications from the *Editio Typica* copyright © 1997 by the United States Catholic Conference, Inc.—Libreria Editrice Vaticana.

Printed in the United States of America

7042

ISBN 978-1-59982-096-5

AUTHOR ACKNOWLEDGMENTS

With great delight, I look forward to the publication of this text and wish to thank those who helped me bring it to fruition. Each is living proof that all being, the very being of this text included, is constituted by relation! I extend my heartfelt gratitude to Margie Thompson, SSJ, my dear friend, Sister, and companion in dialogue, who read, reviewed, and responded to each chapter of this book with an eye to its cogency, accuracy, and accessibility. Her clarifying questions and perceptive comments challenged me, even as her unflagging encouragement and good cheer sustained me. Margie's talent and grace as a professional artist further enhance this text with her compelling work of art *Strange Attractor* as its cover image.

Jerry Ruff and Anselm Academic whose breadth of vision, respect for the Catholic intellectual tradition, receptivity to creative ideas, and commitment to publishing engaging and stimulating texts for the contemporary college student gave this book the marvelous opportunity to reach so rich and vital an audience. I am especially grateful to Kathleen Walsh, my editor, whose literary skills, theological sensibilities, incisive observations, and obvious zest for this project made its completion both expeditious and enjoyable.

My colleagues in theology and philosophy at Barry University, especially Sandra Fairbanks who provided exactly the resources I needed on the philosophical understanding of personhood; Raymond Ward who generously permitted me to "think out loud" with him at particularly perplexing points in this project; and Mark Wedig, OP, whose enlightened and accommodative vision as department chair afforded me the time and space to bring this endeavor to a successful conclusion.

The undergraduate and graduate students at Barry University whose desire to delve into the infinitely knowable mystery of God and willingness to engage the process of theology as "faith seeking understanding" continuously enliven and enrich my work. I thank especially the students in my fall 2011 undergraduate course "The Christian Understanding of God"—Wilner St. Phar, Isaac Washington, Leslie Redmond, Alex Musibay, Kwamain Williams, Shenique King, Orin Harris, Amor del Mar Pagán Irizarry, and Anthony Fabio—for the valuable feedback they gave me concerning the accessibility of the text for upper-level undergraduate students. The enthusiasm and astuteness that they brought to their exploration of and engagement with the theology of the Triune God stimulated profound thought and inestimable delight.

Elizabeth A. Johnson, CSJ, my mentor, colleague, Sister, and friend, whose passion for Divine Mystery, embrace of her vocation of theologian, fidelity to the living tradition, and commitment to the rigors of research inspire and reinforce my own.

Finally, my religious congregation of the Sisters of Saint Joseph of Philadelphia, especially Anne Myers, our President, and our General Council—Mary Dacey, Regina Bell, Carol Zinn, and Constance Gilder—whose wisdom, warmth, and unwavering encouragement hearten and support my ministry as theologian.

Ad majorem Dei gloriam!

PUBLISHER ACKNOWLEDGMENTS

Thank you to the following individuals who reviewed this work in progress:

Kurt Buhring
Saint Mary's College, Notre Dame, Indiana

Suzanne Franck
St. Joseph's College, Patchogue, New York

Catherine Punsalan-Manlimos
Seattle University, Seattle, Washington

CONTENTS

INTRODUCTION 11

Introduction to Part I 25

CHAPTER **1**: To Be Is to Be-in-Relation 27
Introduction .27
Being and Reality 29
Ontology of Substance 31
Toward a Relational Ontology 47
Summary 52
For Further Reading 55

CHAPTER **2**: Cosmic Being as Relation 56
Introduction .56
The Relation of Origin: A Common Creation Story 57
The Relation of Emergence: The Whole Is More than
   the Sum of its Parts 64
Relations of Effect: Bonding in a Creative Cosmos 69
Summary 84
For Further Reading 85

CHAPTER **3**: Human Being as Relation 86
Introduction .86
Defining Personhood 87
Relation of Origin: The *Nature* of Personhood 93
Relation of Effect: The *Nurture* of Personhood 98
Relation of Emergence: Life in Stages 110
Summary 119
For Further Reading 119

CHAPTER **4**: Divine Being as Relation 120
    Introduction 120
    The Rise of Trinitarian Theology 122
    Relation of Origin: The Processions 130
    Relations of Emergence: The Missions. 137
    Relation of Effect: Doctrine of Appropriations 146
    Summary. 155
    For Further Reading 157

CHAPTER **5**: Divine and Cosmic Being in Relation 158
    Introduction 158
    Of Analogies, Models, and Metaphors in Theology . . . 159
    Models of God-World Relationship 165
    Re-Visioning Trinitarian Relation in a Panentheistic Model . 176
    Re-Visioning Trinitarian Action in a Panentheistic Model . . 179
    Summary. 183
    For Further Reading 185

    Introduction to Part II 187

CHAPTER **6**: Creation as Relation in an Evolving Cosmos 189
    Introduction 189
    Theology and Doctrine of Creation 190
    Evolutionary Perspectives on the Cosmos as Creation . . . 195
    Interpreting Creation in an Evolving Cosmos 203
    Interpreting the Divine through an Evolutionary View
      of Creation 207
    Creation in an Evolving Cosmos: Resonances in
      the Tradition 212
    Summary. 222
    For Further Reading 223

CHAPTER **7**: Incarnation as Relation in an Evolving Cosmos. . . . 224
    Introduction 224
    The Doctrine of Incarnation in the Christian Tradition . . . 225
    Evolutionary Perspectives on Human Being 235
    Interpreting incarnation in an Evolving Cosmos. 240

Interpreting the Divine through Evolutionary Incarnation. . 246
Incarnation in an Evolving Cosmos: Resonances
  in the Tradition 252
Summary. 260
For Further Reading 261

CHAPTER **8**: Grace as Relation in an Evolving Cosmos 262
Introduction 262
Theology of Grace 263
Evolutionary Perspectives on Causality and its Effects . . . 272
Interpreting Grace in an Evolving Cosmos 282
Interpreting the Divine through an Evolutionary View
  of Grace 296
Grace in an Evolving Cosmos: Resonances
  in the Tradition 298
Summary. 305
For Further Reading 307

CHAPTER **9**: Living in Trinitarian Relation 308
Introduction 308
Relation: The Symbol that Functions 314
Summary. 329
For Further Reading 331

INDEX. 333

Introduction

his is a book about relations—*intimate relations*—that exist *between* all that is living: between the cosmos and humanity, between the cosmos and God, and between God and humanity. It is also about relations—*essential relations*—that exist *within* all that is living: within an evolving cosmos, within a developing humanity, and within the living God. It is moreover about relations that are fundamentally constitutive of cosmic, human, and divine being and thus provide a clue to the nature of reality itself.

The experience of relation—relatedness, relationality, or relationship—often stimulates a response of curiosity and appeals to us as humans. However, relatedness is not only of curiosity and appeal but also of the very essence of cosmic, human, and divine life. What Margaret Wheatley says of quantum physics in her book *Leadership and the New Science*, ought to be claimed concerning all of life: "Relationships are not just interesting . . . they are *all* there is to reality. . . . None of us exists independent of our relationships with others."[1] Thus, it is with the cosmos and with humans; thus, it is as well with God.

If relatedness is the essence of all life—cosmic, human, and divine—then how is God present and active within the unfolding history of creation? To answer this question in the twenty-first century, we must take into account a worldview shaped by the insights of the sciences, especially those of evolutionary biology and quantum physics. In dialogue with Christian theology, scientific insights have begun to broaden and challenge the way that many people have interpreted

---

1. Margaret Wheatley, *Leadership and the New Science: Discovering Order in a Chaotic World* (San Francisco: Berrett-Koehler, 2000), 34 and 35.

God's presence and action in the world. Such insights concern the age and size of the evolving universe, the complexity and diversity of life on the planet, the inherent creativity of the cosmos, the interplay of law and chance in the development of life forms, the inevitability of death and the emergence of life, the effect of whole systems on their fundamental parts, and the interdependent nature of elements and events at the subatomic level.

Traditionally, Christianity has viewed and described divine action as occasional, episodic interventions that disrupted the laws of nature or human events. Nowhere was this truer than in the divine acts of creation, incarnation, and grace. Creation has generally been thought of as a singular occurrence that happened at a moment forever past, through which the cosmos came into being from nothing by the act of a lone Creator. Christian tradition proclaims the event of the Incarnation in which the Word of God became flesh in Jesus of Nazareth as a once-and-for-all phenomenon that lasted for some 30 years more than 2,000 years ago. Finally, although Christians still consider grace as operative and ongoing in the midst of life, it is most often understood as a *thing that God gives*, rather than as a *way in which God relates* to the world.

Respectful of these understandings, this book, nonetheless, intends to revisit the question of how God is present and active in the world through creation, incarnation, and grace, in dialogue with a wide variety of resources from the Jewish and Christian traditions and the physical, biological, and social sciences. Informed by these disciplines in dialogue with an evolutionary worldview, it proposes that these divine activities are less adequately understood as *discrete and occasional acts* and more fittingly understood as *intimate and enduring relations* between the God and the evolving cosmos. In doing so, it sets forth a view of the Triune God of Christianity as intimately and ceaselessly present and active in the evolving history of the cosmos and dynamically engaged in the full flourishing of creation and its creatures.

What is it about an evolutionary worldview that might enable us to see and speak in new ways about God's interactions with the world? Answering this question requires that we first say something about our human capacity to know and to say anything about God at all!

God as Incomprehensible Mystery

Of all the assertions that religious traditions have made about God, the most fundamental is that God is an incomprehensible mystery. This means that God so utterly transcends the world of our experience that our finite minds are unable to grasp or express anything about God in Godself. Unlike the created world, God is Spirit (John 4:24) and as Spirit cannot be seen, touched, or heard in the same ways in which the physical elements of the natural world can. We must, therefore, observe certain "rules" in our speech about God.

Three such rules are suggested by twentieth-century Catholic theologian Elizabeth A. Johnson. The first rule, as mentioned previously, is that "the reality of the living God is an ineffable mystery beyond all telling. The infinitely creating, redeeming, and indwelling Holy One is so far beyond the world and so deeply within the world as to be literally incomprehensible."[2] As a result of this incomprehensibility, Johnson's second rule indicates that there is "no expression for God [that] can be taken literally."[3] As a result, quoting scholastic theologian and philosopher Thomas Aquinas, Johnson's third rule concludes, "we see the necessity of giving to God many names."[4]

God as Self-Communicating

In view of divine mystery, however, one must then question how persons come to truly know and speak of God. The Christian tradition teaches that persons of faith can come to know the Divine because God has chosen to reveal Godself in freedom and in love. In creation, in human experience, in the sacred writings of the religious traditions, and preeminently in Jesus Christ, God has revealed Godself out of love for creation. Twentieth-century Jesuit theologian Karl Rahner taught that God's very nature is that of free and self-communicating love and that the very existence of the cosmos and

---

2. Elizabeth A. Johnson, *Quest for the Living God: Mapping Frontiers in the Theology of God* (New York: Continuum, 2007), 17.

3. Ibid., 18.

4. Thomas Aquinas, *Summa Contra Gentiles* (*SCG*), 1.31:4. The *SCG* is accessible online in an annotated and abridged version from the *Jacques Maritain Center*, University of Notre Dame; available from *http://www2.nd.edu/Departments/Maritain/etext/gc.htm*.

its creatures is a result of this divine freedom and love. According to Rahner, God communicates *to* human beings *through* all that God has created, both human and nonhuman, and preeminently in Jesus Christ. Therefore, those seeking to explore and express the mystery of the living God must begin in those places through which God reveals Godself. In an evolutionary paradigm, this means, in creation and its creatures.

The Christian understanding of God as Creator and the cosmos as creation begins in the book of Genesis, which proclaims in its opening lines,

> In the beginning when God created the heavens and the earth, the earth was a formless wasteland, and darkness covered the abyss, while a mighty wind swept over the waters. Then God said, 'Let there be light' and there was light. God saw how good the light was. (Genesis 1:1–4a)

"*Then God said.*" God spoke—God communicated Godself—at the advent of creation. While most theologians regard this creation story in Genesis as a form of sacred allegory or myth, it nonetheless expresses an important truth for our attempt to speak of the divine mystery. It reveals God as the source of all creation and all of creation as the self-expression of God. Therefore, we can come to know God by attending carefully to God's self-communication through the natural world. As God's own creation, everything is full of sacred presence; everything has the capacity to reveal the living God.

God as Creator Revealed through Creation

Thomas Aquinas formalized this understanding of how God as Creator can be known through what God creates. In his *Summa Theologiae* (*ST*), Aquinas presented this argument:

> When an effect is better known to us than its cause, from the effect we proceed to the knowledge of the cause. And from every effect the existence of its proper cause can be demonstrated, so long as its effects are better known to us; because every effect depends upon its cause, if the effect exists, the cause must pre-exist. Hence the existence of God,

in so far as it is not self-evident to us, can be demonstrated from those of His effects which are known to us.[5]

In his *SCG*, Aquinas summarized this idea in a simpler fashion: "There is some manner of likeness of creatures to God. . . . [Thus] from the attributes found in creatures we are led to a knowledge of the attributes of God."[6] Theologians term this likeness the analogy of being. The idea of analogy suggests a correspondence between the created order and God because of God's role as the Creator of the cosmos. This analogy between created being and divine being allows us to draw inferences about the attributes of God and the purposes of God based on objects and relationships in the natural order that God created. This is so because, in creating the world, God, whose essence or nature is Being Itself, shares "being" in the form of life and existence with creation. Thus, everything that *has* being participates *in* Being Itself; all that has life and being in creation participates in the very Being of the One who creates. Aquinas explains this in terms of *essence* and *cause*, *participation* and *effect*:

> Whatever is of a certain kind through its essence is the proper cause of what is of such a kind by participation. Thus, fire is the cause of all things that are afire. Now, God alone is actual being through divine essence itself, while other beings are actual beings through participation.[7]

While words constrained by time and space are inadequate to explain this concept fully, one can explain Aquinas's meaning in this way: God, whose essence *is* Being Itself, whose very nature *is* "To Be" without beginning or end and without before or after, causes a creature to come into being by sharing a moment or a portion—and here is where time and space strain our language—of God's Being in the very act of giving life and existence to that creature. In a way analogous to a fire that sets other things aflame by sharing a portion of itself and yet is in no way diminished, God who is *essentially* Being

---

5. Thomas Aquinas, *ST*, I.2.1. The *ST* is accessible online from Kevin Knight, *New Advent*; available from *http://www.newadvent.org/summa/*.

6. Aquinas, *SCG*, 1.33.

7. Ibid., 3:66.7.

causes *a being* to come into existence at a moment in history while in no way diminishing the nature of God. Furthermore, because God as Being causes a creature to come into being, the creature can be said to share in the Being of God and to be a unique manifestation of it. However, because the creature has being in a limited way—there was a time when the creature did not exist, and there will come a time when the creature will no longer exist—the creature cannot be said to exist *as* Being Itself; rather, the creature exists only by participation in it.

Speaking Rightly of God

If the discussion just concluded demonstrates anything, it shows that the limits of human language and concepts make speaking about the mystery of God and the God-world relationship a challenge at best and risky at worst. As T. S. Eliot said, words often "strain, crack, and sometimes break under the burden" of speaking rightly about the incomprehensible mystery of God.[8] Nonetheless, knowledge of God and relationship with God is so significant to human experience that we are literally compelled to speak about God lest the source and end of existence be unacknowledged and unnamed. So while the mystery of God need not leave us speechless, it must make us cautious because no creaturely word or concept, bounded as they are by time and space, can ever fully express the nature, existence, or attributes of God. No matter how fitting it seems, the speech of finite humans inevitably falls short of the infinite Being of God. As Aquinas reminded in the *ST*,

> [No] name belongs to God in the same sense that it belongs to creatures; for instance, wisdom in creatures is a quality, but not in God. . . . When we apply wise to God, we do not mean to signify anything distinct from his essence or power or being. And thus when this term wise is applied to man, in some degree it circumscribes and comprehends the thing signified. . . . Hence, no name is predicated

---

8. T. S. Eliot, "Burnt Norton V," from *Four Quartets. Art of Europe*; available from *http://www.artofeurope.com*.

univocally of God and creatures. Neither, on the other hand, are names applied to God and creatures in a purely equivocal sense. . . . Because if that were so, it follows that from creatures nothing at all could be known or demonstrated about God; for the reasoning would always be exposed to the fallacy of equivocation. Therefore it must be said that these names are said of God and creatures in an analogous sense, that is, according to proportion. For in analogies the idea is not, as it is in univocals, one and the same; yet it is not totally diverse as in equivocals; but the name which is thus used in a multiple sense signifies various proportions to some one thing.[9]

From this, one can see that, while contingent and partial, speech about God is truly appropriate. Here and in other places, Aquinas clearly maintains that one may apply names to God based on human experience[10] and form positive affirmations concerning God.[11] For, in the face of our human experience of this Mystery, nearer to us than we are to ourselves, it is far more misleading to say nothing about God than to humbly attempt to say something, however conditional and inadequate.

This way of understanding the mutual relation between God as Creator and the cosmos as creation is not just reserved to thirteenth-century thinkers like Aquinas. Karl Rahner, as previously noted, pointed out that, because the natural world shares in the Being of God, creation is able to mediate God's communication to us. Furthermore, this analogy of being enables us to express an understanding of God in words and images drawn from the natural world despite the fact that God exceeds anything that we can say or imagine. In so doing, Christians acknowledge that God does not exist in isolated splendor, but in relationship to a cosmos dependent on God for its existence and sustenance. The cosmos speaks eloquently of its Creator—each creature a unique channel of God's self-communication to people of faith.

---

9. Aquinas, *ST*, Ia. 13, a. 5, 64.

10. Ibid., Ia. 13, 3, 62.

11. Ibid., Ia. 13, 12, 7–72.

Theology and Science in Dialogue

In the last century, this belief has received a new dynamism in the dialogue between Christian theology and evolutionary science. This dialogue, however, has not always proceeded smoothly. For many, Sir Francis Bacon's counsel in his 1605 commentary on the human search for the meaning of existence holds true: "Let no [persons] . . . think or maintain, that [they] can search too far or be too well studied in the book of God's word or in the book of God's works . . . only let [them] beware . . . that they do not unwisely mingle or confound these learnings together."[12] While Copernicus' discovery that the sun—not Earth—was the center of the universe changed the way humans understood their place in the universe and the writings of Charles Darwin radically challenged traditional ideas of how life began and develops on our planet, these revolutions in thinking have more often provoked contention rather than cooperation between the two disciplines. Science is accused of being a threat to the biblical and religious traditions. Theology is considered irrelevant to the scientific world of observation, measurement, and prediction. Even in the twenty-first century, the majority of scientists and theologians continue to insist that the two areas of study remain totally separate. This insistence on separation stems from several preconceptions.

Points of Difference

First, many insist upon the separation between theology and science because each allegedly concerns its own distinct realm. Science concerns itself with finite, observable reality, while theology concerns itself with infinite, unfathomable reality. Second, each supposedly serves and is defined by its own objects of study. Science studies natural being and phenomena, while theology focuses on supernatural being and phenomena. Third, each presumably strives for different ends. Science probes the realm of the natural world with a goal of prediction and control. Theology probes the realm beyond the natural order with the goal of personal commitment and moral purpose. Fourth and finally, each characteristically employs its own language system and vocabulary, which hinders communication.

---

12. Sir Francis Bacon in Arthur R. Peacocke, "Rethinking Religious Faith in a World of Science," in *Religion. Science and Public Policy*, ed. Frank T. Birtel (New York: Crossroad, 1987), 3–29 at 4.

Points of Commonality

There are, nevertheless, a growing number of scholars in both theology and science who point out the shortsightedness of this separation and instead emphasize the need for both Christian theology and science to reevaluate and reinterpret their ways of thinking by taking into account the insights and observations of the other. While the differences between the disciplines seem insurmountable, these scholars contend that if one delves beneath the apparent differences, several commonalities between theology and science come to light that make dialogue not only possible but also, in fact, indispensable.

First, both theology and science actually base their claims on what their participants experience and observe in the world. They do this by figuring out the underlying reasons and relationships that seem to produce what they experience and observe. For example, theologian Thomas Aquinas observed phenomena in the natural world that exhibited relationships of cause and effect, such as a hammer driving a nail or a fire burning wood. He noticed that creatures shared natural attributes, such as color or shape or size, but did so in different amounts or to different degrees. He witnessed decay and death in a world of change, yet experienced regularities in nature and saw life constantly sustained and renewed. Based on these observations, Aquinas reasoned that there must be a First Cause on which all other causes depend. He deduced that the varying amounts and degrees of attributes must point to an Ultimate Reality that possesses the fullness of such attributes. He inferred that the transient, yet enduring being of the natural world must depend for its existence upon a Necessary Being who did not change or pass away. He compiled these and other arguments in his *Summa Theologiae* to attempt to answer the question of whether God exists. In each case, Aquinas concluded that the First Cause, Ultimate Reality, and Necessary Being are what "everyone understands to be God."[13]

In a manner not unlike that of Aquinas, English naturalist Charles Darwin used his powers of observation and experience to reason out his proposals about the origin and development of life. He brought these observations and conclusions together eloquently in the final paragraph of his most noted work *On the Origin of Species*

---

13. Aquinas, *ST*, I.2.3.

by Means of Natural Selection, or the Preservation of Favoured Races in the Struggle for Life.

> It is interesting to contemplate an entangled bank, clothed with many plants of many kinds, with birds singing on the bushes, with various insects flitting about, and with worms crawling through the damp earth, and to reflect that these elaborately constructed forms, so different from each other, and dependent on each other in so complex a manner, have all been produced by laws acting around us. These laws, taken in the largest sense, being Growth with Reproduction; Inheritance which is almost implied by reproduction; Variability from the indirect and direct action of the external conditions of life, and from use and disuse; a Ratio of Increase so high as to lead to a Struggle for Life, and as a consequence to Natural Selection, entailing Divergence of Character and the Extinction of less-improved forms. . . . There is grandeur in this view of life, with its several powers, having been originally breathed into a few forms or into one; and that, whilst this planet has gone cycling on according to the fixed law of gravity, from so simple a beginning endless forms most beautiful and most wonderful have been, and are being, evolved.[14]

Beyond their common source material, a second commonality between science and theology is that each claims to speak about and deal with what is real. However, neither theology nor science speaks in a literal way, as if there is a one-to-one correspondence between the words they use and the realities they address. Yet, for each there is *some* correspondence between their words and reality that communicates what they have seen and experienced as accurately as possible. When scientists, for example, speak about the brain, they often use the model of a computer to describe the way the brain works. They employ terms such as *input, output, information processing,* and even *wired* as ways of speaking about brain function without meaning that

---

14. Charles Darwin, *On the Origin of Species by Means of Natural Selection, or the Preservation of Favoured Races in the Struggle for Life* (London: John Murray, 1859), 489–90.

an inspection of the brain would reveal circuitry and memory cards. Theologians also use figurative language when they refer to Jesus as the *Word* or *Lamb* of God, when they speak about the members of the Trinity as *persons*, or when they represent the Creator as *Father*.

Simply because this language is figurative, however, does not mean that it has no basis in reality. As Ian Barbour wrote, although a model, a metaphor, or an analogy is not a literal picture of reality, neither is it simply "useful fiction." Models, metaphors, and analogies are "partial and inadequate ways of imagining what is not observable. They are symbolic representations, for particular purposes, of aspects of reality which are not directly accessible to us."[15] Arthur Peacocke agrees: "Not only does a good model allow logical inferences to be made about possible phenomena . . . but it functions . . . by throwing light forward . . . into new areas of investigation."[16]

It is important to realize that neither Barbour nor Peacocke is talking about the methods of science or theology. Rather, they are speaking about the nature of the language that both theology and science use. An example from science is the way that scientists refer to the theory of the origin of the universe as the Big Bang. Information about these original events came through experiments in chemistry and physics through which data were observed, collected, and interpreted within the scientific worldview. Then, because these events were "aspects of reality which are not directly accessible," events that, obviously, no one had observed directly, scientists extrapolated from this interpreted data a theory about the origin of the universe. When it came to naming this theoretical event, scientists chose a term that gave others a way of "imagining what is not observable"—a *Big Bang*. While by no means intended to be literal, this term enables scientists to communicate the spontaneous, explosive, and dramatic event through which the elements of a nascent cosmos were strewn throughout the vacuum that preexisted what we now understand as "space." Moreover, it does not stretch the point to suggest that a similar dynamic was in play in theology. As ancient religious writers composed the biblical narratives of creation, they

---

15. Ian A. Barbour, *Myths, Models and Paradigms* (London: SCM, 1974), 69.

16. Arthur R. Peacocke, *Theology for a Scientific Age: Being and Becoming—Natural, Divine, and Human* (Minneapolis: Augsburg Fortress, 1993), 31.

based their images and language on their worldview, experience, observation, and interpretation of God and the God-world relationship extrapolated backward.

Hence, whether in science or in theology, the use of such figurative language helps to illuminate critically important aspects of the natural world and of the faith tradition. Without it, neither theology nor science would be able to articulate the meanings and relationships beneath its observations in terms that are understandable and useful for further exploration. In addition, recognizing the figurative nature of theological and scientific language helps to safeguard against literal interpretations. Furthermore, it invites us to expand the models we use and to devise new ways of speaking about God and the God-world relationship. The most important thing to keep in mind is that although such speech expresses profound truth, it is nonetheless limited. It is, as Buddhist Patriarch Huineng reminds us, like a finger pointing to the moon:

> Truth has nothing to do with words. Truth can be likened to the bright moon in the sky. Words, in this case, can be likened to a finger. The finger can point to the moon's location. However, the finger is not the moon. To look at the moon, it is necessary to gaze beyond the finger, right?[17]

These insights point to a third characteristic that theology and science have in common, one that we have met before when talking about the nature of God. That common feature is *mystery*. Mystery truly surrounds and pervades both theology and science. Whether it tries to fathom the wonders of nature or the nature of God, the human mind is, after all, limited. The insights it grasps, the thoughts it formulates, and the language it uses can only know and express what it has been able to experience and observe. The rest depends upon speculation—such as the event of the Big Bang and the Genesis account of the seven days of creation. However, this mystery need not leave us speechless. While the language of theology and science is like "a finger pointing to the moon," it does not call for silence but for humility. This humility comes from the fact that, while all reality

---

17. "Finger Pointing at the Moon," *Stories of Wisdom*; available from *http://www. storiesofwisdom.com/finger-pointing-at-the-moon/.*

is deeply a mystery, reality is continuously communicating itself to us, and thus, it is infinitely knowable. As theologian Sallie McFague wrote, the ways in which theology and science express themselves are like "'houses' to live in for a while, with windows partly open and doors ajar."[18] When a theological or scientific statement "houses" us with hospitality and without restriction, it becomes an acceptable way of speaking about God or about the natural world. However, no statement is ever beyond revision.

Mutually Illuminative Interaction

How might these commonalities between theology and science lead to dialogue and yet preserve the unique character of both theology and science? One way is to look at the relationship between theology and science as one of "mutually illuminative interaction." In this kind of relationship, each area of study illuminates the other. Science illuminates the mysteries of creation. By doing so, science can deepen and expand what creation reveals about its Creator. Theology, on the other hand, illuminates the meanings and purposes that lie beyond the scope of scientific exploration. Such mutually illuminative interaction can produce a paradigm that guides Christian speech about God in an evolutionary cosmos.

In his approach through evolution to the theology of God, twentieth-century scientist and theologian Arthur Peacocke set forth four principles to guide human knowledge and language of God based on the natural world as observed by evolutionary science. First, Peacocke affirmed belief in God as Creator of the cosmos. Second, he maintained, like Aquinas, that if God is the Creator of the cosmos, then the cosmos as creation can reveal the nature and characteristics of its Creator. Peacocke took this idea a step further than Aquinas, however, based on the limits of human imagination and the limitless nature of God. Peacocke proposed that, third, one can *only* speak rightly about God as God is experienced in relation to the cosmos and its creatures, rather than in speculative terms or metaphysical concepts. Therefore, fourth and finally, one must use analogies, metaphors, and models rooted in the analogy of being

---

18. Sallie McFague, *Models of God: Theology for an Ecological, Nuclear Age* (Philadelphia: Fortress 1988), 27.

between Creator and creation to speak about the incomprehensible mystery of God.

God in an Evolving Cosmos

We can now return to our original question: What is it about an evolutionary worldview—one which includes a recognition of the age and size of the evolving universe, the complexity and diversity of life on the planet, the inherent creativity of the cosmos, the interplay of law and chance in the development of life forms, and the inevitability of death and the emergence of life—that might enable us to see and speak in new ways about God's interactions with the world? A simple response holds that evolutionary theory has enabled us to see and understand the cosmos in significantly different ways than the worldview that produced traditional conceptions of the God-world relationship. Because we derive our knowledge and speech about the Infinite Reality of God from our knowledge and speech about the finite reality of the cosmos and its creatures, then the new insights and vocabulary that spring from the evolutionary paradigm of creation not only permit but urge Christians to be open to new ways of thinking and speaking about God and God-world relationships. They do so in the spirit of the invitation God offered to Isaiah: "See, I am doing something new! Now it springs forth, do you not perceive it?" (Isaiah 43:19) And because, as Aquinas affirmed, "from every effect the existence of its proper cause can be demonstrated," the new perception of the entities, structures, and processes of the cosmos that springs from an evolutionary understanding invites us see anew the living God in the intimate relations of creation, incarnation, and grace revealed in the evolving cosmos.

As we see in the chapters that follow, a wide variety of scientific disciplines in dialogue with the wisdom of Judaism and of the rich and diverse traditions within Christianity affirm that the nature of this cosmos, its creatures, and its Creator is *essentially* relational, *intimately* relational. Moreover, the relations existing within and between the entities of an evolving cosmos and within and between its creatures ultimately reflect relations within the living God and between the living God and the cosmos—relations traditionally termed *creation*, *incarnation*, and *grace*.

Introduction to

PART I

The first part of this book sets forth the concept of relational ontology, the philosophical study of the nature of being as constituted by essential relations. It examines the way this concept realizes itself in cosmic, human, and divine being through relations of origin, effect, and emergence. By design, the chapters on the cosmos and the human person focus primarily on philosophy and on the natural, physical, behavioral, and social sciences to substantiate claims about the relational nature of all reality. In doing so, these chapters resist the temptation to speak from a theological perspective in order to source their claims in a broader spectrum of disciplines and, thus, enlarge their relevance and base of support for readers not rooted in the Christian tradition. With chapter 4, on divine being, however, the line of thought takes a decided turn toward the theological and continues on that line throughout the remainder of the text. Concepts from these early chapters on cosmic, human, and divine being return in dialogue with Christian theologies and doctrines to examine ways in which the Triune Christian God interacts with the cosmos and its creatures in an evolutionary world. As a result, relations between and among cosmic, human, and divine beings find expression in perhaps new and surprising ways that deepen and amplify the reality—and the mystery—of relation within and among all being, relations that the Christian tradition terms *creation*, *incarnation*, and *grace*.

Chapter 1

TO BE IS TO BE-IN-RELATION

INTRODUCTION

In a famous Shakespearean soliloquy, Hamlet, prince of Denmark, broods over his continuing existence:

> To be, or not to be: that is the question:
> Whether 'tis nobler in the mind to suffer
> The slings and arrows of outrageous fortune,
> Or to take arms against a sea of troubles,
> And by opposing end them?
> . . . .
> To grunt and sweat under a weary life,
> But that the dread of something after death,
> The undiscover'd country from whose bourn
> No traveller returns, puzzles the will
> And makes us rather bear those ills we have
> Than fly to others that we know not of?[1]

---

1. "The Soliloquy in Hamlet" by William Shakespeare; available from *http://www.friesian.com/notes/hamlet.htm*.

But even those who have not reached the brink of melancholy over which Hamlet peers still puzzle over the essential questions of what it means "to be" in the face of "the slings and arrows of outrageous fortune" or the "grunt and sweat" of life or "the dread of something after death." We ponder: "Why is there something rather than nothing? Why am I here? What is my purpose? Where have we come from, and where are we going? What does it mean 'to be'?" These questions about the meaning and purpose of life simmer subconsciously in the minds and hearts of humans. Now and then, these existential questions churn and bubble up into consciousness at critical junctures that require decision or direction. Conscious or not, they nonetheless shade and contour the ways in which we see the being within and around us and, for believers, the Being beneath and beyond us.

This first chapter explores the question of being, the issue of what constitutes reality, and the ways in which being and reality have been studied, understood, and described in the philosophical and, by extension, theological traditions. It investigates the nature of being through the branch of philosophy known as ontology and examines philosophy's traditional accounts of what constitutes the nature of reality.

These accounts, classically constructed by Aristotle in his *Categories* and *Metaphysics* and by Plato in his *Phaedo*, have exerted tremendous influence in the centuries since their formulation. Nonetheless, as this chapter reveals, the descriptions and classifications of the reality of being offered by these thinkers have limitations. Ontology reflects the level of knowledge and worldview of a given period in history; thus, each ontological proposal must be evaluated to see if it stands the test of time. Are the ontological systems of Aristotle and Plato— and those thinkers who follow their leads—adequate for *this* time in history? Are traditional accounts of what constitutes the reality of being consonant with an evolutionary worldview in which the reality of the cosmos is understood not as static in being but as dynamic in becoming? Are these accounts consistent with the insights of quantum physics that have raised questions about what constitutes the nature and reality of being at the subatomic level?

This chapter further inquires whether the accounts offered by Plato and Aristotle adequately address the anthropological, psychological, and sociological perspectives on human being that emphasize the impact of family, society, and culture on the development of human persons. Finally, the chapter questions whether these philosophical accounts present a theologically valid and morally acceptable conception of the Divine consistent with God as Trinity and responsive to a suffering world. A theology for *this* time in history must take into consideration all the data and interpretations that the Christian tradition and the natural and social sciences have to offer today—even as philosophy and theology did in the time of Plato and Aristotle—if it is to speak credibly about the nature and reality of natural, human, and divine being and about the ways in which the cosmos, the human, and the Divine relate and interact.

BEING AND REALITY

Questions about the nature and constitution of reality have been studied in several academic disciplines, including the natural sciences, the social sciences, theology, and philosophy. Philosophy, in particular, has wrestled for centuries over the meaning of *reality* and "being *qua* being" (being *as* being), in the words of Aristotle, in the philosophical discipline known as *metaphysics*. Literally, the term *metaphysics* means, "beyond or outside of the physical" and refers to "a division of philosophy that is concerned with the fundamental nature of reality and being and that includes ontology, cosmology [the study of the origins of the universe], and often epistemology [the study of the nature of knowledge and how it is acquired]."[2] According to professor of philosophy Michael J. Loux, who is well known for his writing on metaphysics,

> What is distinctive about metaphysics is the way in which it examines those objects; it examines them from a particular perspective, from the perspective of their being beings or things that exist. So metaphysics considers things as beings or as existents and attempts to specify the properties or features they exhibit just insofar as they are beings or existents.[3]

2. "Metaphysics," *Merriam-Webster Online Dictionary* 2009; available from *http://www.merriam-webster.com/dictionary/metaphysics*.

3. Michael J. Loux, *Metaphysics. A Contemporary Introduction* (New York: Routledge, 2006), 3.

Moreover, as a study of beings or existents, metaphysics is also concerned with "first causes" of the creative processes, structures, and entities of the cosmos. Hence, the scope of metaphysics extends beyond natural or human being and reality to explore the very being and reality of God.

Closely related to metaphysics—and contained in its very definition—is the subject of ontology, the branch of metaphysics concerned with the nature of being. Described by Nicolai Hartmann, "ontology has to do with fundamental assertions about being as such . . . [that] we call categories of being."[4] Moreover, because it concerns the essential nature of everything that exists, the study of ontology does not exist as an independent branch of study but exists in dialogue with other means by which humans understand their reality. However, as discussed previously, because we understand reality within a particular worldview, "Ontology [too] mirrors . . . the level of our knowledge of the world at any given time."[5]

Hartmann's claim that ontology mirrors our worldview is demonstrated in the divergent viewpoints of two of the most noted philosophers in history, Plato and Aristotle. A student of Socrates and teacher of Aristotle, Plato (429–347 BCE) is arguably one of the most influential thinkers and writers in the history of philosophy. His philosophical thought was deeply shaped by both the political events and intellectual movements of his time, and his works, such as the *Republic* and *Phaedo*, remain influential to this day. In response to the question of what constitutes the being of the cosmos, Plato surmised that the general structures of the world derived from an ideal world of Forms or Ideas. Existing in the perfect realm of the mind, the Form or Idea of an entity is an abstract, eternal, and changeless paradigm of the objects and structures that exist only imperfectly in the world of experience. For Plato, it is the abstract Form or Idea that is the *really* real, not the object perceived by the senses, which is limited by time and space and is, therefore, defective. In his thinking, "the world was essentially intelligible, and so it must be the intellect and not the senses that had the ultimate 'vision' of this true being. The intellect

---

4. Nicolai Hartmann, *New Ways of Ontology*, trans. Reinhard C. Kuhn (Chicago: Henry Regnery, 1953), 13–14.

5. Raul Corazzon "Introduction," *Birth of a New Science: The History of Ontology from Suarez to Kant*; available from *http://www.ontology-2.com/history.htm*.

had to use the information of the senses to read what was behind, and beyond, sensation. . . . The forms that objects had here below were, therefore, imperfect cases of the perfect case or form that exists in the other intellectual realm."[6] Hence, in the quest to determine what constitutes reality or what best represents the essential nature of reality, Plato does not begin his journey in the experiential realm of tangible existence, but in the intellectual world of ideal Forms.

In response to the same question, however, Plato's student Aristotle came to a different conclusion. Like his teacher, Aristotle (384–322 BCE) made a profound impact on Western thought and wrote on such varied topics as logic, morality, aesthetics, science, and politics, as well as philosophy and metaphysics. Nevertheless, unlike his teacher, when Aristotle considered the nature of reality, he rejected Plato's theory of intellectual forms and asserted that the nature of being could only be identified through sense experience and knowledge of the world. Real being for Aristotle is not in the abstract form, but rather in the concrete individual thing; it is not in the universal concept, but rather in the particular object perceived by the senses. Therefore, in his quest to determine what constitutes reality or what best represents the essential nature of reality, Aristotle emphasized empirical observation and sense perception, rather than focusing on the realm of the intellect. Nevertheless, despite their different starting points and their different conclusions as to what is "the *really* real," both Plato and Aristotle referred to "substance" as what constitutes reality.

ONTOLOGY OF SUBSTANCE

While Plato, Aristotle, and their contemporaries commonly used the term *substance* in their philosophical analysis, it was Aristotle's account of substance that held influence for centuries after him.[7] For

---

6. Stephen Mc Grogan, "Plato's Theories of Forms," *Metaphysics*; available from *http://metaphysics.suite101.com/article.cfm/platos_theory_of_the_forms*.

7. The understanding of *substance* in philosophy has gone through many metamorphoses in the centuries since Aristotle. For some helpful overviews, see "Substance," *The Catholic Encyclopedia*; available at *http://www.catholic.org/encyclopedia/view.php?id=11137* or "Substance," *Stanford Encyclopedia of Philosophy*; available from *http://plato.stanford.edu/entries/substance/*.

this reason, his explanation serves as the basis for understanding the term in this text.

Definition of Substance

Because of his starting point in empirical reality, Aristotle first uses the term *substance* to refer to a particular individual or to a particular thing.[8] As such, "'substances' are the things which exist in their own right."[9] Aristotle named such individual entities "primary substances." Moreover, these primary substances can have particular qualities attributed to them, such as color or size. These qualities are said to be predicated of particular individuals, but in themselves are general terms. In Aristotle's schema, they "are said to be 'present in' primary substances, that is, they cannot exist independently or apart from individuals."[10] For example, this book is a primary substance called *Trinity in Relation*. Beyond that, qualities such as thick or thin, large or small, clear or confusing, costly or inexpensive can be predicated of it. Nonetheless, these qualities have no existence unless realized in a particular thing or individual. Aristotle called these qualities present in primary substances "accidents." The accidents predicated of a primary substance both distinguish one primary substance from another and classify it with another. Hence, the Granny Smith apple and the Macoun apple on a counter in a kitchen are each a primary substance. On the one hand, the Granny Smith has the qualities of green, hard, and tart, whereas the Macoun has the qualities of red, juicy, and sweet. These qualities, or predicates, differentiate the two primary substances from each other. Nonetheless, both of these primary substances are apples and, thus, can be classified with each other. In this way, qualities, or predicates, can identify both differences and similarities among various primary substances.

This example leads to another of Aristotle's central ideas about the nature of reality. As we have seen, qualities not only distinguish primary substances; they also classify them into *kinds* of substances.

---

8. Diogenes Allen and Eric O. Springsted, *Philosophy for Understanding Theology* (Louisville, KY: Westminster John Knox Press, 2007), 65.

9. "Substance," in *Routledge Encyclopedia of Philosophy*, ed. Edward Craig (London, Routledge, 1998), 205.

10. Allen and Springsted, *Philosophy*, 65.

Despite their differences, Granny Smith and Macoun share something essential between them; they are both *kinds* of apples. Hence, *apple* can be predicated of both of these primary substances and indicates to what group of substance each belongs. One can think of this in terms of the taxonomy used in the sciences to classify plants and animals according to their presumed relationships. In a scientific taxonomy, classifications move from the more general categories of domain, kingdom, and phylum to the more precise categories of genus and species. In a similar fashion, Aristotle recognized that primary substances could be classified through successive levels of specificity, from species to genus and beyond. These classifications of substances Aristotle termed *secondary substances.*

Returning to the apple, previously considered, we could differentiate the secondary substance or classification of species into *Malus domestica*, like the domestic Granny Smith and Macoun, or the *Malus sieversii*, their wild ancestor found in Central Asia. Despite the difference in their secondary substance or classification at the level of species, they share secondary substances or classifications higher in the taxonomy: kingdom Plantae, division Magnoliophyta, class Magnoliopsida, order Rosales, family Rosaceae, subfamily Maloideae or Spiraeoideae, tribe Maleae, and genus *Malus.* Furthermore, their unique product names—Granny Smith and Macoun—constitute another kind of secondary substance or classification.

What is important to remember in this discussion is that the meaning of substance in philosophical usage is not the same as the meaning of substance in general usage. In general usage, a substance is the physical matter of which a person or thing exists. Its substance is an aspect or a quality of a larger more complete whole. A statue is a statue whether its substance is concrete or marble. A chair is a chair whether its substance is plastic or wood. It follows then that a substance is not specific or unique to a particular person or thing. All kinds of things are made of comparable substances. Wood is a substance that we use to make tables and chairs. Plastic is a substance that we use to make spaceships and picnic utensils. Thus, in general use, substance does not indicate anyone or anything in particular. In philosophical usage, however, the word *substance* has a particularity to it. As a primary substance, it refers to a particular individual or to a particular thing. As a secondary substance, it refers to specific attributes that characterize that particular individual or thing. The following quote effectively summarizes the preceding discussion and bears citing at length:

> The most important things we predicate of an individual . . . are its genus and species. They give us its essence; they tell us *what* the individual is; they tell us the *kind* of being it is. . . . The other things we predicate of a primary substance do not tell us the *kind* of thing it is. So there are two types of predicates: those that tell us the kind of thing that each individual thing is and those that do not. Secondary substances tell us what a substance is *essentially*; the other predicates tell us what it is *accidentally*. . . . [Thus] we have a major division between substance and accidents (between individuals and what is present in them). We have a distinction between substances themselves: individual substances (primary substances) and *kinds* of substances (secondary substances). Genera and species . . . and accidents are predicated of primary substances. But only genera and species give us what is essential to a primary substance, that is, tell us what a primary substance *must* have in order to be that particular kind of reality.[11]

In *Categories*, one of his earlier writings, Aristotle enumerates ten categories that weave throughout his discussion of substance and accident. The first of these categories is substance and includes both primary and secondary substances. The other nine categories represent logical groupings of the general qualities that can be predicated of substances. These categories are quantity, quality, relation, place, time, posture, possession, action, and being acted upon. Applied to our Granny Smith apple, one could say "The Granny Smith apple was large, green, next to the Macoun apple, on the countertop, at lunchtime, on its side, with a split skin, leaking juice, and sliced for a pie." One might ask, however, whether this description—in terms of primary substance, secondary substance, and accidents—reveals anything more than a sense perception of the apple and leaves open

---

11. Ibid., 66.

the question of its essential reality. If it does, at least, give a sense perception of the apple—or the person, the tree, the mountain, or the cat—it has met Aristotle's understanding of what constitutes "the real." Nonetheless, does more than what is perceived through the senses not constitute reality—natural, human, and divine? Furthermore, how does sense perception assist in knowing the reality of what is immaterial or spiritual, hence, the reality of God?

Duality of Substance

Beyond the notions of substance and accidents, philosophy and theology have further sought to characterize the nature of reality in still more encompassing categories. One such characterization attempted to classify kinds of reality into broad and dichotomous categories that resulted in a variety of arrangements called "dualisms." The term *dualism* is a wide-ranging designation that has had a variety of applications in the history of thought. Its references include mind-body dualism, epistemological dualism, metaphysical or ontological dualism, ethical dualism, and religious dualism, to name but a few. In general, dualism points to the theory or belief that "for some particular domain, there are two fundamental kinds or categories of things or principles."[12] Hence, as noted previously, dualisms are usually expressed in terms of oppositions: good or evil, mind or body, supernatural or natural, spirit or flesh, light or darkness, and the like. This section focuses on metaphysical or ontological dualism, described as a "philosophical system positing two basic non-reducible substances, typically matter (or body) and spirit (or soul)."[13] This is to say that the fundamental essence of any reality is either material in nature or spiritual in nature and never a combination of the two. The history of dualism in philosophical thought stretches from before the time of Socrates (469–399 BCE) to the present, with a particular ascendancy in the writing of René Descartes (1596–1650 CE). More than one hundred years before the time of Plato, philosophers such as Anaximander, Heracleitus, Empedocles, and Anaxagoras claimed

12. Howard Robinson, "Dualism," *Stanford Encyclopedia of Philosophy* (October 10, 2007); available from *http://plato.stanford.edu/entries/dualism/*.

13. "Dualism—Challenges to Dualism, Bibliography," *Science Encyclopedia: The History of Ideas, Vol. 2*; available from *http://science.jrank.org/pages/7636/Dualism.html*.

the existence of opposed natural substances that played a role in the development of the world. However, Plato can be credited with a classical formulation in his metaphysics of an ideal world of Forms.

In Plato's *Phaedo*, a dialogue between the characters identified as "Socrates" and "Cebes" represent Plato's reasoning about "Being in itself" as opposed to "the many beautiful things" perceived by the senses. Socrates proposes the following:

> The Being in itself which in our questions and answers we characterise as real existence—is that always in the same state and with the same aspect, or different at different times? Absolute equality, absolute beauty, absolute every thing which is—do these ever admit change of any kind whatever? Or does each of them of which we predicate real existence, uniform in its pure simplicity, constantly preserve the same aspect and condition and never in any way on any occasion whatever admit any variation? . . . But what of the many beautiful things, men for instance, or horses, or clothes, or any other whatever of the same kind . . . or all that bear the same name with the ideas? Are they permanent in their condition? Or just the reverse of the others, do they never . . . at all preserve any constancy, either in themselves or in their relations to one another? . . . Then let us assume . . . two kinds of existing things, one visible and the other invisible. . . . And the invisible constant and immutable, but the visible subject to perpetual change.[14]

For Plato, the real and true substances are the eternal Forms of "Being itself" and sense objects are merely deficient representations of them. Moreover, the Forms are unchangeable universals, while their copies are no more than passing reflections.

Despite the influence of Plato's metaphysical dualism, some aspects of his thinking have been opposed by noted philosophers. Aristotle did not accept Plato's dualism that Forms exist independently of their expression in individual entities. However, even with Aristotle's emphasis on the material nature of reality, he still believed

---

14. Plato, *Phaedo*, trans. E. M. Cope (Cambridge, MA: Harvard University Press, 1875), 41–42.

that the intellect within a material person must itself be immaterial. He reasoned that if the intellect itself were material in substance like the body that it inhabits, it could not grasp anything that was immaterial, such as concepts, ideas, or abstractions.[15] Building on Aristotelian thought, Thomas Aquinas distinguished between the soul of the human person—which, like Aristotle, he considered the "form"—and the person him- or herself. For Aquinas, the "soul" was only the "person" when united with the body, as the body was the carrier of the sense images that contribute to the wholeness of human "personhood."[16] Immanuel Kant denied that humans possessed the capacity to know "the thing-in-itself" or the "noumenon." Humans can only know the conscious experience of the thing-in-itself or the "phenomenon."[17]

This discussion of ontological dualism would be incomplete, however, without reference to the dichotomy of matter and spirit proposed by seventeenth-century philosopher René Descartes. "Cartesian dualism," as it is called, has spawned countless interpretations, responses, refutations, and defenses in the centuries since he expounded his theories.[18] In Descartes' own words, "I recognize only two ultimate classes of things: first, intellectual or thinking things, i.e. those which pertain to mind or thinking substance; and, secondly, material things, i.e. those which pertain to extended substance or body."[19] He arrived at this recognition after searching for an absolute certainty upon which to base his further quest for knowledge. The one certainty he found indisputable is expressed in his famous statement, "*Cogito ergo sum*," which means, "I think therefore I am."

Through his search for absolute certainty, Descartes arrives at the indisputable fact that he is a thinking being. The reality of his body could be doubted, but not the reality of his mind. From this,

15. Aristotle, *De Anima* III, 4; available from *http://classics.mit.edu/Aristotle/ soul.3.iii.html*.

16. Robinson, "Dualism."

17. M. Alan Kazlev, "Dualism," *Kheper: Worldviews*; available from *http://www. kheper.net/topics/worldviews/dualism.htm*.

18. For a survey of and responses to such interpretations *and* misinterpretations, see Gordon P. Baker and Katherine J. Morris, *Descartes' Dualism* (New York: Routledge, 2002).

19. René Descartes, *Principles* I.48, in *The Philosophical Writings of Descartes: Vol. 1*, trans. John Cottingham, Robert Stoothoff, and Dugald Murdoch (Cambridge: Cambridge University Press, 1986), 208.

Descartes concluded that the mind and body were separate entities. The mind was a "thinking thing" and an immaterial substance,
whereas the body was a nonthinking thing and a material substance.
Such "substance dualism" suggested to him that the mind can exist
apart from the body, and it reinforced the Platonic notion that the
soul, as immortal, occupies a realm of existence distinct from that of
the physical world, as, by extension, does God.

Consequences of Substance Ontology

The propositions of substance ontology with the ontological dualisms that often accompany them have had far-ranging consequences
in the disciplines of cosmology, anthropology, and theology. While
some propositions have benefited the aims of these disciplines, others
have been problematic in the light of contemporary understandings
of the cosmos, the human person, and the Christian God.

The Problem of Stasis

Plato's theory of Forms and Aristotle's empirical approach present
lucid arguments for affirming the reality of both material and immaterial being. Nonetheless, their substance ontology implies that cosmic
and human beings are static entities whose essence and identity do not
change over time, because in substance ontology what constitutes a
person or thing is a particular nature with more or less stable attributes.
If you consider the apples that have journeyed with us through this
chapter, the attributes of the apple such as large, red, crisp, and sweet
are of no enduring significance for its identity, so to speak. Comparing
it to an apple that is small, green, hard, and tart is irrelevant in substance ontology for which an apple is an apple is an apple! Hence, even
if the attributes of a being change, whether that being is a person or
thing, the characteristics that common sense suggests make individuals
distinct from each other have no impact. Regardless of the attributes,
the identities of beings categorized as similar in substance are indistinguishable from one another ontologically. As the upcoming chapters clearly demonstrate, however, the evolutionary and social sciences
view life forms as dynamic, as beings in the process of becoming over
time. The attributes they develop or discard have bearing on the reality
of the person or thing in question. The size, shape, color, and weight
of an object, as well as the ethnicity, race, height, and location of a

person constitute in large measure the reality of an individual over time. When this idea of stasis extends to the Divine, as both Plato and Aristotle have done, the Being of God is conceived in terms of immutability (inability to change) and impassibility (inability to be moved or affected). This is clearly inconsistent with the biblical tradition of the living God who is experienced in dynamic, personal, and passionate relationship with creation and its creatures.

The Problem of Self-Sufficiency

In a famous meditation in his work *Devotions upon Emergent Occasions*, poet John Donne reflected, "No man is an island, entire of itself; every man is a piece of the continent, a part of the main. . . . Any man's death diminishes me, because I am involved in mankind; and therefore never send to know for whom the bell tolls; it tolls for thee."[20] In this quote, Donne maintained that neither humans nor any other life form exists in splendid isolation from others, but in integral, effective relationship. Neither humans nor any other life form, therefore, is sufficient unto itself, needing nor desiring any other.

Nevertheless, "the traditional study of ontology has been dominated by the concept of 'substance' which embodies such notions as self-subsistence, self-maintenance, [and] unchanging presence as an independent self."[21] Thus, within their conceptions of substance ontology, Plato viewed the individual as simply a passing instance of a universal, and Aristotle considered the individual as an independent entity with particular qualities. Interaction and relationship with other cosmic, human, or divine beings were not only unnecessary but also, if occurring, were patently ineffective. Autonomy and independence were the rule, and the more autonomous and independent an individual proved to be, the more valued and perfected is that individual. In contrast to this unbridled autonomy, however, contemporary cosmology, physics, psychology, sociology, and anthropology have consistently emphasized the critical roles of interdependence rather than independence, of interrelationship rather than self-sufficiency, and of dynamism rather than immutability as the reality of the cosmic and

20. John Donne, "Meditation XVII," *Devotions upon Emergent Occasions*; available from *http://isu.indstate.edu/ilnprof/ENG451/ISLAND/text.html*.

21. G. Douglas Pratt, "Being and God: An Ontological-Relational Approach to the Concept of God," 36–38, in *The Religious Dimension* (Auckland, New Zealand: Rep Prep, 1976), 37.

human. Hence, human being, as well as cosmic being, "is neither a self-sufficient . . . substance nor an autonomous individual . . . but a being . . . [which] lives . . . only in I-Thou-We relations."[22]

Philosophers applied this attribute of self-sufficiency, moreover, not only to cosmic and human beings but also to the Divine. When substance ontology is applied to the Divine, God is conceived as "an objective, metaphysical, self-existent Being."[23] This should not be surprising "because [if] independence and self-subsistence are the basic characters of substantial being, its perfect embodiment must be self-produced or unproduced, uncaused, uncreated."[24] Despite the many twists and turns in the historical course of theology, this philosophical conception of the Divine has endured, although not without its critics. A famous critique of this conception of the Divine came from Blaise Pascal (1623–1662) who contrasted the God of Abraham, Isaac, and Jacob—the God of the Bible—with the God of the philosophers like Plato and Aristotle. While some belie this contrast, the fundamental disparity is this:

> The [God of the philosophers] is allegedly only a human conception—a product of rational theologizing, with no explicit basis in biblical revelation. While the philosophers' God is variously conceived, it is usually said to be, among other things, absolutely unlimited in all respects, wholly other, absolutely simple, immaterial, nonspatial, nontemporal, immutable, and impassible. By way of contrast, the biblical record describes the God of Abraham, Isaac, and Jacob as "the living God" who created man in his "own image and likeness" (Genesis 1:26), who spoke with Moses "face to face, as a man speaketh unto his friend" (Exodus 33:11). He is the loving God who is profoundly "touched with the feeling of our infirmities" (Hebrews 4:15) and salvifically involved in our individual and collective lives.[25]

22. Walter Kasper, *The God of Jesus Christ*, trans. Matthew J. O'Connell (New York: Crossroad, 1984), 290.

23. J. A. T. Robinson, *Exploration into God* (London: SCM, 1967), 61.

24. Magda King, *Heidegger's Philosophy* (Oxford: Basil Blackwell, 1964), 16.

25. David W. Paulsen, "The God of Abraham, Isaac, and (William) James," *The Journal of Speculative Philosophy* 13.2 (1999): 114–146, at 114.

Beyond these and other biblical warrants for questioning the philosophical self-sufficiency of God, several contemporary Christian theologians point to the core belief in God as Trinity. Such a pointing does not assert a God who lives as a solitary monad or unitary Being in a state of splendid isolation, but a God whose very essence and existence is characterized by relationship through which a diversity of Divine Persons exists as the unity of one God.

The Problem of Dualism

Indisputably the dualism in Platonic and Aristotelian metaphysics has preserved the ontological distinctions between substances of different orders and different species. Nonetheless, it has done so at the price of equality and at the cost of union.

The Price of Equality

At the time of Plato and Aristotle, people believed in a hierarchy of being with a corresponding hierarchy of value or of goodness. One of Plato's interpreters, Augustine of Hippo (354–430 CE), carried the notion forward into Christian theology. According to the hierarchy of being, "living beings are higher than nonliving, while within the category of the living, sentient beings are higher than non-sentient, rational higher than nonrational, and so on through the order of natural beings, and up the scale to god in Augustine's version. So far as the order of nature is concerned, humans are at the apex of the hierarchy."[26]

This perspective, with some assistance from the biblical creation stories, has contributed to the hierarchy of the human over the material world in which the nonhuman is subordinate to the human, serves the needs of the human, and has, therefore, only instrumental value to the human. Some suggest this hierarchical arrangement has contributed to the ecological crisis and the despoliation of the natural environment. Contemporary cosmology and evolutionary biology reject this anthropocentric perspective. Contemporary cosmology clearly tells a creation story in which the cosmos and its creatures share a common origin in an original singularity, a "primeval, unimaginably condensed

---

26. Ted Benton, "Realism about the Value of Nature?" in *Defending Objectivity: Essays in Honour of Andrew Collier*, edited by Margaret S. Archer and William Outhwaite (London: Routledge, 2004), 245, as it appears in the original.

mass of fundamental particles and energy," consisting of the most basic subatomic elements of matter-energy-space-time.[27] Not only does this common origin belie a substantial distinction between humans and the rest of the material world but also in tandem with evolutionary biology, it also implies an *inverse* hierarchy of being in which humans, the last to arrive on the scene, are critically dependent on the natural world for their sustenance and survival. Thus, the story of contemporary cosmology and evolutionary biology indicates that reality shares a common origin, a common nature, and an inherent relation and calls into question the ontological hierarchy based on substance.

The ontological hierarchy of the divine, human, and nonhuman also implies a dualism between spirit and matter. Though part of the natural world, humans occupy a higher place in the hierarchy of being not only because they are animate realities, as opposed to inanimate realities but also because humans are deemed to possess rationality, freedom, and a soul—that spiritual element within matter connecting them to the immaterial world of the supernatural. In addition to being immaterial, the soul is also considered to be immortal, destined to return after the death of the body to the spiritual realm from which it came.

While a material body and an immaterial soul clearly represent a dualism of substance, the union of body and soul is essential to what it means to be human. To explain how these two irreducible and opposite substances can nonetheless coexist in one being, adherents of substance ontology have proposed a variety of theories explaining how the spiritual soul and the material body are united. For Plato, the human was a sum of separate parts. For Augustine, the human was composed of a soul and body; but the soul was not the body, and the body was not the soul. Hence, no real union took place. Aristotle believed humans were composites of form and matter, which called into question the incorruptibility of the soul after the death of the body. Aquinas attempted to resolve the problem of soul-body dualism by proposing that the soul is the form and substance of the body and elevates the body to a spiritual existence.

The dualism between the mind and body has posed problems for human existence and has had other problematic effects. The

---

27. Arthur Peacocke, "Theology and Science Today," in *Cosmos and Creation: Science and Theology in Consonance*, ed. Ted Peters (Nashville, TN: Abingdon, 1989), 30.

problems stem from the fact that mind and body/matter and spirit are not only conceived dualistically but also interpreted hierarchically with the mind valued over the body and spirit valued over matter. This split leads to several negative consequences. First, it has been blamed for the denial and, in fact, denigration of the body. This view sees the body as the prison of the immaterial and infinite soul, which ceaselessly yearns for release. Hence, the body—its needs and well-being—has been subjected to indifference at best and abuse at worst, for the soul and its salvation are of primary importance. Such a viewpoint has mired countless people in oppression and suffering and left them seeking the world to come instead of rightfully demanding justice in the world here and now. Moreover, in patriarchal societies, the spirit/matter dualism has translated into a male/female dualism, which associates men with the spiritual, the rational, and the godly; and women with the natural, the nonrational, and the earthly. Like Earth and its resources, women were perceived as having only instrumental value to satisfy the needs of men, rather than sharing the intrinsic value born of the same substance, the same dignity, and the same potential as men.

Finally, the spirit/matter dualism has posed difficulties for conceiving how God might be present and active in the natural world, both human and nonhuman. According to substance ontology, when primary substances of the same order unite, they do not retain their original substances but become a new substance. For example, adding the substance tin to the substance copper makes bronze; adding the substance zinc to the substance copper results in brass. In the animal world, a cama is the offspring of a camel and llama; in the world of fruit, a grapple emerges from crossing a grape and apple. One often finds examples of this sort of hybridity in the natural world. These examples highlight the point that, in substance ontology, the union of two substances compromises the integrity of each of the original substances.

The Cost of Union

The issue becomes more complex, however, when one contemplates the possibilities for union of God with the world. The substance of God, as noted previously, is immaterial, eternal, simple, immutable, impassible, and necessary (not dependent on anything else for its origin or sustenance). On the contrary, the substance of the natural world is material, temporal, compound, contingent, changeable, and able to be affected. Because of this substance dualism between God and the cosmos, philosophers have generally conceived of God's presence and action in the world through the two paradigms of transcendence and immanence. These paradigms, in turn, have been expressed in the beliefs of deism, theism, and pantheism.

The paradigm of transcendence asserts the ontological distinction between God and the world or between Creator and creation. Its extreme form is deism, the belief that God created a law-abiding universe that God then left to run on its own. It stresses the unequivocal transcendence of God and allows no interaction or involvement between God and the world. Christian theology has tended to moderate this extremism while still emphasizing divine transcendence. Thus, it has tended toward theism, the view that God is a personal and purposeful eternal being who principally transcends the world and yet acts immanently within it. In this paradigm, God interacts with the world through particular acts of special providence or miracles that counter the freedoms, the natural laws, or the natural processes that God put in place. These interventions are perceived as episodic or intermittent, which begs the question of whether God's power and providence toward creation happens only on occasion or is in fact an ever-present and ever-active relationship. Finally, although theism incorporates both the transcendent and immanent aspects of the divine nature, it contends in its classical form that while God affects and transforms the universe, the universe cannot affect God.[28]

---

28. As Aquinas indicates in his *ST*, "Since therefore God is outside the whole order of creation, and all creatures are ordered to Him, and not conversely, it is manifest that creatures are really related to God Himself; whereas in God there is no real relation to creatures, but a relation only in idea, inasmuch as creatures are referred to Him. Thus there is nothing to prevent these names which import relation to the creature from being predicated of God temporally, not by reason of any change in Him, but by reason of the change of the creature; as a column is on the right of an animal, without change in itself, but by change in the animal." (*ST*, Ia. 13. 7) And further, "Therefore there is no real relation in God to the creature; whereas in creatures there is a real relation to God; because creatures are contained under the divine order, and their very nature entails dependence on God." Thomas Aquinas, *ST*, Ia. 28. 1, trans. Fathers of the English Dominican Province; online ed. Kevin Knight; available from *www.newadvent.org/summa/*.

In contrast, the paradigm of immanence asserts that God as God is truly present in the created world. Its extreme form is pantheism, a belief that identifies God with the totality of nature, with the laws of nature, or as the world soul inherent in nature. In direct contrast to deism, pantheism stresses the immanence of God in the universe, a universe that God in no way transcends. While this model responds to questions of divine intervention, presence, power, and providence, it compromises the ontological otherness of God in the following ways: As noted previously, substance ontology holds that the union of two substances of the *same* order produces a new one that subsumes the former substances. Perceiving God and the world as substances within the same order would result in pantheism. However, that the substance of God and the substance of the world are of two *different* orders precludes the possibility for union. This is reflected in the following explanation concerning the capacity of the union of the human mind and the Divine:

> Finite substance remains finite, and eternally distinct from the Absolute; the Absolute is the sole fountain and source of knowledge which alone can harmonize the antithesis of thought and its object. . . . Although there can be no interpenetration of mind and matter—the two substances being mutually opposed—yet there can be a true and permanent union between the mind of man and the Absolute, both being of spiritual substance. . . . Spiritual and extended material substances are diametrically opposed.[29]

Hence, in substance ontology, true God cannot remain true God and be truly immanent in the cosmos. Conversely, true cosmos cannot remain true cosmos and be conceived as filled with the being of God. Thus, substance ontology with its dualisms denies the affirmation that the living and true God indwells the cosmos and its creatures. Rather, it offers a "God of the gaps" in which the Divine is intrusive rather than intrinsic to the ongoing life and creativity of the cosmos. Moreover, it has critical consequences for Christian belief in the

---

29. See "Malebranche," in *The Dictionary of Sects, Heresies, Ecclesiastical Parties and Schools of Religious Thought*, edited by John Henry Blunt (Whitefish, MT: Kessinger, 2003), 284–5.

Incarnation, the belief that the Word of God became flesh in Jesus of Nazareth proclaimed the Christ.

An essential part of the doctrine of the Incarnation is belief in the hypostatic union. This belief held that Jesus the Christ possessed both a fully divine nature (a spiritual substance) and a fully human nature (a material substance) *fully united* in one person. Because this belief concerned the thoroughly unique event of the union of divine and human natures, this was clearly a step beyond the quandary of how body and soul could be united in one person. Here the question concerned how Christians could talk about the union of two irreducibly different substances—one fully human and one fully divine—in one person in a way that did not compromise the integrity of either. In response to this unique and unrepeatable event, the church fathers did not try to explain or reconcile the hypostatic union in philosophical terms, because it exceeded anything their categories had ever conceived. Neither did they attempt to clarify why the union of two substances did not result in an entirely new substance. Rather, the Council of Chalcedon in 451 CE chose to make a definitive pronouncement to be held on the basis of faith that, nonetheless, acknowledged and retained the principal terms of the ontology of substance by keeping the natures (substances) unconfused, unchanged, indivisible, and distinct:

> We also teach that we apprehend this one and only Christ-Son, Lord, only-begotten—*in two natures*; and we do this *without confusing the two natures, without transmuting one nature into the other, without dividing them into two separate categories, without contrasting them according to area or function. The distinctiveness of each nature is not nullified by the union. Instead, the "properties" of each nature are conserved and both natures concur in one "person" and in one reality* [hypostasis]. They are not divided or cut into two persons, but are together the one and only and only-begotten Word [Logos], God, the Lord Jesus Christ.[30]

---

30. "The Council of Chalcedon (451 AD): Definition concerning the two natures of Christ," *Eternal Word Television Network*; available from *http://www.ewtn.com/library/COUNCILS/CHALCHRI.HTM*, italics added.

As this Christological conundrum illustrates and upcoming chapters of this book demonstrate, many of the tenets and implications of substance ontology are inconsistent with contemporary understandings of cosmic, human, and divine being. Substance ontology cannot adequately conceive of a God-world relationship that works with an evolutionary worldview, that responds to the deepest yearning of the human heart for unconditional love and union, and that acknowledges the intimate and enduring presence and action of the Divine in all of reality and history. At this point of impasse, this book seeks an alternative that can move the understanding of cosmic, human, and divine reality forward. The alternative it proposes is the ontology of relation.

TOWARD A RELATIONAL ONTOLOGY

Relational ontology asserts that mutual relation rather than substance constitutes, classifies, and distinguishes the very being of all that exists. In contrast to substance ontology, a relational ontology upholds the distinction between the Creator and the created, and between creatures themselves, without insisting on a radical separation in order to maintain their own individual selfhood. It does not demand this separation because relational ontology contends that the ontological distinction between Creator and created and, in fact, between creatures themselves is a distinction of *subjects* rather than *substances*. The shift from substance to relational ontology is a shift from interpreting persons and things as discrete objects according to their primary and secondary substances in isolation to interpreting persons and things as subjects in active and interactive relation to all other subjects—cosmic, human, and divine.

The Theological Basis for Relational Ontology

Theologians often trace the basis for relational ontology to Thomas Aquinas and his reflection on whether the term *person* signifies *relation* in the Trinity. According to Aquinas, "a divine person signifies a relation as subsisting . . . although in truth that which subsists in the divine nature is the divine nature itself."[31] A close reading of this

---

31. Aquinas, *ST*, Ia.29.4.

passage from the *ST* reveals Aquinas's insight that the *nature* of God, the *reality* of God, is essentially *relational*. As Trinity, the three Persons share one divine nature but are distinguished as Persons by their relation to one another. In traditional language, the three Persons are distinguished by the relations of Father to Son, Son to Father, Father and Son to Holy Spirit, Holy Spirit to Father and Son; nonetheless, all are one God. The key point here for relational ontology is that these divine relations are not distinct from the divine nature but, in fact, subsist within it and are the divine nature itself.

This assertion by Aquinas has ramifications for both human and cosmic being. Christians profess, on the basis of Scripture, that humans are made in the image and likeness of God. Therefore, if the reality and the very nature of the God in whom we believe is constituted by relation—is relation itself—then, by extension, human reality and the very nature of human being itself is constituted by and is relation. Furthermore, Christians profess that God is Creator, the very Source and Ground of Being for all created being. This leads logically to the following propositions:

If God is the Source of Being for the being of all creation, *then* the being of all creation shares in the Being of God.

If God's Being *by nature* is relational, *then* the being of all creation *by nature* is relational.

Aquinas spoke eloquently of this essential relationship between divine being and created being. In the *ST*, Aquinas calls the essential relation between God and creation *participation*, and it is not participation reserved simply to humanity. "Because the divine goodness could not be adequately represented by one creature alone," Aquinas stated, "God produced many and diverse creatures. . . . Thus the whole universe together participates in divine goodness more perfectly, and represents it better, than any single creature whatsoever."[32]

Expanding the Foundations of Relational Ontology

For some, the claims that are made in the preceding section rate as mere theological speculation. Nevertheless, this conclusion would

---

32. Ibid., *ST*, Ia.47.1.

be ill-founded. For as the chapters that follow show, beyond the claims made on the basis of the relational nature of the Christian God, the relations that constitute the very life of the cosmic and human have been observed, studied, described, and demonstrated empirically by the physical and social sciences. In the chapters that follow, insights about the universe from contemporary cosmology, evolutionary biology, and physics; about humans from sociology and psychology; and about God from classical and contemporary theology essentially affirm the relational nature of all being. Whether we consider cosmic, human, or divine being, three categories of "constitutive" or "essential" relationship—that is, a relationship so integral to the very nature of a being that, without this relationship, the being would no longer be itself—shape the content throughout this book. These are (1) a *relation of origin*, (2) a *relation of emergence*, and (3) a *relation of effect*.

Relation of Origin

As the term implies, a *relation of origin* stems from the fact that various entities share a common source of being that inextricably binds them together ontologically and existentially. Because of this common origin, particular qualities can be gleaned from, presumed of, and/or applied to the group as a whole. One example of a relation of origin from the perspective of the cosmos is the "common creation story." This story looks to a time in the order of approximately 13.7 billion years ago when the cosmos was no more than a fraction of a second old and took the form of a compressed fireball, consisting of the most basic subatomic elements of matter-energy-space-time.[33] All elements of matter, energy, space, and time that would ever exist erupted as a single quantum gift of existence from what scientists have termed the Big Bang. From this original unity came "conditions of chemical composition and temperature and radiation, permitting, through the interplay of chance and necessity, the coming into being of replicating molecules and [all] life . . . on planet Earth."[34]

---

33. Peacocke, "Theology and Science Today," 30.

34. John Polkinghorne, *One World: The Interaction of Science and Theology* (London: SPCK, 1986), 56.

Relation of Emergence

The second kind of relation is the *relation of emergence.* In evolutionary theory, the principle of emergence implies that "the whole is more than the sum of its parts." It refers to the reality that certain novel forms of life that emerge or develop from more elemental forms of life are not reducible or explainable in terms of the form or elements that preceded them. These emergent forms, therefore, require new language and concepts capable of describing them accurately in new and nonreductionist ways. Nevertheless, they bear an inherent relation to the forms that preceded them, for the creative potential of the earlier levels of organization become actualized in these surprising new forms over great expanses of time.

In this book, for example, letters join as words; words link into sentences; sentences combine into paragraphs; paragraphs build into chapters; and so on until the emergence of the finished product, which is more than the simple sum of the parts that composed it. A similar dynamic occurs in any creative activity, whether the result becomes a symphony, a painting, a skyscraper, or a newborn child. None of these outcomes or effects can be reduced to their component parts. Yet none of them could have come into being without the relations that preceded them and none of them exist independent of their inherent relations.

Relation of Effect

Finally, the *relation of effect* suggests that the entity is a unique outcome or *effect* of the relationship among the elements that constitute it, such that, without the relationship of the elements, the effect or outcome would not exist. The *relation of effect* reveals itself in the very particle structure of matter at the subatomic level. As atomic physicist Henry Stapp has pointed out, "An elementary particle is not an independently existing unanalyzable entity. It is, in essence, a set of relationships that reach outward to other things."[35] Werner Heisenberg, one of the founders of quantum theory, substantiates

---

35. Henry Stapp, in Frithjof Capra, "The New Vision of Reality: Toward a Synthesis of Eastern Wisdom and Modern Science," in *Ancient Wisdom and Modern Science,* ed. Stanislav Grof (Albany, NY: State University of New York Press, 1984), 135–148 at 138.

Stapp's insight and contends, "The world thus appears as a complicated tissue of events, in which connections of different kinds alternate or overlap or combine and thereby determine the texture of the whole."[36]

Why These Three Relations?

While many other relationships exist among and within beings, there are compelling reasons for concentrating on these three. First, each applies to relations within all the categories of being to be discussed—nonhuman, human, and divine. Second, all three describe a relational concept applicable to a broad range of beings within each category itself. Third, each one identifies relations that are recognizably constitutive or essential. Without the relation, the entity would either become something entirely other or cease to be at all. Fourth, each relationship is supported by the data gathered by the discipline that studies each of the beings we consider in the chapters to come—the disciplines of evolutionary and physical sciences, of social and behavioral sciences, and of Christian theology. Finally, because of their pervasiveness, the three relations enable logical and coherent connections and inferences to be drawn among and about the nonhuman, human, and divine realms of being that are explored.

The chapters that follow examine these three relations in greater detail and apply them to cosmic, human, and divine being. The insights of the evolutionary and physical sciences and of cosmology point out the essential relatedness of cosmic being from the subatomic level to the expanses of the universe. Psychologists offer psychosocial theories of personality that affirm the indispensability of interpersonal, social, and environmental relationships in constituting human personhood over the course of a lifetime.

While each of the disciplines above sketches out its own foundation for its claims of how relationality is constitutive of cosmic and human being, Christian theologians, following Aquinas, ground their claims about the essential relationality of cosmic and human being in the essential relationality of God as Trinity. If God who is

---

36. Werner Heisenberg, *Physics and Philosophy: The Revolution in Modern Science* (New York: Harper, 1958), 96.

Being Itself is, as Trinity, relational by nature, then, as the Source of all created being, this Triune God constitutes the being of creation itself as relational.

SUMMARY

The nature and constitution of reality have provoked significant questions and answers in many academic disciplines, including the natural sciences, the social sciences, theology, and philosophy. As this chapter demonstrated, the philosophical discipline of metaphysics is noteworthy in this regard because it has wrestled for centuries over the meaning of *reality* and *being* qua *being*. The origin of the most common response of metaphysics to the question of reality and being derives from the work of Plato and Aristotle, both of whom posit the notion of substance as what constitutes reality.

Because of its starting point in empirical reality, Aristotle's understanding of substance served as the foundation for this chapter's exploration of the ontology of substance. Demonstrating how Aristotle used the term *primary substance* to refer to a particular individual or to a particular thing existing in its own right, the term *secondary substance* to discuss the categories into which these are classified, and the term *accidents* to refer to the particular qualities attributed to them, this chapter, nonetheless, asked whether this description of being in terms of *primary substance, secondary substance,* and *accidents* reveals anything more than a sense perception of an entity and leaves open the question of its essential reality. It further questioned how sense perception assisted one in knowing the reality of what is immaterial or spiritual, such as the reality of God. Moreover, it discussed several dilemmas inherent in substance ontology that have been problematic in the light of contemporary understandings of the cosmos, the human person, and the Christian God.

The first was the problem of stasis, which implied that cosmic and human beings are static entities and that what constitutes a person or thing is a particular nature with more or less stable attributes. Following from the problem of stasis was the problem of self-sufficiency, which asserted that the more autonomous and independent an individual proved to be, the more valued and perfected it is—an assertion, however, challenged by contemporary cosmology, physics, psychology, sociology, and anthropology that have consistently emphasized the critical roles of interdependence, of interrelationship, and of dynamism in living entities and systems. Substance ontology also carried the problem of dualism. First, this dualism of substances was hierarchical, with a corresponding hierarchy of value or of goodness. The fact that mind and body/matter and spirit, for example, are not only conceived dualistically but also interpreted hierarchically posed difficulties for conceiving the value of the natural world. Moreover, the fact that spiritual and material substances cannot intermingle raised questions of how God might be present and active in the lives of human and nonhuman beings. Thus, adherence to substance ontology also comes at the cost of union between God and the world. In substance ontology, God cannot remain truly God and be immanent in the cosmos, and the cosmos cannot remain truly cosmos and filled with the being of God.

Because substance ontology, therefore, can neither adequately address a relational contemporary worldview nor respond to the deepest yearning of the human heart for union with the Divine nor acknowledge the intimate and enduring presence and action of the Divine in all of reality and history, this chapter proposed an alternative ontology, that of an ontology of relation. Relational ontology asserts that it is the relations within and between all that exists that constitute, classify, and distinguish the very being of each existent. While theology traces the basis for relational ontology to Thomas Aquinas's teaching on the Being of the Trinity, insights from contemporary cosmology, evolutionary biology, and physics, as well as from sociology and psychology affirm the relational nature of the universe. Moreover, three particular relations exist that arguably constitute all forms of being, whether cosmic, human, or divine. The first is the relation of origin that stems from the reality that various entities share a common source of being that inextricably binds and constitutes them ontologically and existentially. The second is the relation of emergence that contends that while novel forms of life emerge or develop from more elemental forms of life and bear an inherent relation to the forms that preceded them, they are not reducible or explainable in terms of the form or elements that preceded them. They, therefore, require new language and concepts capable of describing them accurately as the creative potential of the earlier levels of organization become actualized in these surprising new forms over great expanses of time. Finally, the relation of effect suggests that an entity is a unique outcome or effect of the relationship among the elements that constitute it, such that, without the relationship of the elements, the effect or outcome would not exist.

The chapters that follow demonstrate that, when heard in the timbre of relational ontology, the scholarly claims of the evolutionary and physical sciences, of sociological and psychosocial theory, and of classical and contemporary theology ring with a singular resonance. They all affirm the principal point of the following statement based on quantum physics and chaos theory, namely, that we are, *in essence*, our relationships:

> The universe that quantum physics and chaotic dynamics reveal is a fundamentally relational universe where subject and object are interpenetrating presences. In a relational universe, to speak of 'an object' is to speak in a short-handed way of patterns of complex, dynamically interpenetrating relationships. These relationships are dynamic and nonlinear. The relational universe is not the world of discrete, atomistic objects that behave deterministically, therefore predictably, according to linear causality. As A interacts with B, the identity of A changes to reflect its interaction with B. Likewise for B. As A and B continue to interact, along with innumerable others, changes to their "identity" complexify beyond measure and prediction. . . . All of us, including non-human beings, are our relationships. We are nothing other than our relationships—with each other, with the world. We are patterns that connect.[37]

37. Heesoon Bai and Hartley Banack, "'To See a World in a Grain of Sand': Complexity Ethics and Moral Education," *Complicity: An International Journal of Complexity and Education* 3:1 (2006): 5–20 at 9–10.

FOR FURTHER READING

Kasper, Walter. *The God of Jesus Christ*. Translated by Matthew J. O'Connell. New York: Crossroad, 1984.

Peacocke, Arthur. "Theology and Science Today." In *Cosmos and Creation: Science and Theology in Consonance*, edited by Ted Peters. Nashville, TN: Abingdon, 1989.

Polkinghorne, John. *One World: The Interaction of Science and Theology*. London: SPCK, 1986.

Chapter 2

COSMIC BEING AS RELATION

"All of us, including non-human beings, are our relationships.
We are nothing other than our relationships—with each other,
with the world. We are patterns that connect."[1]

INTRODUCTION

This chapter explores the relationships that constitute the essential nature of the "nonhuman beings" included in this quote. Such non-human beings include all the animate and inanimate, organic and inorganic forms that populate and inhabit the cosmos and that have done so in more elemental or primitive forms for millennia before the appearance of humans. In developing the idea of the relational nature of the cosmos—a name that signifies a harmonious system or whole—this chapter applies the three categories of relationship defined at the conclusion of the first chapter: (1) a *relation of origin*, (2) a *relation of emergence*, and (3) a *relation of effect*. Recall that these relationships are considered "constitutive" or "essential." This means that the relationship is so elemental to the very nature of a particular being that without this relationship the being would no longer be itself.

---

1. Bai and Banack, "To See a World in a Grain of Sand," 10.

THE RELATION OF ORIGIN:
A COMMON CREATION STORY

As the name implies, a *relation of origin* stems from the fact that various entities share a common source of being that inextricably binds them together ontologically (by nature) and existentially (in existence). Because of this common origin, particular qualities can be gleaned from and applied to the group as a whole. In this chapter, the principal relation of origin to be considered is that of the "common creation story."

The common creation story looks to a time approximately 13.7 billion years ago. When no more than a fraction of a second old, the cosmos took the form of a compressed fireball, a "primeval, unimaginably condensed mass of fundamental particles and energy," consisting of the most basic subatomic elements of matter-energy-space-time.[2] Then, as described by Arthur Peacocke's poetic rendition of the epic of evolution,

> Obeying its given laws and with one intensely hot surge
> > of energy—
> > a hot Big Bang—
> > [an] Other exploded as the universe
> > from a point twelve or so billion years ago in our time,
> > > thereby making space.
> Vibrating fundamental particles appeared, expanded
> > and expanded
> > and cooled into clouds of gas, bathed in radiant light.
> Still the universe went on expanding and condensing
> > into swirling whirlpools of matter and light—
> > > a billion galaxies.
> Five billion years ago, one star in one galaxy—our Sun—
> > attracted round it matter as planets.
> One of them was our Earth.

---

2. Peacocke, "Theology and Science Today," 30.

On Earth, the assembly of atoms and the temperatures became
    just right
  to allow water and solid rock to form.
Continents and mountains grew
    and in some wet crevice, or pool, or deep in the sea,
      just over three billion years ago,
      some molecules became large and complex enough to make
        copies of themselves
    and so the first specks of life.
Life multiplied in the seas, diversifying and becoming more and
    more complex.
Five hundred million years ago,
    creatures with solid skeletons, the vertebrates, appeared.
On land, green plants changed the atmosphere
    by making oxygen.
Then 300 million years ago, certain fish learned to crawl from
    the sea
  and live on the edge of land, breathing oxygen from the air.
Now life burst into many forms—
    reptiles and mammals (and dinosaurs) on land,
    flying reptiles and birds in the air.
Over millions of years,
    the mammals began to develop complex brains that enabled
      them to learn.
Among these were creatures who lived in trees.
From these our first ancestors derived and then,
    only 40,000 years ago,
    the first men and women appeared.[3]

Darwin and Evolution

While the details of this evolutionary epic have derived from
the efforts of countless natural and physical scientists who have

---

3. Peacocke, "The Challenge and Stimulus," 89–90.

persistently worked to establish the validity of its fundamental elements within their scientific fields, the paradigm that shapes it is largely associated with British naturalist Charles Darwin. However, the path to this validation for Darwin himself was not without obstacles. At the outset, Darwin's fellow naturalists were skeptical about an evolutionary worldview. In his seminal 1859 work, *On the Origin of Species by Means of Natural Selection, or the Preservation of Favoured Races in the Struggle for Life*,[4] Darwin characterized the prevailing perspectives at the time of history in which he wrote:

> Until recently the great majority of naturalists believed that species were immutable productions, and had been separately created. This view has been ably maintained by many authors. Some few naturalists, on the other hand, have believed that species undergo modification, and that the existing forms of life are the descendants by true generation of pre-existing forms.[5]

His studies in South America, the Galapagos Islands, and the Pacific coral reefs aboard the H.M.S. *Beagle*, however, led Darwin to a different and ultimately revolutionary conclusion:

> I can entertain no doubt . . . that the view which most naturalists until recently entertained, and which I formerly entertained—namely, that each species has been independently created—is erroneous. I am fully convinced that species are not immutable; but that those belonging to what are called the same genera are lineal descendants of some other and generally extinct species, in the same manner as the acknowledged varieties of any one species are the descendants of that species. Furthermore, I am convinced that natural selection has been the most important, but not the exclusive, means of modification.[6]

---

4. Charles Darwin, *On the Origin of Species by Means of Natural Selection, or the Preservation of Favoured Races in the Struggle for Life* [book online] (London: John Murray, 1872); available from *http://www.literature.org/authors/darwin-charles/the-origin-of-species-6th-edition/*.

5. Ibid.

6. Ibid.

Since that time, both history and science have clearly given witness to the legitimacy and endurance of Darwin's conviction. In fewer than two hundred years and in the face of challenges from certain religious traditions and segments of the scientific community, the fundamental validity of the evolutionary worldview has been so sufficiently established that many of those living in the twenty-first century find it no longer possible to operate solely within the biblical worldview that shaped the understanding of the creation of the universe for thousands of years.

For the purposes of this book, Darwin's theory of the evolution of species may be summarized in two propositions: First, Darwin theorized that all organisms, past, present, and future, have a common descent from earlier living systems. Second, Darwin proposed that different species of such organisms derive from prior species through the process of natural selection.[7] This process of selection, according to Darwin, follows from "the struggle for life:"

> Owing to this struggle, variations, however slight and from whatever cause proceeding, if they be in any degree profitable to the individuals of a species . . . will tend to the preservation of such individuals, and will generally be inherited by the offspring. The offspring, also, will thus have a better chance of surviving.[8]

Darwin recognized that his theory would raise objections from others who studied such variations in species. He pointed out, for example, that "naturalists continually refer to external conditions, such as climate, food, etc., as the only possible cause of variation." However, Darwin thought that this was a very limited perspective, one that was, in fact, "preposterous." Marveling at the array of bodily and behavioral adaptations that he observed in nature, Darwin thought it unreasonable "to attribute to mere external conditions, the structure, for instance, of the woodpecker, with its feet, tail, beak, and tongue, so admirably adapted to catch insects under the bark of trees."[9]

---

7. Peacocke, *Theology for a Scientific Age*, 56.

8. Darwin, *On the Origin of Species*, available from *http://www.literature.org/ authors/darwin-charles/the-origin-of-species-6th-edition/chapter-03.html*.

9. Ibid.

Nevertheless, Darwin lacked the scientific evidence to validate his theory of natural selection and his intuition about its cause. That would be left to nineteenth-century biologist Gregor Mendel, who identified the laws of heredity and the science of genetics. The dynamics of the process of heredity would be further clarified by the twentieth-century discovery by James Dewey Watson and Francis Crick of the helical structure of the DNA molecule, the carrier of genetic information. Hence, when one combines Darwin's theory of evolution with Mendel's theory of genetics and Watson and Crick's discovery of the DNA molecule, one arrives at an understanding of the dynamic that Darwin proposed.

The process Darwin termed *natural selection* occurs on the basis of naturally occurring genetic variations within individuals in populations. When this genetic variation enables a particular member of a species to adapt to its environment, to obtain sufficient nourishment, to survive its potential challenges, and thus, to reproduce itself, then that particular specimen of the species thrives while others not so adapted fail. Generally speaking, the main impetus for the genetic variations that occur and that result in the appearance or disappearance of certain species comes from random genetic mutations within the organism and within its population. However, because such mutations are both random and rare, evolution is a slow, gradual process, requiring great expanses of time.

Law and Chance in the Evolutionary Process

Over time, scientists have observed that the process by which these genetic variations result in evolutionary creativity involves the dynamic relationship between law and chance. This dynamic results in remarkable continuity of form throughout the ages even as it produces novelty in the transition from one form of organization to another. Think of the continuity and the novelty in the development of humans throughout the ages. This genus and species developed from *Homo habilis*, the "handy" hominid; to *Homo erectus*, the "standing" hominid; to *Homo sapiens*, the "wise or intelligent" hominid—with all the variation in between. Continuity among these creatures occurred because natural laws such as heredity governed the general processes that produced each form of the genus *Homo*. Because such laws apply to and, in fact, govern the life and development of not only human forms of life but also myriads of other forms of cosmic life, they produce an overarching and enduring relationship among these human life forms and forge bonds between humans and the great diversity of other life forms.

This relationship stretches back to the beginning of the universe when such natural laws guided the rates and possibilities of cosmic change as it developed from hydrogen nuclei to heavier atoms to small molecules to macromolecules, then through aggregates of molecules to primitive cells to living organisms and beyond—forming an indissoluble relationship among all the cosmic forms that have ever existed and, in fact, will ever exist. Even when novel forms emerge from chance variations and mutations that occur unpredictably at the subatomic level—such as the novelty that distinguishes the handy, standing, and intelligent hominid—such new forms become observable and inheritable because these variations and mutations are swept into the dynamism of natural law at the macroscopic level, laws that link life forms to one another in the processes by which they develop and become more complex. This view of evolutionary creativity—a view that emphasizes the dynamic of law and chance that preserves robust life forms and produces novel ones—belies the caricature of "nature red in tooth and claw" often used to summarize the evolution of species. "The view of evolution as chronic bloody competition among individuals and species," according to biologist Lynn Margulis and writer Dorian Sagan, "dissolves before a new view of continual cooperation, strong interaction, and mutual dependence among life forms. Life did not take over the globe by combat but by networking."[10]

The form of natural law demonstrated previously is genetic theory. The combination and recombination of dominant and recessive genes over many generations are generally predictable, which has been a great boon to breeders of plants and animals alike. In the midst of the experimentation, observation, and research that identified natural laws such as that of genetics, however, scientists discovered that the relationship of natural law between life forms was not

---

10. Lynn Margulis and Dorion Sagan, *Microcosmos: Four Billion Years of Evolution from our Microbial Ancestors* (Berkeley, CA: University of California, 1997), 29.

the only dynamic in play. Because of unexpected variations of life forms within a particular species, which at times resulted in variations within species or in the origin of a whole new species, scientists conjectured that another relationship operated to produce these novel forms. That relationship was the interplay between natural law and the operation of chance.

Evolutionary biologists apply the term *chance* to either of two scientific circumstances: On one hand, scientists term a situation *chance* when there is scientific ignorance concerning the conditions and variables that cause a particular outcome. On the other hand, a chance occurrence may result from the intersection of two otherwise unrelated causes that interact to produce a new outcome. In this second case, while scientists can explain each cause in itself, no predictable connection between these causes was made before the point at which they intersect.

Classic examples of this second kind of chance usually involve the influence of environmental variables on life forms in that environment. An often repeated story is that of the peppered moth. In England during the mid-nineteenth century, the peppered moth primarily produced offspring with light colored wings, with an occasional dark-winged variation. As the story goes, when flying around,

> The little moths [both light- and dark-winged] would alight on the light-colored tree trunks; and birds, able to see the darker ones more easily, ate them and tended to ignore the light-colored varieties. . . . In the 1850s, about 98% of the uneaten peppered moths were the light variety; [nevertheless], because of recessive and dominant genes, peppered moths regularly produced both varieties as offspring.[11]

However, the smoke and grime that resulted from the Industrial Revolution made the tree trunks darker, and the light-winged moths became easy prey while the dark-winged moths, less visible to the birds, were able to survive. By the 1950s, approximately 98 percent of

---

11. Vance Ferrell, "Natural Selection," in *Science vs. Evolution*; available from *http://www.pathlights.com/ce_encyclopedia/sci-ev/sci_vs_ev_9.htm*.

the peppered moths were the dark variety.[12] In the light of Darwin's theory of natural selection, this outcome now makes sense. Nonetheless, at the time, no prevailing paradigm applied that would have enabled scientists to foresee or predict the outcome of this random crossing of environment and inhabitants.

Through such relationships between law and chance, this common creation story continues to unfold. It began as a single quantum gift of existence through which all the elements of matter, energy, space, and time that would ever exist erupted into being. Over eons of time and expanses of space, from this original unity came diversity. From primeval darkness came light. Stretching out from the Big Bang, the process of the evolution of life involved "a continuous, almost kaleidoscopic, recombination of the component units of the universe into an increasing diversity of forms."[13] Relationships and interrelationships exponentially multiplied, each unique and yet each inextricably interwoven in a grand web of existence! As a result of this process,

> . . . the universe is complexly interconnected, everything being related to everything else to some degree. . . . The story of biological evolution, moreover, makes evident that we humans share with all other living creatures a common genetic ancestry tracing back to the original single-celled creatures in the ancient sea. Bacteria, pine trees, blueberries, horses, the great gray whales—we are all kin in the great community of life.[14]

THE RELATION OF EMERGENCE: THE WHOLE IS MORE THAN THE SUM OF ITS PARTS

It is evolutionary theory itself that generates the principle and *relation of emergence*. The term *emergence* implies that "the whole is more than the sum of its parts." It refers to the reality that certain novel

---

12. Ibid.

13. Arthur Peacocke, "God as the Creator of the World of Science," in *Interpreting the Universe as Creation*, ed. V. Brummer (Kampen, Netherlands: Kok Pharos, 1991), 103.

14. Johnson, *Quest for the Living God*, 184.

forms of life that develop—emerge—from more elemental forms of life are not reducible or explainable in terms of the form or elements that preceded them, but neither are they independent of them. These emergent forms, however, differ so significantly from the forms that preceded them that new vocabulary and concepts are required in order to describe them accurately in new and nonreductionist ways. Nevertheless, the "novel" bears an inherent relation to the forms that preceded it because in these surprising new forms, called "emergents," the creative potential of the earlier levels of existence actualizes itself over great expanses of time.

Examples of emergence span the cosmos itself. They include a diversity of phenomena such as the formation of hurricanes and sand dunes, the construction of ant colonies and termite mounds, and the development of organisms and consciousness. Consider this description of the emergence of a hurricane from the science series *NOVA*:

> Take a small atmospheric disturbance whirling around in a stretch of warm tropical ocean, at least 80°F. Make sure it's 300 miles or more from the equator so it's sufficiently stirred by the Earth's rotation. Season it with evaporating seawater, which condenses when it rises high enough into the atmosphere. Lower the atmospheric pressure near the surface. What do you get? The emergent happening known as a hurricane, with its emergent attributes (e.g., winds of at least 74 miles per hour) and its emergent behaviors (e.g., an ability to suddenly alter course).[15]

Billions of neurons emerge as consciousness; buyers, sellers, and myriad transactions emerge as the stock market; parents and children emerge as a family; multitudes of families emerge as societies. From the mundane to the sublime, each of these is an example of emergence that impacts daily lives.

Emergence in the cosmos is creative in ways analogous to human creativity. Human creativity continually produces sounds, words, objects, and events by building relationships between more rudimentary elements resulting in constructions not necessarily predictable in

---

15. Peter Tyson, "Emergence: Everyday Examples," *NOVA scienceNOW*, available from *http://www.pbs.org/wgbh/nova/sciencenow/3410/03-ever-nf.html.*

advance. Such a dynamic occurs in any creative activity, whether the result becomes a symphony, a painting, a skyscraper, or a newborn child. None of these outcomes or effects can be reduced to their component parts. Yet none of them could have come into being without the relations that preceded them and none of them exist independently of their inherent relations.

Varied as they are, common threads bind the preceding examples of emergence from both cosmic and human creativity together. In general terms, there are four overarching characteristics of emergent forms: First, in each emergent form, "there are a number of nested levels of detail, each of which has properties different from those levels that comprise it, and so needs a new holistic type of description or label to be applied."[16] Think for a moment of an ant colony.

> Ants are not mental giants, and they can't see the big picture. Yet out of their simple behaviors . . . arises a classic example of emergence: the ant colony. The colony exhibits an extraordinary ability to explore and exploit its surroundings. It is aware of and reacts to food sources, floods, enemies, and other phenomena, over a substantial piece of ground. Each ant dies after days or months, but the colony survives for years, becoming more stable and organized over time.[17]

The levels of details in the construction of an ant colony include instinctive behavior, surrounding environment, sources of food, presence of enemies, and potential for natural disaster. Each of these levels presents itself uniquely and each has a complexity all its own. Yet when taken together, what emerges is more than the sum of each of these discrete levels; it is in fact an integrated whole—a colony—that is wholly related to the levels that comprise it, but which is indescribable by language that applies to any one level alone.

Second, while the properties of an emergent cannot be reduced to the levels that precede it, the examples presented demonstrate that if one were to remove any of the preceding levels, the emergent itself

---

16. Chris Lucas, "Emergence and Evolution—Constraints on Form," *The Complexity & Artificial Life Research Concept*; available from *http://www.calresco.org/emerge.htm*.

17. Tyson, "Emergence: Everyday Examples."

would no longer exist. Scientists call this state of an emergent *supervenience*, defined as relational dependency among sets of properties. The state of supervenience can be demonstrated by considering the previous example of the hurricane. In the absence of a particular level of wind velocity, atmospheric pressure, or water temperature, the hurricane cannot develop because the elements necessary for its emergence were absent. Thus, although a hurricane cannot be *reduced to* a particular level of wind, pressure, or temperature, without any one of these elements, the emergent hurricane would not exist. Consequently, the property of supervenience leads to a third characteristic of an emergent form, the one expressed in the subtitle of this section: "The whole is more than the sum of its parts." This phrase means that the novel life form is not just an accumulation of the elements and structures from which it emerges. The hurricane, the ant colony, and this book represent a collection of parts to be sure, but the product is the result of complex relations and interactions among these parts to produce the novel form. Because of the essential relation and interactions among the parts, the emergent presents itself as a wholly unique and irreducible manifestation of the dynamic interrelationship among its components parts.

Fourth and finally, a mutually causal relationship exists between an emergent and its component parts. The nature of this relationship is captured by the term *whole-part interaction*. This *whole-part interaction* first describes a type of causality that scientists have observed repeatedly, namely, that the properties, behaviors, and interrelationships of the parts of a system influence the properties, behaviors, and interrelationships of the whole of the system. Examples are myriad and easy to imagine. Consider a computer, a cell phone, a car, or a human body. If any of the component parts of these "systems" stops functioning, the system itself ceases to function properly. If a microchip fails or a fan belt cracks or a heart stops beating, the whole system fails as well. It does so *precisely* because the interrelationship of its component parts constitutes the being of the system as a whole and if the component parts are not able to relate, the being of the system is affected. This seems to be common sense.

However, emergence demonstrates a further phenomenon. Not only does the state of each component affect the system as a whole but also the state of the system as a whole affects the behavior of the component parts. Again, it does so *precisely* because the being of the system as a whole has an essential relationship with its component parts.

Place a beaker of water on a burner in a lab. The heat from the burner affects the system as a whole—the water—and ultimately excites the hydrogen and oxygen whose relationship constitutes the water. This excitement changes the behavior of the molecules and causes the formation of bubbles. These bubbles rapidly and chaotically rise to the surface of the water but then remarkably organize into a regular pattern of movement as long as the heat remains. Remove the heat and the component parts eventually settle into the state they were in prior to the heat that affected the system as a whole. Hence, the effects exerted on the system of water as a whole caused the molecules to behave differently than if they were in isolation.

Furthermore, in some cases the parts are impaired because of the state of the system. All the component parts of a computer may be functional but in the absence of a proper operating system or integrative program, the parts do not relate properly, and the whole cannot function as it ought. In the human body, the heart may be healthy, the arms and legs may be strong, and the lungs may be capable, but if the brain—the organizing system, so to speak—fails to send signals that enable these parts to interrelate with one another and with other vital components of the whole, neither the organs nor the body functions properly. Clearly, realities existing at lower levels ("the parts") not only affect the realities existing at higher levels ("the whole") but also they are affected by them.

Through this discussion of emergence, one can see that the history of nature is "a nexus of evolving forms," dynamic in character and always in process. In view of evolutionary emergence, "the 'being' of the world is always also a 'becoming' and there is always a story to be told, especially as matter becomes living and then conscious, and eventually, social too."[18] Because of this phenomenon of ongoing emergence, scientists have long questioned whether there are trends in the evolutionary process. Some see the evolution of life as "a copiously branching bush, continually pruned by the grim reaper of extinction, not a ladder of predictable progress."[19] Others maintain

---

18. Peacocke, "God as the Creator of the World of Science," 102.

19. Stephen J. Gould, *Wonderful Life: The Burgess Shale and the Nature of History* (London: Penguin, 1989), 35.

that evolution has a precise orientation toward the emergence of humanity, such that all of the eons of inorganic and organic development had little intrinsic value of their own.[20] A less radical form of this perspective asserts that, since the emergence of new forms appears over time to result in a hierarchy of organization and complexity, there is a propensity to see all emergence as tending toward humanity. Critics of this thinking declare that such a perspective makes too much of humanity as the measure of the creative process. Rather, these critics urge that research assess cosmic and biological development using criteria that do not assume that humanity is the climax or the culmination of the process. Regardless of one's position concerning trends in evolutionary emergence, one thing is plain, as chemical engineer and philosopher of science Kenneth Denbigh (1911–2004) observed: "Cosmic evolution has been attended by a great increase in the richness and diversity of forms . . . [which] has made its appearance out of homogeneity. . . . [This] is an inventive process and is one that is still continuing."[21] And this process is constituted by relationship!

RELATIONS OF EFFECT: BONDING IN A CREATIVE COSMOS

The *relation of effect* bears an innate connection to the *relation of emergence* because the relation of effect essentially defines the dynamic that underlies the process of emergence. Like the relation of emergence, a relation of effect exists among the essential elements that make up a particular entity, and the entity itself is a unique outcome or effect of the relationship among the elements that constitute it. Without the relationship of the elements, the effect or outcome would not exist. There is, however, a difference between the relation of emergence and the relation of effect.

Not every relation of effect results in an emergent form, that is, a form so novel that it cannot fully be described by reference to the

---

20. See Theodosius Dobzhansky, "Teilhard de Chardin and the Orientation of Evolution: A Critical Essay," in *Process Theology: Basic Writings*, ed. Ewert Cousins (New York: Newman, 1971), 229–48.

21. Kenneth Denbigh, *An Inventive Universe* (London: Hutchinson, 1975), 156.

elements that constitute it. The *American Naturalist* journal reported on the case of a genetic mutation that occurred in the flycatcher bird population in the Solomon Islands. According to this report, such genetic mutations occur with some frequency and often lead to a striking color change in a particular flycatcher's underbelly and/or to its song variation. On a case by case basis, this color change or song variation results from and is explained by a simple relation of cause and effect. The mutated gene is the particular cause of either the effect of a change in belly color or of a variation in song within a specific bird.

However, consider that the basis of belly color and song is how flycatchers find their mates. If the color and song differences produced by these gene mutations prevent flycatchers from recognizing potential mating partners, then the color and song deviations carried by these unique specimens within a species eventually die out. On the other hand, suppose that the flycatchers carrying the genetic mutation somehow mate with one another, and the genetic mutation is passed on to another generation, which ultimately reproduces a subsequent generation in turn. This reproductive sequence can eventually lead to the emergence of a new species, one differentiated by belly color and song style and, thus, requiring different taxonomical classification. As one can surmise from this example, there are myriad entities in the cosmos that result from the relation of effect between or within their constituent parts and the effect that comes about can be described precisely in terms of the parts or events that occasioned them. While the effect is an unusual form, like the flycatcher with a different coloration or song, as an occasional or isolated effect, it does not require a wholly new classification or vocabulary to account for it. Nonetheless, when a certain synchronicity of events occurs, such as mating between these unusual forms, such isolated effects can multiply in complex and wondrous sequences that result in a new emergent form that requires new classification and vocabulary.[22]

Clearly, many of the entities, structures, and events one experiences each day result from one type of relation of effect known as a cause-and-effect relationship. Examples of this kind of relation are innumerable and documented in all the natural sciences.

22. "DNA Mutation in Birds Can Lead to Evolution of New Species," *Thaindian News*; available from *http://www.thaindian.com/newsportal/health/dna-mutation-in-birds-can-lead-to-evolution-of-new-species_100228228.html.*

Biology

The field of biology deals with different types of relations of effects. Biologists have differentiated these relations as either functional or evolutionary.[23] In functional biology, the scientist studies the operations and relationships among elements within organisms and seeks how something functions by means of those relationships. Evolutionary biology studies every organism as embedded in relationships—to a species, to a historical period, and to a chain of events stretching back millions of years. Accordingly,

> To find the causes for the existing characteristics, and particularly adaptations, of organisms is the main preoccupation of the evolutionary biologist. He is impressed by the enormous diversity of the organic world. He wants to know the reasons for this diversity as well as the pathways by which it has been achieved. He studies the forces that bring about changes in faunas and floras (as in part documented by paleontology), and he studies the steps by which the miraculous adaptations so characteristic of every aspect of the organic world have evolved.[24]

Regardless of the type of biology considered, the cause-and-effect relationships are complex. Sometimes biologists can trace inherited diseases such as Down syndrome, color blindness, and sickle cell anemia to particular genes and to certain chromosomal mutations. They can link disorders like scurvy or rickets to specific nutritional deficiencies in vitamins C and D, respectively. However, seldom does the biologist find a single exclusive cause for the effects and behaviors of most biological organisms. Consider the following example. A biologist asks, "What causes birds to migrate in winter?" The answer can be any one of a number of cause-and-effect relations or a combination of them all. The winter absence of insects that serve as food for the birds is an ecological cause for migration. A genetic cause stems from the constitution that disposes the migrating bird to respond to certain stimuli through the act of migration. A decrease in the number of daylight hours triggers an internal physiological cause of migration,

---

23. Lynn Hankinson-Nelson, "Cause and Effect in Biology;" available from *http://faculty.washington.edu/lynnhank/Mayr2.pdf*.

24. Ibid.

while a drop in temperature provides an external physiological cause to migrate. However, while the specific or predominant cause for a particular effect may be difficult to pinpoint, the relation of effect still triggers a capacity intrinsic to the nature of the organism.

Genetics

The science of genetics explores relations of effect that underlie several of the scientific phenomena discussed previously. Geneticists affirm the constitutive effect of the relations between dominant and recessive genes in the transmission of hereditary characteristics. Physical or biochemical characteristics in an organism associated with a dominant gene are observable whether or not the gene is coupled with (that is, related to) an alternative recessive gene. Traits associated with the recessive gene, however, are observable only when two recessive genes are coupled or related. In the example of the peppered moth, the gene that produced light wings was and remained genetically dominant. That environmental variables made the trait of dark wings more observable over time did not result from a change in the genetic relation of effect, because light-winged moths continued to propagate. However, because the light-winged moths did not survive in great enough numbers to reproduce and pass on the dominant light-wing gene, the trait became less observable. On the other hand, because the dark-winged moths—which by the genetic relation of effect had to have possessed two recessive genes for dark-colored wings to have expressed the dark wings—survived, the probability increased that the two recessive genes for dark-wingedness would combine and produce more dark-winged offspring. The bottom line is this: the constitutive genetic relation of effect between dominant and recessive genes did not change; only the probability of observing the effect of the recessive genes increased because these offspring were more likely to survive and reproduce.

Chemistry

Chemistry deals with multitudinous cause-and-effect relationships between chemical bonds and the effects of these combinations in cosmic existence. They include the familiar organic compounds of water (H_2O) and cholesterol ($C_{27}H_{46}O$), the formation of real sugars such as sucrose ($C_{12}H_{22}O_{11}$) and glucose ($C_6H_{12}O_6$), and of artificial sweeteners such as aspartame ($C_{14}H_{18}N_2O_5$) and saccharin ($C_7H_5NO_3S$). Chemical reactions also occur in a cause-and-effect fashion. Mixing acid with bleach results in a highly toxic chlorine gas; combining nitric acid with combustible materials such as alcohol and other common solvents results in fire. Whether a compound or a combustible, each is an effect of the causal relation between the elements that produced it, and each is describable precisely in terms of those related elements.

Physics

For centuries, the science of physics interpreted the cosmos within the cause-and-effect dynamic. Concerned with the study of matter and the analysis of nature, physicists seek to understand the nature and behavior of the universe. According to H. D. Young and R. A. Freedman, physicists like themselves "observe the phenomena of nature and try to find patterns and principles that relate these phenomena. These patterns are called physical theories or, when they are very well established and of broad use, physical laws or principles."[25] Note that by its very definition, physics concerns itself with the phenomena of "patterns and principles that relate." These patterns and principles lend themselves to the relative, rather than absolute, character of motion, velocity, mass, and the like, as well as the interdependence of matter, time, and space.

Classical Newtonian Physics

Initially, the phenomena physicists observed were limited to the macroscopic world, that is, the world observable by the naked eye and one that extended to the planets, stars, and galaxies. They interpreted the world through classical mechanics, a field of physics that traces its origins to Sir Isaac Newton (1643–1747). Based on his experimentation with sensory observations, Newton set forth his 1687 *Philosophiae Naturalis Principia Mathematica* which is regarded as foundational in the scientific revolution. These rules described a universe that operated according to repeatable and identifiable relations of causes and effects that yielded qualities universal to "all bodies whatsoever."

---

25. H. D. Young and R. A. Freedman, *University Physics with Modern Physics* (Reading, MA: Addison-Wesley, 2004), 2.

The model of the universe typically associated with Newton's worldview is that of a "clockwork universe." It constituted a model unique in its ability to predict and interpret any given situation, consistent in its conclusions regardless of time or place, and independent of the observer's presence and expectations.[26] Within this Newtonian perspective, which dominated Western thought for more than two-and-half centuries, *matter* (the stuff of the world) possessed *energy*, with a location in *space* at a particular *time*. This worldview applied well to phenomena observable by the naked eye. However, physicists soon discovered through the use of advanced tools for observation and measurement that Newton's conclusions tended to be less reliable in the domains of the very small (the subatomic level), the very fast (speeds close to light), and the very large (the cosmic level).[27] Observations and measurements of phenomena within these ranges failed to agree with Newton's predictions or mechanics. Twentieth-century mathematician and physicist Albert Einstein (1879–1955) demonstrated that interrelations among time, space, and the velocity of light affected the observation and measurement of matter and energy.

Consider the application of Einstein's theory of special relativity to events taking place at the speed of light. At this speed, for example, the ticking rate of a clock or the length of a yardstick is not absolute, but is *relative* to the motion of the one observing that clock or yardstick. According to special relativity, moving clocks tick more slowly than clocks at rest and yardsticks in motion appear shorter than yardsticks at rest. Compare this with the Newtonian worldview that considered time to be one-dimensional, continuous, and independent of objects and events—that is, time as absolute and unrelated to other factors. Contradicting Newton's principles, which held that space is uniform, three-dimensional, and infinite, Einstein's theory of general relativity demonstrated that space and time are also interrelated and that the relation between them affects the observation, measurement, and interpretation of phenomena. In addition to motion's effect on observation and measurement discussed in special relativity, the theory of general relativity proposed that gravity can also affect the relationship of time and of space.

---

26. "Newton," University of Dallas; available from *http://phys.udallas.edu*.

27. Peacocke, *Theology for a Scientific Age*, 29–30.

In addition to discrepancies observed by physicists in the realm of the very fast, scientists also observed fundamental discrepancies when trying to apply Newtonian mechanics to the realm of the very small, that is, at the atomic and subatomic levels. For example, experiments conducted by physicist Werner Heisenberg (1901–1976) challenged Newton's principles concerning the physical structure of objects and the predictability of their attributes at the atomic and subatomic levels. The outcome of his experiments resulted in what has been termed *the uncertainty relation* between attributes of particles at the subatomic level. During his experiments, Heisenberg observed that when he determined the position of a certain particle, he was unable to determine simultaneously the momentum (the measure of motion) of that same particle. Conversely, when he determined the momentum of a particle, he was unable to simultaneously locate the position of that particle. According to Heisenberg himself, "The more precisely the position is determined, the less precisely the momentum is known in this instant, and vice versa."[28]

The implication of repeated experiments that yielded the same results was revolutionary! They contradicted Newton's assertion that observation and measurement were independent of the presence and expectations of the observer. Rather, Heisenberg's experiments demonstrated that the act of observing alters the reality being observed; he showed that the *relation* between the observer and the observed actually altered reality at the subatomic level. Physicists "learned that . . . on the level of individual atomic processes the scientist now finds that he in fact has a role in the creation of the world that he is describing."[29] This makes scientists, in the words of Heisenberg's associate Neils Bohr (1885–1962), "both onlookers and actors in the great drama of existence."[30] In other words, the relation between the observer and what he or she observes affects both the reality of the observed and the observation itself.

---

28. David Cassidy, "Quantum Mechanics: The Uncertainty Principle," *American Institute of Physics*; available from *http://www.aip.org/history/heisenberg/p08.htm*.

29. Richard Schlegel, "The Impossible Spectator in Physics," *Centennial Review* 19 (1975): 217–231 at 218.

30. Neils Bohr, *Atomic Theory and Description of Nature* (Cambridge: Cambridge University, 1934), 119.

Relational Quantum Mechanics

Attempts to explain phenomena, such as those discussed previously, has led to the development of a theory of physics termed *relational quantum mechanics* (RQM), which deals with the mechanics of the atomic and subatomic world. This is a world common to all matter of any kind, both human and nonhuman. Inspired by the work of scientists such as Heisenberg, "The notion rejected [by RQM] is the notion of absolute, or observer-independent, state of a system; equivalently, the notion of observer-independent values of physical quantities."[31] Einstein and others had already demonstrated that the dimensions of the physical world such as time, space, energy, motion, and mass are not absolute as presumed by Newton but are, in fact, relative to one another. In response to this altered worldview, RQM sought to provide a systematic theory that takes into account this shift in perspective that was already well documented in scientific circles.

While RQM is neither the only interpretation of reality in a post-Newtonian worldview nor the only interpretation of reality at the atomic and subatomic levels, so compelling are the fundamentals of RQM that it has garnered support among a variety of scholars in several different fields of study. Princeton mathematician Simon Kochen advocates "dropping the assumption of the absoluteness of physical properties of interacting systems. . . . Thus quantum mechanical properties acquire an interactive or relational character."[32] Author and lecturer Margaret Wheatley, in her book *Leadership and the New Science*, states, that when she considers partnership, management, and organization in the corporate world, "quantum physics quickly returns me to a central truth. We live in a universe where relationships are primary. . . . Nothing exists independently of its relationships."[33] Rather than incidental or accidental, "In the quantum world, relationships are not just interesting; to many physicists, they are *all* there is to reality."[34] Noted German physicist

31. Carlo Rovelli, "Relational Quantum Mechanics," *International Journal of Theoretical Physics* 35 (1996): 1637–1678 at 1.

32. Simon Kochen, "The Interpretation of Quantum Mechanics," in Rovelli, "Relational Quantum Mechanics."

33. Wheatley, *Leadership and the New Science*, 70–71.

34. Ibid., emphasis in the original, 25.

Max Planck (1858–1947), who is often called the father of quantum physics, summarizes the preceding points nicely: "Modern physics has taught us that the nature of any system cannot be discovered by dividing it into its component parts and studying each part by itself. . . . We must keep our attention fixed on the whole and on the interconnection between the parts."[35]

In his writing, philosopher Juan Ferret explicitly makes the connection between relational quantum mechanics and the relational nature of being. He emphasizes RQM's proposition that "a system can only become a system in interaction with at least one other system" and "that the dynamical interactions [between systems] will be crucial for accounting for the state of the system."[36] To pinpoint clearly RQM's ontological significance within the world of physics and beyond, Ferret differentiates the meaning of the term *relativity* as used in the theories of Einstein and the term *relationality* as used in the theory of RQM. To do so, Ferret uses the philosophical ideas belonging to his own discipline, and the distinction he makes proves crucial for the claim made in this chapter—namely, that relation is *constitutive* of what a being or, in Ferret's terms, a system *is*. According to Ferret,

> A main difference between the relative and the relational is that the *relative is primarily epistemological* while the *relational is primarily ontological.* By relational we mean that the reference frame is not solely an epistemic tool for being able to talk meaningfully of or measure position, velocity, or energy, but rather that the reference frame has some ontological significance for the account of the properties of the system and, of course, the system itself. *This means that the system, to be a system, needs another system to interact or relate.*[37]

According to this distinction, while *relativity* as used in physics is a way to *know* or *observe* something about the way a being exists

---

35. Max Planck, "The Global Noetic Repertoire," *The Institute for Contemporary Ancient* learning; available from *http://www.beyondthematrix.com/inst/ICAL--The%20 Global%20Noetic%20Repertoire.html.*

36. Juan Ferret, "The Ontological Import of Relational Quantum Mechanics," *The Berkeley Electronic Press*; available from *http://works.bepress.com/cgi/viewcontent.cgi? article=1007&context=juan_ferret: 2–3.*

37. Ibid., emphasis added, 5.

(epistemology), *relationality* as used in quantum mechanics is about what constitutes the *nature* of what that being actually *is* (ontology). To say that something is *relative*, in other words, tells us something about how a particular being exists in the world as it is affected by time, space, motion, and the like, but to speak of *relationality* tells us about the nature of its being in itself. Moreover, this relationality is one of *effect* because, in Ferret's words and faithful to RQM theory, "the system, to be a system, needs another system to interact or relate" with it and thus to have a constitutive effect on it.

As an example of this wondrous reality of the constitutive nature of the relation of effect, consider the curious case of the electron. Its nature presents such a conundrum that the renowned Italian physicist Enrico Fermi concluded his paper on the quantum theory of radiation with the statement, "In conclusion, we may therefore say that practically all the problems in radiation theory which do not involve the structure of the electron have their satisfactory explanation; while the problems connected with the internal properties of the electron are still very far from their solution."[38] What is it that makes the nature of the electron such a puzzlement?

The word *electron* was first used in 1894 by Irish physicist George Johnstone Stoney (1826–1911) to describe a specific unit of electrical charge. However, credit for discovering the subatomic element to which the word *electron* now refers goes to British physicist J. J. Thomson (1856–1940), who identified the electron in a series of experiments with cathode rays in 1897. During this experiment, Thomson bent the cathode rays by means of a magnetic field and found that the rays consisted of numerous tiny negatively charged particles much smaller than the atom, which at the time had been considered the smallest of the building blocks of matter. Over time, these particles came to be called electrons. Following this discovery, "One experiment after another was performed which proved conclusively the existence of these little things." However, strangely enough "no one knew exactly what they looked like, or what their function was, or why they existed at all."[39]

---

38. Enrico Fermi, "Quantum Theory of Radiation," *Reviews of Modern Physics* 4 (1932): 87–132 at 132.

39. Isaac Mc Phee, "The Discovery of the Electron: J. J. Thompson and the First Subatomic Particle," *Suite 101*, available from *http://www.suite101.com/content/the-discovery-of-the-electron-a45714#ixzz0zo8JZXqvf.*

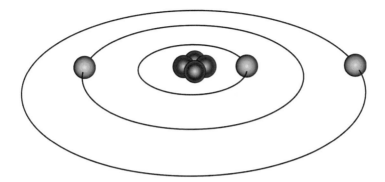

Figure 2.1 An Orbital Particle Model of an Electron

© Trevor Ponman, School of Physics & Astronomy, University
of Birmingham. Used with permission.

While such experiments seemed to indicate that electrons have both mass and momentum, if a scientist hits an electron with a photon of energy to find its location, he or she could not be certain of what happens as a result. Why? The answer lies within Heisenberg's uncertainty principle, which states that one cannot know both the position and the momentum of an electron—or of any other subatomic particle under observation—at the same time. Simply stated, if the photon shows the position of the electron, its subsequent momentum is a mystery; if one follows its momentum, then one loses track of its position. As a consequence, scientists can speak only of the probability of finding that electron in a particular area, with no certainty or regularity of its position. "Thus," states nuclear biologist John Blamire, "we can no longer think of electrons as 'planets orbiting an atomic center.'" (See Figure 2.1) Rather, we find that "electrons . . . exist . . . as diffuse waves of probability."[40] (See Figure 2.2)

How is it, though, that electrons, once considered to be particle-like bundles of energy, exhibit the characteristics of waves? To answer this question, numerous scientists and science classes—since the early 1900s have conducted an experiment dubbed the double-slit experiment. Using a method similar to spraying pellets through slits in a screen, scientists have conducted the double-slit experiment with a variety of particles, waves, and electrons.

---

40. John Blamire "Physical Structure," *Science @ a Distance;* available from *http://www.brooklyn.cuny.edu/bc/ahp/AVC/PhysStruc/VCB_PS_HP.html.*

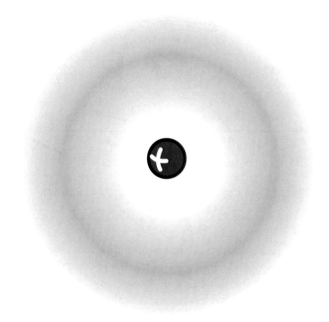

Figure 2.2 A Wave Model of an Electron

© John Norton. http://www.pitt.edu/~jdnorton/teaching/HPS_0410/chapters/index.html. Used with permission.

First, imagine a scientist spraying solid pellets through two slits in a panel, aimed at a solid wall behind it. As one might expect, the pellets go through the two slits in the panels and make a pattern of two more or less straight lines on the wall (Figure 2.3).

Next, imagine a scientist propels rippling waves of water through the double-slit panel onto the wall behind it. When the ripples hit each slit, two new sets of ripples form, which, in turn, interfere with each other. The pattern formed on the wall reflects both the two sets of ripples and the interference between them (Figure 2.4).

Now, the scientist moves from pellets and ripples to electrons and discovers what American physicist Richard Feynman (1918–1988) discovered in his version of the double-slit experiment.[41]

41. See Richard Feynman, *The Character of Physical Law* (Cambridge, MA: MIT, 1965), Ch. 6 and Richard P. Feynman, Robert B. Leighton and Matthew Sands, *The Feynman Lectures on Physics*, Vol. III (Reading, MA: Addison-Wesley, 1963), Ch. 1.

Figure 2.3 Double-Slit Experiment with Pellets.

When Feynman propelled electron particles—which are clearly more like pellets than like ripples of water—toward the two slits, the electron particles enter the two slits independently, like the pellets in the first phase of the experiment. However, instead of getting a pattern like that in Figure 2.3, the pattern that resulted was an interference pattern like the one in Figure 2.4, produced by waves (Figure 2.5).

Feynman now decided to take a closer look at this curious phenomenon. He repeated the particle experiment and, using a light source, he "observed" the electrons as they passed through the slits and determined that they did so independently as pellets do. To his amazement, however, when he looked at the pattern on the wall, he did not see the wave-interference pattern; rather, he saw the pellet pattern of Figure 2.3. Like Heisenberg, Bohr, and Schlegel, he found that the very act of observing the electrons altered their reality! As science writer Stephen Whitt explains, "When we look, the electrons

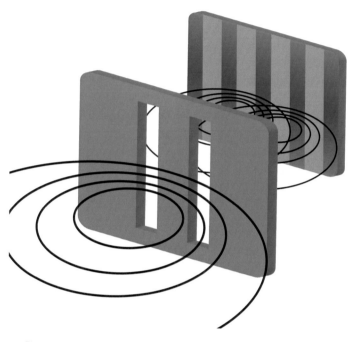

Figure 2.4 Double-Slit Experiment with Rippling Waves of Water

do one thing. . . . When we don't look, they do something entirely different. . . . We get the sense that nature is playing with us." Whitt continues:

> Feynman then shows how by using less intense light, or light of a longer wavelength, the bullet pattern gradually, bullet by bullet, morphs into the water pattern. . . . We try to look with just enough force to see what's going on, and [nature] turns the electrons into bullets. We look with just too little force to see what's going on, and the electrons turn back into water waves again!

Moreover, if the experimenter closes one slit and watches, the electrons make a pellet pattern; reopen the second slit and don't watch and a wave pattern returns. Thus, Whitt concludes, "When we're looking, electrons go through one slit or the other. . . . When we're

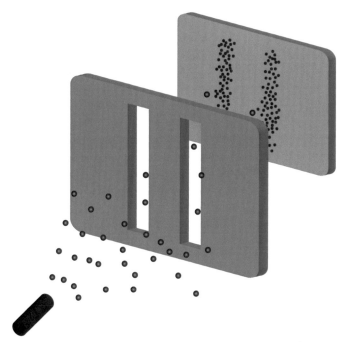

Figure 2.5 Double-Slit Experiment with Electron Particles.

not looking, something strange happens, and we just don't know what it is."[42]

What do all these examples about the life of the electron have to say about the relation of effect explored in this section? Simply, they tell us that the only way to talk about nature of the electron—an elementary particle arguably as old as the universe and as fundamental a constituent of matter as exists—is in terms of its relationships! This reality led quantum physicist David Bohm (1917–1992) to conclude, "Thus, under all circumstances, we picture the electron as something that is itself not very definite in nature but that is continually producing effects which, whether they are actually observed by any human observers or not, call for the interpretation that the electron has a nature that varies in response to the environment."[43] Indeed,

42. Stephen Whitt, "The Experiment with Two Holes," *Turtle Universe*; available from *http://stephenwhitt.wordpress.com/2008/12/17/the-experiment-with-two-holes*.

43. David Bohm, *Quantum Theory* (New York: Prentice-Hall, 1951), 610.

the very being of the electron, the primordial element of all material being itself, *is* an effect of its relations and *has* an effect in its relation to each and all of the inhabitants of its subatomic world!

SUMMARY

Thus begins the exploration into how different types of relations constitute the nature of being—natural, human, and divine. As a first step, this chapter focused on natural being. Through many examples, it demonstrated how relations of origin, emergence, and effect are not only common to all natural beings but also constitutive of their very nature. The relation of origin shared by the natural world, including humans, stems from the common creation story, which continues to unfold. Stretching out from "the Big Bang," relationships and inter-relationships have exponentially multiplied, each unique and yet each inextricably interwoven in a grand web of existence.

This common creation story is continued and enhanced through the relation of emergence. This chapter described how novel forms of life develop from more elemental forms of life. They are so novel that they are not reducible or explainable in terms of the elements that preceded them; however, their novelty does not make them independent of their ancestry. Through the relation of emergence, the creative potential of the earlier levels of existence actualizes itself in new forms and structures over great expanses of time.

Finally, multiple examples from the physical sciences demonstrated how a relation of effect exists among the elements of particular entities and how each entity is a unique outcome or effect of the relationship among the elements that constitute it. Without the relationship of the elements, the effect or outcome would not exist. The nature of numerous beings in the cosmos results from the relation of effect termed *cause-and-effect relationships*. While sometimes complex, these relationships are nonetheless innumerable, well documented, and generally understood within the world observable to the naked eye. However, as quantum physics demonstrates, there are some relations of effect shaping the nature of being in the subatomic world that, although observable and documented, involve dynamics that retain a sense of mystery around the effects they produce. While the dynamics remain mysterious, the outcomes are, nonetheless, clear: The cosmos exists as relationships, as essential patterns that connect.

FOR FURTHER READING

Darwin, Charles. *On the Origin of Species by Means of Natural Selection, or the Preservation of Favoured Races in the Struggle for Life*. London: John Murray, 1859.

Johnson, Elizabeth A. *Quest for the Living God: Mapping Frontiers in the Theology of God*. New York: Continuum, 2007.

Peacocke, Arthur. *Theology for a Scientific Age: Being and Becoming—Natural, Divine, and Human*. Minneapolis: Augsburg Fortress, 1993.

Chapter 3

HUMAN BEING AS RELATION

"To be an isolated, autonomous individual is, literally, to have no humanity, no identity, no self; it is to be no-thing, a no-body. For personhood presupposes relationality; my humanity is defined by my relationships with others."[1]

INTRODUCTION

Because humans are part and parcel of the evolving cosmos, because the universe through its own inherent structures and processes and from its own intrinsic "stuff" has generated a distinctively personal entity called humanity, we as humans share in the essential relations that constitute the cosmos itself. We trace our origin to the common creation story. We recognize that the processes of law and chance that produced a great diversity of life forms throughout cosmic history produced us as well. Hence, there is an indissoluble relationship among all the life forms that have ever existed and, in fact, will ever exist. We acknowledge our emergence from more elemental forms of life and grasp our inherent relation to the forms that preceded us.

---

1. Roberto S. Goizueta, *Caminemos Con Jesus: Toward a Hispanic/Latino Theology of Accompaniment* (Maryknoll, NY: Orbis Books, 1995), 50–51.

We marvel at the creative potential inherent in these earlier levels of existence that became actualized in us over great expanses of time. Finally, we understand our existence as the outcome of myriad cause-and-effect interactions associated with the principles and patterns of biology, genetics, chemistry, and physics that cooperated to produce our being from the micro to macro level. For all these reasons, as Arthur Peacocke observed,

> Far from [human] presence in the universe being a curious and inexplicable surd, we find we are remarkably and intimately related to it on the basis of this contemporary scientific evidence which is "indicative of a far greater degree of [humanity's] total involvement with the universe" than ever before envisaged.[2]

Nonetheless, while humans are inextricably woven into the relational fabric of the universe as a whole, we experience further levels of relation by virtue that we are not simply natural. We are also, in fact, *personal*. That personal difference, however, is not easily definable. What exactly does it mean to be a "person"? How does one define *personhood*? Is it synonymous with being *human*, or does it imply a further composite of characteristics and capacities? The answer to these questions depends in large measure on the academic discipline to which one poses them.

DEFINING PERSONHOOD

Defining what it means to be a person is by no means simple. There is a wide array of approaches and responses—many interrelated—that various disciplines give to the question of personhood. To introduce the complexity of the topic of personhood, this chapter begins by exploring the philosophical perspectives that provide the theoretical basis for understanding personhood not only in philosophy but also in fields such as biology, psychology, sociology, and theology as well.

---

2. Arthur Peacocke, *Creation and the World of Science: The Bampton Lectures 1978* (Peacocke, *Creation and the World of Science*) (Oxford: Clarendon, 1979) with internal quote by Bernard Lovell, "In the Centre of Immensities," 68.

Philosophy

Much of the dialogue concerning personhood or selfhood rests on, references, or implies certain metaphysical principles from the discipline of philosophy. Nonetheless, a survey of the concept of person in philosophy demonstrates that philosophical principles have themselves evolved throughout the ages from early notions in ancient Greece to contemporary usage today.[3]

Greek Roots

According to philosopher William O. Stephens, the philosophical concept of person began in ancient Greece with the word *prosōpeion* (cognate: *prosōpon*), meaning, among other things, *mask, face, countenance, character, role*, or *legal entity*. These various meanings, however, can tend to cloud rather than to clarify the term. For example, the Stoic teacher Epictetus, in a series of discourses throughout the late first and early second centuries, uses the same term *prosōpon* to refer to an actor's mask, a government post, an individual's character, and a series of roles. Within these uses of *prosōpon*, Epictetus, at times, clearly refers to roles or states into which one is born, which arise from genetic predisposition, or which are determined by class structure or social status. At other times, however, he uses *prosōpon* to refer to more generic states of individuals, such as being a beggar or a cripple or a governor or a senator. Moreover, Epictetus uses the same term to refer to what Stephens calls "the power of *individualization*," which adds to the concept of *prosōpon* "the notion of self-worth, or the sense of self-propriety, that is, one's stand on what befits oneself and what does not."[4] Hence, rather than narrowing the meaning of *prosōpon* (*person*) to a well-defined set of attributes or capacities, the earliest Greek understanding reveals that personhood represents a complex of interactive elements including genetic makeup, social standing, and psychological self-consciousness.

---

3. William O. Stephens, "Masks, Androids, and Primates: The Evolution of the Concept of 'Person,'" in *The Persons: Readings in Human Nature*, ed. William O. Stephens (Saddle River, NJ: Pearson, 2006), 397.

4. Ibid., 397–99 at 399.

Focus on Rationality

In the sixth-century, the Christian philosopher Boethius advanced a definition of person that would characterize notions of personhood for centuries to come. According to Boethius, "Person is an *individual substance of rational nature* (*naturae rationalis individua substantia*)"; furthermore, he contended, "Man alone is among the material beings person, he alone having a rational nature."[5] With this, Boethius signaled a shift toward rationality that became, according to classical scholar A. A. Long, the standard by which "to distinguish human beings, individually or collectively, from other animals . . . by virtue of reason, reflection and (self-) consciousness (as in Locke and Leibnitz), or as being 'ends in themselves' (as in Kant), or as in some modern accounts, such as those of Frankfurt and Dennett, which take person to be an essentially normative concept."[6]

Noteworthy among those expounding this normative concept of person as rational being was seventeenth-century mathematician and scientist René Descartes. He developed a dualistic conception of the human person as composed of a material body (*res extensa*) and a rational soul (*res cogitans*), which are independent of each other and irreducible to the other.[7] In his *Treatise on Man*, Descartes described the material body as "nothing but a statue or machine made of earth . . . [in which] God . . . places . . . all the parts required to make it walk, eat, breathe, and indeed to imitate all of those functions which can be imagined to proceed from matter,"[8] common to humans and animals as well. The *rational soul* or *mind*, however, was reserved to persons alone. It is through the rational soul that humans possess and exercise such attributes as freedom, intelligence, responsibility, virtue, and vice.[9]

---

5. Boethius, *De Persona et Duabus Naturis*, ii, iii, in P.L., LXIV, 1342 sqq., cited in J. Margaret Datiles, "What Exactly is 'Constitutional Personhood'? The Definition of Personhood and Its Role in the Life Debate,"*Americans United for Life*, available from *http://www.aul.org/2010/04/what-exactly-is-%E2%80%9Cconstitutional-personhood%E2%80%9D-the-definition-of-personhood-and-its-role-in-the-life-debate/*.

6. A. A. Long, "Stoic Philosophers on Persons, Property-ownership and Community," in *Aristotle and After: Bulletin of the Institute of Classical Studies* 68 (1997): 13–31 at 13–14.

7. Cf. chapter 1 of this book in the section "The Problem of Dualism."

8. René Descartes, *Treatise on Man*, in Stephens, *Person*, 68.

9. G. P. Baker and Katherine J. Morris, *Descartes' Dualism* (Florence, KY: Routledge, 1995), 214.

British philosopher John Locke expanded this notion of the person based on rationality in his 1689 work *An Essay Concerning Human Understanding*. His definition of personhood included not only the possession of rationality but also the use of it through, for example, constructing accounts about the self and the world or devising plans or strategies and acting upon them.[10] Thus, for Locke, a person is a "thinking intelligent Being, that has reason and reflection, and can consider itself as itself . . . in different times and places; which it does only by that consciousness, which is inseparable from thinking."[11] The essence of his definition of personhood, moreover, is implied in the phrase "in different times and places." This phrase entails for Locke a *continuity of consciousness* that constitutes one's personal identity or "the sameness of a rational being." This continuity of consciousness reaches from one's present back into one's past, relating memories, thoughts, and experiences to one another in such a way as to provide an unbroken linkage that assures the human that "it is the same *self* now as it was then." [12] For Locke, therefore, one's personal identity is a holistic construct that unites the different elements of one's existence over time.[13]

In view of the complexity evident in the considerations of personhood, twentieth-century philosopher Daniel C. Dennett wondered if there might not be more than one concept of person that would call for a more nuanced understanding of personhood than can be communicated in any one concept.[14] Building on the work of John Locke, Dennett proposed two notions of personhood: that of metaphysical personhood and that of moral personhood. Presuming that metaphysical personhood is a necessary condition for moral personhood, Dennett outlined six necessary conditions for personhood: (1) a person is rational, (2) a person has certain psychological or mental capabilities (intentionality), (3) a person is one who is perceived or

---

10. See Charles Taylor, "The Concept of a Person," in Volume One of *Philosophical Papers* (Cambridge: Cambridge University Press, 1985), 97–114.

11. John Locke, *An Essay Concerning Human Understanding*, 2.27, 9, in Datiles, "What Exactly Is 'Constitutional Personhood'?"

12. Ibid., in Stephens, *Person*, 82, italics in the original.

13. See Gottfried Leibnitz, *New Essays on the Human Understanding*, trans. P. Remnant and J. Bennett (Cambridge: Cambridge University Press, 1981), 232–47.

14. Daniel C. Dennett, "Conditions of Personhood," in Stephens, *Person*, 227.

treated as a person by others (one toward whom a particular stance is taken), (4) a person is capable of behaving as a person toward another (reciprocity), (5) a person is capable of verbal communication, and (6) a person is conscious or self-conscious in a way that no other species demonstrates.[15]

Dennett's point is that many complex conditions and interrelations constitute whether one recognizes oneself or another as "personal." Because of the complexity of interaction among these themes, the simple presence or absence of any of these conditions is not sufficient for the attribution of personhood. Whether attributed to oneself or to another, personhood is conditioned by mental capacity, psychological state, social interaction, mutual exchange, verbal interaction, and self-awareness. Furthermore, decisions concerning the attribution of personhood depend upon the presuppositions of the decision makers. Hence, philosophers such as Jane English warn against presupposing "that the concept of a person can be captured in a straightjacket of necessary and/or sufficient conditions." Instead, the term *person* implies "a cluster of features, of which rationality, having a self-concept, and being conceived of humans are only a part."[16]

Person as Relation

Even a cursory overview of the philosophical viewpoints about what constitutes a person shows that these perspectives are diverse and wide-ranging. Nonetheless, these philosophical insights indicate that the reality of personhood involves the influences of various kinds of relations. Such relations include the existential relations between rationality, intentionality, and self-consciousness; between the rational soul and the material body; and between the continuity of self-consciousness and changes in time and space. They extend to cognitive relations among successive perceptions unified by common end, resemblance, and causation. The question is how these relations relate to the constituents of origin, effect, and

---

15. Ibid., 228–29.

16. Jane English, "Abortion and the Concept of a Person," *Canadian Journal of Philosophy* 5, no. 2 (October 1974): 233–43 at 234.

emergence proposed by this text. How do these internal relations among cognitive structures in the human connect to other internal and external relations with self and others that are critical in constituting one's personhood?

The difficulty of parsing the influences of such internal and external relations on personhood has historically been the subject of great debate. This debate is known as the "nature-nurture" controversy, and it has intermittently swelled and ebbed within the biological, social, and behavioral sciences for many years. The controversy deals with the question of whether heredity (nature) or environment (nurture) is the more influential in shaping the essential characteristics and behaviors that constitute our sense of self as person. At the "nature" extreme is the notion of a biological determinism, glibly expressed as "biology is destiny."[17] This perspective envisions human personhood as essentially controlled by one's genes to the exclusion of environmental influence. At the "nurture" extreme is the assertion that the human person is essentially a *tabula rasa*, or "blank slate." This denotes the idea that the human person is born devoid of inherent mental content, which equates to being devoid of personhood.[18]

A relational ontology in an evolving cosmos, however, suggests that the reality of human personhood derives not from either extreme of nature or nurture, but from a fruitful interaction between the two. Therefore, this chapter explores the influence of nature in its section on the relation of origin and the influence of nurture in its section on the relation of effect. In its section on the relation of emergence, moreover, it demonstrates that these personal relations interact in an interpersonal, social context in which eight stages of interdependent development characterize the emergence of the person throughout life from birth to death.

---

17. A related concept is "anatomy is destiny." See Sigmund Freud, "The Dissolution of the Oedipus Complex," in *The Freud Reader*, ed. Peter Gay (London: W. W. Norton & Company, 1995), 661–66.

18. "Let us then suppose the mind to be, as we say, white paper void of all characters, without any ideas. How comes it to be furnished? Whence has it all the materials of reason and knowledge? To this I answer, in one word, from EXPERIENCE." See John Locke, *An Essay Concerning Human Understanding*, Vol.1 (New York: Dover, 1959), 121–5 for a fuller explanation.

RELATION OF ORIGIN:
THE *NATURE* OF PERSONHOOD

In its discussion of the pepper moth, chapter 2 discussed how the genetic relations between dominant and recessive genes transmitted a number of hereditary characteristics, which are generally predictable over many generations. Like the pepper moth, humans have physical characteristics that are largely genetically determined through the inheritance of certain genes from one's biological parents that contribute in significant ways to their lives and well-being, as well as to their self-perceptions and self-esteem. This stems from the fact that the human being is a self-conscious and self-reflective creature and, because of this, perceptions about genetic capacities and characteristics often influence understanding of one's own personhood. Hence, to the extent that the conception of one's personhood is shaped by these heritable capacities and characteristics, the person is constituted by his or her *relation of origin*. Following, two aspects of the person's relation of origin are considered: biological constitution and the experience of embodiment to which this constitution often gives rise.

Biological Constitution

While the meaning of personhood is not reducible to biological constitution, there is a consensus that any discussion of personhood must begin by defining what it means to be human.[19] Biologists indicate that when a sperm and an ovum of the species *Homo sapiens* unite to produce a zygote, "a genetically unique biologically human entity is brought into existence."[20] Over time and with proper nurturance, this biologically human entity develops into a member of the species *Homo sapiens*, "distinguishable from other nonhuman entities."[21] On this basis, human parents are conceiving what constitutes a human. However, while there is consensus on what constitutes a biological *human*, there is no general agreement

---

19. Edwin Hui, *At the Beginning of Life: Dilemmas in Theological Bioethics* (Downers Grove, IL: InterVarsity Press, 2002), 58.

20. Ibid.

21. Ibid.

on whether biological humanity is the sole and sufficient condition for what constitutes a *person*.

One bioethicist who supports the correspondence between biological humanness and human personhood is Edwin Hui. In his book *At the Beginning of Life*, Hui discusses four genetic arguments to support his contention that biological humanness is tantamount to human personhood. He bases his argument upon fundamental relations between the zygote and the various stages of the human that eventually grows into adulthood.

Hui's first argument maintains that the distinctive genetic endowment of the zygote is so significant to the unique identity of a human life that to be *this specific human* is to be a *person*. This ontological uniqueness stems from the uniqueness of the deoxyribonucleic acid (DNA) molecule that controls the production of all other cells in the body. His second argument centers on the continuity between this unique zygote and the future adult. Hui contends that genetic individuality provides an indissoluble linkage between the identity of the adult and that of the zygote from which that person developed. The third argument Hui presents builds on the zygote's self-development through the impetus of its unique DNA. "According to its unique genetic endowment," Hui asserts, "the zygote possesses an inherent and naturally active capacity, encoded in its genome, to control and coordinate its systematic development and differentiation throughout the entire life process from fertilization onward."[22] The verbs *controlling, coordinating, maintaining*, and *developing* and the descriptors *inherent, natural, autonomous*, and *intrinsic* signal Hui's fourth argument. According to Hui, the very capacities encoded and actualized in the zygote are the same capacities evident in the developed adult.

To be fair, many biologists, geneticists, bioethicists, and philosophers challenge Hui's arguments. Some thinkers object to his claims on the basis of the possibility of twinning in the zygote.[23] Others contest Hui's argument on the philosophical basis of the lack of self-consciousness in the fetus that constitutes personhood in the

---

22. Ibid., 60.

23. Francis Beckwith, "What Does it Mean to Be Human?" *Christian Research Journal* 26:3 (2003): 1–7 at 3.

developed adult.[24] Related to the presence of consciousness, still others argue that, because the fetus cannot be shown to have continuous memories of their embryonic experiences, the fetus cannot be recognized as a "person."[25]

However, others such as professor of philosophy Patrick Lee defend Hui's contentions. Lee affirms that there is evidence that the early embryo is a unified being, as the "early embryo . . . behaves like a single organism with an intrinsic goal directedness for which its cellular parts interact."[26] Historian and lawyer Anthony Fisher adds, "the evidence also shows that the time [when cell differentiation] begins is determined from within by a 'clock mechanism' intrinsic to the developing embryo."[27] Because of this, the early embryo can be considered an ontological unity whose biological parts work together for the growth, development, and continued existence of the whole. Observations such as these show that embryonic "cells function in concert with what the early embryo's intrinsically directed nature has instructed them to do. The unfolding is orderly and goal-directed with the end being the continuing development and subsistence of the embryo itself as a *whole*."[28]

The Experience of Embodiment

Biological and genetic factors such as those described previously result in a plethora of physical traits inherited from one's biological parents such as eye color, hair color, skin tone, height, bone structure, blood type, and the like. What part do such traits play in our personhood? They shape the embodiment through which our essential personhood is incarnated, communicated, and mediated to the world around us and to our very selves. Because the mind, spirit, and body of the human person is an integrated whole, the influences that affect

---

24. Michael Tooley, *Abortion and Infanticide* (New York: Oxford, 1983): 118–21.

25. Hui, *At the Beginning of Life*, 72.

26. Beckwith, "What Does it Mean to Be Human," 4.

27. Anthony Fisher, "When Did I Begin? Revisited," *Linacre Quarterly* 58 (1991): 59–68 at 60.

28. Beckwith, "What Does it Mean to Be Human," 4, referencing Patrick Lee, *Abortion and Unborn Human Life* (Washington, DC: The Catholic University of America Press, 1996), 96.

and shape the physical aspects of the human affect and shape the whole person. This means that what constitutes one physically has ramifications for every aspect of one's self.

How one experiences his or her body shape, size, characteristics, or well-being affects how one sees oneself as a person. Often this sense of self is not simply a matter of an objective or impassive statement regarding one's height, weight, eye color, hair texture, and the like. Because our bodies mediate who we are as persons to the rest of the world and because our bodies are inextricably connected to our mind and spirit, the feedback we receive for our cultural milieu or social group about our bodies tends to significantly affect our sense of self as person. While we may give lip service to the idea that physical features are only skin deep, society clearly communicates that certain genetically determined characteristics and body types are more desirable. Our mind then—consciously, subconsciously, and even unconsciously—translates these messages into assessments of ourselves as persons.

In addition to exploring the biological dimensions of human personhood, the work of bioethicist Edwin Hui also touches upon the theme of embodiment and its effects on personhood. He focuses on the hierarchical dualism that has devalued the human body and elevated the human spirit to the extent that the body is "something from which the person should be freed or, failing that, upon which disciplines should be imposed."[29] In contrast to this dualism, Hui points out that "far from experiencing the body as inert material, the self experiences the body both as familiar and strange, mine and other, intimate yet alien—a dialectical phenomenon that Richard Zaner considers as 'the core of human body-as-experienced.'"[30] Despite this ambiguity, phenomenologists like Zaner contend that the body provides one's essential sense of being a human person. It announces one's presence and expresses thoughts, feelings, and actions throughout the life of the human person. "Hence," Hui contends, "the body is far from . . . neutral."[31] This means that respect for the person

---

29. Hui, *At the Beginning of Life*, 74.

30. Ibid., 75, internal quote from Richard Zaner, "Body—I. Embodiment: The Phenomenological Tradition," in *Encyclopedia of Bioethics*, ed. Warren Reich (New York: Macmillan, 1995), 1:292.

31. Ibid.

entails respect for the embodied person."[32] Hui notes that one's sense of full personhood is also diminished by bodily violation or injury to the extent that "one hardly feels that one is a full person if . . . one's body is in any way compromised."[33] Moreover, genetic research contends that it is "more obvious than ever that there is no human self that stands outside the processes of biology, unaffected by them."[34]

In a very perceptive and sensitive description of the relationship of human embodiment and the constitution of one's personhood, Hui offers six ways in which one's body is "the hinge . . . for the relationship between the human being and his self, neighbors, and the world."[35] First, as the *basis of one's presence and action*, the body is the "center from which one's action is originated . . . and the basis for the self-presence of the human being and person."[36] It is through our bodies that we are located in space and in relation to other objects and persons in the world; our bodies make our personhood present in and to the world itself. Second, the body is the *basis for communication* to and with the world around us. We communicate through our physical ability to speak and to hear, as well as through nonverbal and nonauditory communication. The body enables us to smile or frown, show surprise or disappointment; it enables us to touch and to caress, to kiss and to cry. Third, the body is *the basis of one's identity, particularity*, and *self-consciousness*. It mediates the world to our personal consciousness and mediates our personal consciousness to the world. Fourth, as the body does so, it becomes *the basis of personal history*. Bodily structures and processes synthesize and integrate our personal experiences over time, which enables us to experience and establish historical individuality.

Fifth, the body is *the basis for relation*. The body makes it possible to interact with others; it mediates feelings, desires, and intentions with a clarity and intensity inexpressible in mere thought or word. Finally, the body is *the basis of sexuality*. Our embodied sexuality

---

32. Hui, *In the Beginning of Life*, 75 (emphasis added).

33. Ibid., 76.

34. Roger Lincoln Shinn, *The New Genetics: Challenges for Science, Faith, and Politics* (London: Moyer Bell, 1996), 51.

35. Hui, *In the Beginning of Life*, 83.

36. Ibid., 76.

provides the ability to tangibly give and receive love, to incarnate the essential relationality of human personhood through "the personal power to *share* (physically, psychically, and spiritually) *the gift of self* with self and with others."[37] This sexual relation, moreover, provides the opportunity for a more marvelous relation still—that of "the privilege of living bodily within another human being, to share flesh and blood with the utmost degree of intimacy and immediacy."[38] Can any relation be more essential, integral, or constitutive of personhood than this?

RELATION OF EFFECT: THE *NURTURE* OF PERSONHOOD

As the experiences of embodiment demonstrate, the intrinsic *relation of origin* termed *nature* remains inseparable from the extrinsic *relation of effect* termed *nurture*. From the moment of conception, our personhood is developing not only in relation to factors unique to one's own self but also to factors that interminably affect us from beyond oneself. Although our embodiment is uniquely our own, it, nonetheless, connects to the other. The effects of the other, of the environment, further constitute one's sense of personhood. It begins with the first environment that affects and shapes us as persons—our mother's womb.

Prenatal Influence

The health, well-being, and behaviors of the mother affect the developing fetus as the very first environment inhabited by the infant. Like the environmental effects the child experiences throughout life, these influences both positively and negatively impact the developing child. Physically, the unborn child is wholly dependent upon the nutritional intake and health of the mother; emotionally, the child is affected by any anxiety or stress the mother may experience.

---

37. Mary Timothy Prokes, *Toward a Theology of the Body* (Grand Rapids, MI: Eerdmans, 1996), 95.

38. Hui, *In the Beginning of Life*, 79.

Moreover, because they impact the fetal environment, cigarette smoking, alcohol consumption, or drug abuse by the mother can have deleterious effects on the unborn child depending on the stage of fetal development.[39] However, particular kinds of positive stimulation impact the developing fetus as well. Because of its nascent auditory, tactile, and mental capacities, the fetus senses and responds to various kinds of stimulation even *in utero*. Studies have demonstrated that "long before the development of advanced brain structures, prenates . . . [seem to] react to individual voices, stories, music, and even simple interaction with parents."[40] Clearly, because positive and negative stimulation plays such a significant role in the development of consciousness and, thus, self-consciousness, nascent personhood develops even in this most primitive of human environments.

Social Location

Beyond the intimacy of the fetal environment, there is a complex of influences, experiences, and circumstances that impact an individual as he or she lives, develops, and works. The social and behavioral sciences use the term *social location* to refer to this complex of factors. One's location includes one's gender, race, ethnicity, and language. It is affected by the family system in which one is raised, the historical period in which one grows up, the philosophy and worldview of one's era, the social and economic status that one either enjoys or endures, and the religious tradition that one embraces as one's own. Location is further shaped by sexual orientation, marital status, level of education, and country of origin, as well as by any and all of the life experiences and events that have formed, informed, and transformed the existence of each person. In a word, *social location* encompasses the constellation of external effects that shape one's self-understanding as person.

In many cases, social location affects one's sense of personhood differently depending on the value a particular society, culture, or historical period places on particular characteristics of personhood and

39. Ibid., 232–35.

40. "Prenatal Attachment and Stimulation," *Developmental Psychology Student Netletter*; available from *http://www.mesacc.edu/dept/d46/psy/dev/Spring02/prenatal/attachment.html*.

social standing. Those possessing a certain valued characteristic or who belong to a valued stratum of society have their sense of personhood reinforced in a positive way by those associations. Those who do not have their sense of personhood diminished. In contemporary America and other industrialized nations around the world, for example, it is socially advantageous to possess a certain level of wealth, education, and class. Different cultures place different values on particular body types, ethnic backgrounds, and skin tones. To the extent that one's culture, society, or peer group values the personal characteristic that one possesses, to that extent is one's sense of personhood—for good or ill—reinforced; to the extent that one does not possess such characteristics, one's sense of self is diminished. While each experience that an individual has within his or her social location constitutes some aspect of her or his personhood, several categories of effects stand out as particularly influential in shaping one's sense of self. These include family of origin, race, ethnicity, gender, and economic status.

Undoubtedly, the effects of these categories can be extremely positive on personal development. A safe and supportive home life that models mutuality in gender roles disposes individuals to fruitful relationships and personal integrity. Racial and ethnic identity enriches individuals with a cultural heritage and communal bond. Economic stability provides educational, social, and occupational opportunities and freedom from financial stress and anxiety. In all these ways, these effects bolster one's sense of personhood, especially when experiences within these relations are generally balanced and healthy. When they are not, the effects can be devastating.

Family Structure and Social System

Under ordinary circumstances, each individual comes into this world as part of a family structure and social system. The most rudimentary unity of this structure and system is the family of origin, typically defined as a family or kinship group related by blood or genetic ties or, more simply, the family into which one is born. Styles of interaction within the family affect our ongoing relationship with both self and others. While these interactions vary within different cultures and between family systems, they tend to perpetuate themselves throughout life and affect one's sense of the contours and value of one's personhood. They "establish patterns for individuals within the family of how, when, and to whom to relate."[41]

Nevertheless, although relationships within the family constitute one's sense of personhood in essential ways, developing personhood also takes place within a broader social system of relationship with friends, classmates, colleagues, and the like. Several twentieth-century philosophers contend that, rather than the personal self's being constituted principally through relations produced by self-reflective rationality, personhood requires relation toward the Other in order to constitute one's sense of self. Moving beyond the earlier emphases on individual rationality, psychological states, and mental capacities, philosopher John Macmurray envisioned the personal self as an agent and a doer, constituted by relationship with others.[42] As agent, the personal self is an embodied and operative being, directed ecstatically outward toward other persons and toward an entirely personal world.[43] Rather than being constituted as an autonomous substance containing an individual center of consciousness (Boethius), to be a person is to be agential, constructing oneself through actions in relations. Because personhood is located in relationality rather than rationality, moreover, even an infant at the mother's breast—whose individual rationality, psychological state, and mental capacity is largely indeterminable—is, nonetheless, constituting him- or herself as a person through intimate and agential relationship with the mother.[44]

As this series of relationships in a person's life influences the individual's sense of self, openness to relationships and encounters with others aid the developing person in differentiating oneself within the context of these relationships. Such influences help to determine the contours of "me" and "not me" in much the same way as embodiment helps one to determine what is uniquely "mine" from what is "not mine." In so doing, the personal self is constituted

---

41. Philip Rich, "Differentiation of Self in the Therapist's Family of Origin"; available from *http://www.infolizer.com/i8om5ep1a7g5esa19nmi3ci8a15ed4u/Differentiation-of-self-in-the-therapists-family-of-origin.html.*

42. John Macmurray, *The Self as Agent* (New York: Harper and Brothers, 1957), 11.

43. Ibid., 100–102.

44. John Macmurray, *Persons in Relation* (New York: Harper Brothers, 1961), 61.

in response to feedback received from others.[45] When the feedback accepts and affirms one's uniqueness, capability, and worth, the individual develops a positive sense of self and behaves in ways consistent with his or her own value system and self-image. If, however, the individual experiences rejection and criticism of one's actions or one's values, the developing person senses that one's personhood is flawed and has no value to others. These experiences can result in dissonance and confusion about one's personhood. To reach fullness of personhood, however, depends on maintaining an openness to experience, a trust in one's judgment to choose appropriate behavior and responses, freedom of choice, creativity, reliability and constructiveness. As psychotherapist Carl Rogers cautions, "This process of the good life is not, I am convinced, a life for the faint-hearted. It involves the stretching and growing of becoming more and more of one's potentialities. It involves the courage to be. It means launching oneself fully into the stream of life"[46]—a life in relation to others.

Cultural Conditioning

Cultural conditioning refers to the often unconscious process through which humans are socialized to adopt particular patterns of thought, values, and behaviors held by a specific culture. In his essay "Culture and the Individual," English novelist Aldous Huxley points out the paradoxical relation of effect culture exerts on an individual's sense of personhood:

> Between culture and the individual the relationship is, and always has been, strangely ambivalent. We are at once the beneficiaries of our culture and its victims. . . . It is to language and culture that we owe our humanity. And "What a piece of work is a man!" says Hamlet: "How noble in reason! how infinite in faculties! . . . in action how like an angel!"[47]

---

45. R. M. Ryckman, *Theories of Personality* (Pacific Grove, CA: Brooks Cole Publishing, 1993), 106.

46. Carl Rogers, *On Becoming a Person: A Therapist's View of Psychotherapy* (London: Constable Carl, 1961), 196.

47. Aldous Huxley, "Culture and the Individual," *Scribd.com*; available from *http://www.scribd.com/doc/9638444/LSD-The-ConsciousnessExpanding-Drug#outer_page_38*.

However, warns Huxley, "in the intervals of being noble, rational and potentially infinite," the impact of human culture and its conditioning "plays such fantastic tricks before high heaven as make the angels weep."[48] This type of cultural conditioning "as makes the angels weep" manifests itself in biases, prejudices, and discriminatory practices that often wreak havoc on the constitution of human personhood. In the extreme, they become forms of oppression and injustice against a particular race, gender, economic group, or ethnicity and express themselves as racism, sexism, poverty, and xenophobia.

Race

The effect of race in the constitution of one's personhood varies among cultures and societies throughout the world. As a biological aspect of oneself, race certainly shapes one's fundamental concept of personhood. However, because differences within and between races are variously valued and devalued throughout the world, its effect upon the constitution of personhood stretches far beyond its biological basis. While similarities in race and ethnicity create and enhance experiences of community, solidarity, and collective memory, differences in race and ethnicity can produce division, discord, and disjointed discourse. In their most radical form, racial differences underpin the system of discrimination and oppression called racism. Racism has been present throughout history in all regions of the world from the rise of tribal systems to the present. Despite its ubiquity, the origins of the phenomenon are often disputed. Nonetheless, its ramifications are clear. Racism infects both actions and attitudes.

As an action, racism entails the systematic exclusion of a particular race from equal access to political, economic, and social power. Institutionalized racism prohibits equal access to political participation and power, to employment, to ownership of property, to adequate health care, to equal education, to businesses such as theaters, restaurants, and hotels, and to public places such as swimming pools and libraries. Racism as an attitude is the distorted mindset that one's own racial group is superior to another. It manifests itself as prejudice, bigotry, and discrimination against another racial group. Prejudice is the act of making negative judgments about an individual because of

---

48. Ibid.

the group to which he or she belongs. Such judgments are generally not based on specific experiences or knowledge of individuals within a group but on the stereotypical projection of particular beliefs or ideas upon an individual without prior knowledge and without an examination of the facts of a situation. In its extreme form, prejudice is called bigotry, an irrational hatred of persons from a different racial or ethnic group than one's own.

History has given us a number of examples of institutionalized racism that have had deleterious effects on the development of personhood in individuals and in communities. In the United States, for example, one trajectory of racism traces itself to the scandal of slavery when the first African slaves were brought to Virginia between 1607 and 1619. Between the sixteenth and nineteenth centuries, estimates are that more than 650,000 Africans were enslaved in the United States.[49] Although slavery as an institution was ended by law in 1865 with the passage of the Thirteenth Amendment and subsequent legislation continued to extend equal rights under the law to black Americans, racism toward black men and women has endured into the twenty-first century. Black households in the United States had the lowest median income in 2005 ($30,858) among race groups. In 2005, African Americans had 2.3 times the infant mortality rate of white Americans, and the suicide rate for black Americans of all ages was 5.25 per 100,000—about half the overall U.S. rate of 10.75 per 100,000. Black teenagers comprise 36.7 percent of all tenth-grade high school dropouts, and black Americans are jailed at five times the rate of whites.[50]

---

49. For further information, see Ronald Segal, *The Black Diaspora: Five Centuries of the Black Experience Outside Africa* (New York: Farrar, Straus and Giroux, 1995) and Kwame Anthony Appiah and Henry Louis Gates Jr. (eds.) *Africana: The Encyclopedia of the African and African American Experience* (New York: Basic Civitas Books, 1999).

50. These are other pertinent statistics may be obtained from the Web site of U.S. Department of Health and Human Services Office of Minority Health at *http://www.omhrc.gov* from the Web site of the U.S. Census Bureau at *http://www.census.gov/* and from the U.S. Department of Education Web site at *http://www.ed.gov*. Data on the rates of suicides among black Americans were obtained from the study "Suicide among Black Americans" funded by the Suicide Prevention Resource Center under the auspices of the U.S. Department of Health and Human Services. Results are available from *http://74.125.47.132/search?q =cache:BdNRfpWIr0wJ:www.sprc.org/library/black.am.facts.pdf+black+Americans+statistics&cd=2&hl=en&ct=clnk&gl=us.*

Clearly, such racist realities have a negative impact on the constitution of personhood for those individuals who are subjected to such bigotry and oppression. In an address commemorating African American History Month, psychiatrist Alvin Poussaint pointed out that racism "has a whole psychological impact. There becomes a burden of proof on blacks to show that they are OK; a burden of proof to show that they are competent."[51] The struggle for civil rights, therefore, "has been to make a black life count as much as a white life." The significance is this: "When a relative value is placed on a life, it sends a message to persons doing the oppressing, as well as to the persons being victimized. In turn, the victim learns to devalue their own life" and, by extension, their very personhood.

Gender

Despite many transnational and cross-cultural advances in the status of women within the last fifty years, men continue to enjoy higher social status and value in societies throughout the world, which serves to constitute their sense of person more positively than that of women. In addition, the emotional, physical, and psychological dimensions stereotypically associated with men such as physical strength, rationality, analytical ability, dispassion, and emotional control continue to be valued more highly than characteristics stereotypically attributed to women such as frailty, affectivity, emotionality, passion, and acquiescence. While life experience and scholarly research indicate that none of these characteristics is innately more associated with one gender or the other and that these values and attributes are clearly inculcated by nurture from the very beginning of life, the social stereotypes endure. The behaviors and decisions that stem from these stereotypes, moreover, have serious consequences for women's health and well-being and, by extension, women's sense of self.

The following facts culled by the *Women's Learning Partnership* organization elucidate several consequences of being born into the world today as female. Of the 855,000,000 people in the world

---

51. Excerpts from Alvin Poussaint, "Afro-American Scholars: Leaders, Activists, and Writers," in Lucy D. Suddreth, "How Racism Affects Everyone," *The Library of Congress Information Bulletin*; available from *http://www.loc.gov/loc/lcib/93/9304/racism.html*.

who are illiterate, 70 percent of them are female. Parents in countries such as China and India sometimes use sex determination tests to find out if their fetus is a girl. Of 8,000 fetuses aborted at a Bombay clinic, 7,999 were female. Nearly half of all people living with HIV/AIDS are women and girls. On average and across the world, women work more hours than men each week, sometimes as much as 35 hours more, but their work is often unpaid and unaccounted for. Where women do the same work as men, they are paid 30 to 40 percent less than men. In the United Kingdom, Italy, Germany, and France, women are paid 75 percent of men's wages, whereas in Vietnam, Sri Lanka, Tanzania, and Australia women earn 90 percent of men's wages. Moreover, while women produce nearly 80 percent of the food on the planet, they receive less than 10 percent of agricultural assistance. In addition, the majority of the world's women cannot own, inherit, or control property, land, and wealth on an equal basis with men. Thus, 75 percent of the refugees and internally displaced in the world are women who have lost their families and their homes.[52]

As these statistics show, both the mindset of patriarchy and the distorted system of beliefs that supports it—called sexism—are alive and well and continue to deprive women of status, participation, and opportunity in every sphere of public and private life. Multiple studies show that such deprivation produces feelings of depression, anger, disgust, and guilt; low self-esteem, eating disorders, and generalized psychological distress.[53] Clearly, experiences of sexism have a negative relation of effect on women's sense of personhood.

A corollary of sexism is heterosexism which is sexual discrimination or prejudice based on the assumption that heterosexuality is the norm. Similar to the scourge of sexism that implicitly assumes that the male is the norm, heterosexism spawns a whole constellation of stereotypes, misconceptions, and prejudices that deprive gay, lesbian, bisexual, transsexual, and transgender persons of human rights, of social status and equality, of economic opportunities, and of access

---

52. "Human Rights Facts and Figures," *Women's Learning Partnership for Rights, Development and Peace;* available from *http://www.learningpartnership.org/en/resources/facts/humanrights.*

53. Bonnie Moradi and Linda Mezydlo Subich, "Perceived Sexist Events and Feminist Identity Development Attitudes: Links to Women's Psychological Distress," *The Counseling Psychologist,* 30, no. 1 (2002): 44–65.

to many spheres of public and private life. Examples of institution-alized heterosexism include the denial of the right to marriage, to custody and adoption of children, to benefits from Social Security, and to other rights accorded to heterosexual spouses. In recent years, laws have been passed that have essentially legalized discrimina-tion based on sexual orientation in the areas of health care, housing, and employment. Moreover, so-called "marriage protection acts" or "defense of marriage acts" have sought to restrict the right of homo-sexuals to marry by defining marriage as a legal union between one man and one woman.[54]

Like sexism, heterosexism also produces deleterious effects on the self-esteem and well-being of homosexual persons from school-age through adulthood. Results from the National Youth Risk Behav-ior Survey conducted in 2003 by the Massachusetts Department of Education reported that "LGBT students, when compared with their heterosexual peers, were: over 5 times more likely to have attempted suicide in the past year; over 3 times more likely to have skipped school in the past month because they felt unsafe at or en route to school; and over 3 times more likely to have been threatened or injured with a weapon at school in the past year."[55] Research with col-lege students "concluded that diminished self-esteem, greater psycho-logical distress, and suicidality were associated with reports of greater victimization based on sexual-minority status."[56] In a study on sexual minorities in the workplace, the experience of heterosexism linked with lower health and well-being, greater anxiety and depression, social withdrawal, and lower life satisfaction and physical health for respondents. While heterosexism surely militates against the forma-tion of a healthy sense of personhood in gay, lesbian, bisexual, trans-sexual, and transgender persons, positive nurturance and relationships

---

54. See, for example, the text of "Public Law 104-199—Defense of Marriage Act," *U.S. Government Printing Office*; available from *http://www.gpo.gov/fdsys/pkg/PLAW-104publ199/html/PLAW-104publ199.htm*.

55. "Statistics," *Lesbian Gay Bisexual Transgender Center, Case Western Reserve Uni-versity*; available from *http://case.edu/lgbt/safezone/statistics.html*.

56. Perry Silverschanz, Lilia M. Cortina, Julie Konik, and Vicki J. Magley, "Slurs, Snubs, and Queer Jokes: Incidence and Impact of Heterosexist Harassment in Academia;" available from *http://www.lsa.umich.edu/psych/lilia-cortina-lab/silver schanz%20et%20al.%202008%20.pdf*: 181.

at all stages of life can, nonetheless, serve to "promote self-esteem and a sense of value and worth . . . help . . . develop a sense of identity . . . [and] teach survival skills to cope in the larger world."[57]

Economic Status

In 2005, the wealthiest 20 percent of the world's population accounted for almost 80 percent of consumption. Nearly a billion people survive on less than one dollar per day, and 80 percent of people throughout the world live on less than ten dollars a day. More than a billion people in developing countries have inadequate access to water and basic sanitation. A quarter of all humanity lives without electricity. Twenty-five thousand children under the age of five die from poverty-related causes each day. While six billion dollars annually would provide basic education for all and nine billion dollars would provide access to water and sanitation for all, eight billion dollars is spent on cosmetics in the United States. In Europe, eleven billion dollars is spent annually on ice cream alone. Although seventeen billion dollars is spent annually on pet foods in Europe and the United States, thirteen billion dollars would provide basic health and nutrition for all.[58] Today in the United States, estimates indicate that more than 35 million Americans or 14 percent of the population live in poverty.

As pervasive a social phenomenon as it is, poverty is equally complex, especially with regard to its causes. Nonetheless, the consequences for the constitution of personhood are clear.[59] Infants born into poverty have lower birth weight, greater mental and physical disabilities, and a higher incidence of mortality than those growing up in better financial circumstances. Children raised in financially impoverished circumstances have more frequent and more severe health problems and, thus, miss more school because of sickness. Poverty is associated with more incidences of violence and abuse in families, sometimes leading to death. In extreme circumstances,

---

57. Connie R. Matthews and Eve M. Adams, "Social Justice Approach to Prevent Mental Health Effects of Heterosexism: A Social Justice Approach to Preventing the Negative Consequences of Heterosexism," *Medscape*; available from *http://www.medscape.com/viewarticle/586710_3*.

58. Anup Shah, "Poverty Facts and Stats," *Global Issues*; available from *http://www.globalissues. org/article/26/poverty-facts-and-stats*.

59. "Causes and Effects of Poverty," *CliffsNotes.com*; available from *http://www.cliffsnotes.com/ study_guide/topicArticleId-26957,articleId-26882.html*.

poverty can result in homelessness, which exacerbates an already difficult family situation. Children of homelessness suffer malnutrition as well as disruption in family, school, and social relationships.[60] If, in fact, one's personhood is shaped by stable relationships, positive interactions with family and social system, and healthy embodiment and well-being, then the effects of poverty wreak havoc on the development of a full-functioning and fully flourishing person.

Ethnicity

Ethnic heritage is a significant factor in the life of a person. It enables one to stretch beyond the here and now to embrace and be embraced by shared ancestry, language, memories, traditions, symbols, and rituals that stretch for centuries and enrich one's life with depth and breadth of meaning. Each citizen of the United States, for example, can trace his or her ancestry to those who were once aliens and strangers in this land, exiled because of political, economic, or social oppressions in their country of origin. Nonetheless, the history of immigration from the sixteenth century through the early-twentieth century has occurred within decidedly shifting worldviews. As a result, attitudes toward cultural and ethnic diversity have varied from one historical epoch to another and from one generation to the next.

While enculturation was largely expected of European immigrants, and acclimation was highly valued in the public sector, many racial and ethnic groups determinedly and publicly embrace and celebrate their diversity of culture, language, and tradition. Their ancestral heritages are a source of pride and require preservation. In recent years, however, some local, state, and national legislators have attempted, with varying degrees of success, to reinstate the expectation of assimilation and enculturation by introducing legislation to impose English as the national language and to eliminate multilingual signage, forms, and education. Such radical retrenchment presumes homogeneity in American history and culture that has never existed. Moreover, it reveals a lack of remembrance on the part of many American citizens whose separation from their immigrant past can often be measured in generations rather than

---

60. Ibid.

in centuries and whose nationalistic protests cannot obscure that, in its lived reality, the United States has been and remains a culturally plural society.

At the root of much discriminatory behavior is xenophobia or the fear of the stranger. Such fear creates negative images that lead to stereotypes about people whose language, facial features, or skin color identify them as Asian, Arab, African, Hispanic, or Latino. Undoubtedly, recent experiences of international and domestic terrorism in the United States have amplified xenophobic fears. Regrettably, these fears have been intensified through political and ideological rhetoric and have mushroomed into bigotry, profiling, violence, and injustice.

Caught in the midst of these dynamics are individuals trying to forge a positive sense of their personhood in relation to their ethnic group as well as to the family, social system, and larger society of which they are a part. With them, those exploring their identities within the relations of effect of race, gender, and economic status navigate a shifting terrain of phenomena, events, and relationships. The outcome of their exploration depends upon the stability of their foothold within the matrices of their relations.

RELATION OF EMERGENCE: LIFE IN STAGES

Introduction

As discussed in chapter 2, emergence refers to the reality that certain novel forms of life that develop from more elemental forms of life are not reducible to the form that preceded them, but neither are they independent of them. How does the relation of emergence apply to human personhood? In the earlier discussion of the biological dimensions of personhood, Edwin Hui based his arguments concerning humanness and personhood on the fundamental and indissoluble relations among the various stages of the human that emerges into adulthood. Coming from a psychosocial theory of human personality development, psychoanalyst Erik Erikson makes a similar contention about continuity and novelty within the developing human person.

Erikson's Psychosocial Theory of Development

According to Erik Erikson, the human personality develops psychosocially by means of interpersonal interaction between the individual and his or her family and social system, which Erikson perceived as reflecting the values of the broader culture. Erikson postulated that through interpersonal interactions within one's social context, the human person progresses through eight psychological stages of a life cycle by resolving a series of "crises" that arise through such interactions. These crises are not traumatic events; rather, they are optimal moments in human development through which human personhood emerges. Each stage, moreover, lays the foundation for the next developmental stage. Erikson describes these crises in terms of eight sets of contrasting values associated with each stage of a person's life cycle as seen in the following table.

TABLE 3.1: EIGHT STAGES OF THE PSYCHOSOCIAL THEORY OF PERSONALITY DEVELOPMENT[61]			
Stage	**Age Span**	**Crisis**	**Outcome**
One	0–18 months	trust vs. mistrust	hope
Two	18 months–3 years	autonomy vs. doubt/ shame	will and courage
Three	3–5 years	initiative vs. guilt	independence and purpose
Four	6–12 years	competence vs. inferiority	competence
Five	12–18 years	identity vs. role diffusion	fidelity and devotion
Six	18–35 years	intimacy vs. isolation	love and affiliation
Seven	35–65 years	generativity vs. stagnation	productivity and care
Eight	65 years–death	integrity vs. despair	wisdom

Because the resolution of each crisis affects the capacity of the human person to resolve successfully subsequent critical stages, the

61. Erik Erikson introduced his psychosocial theory of personality development in his book *Childhood and Society* (New York: Norton, 1950). He further refined it in subsequent publications, including *Identity: Youth and Crisis* (New York: Norton, 1968). The information in this chart is culled from commentaries on his work.

sense of personhood that emerges from each critical stage is essentially related to the sense of personhood preceding it. Nevertheless, because the resolution of each crisis results in the acquisition of new psychological, emotional, social, and sometimes physical capacities in the developing person, each stage is emergent, requiring a new vocabulary to describe the personal outcome adequately. Rather than being relegated to the technical language of psychology or sociology, these emergent distinctions are expressed in the common references used for the developing person, including infant, toddler, preschooler, youngster, adolescent, young adult, adult, and elder. Each descriptor correlates with a recognizable stage of life and provokes a constellation of attributes and abilities generally consistent with each stage or grouping.

Stage One: Infancy: 0–18 Months: Trust vs. Mistrust

The principal human relationships within the first year of a child's life are with the child's caregivers, ordinarily the parents and particularly the mother. During this stage, the infant is fully dependent upon others for food, sustenance, and comfort. Because parental and family relationships and interactions virtually constitute their world, infants develop their first impressions about the broader world around them based on their experiences of the family. When the infant experiences her or his caretakers as dependable, nurturing, responsive, warm, and affectionate, when the infant senses that his or her parents consistently satisfy basic needs, then the infant begins to develop a sense that the parents, the family, and, literally, the world and those in it are worthy of his or her *trust*. With this sense of trust, moreover, comes the *quality of hope*—the feeling that what is desired can be obtained and that what is needed will be provided. If, however, the parents or the home environment is characterized by neglect or even abuse, then the infant becomes insecure and develops a sense of *mistrust* in the world. As a result, the world the infant comes to anticipate is unreliable, unpredictable, and even dangerous, leading to a disposition of insecurity and even despair.

Stage Two: Toddler: 18 Months–3 Years: Autonomy vs. Shame and Doubt

During toddlerhood, the primary relationships and interactions for a developing child continue to be with parents and family. During this time, the toddler's motor skills begin to develop and with them the ability to navigate the environment. These are also the day care years, which, in our contemporary world, often broaden the scope of the child's relational world to include playmates and day care personnel and friends. Nonetheless, the toddler's parents are still who provide the secure foundation for the child's excursions into the world.

Because of their developing motor skills, toddlers are now able to assert their burgeoning independence and meet some of their own needs. Toddlers acquire the basic mobility skills of crawling, standing, walking, and running and of self-care such as washing, feeding, and toilet training. They eagerly explore their home, neighborhood, and care environments with eyes, hands, feet, and mouths. This is also the phase of the "terrible twos" when toddlers readily make their wishes known, master the word "No!" and find many opportunities to use it. If parents, siblings, and caretakers respond to these self-asserting behaviors in the toddler with patience, encouragement, and affirmation, setting limits when appropriate, then the toddler begin to develop personal *autonomy*, a sense of one's ability to handle the challenges and problems they encounter, as well as a rudimentary idea of right and wrong. Based on their sense of autonomy, toddlers manifest the *qualities of will and courage* as the capacity to make decisions, to have confidence in them, and to move forward in spite of fear or misgivings. If, however, these significant others are overly rigid or restrictive in their responses toward such overtures of independence or if they harshly criticize or ridicule the toddler's attempts at self-assertion, then the toddler develops self-*doubt or shame*. Such shame and doubt often lead to a sense of inadequacy about one's abilities and a tendency toward overdependence on the help or opinion of others.

Stage Three: Preschooler: 3–5 Years: Initiative vs. Guilt

The stage of toddlerhood advances rapidly into the preschool years, during which the interactions, skills, and opportunities of the developing child expand into exciting and unfamiliar territories, although the basic family unit still provides the most significant relationships. Preschoolers can now begin to test out some of the social skills that help them to cope with playmates and schoolmates. During this stage, children not only participate in goings-on planned by parents, teachers, or playmates but also initiate role-play projects or pursuits in which others take part. Some of these pursuits require the child to take risks—to ride a bike, to cross a street, to make new friends, to communicate ideas, or to exhibit fledgling leadership. In these areas of life children frequently take their cues in behavior, language, and choices from their parents or significant adults in their lives and never cease to delight and disturb by incessantly asking, "Why?"

When these self-starts and overtures made by three- to five-year-olds are met by encouragement, interest, and participation by the significant others in their lives, preschoolers develop *initiative*, a personal sense of their capacity to plan and undertake activities, make decisions, take risks, engage others cooperatively, and exercise leadership. A strong sense of personal initiative results in the *qualities of independence and purpose*, through which children's self-reliance and motivation emerge in meeting the complexities of their expanding universe. If their initiatives are thwarted by unwarranted disapproval or undue control, then the child develops a sense of *guilt*. "Immobilized by guilt, [the child] is fearful . . . and is restricted both in the development of play skills and in imagination."[62]

Stage Four: School-Age Child: 6–12 Years: Industry vs. Inferiority

As children fully enter the school-age period, the influence that their parents once exercised is moderated to some extent by significant relationships within the school and neighborhood communities. Teachers, in particular, play an expanding and important role in the child's developing personhood. Because of growth in their perceptual and cognitive capacities, children at this stage are more aware of themselves as individuals. Moreover, because of their exposure to persons and situations outside the familiarity of their family structure, school-age children begin to grasp the meaning and complexity of experiences and events, articulate moral norms and attitudes, and perceive social, cultural, and personal differences.[63] Having resolved the crisis of their previous stage, they exhibit initiative in starting,

---

62. "Developmental Milestone," *Child Welfare Manual*; available from *http://www.dss.mo.gov /cd/info/cwmanual/section7/ch1_33/sec7ch4.htm.*

63. K. Eileen Allen and Lynn R. Marotz, *Developmental Profiles: Pre-birth through Twelve* (Florence, KY: Cengage Learning, 2009), 193.

carrying through, and bringing projects to completion, and they experience pride in a job well done.

Given the opportunity to demonstrate such abilities, praised for their accomplishments consistent with such abilities, and encouraged to expand their reach and attempt still greater things, school-age children develop *industry* accompanied by diligence, perseverance, and follow-through. This instills in the child the *quality of competence*, that is, the sense of possessing the skills, capacities, and knowledge through which one feels well qualified and equipped to meet the requirements of one's state in life. Conversely, if their peers discourage children's initiatives, if their accomplishments fail to meet the unrealistic expectation of parents or teachers, or if they experience ridicule or rejection, they may suffer from a sense of *inferiority*, which has significant impact on their self-concept and self-esteem.

Stage Five: Adolescent: 12–18 Years: Identity vs. Role Confusion

Adolescence is a time of transition, a time when adulthood slowly emerges from childhood in the midst of significant social interactions and relationships, shifts in the moral landscape, and struggles to find and establish a unique and authentic sense of self. Nonetheless, though transitional, the passage through the period of adolescence proves critical and often decisive in shaping and validating one's emerging sense of personhood, one's capacity for enduring relationship, and one's commitment to principles and responsibilities.

During adolescence, therefore, the individual contemplates and, at times, even broods over the kind of person he or she will be and the role she or he wishes to play in the adult world. Adolescents are concerned with how they appear to others, how they fit into a social group or society in general, or what others think or say about them. When in the midst of the bio-psycho-social forces that swirl around them, adolescents explore their potentialities, establish their identity upon their findings, and emerge with that deep awareness of who they are. They can develop the quality of *fidelity*, "the ability to sustain loyalties freely pledged in spite of the inevitable contradictions and confusions of value systems."[64] Those less grounded

---

64. Richard Stevens, *Erik Erikson: An Introduction* (New York: St. Martin's Press, 1983), 50.

in that awareness, however, experience *role confusion* (*diffusion*). In the face of unresolved conflicts, the adolescent can experience self-consciousness and self-doubt, rather than self-certainty; be plagued by feeling of inferiority, rather than achievement; and engage in negative behaviors such as delinquency, rather than in constructive and productive roles. If, however, the adolescent can answer satisfactorily for him- or herself, "Who am I?" "What have I got?" and "What am I going to do with it?" he or she has established an identity on which to base the remaining stages of an emerging life.[65]

Stage Six: Young Adult: 18–35 Years: Intimacy vs. Isolation

In 2004, the Australian punk band The Living End recorded the single "I Can't Give You What I Haven't Got."[66] In a very real way, the title of this song expresses the dilemma inherent in the emergence from the crisis of identity into readiness for the decision of either intimacy or isolation. The reason is this: If I do not know who I am in myself, who can I be for another? If I do not embrace my own identity, how can I give myself to another? These questions confront young adults who enter this sixth stage of life in which they are drawn to seek meaningful and reciprocal intimate relationships and to share their own unique personhood in devoted friendships and in marriage.

At this stage, the principal relational sphere is with other young adults like themselves. Increasingly secure in one's personal self, the young adult ventures out to explore the possibility of finding security and *intimacy* with another. When able to enter into such a mutually satisfying relationship with another, the young adult begins to develop the qualities of love and affiliation, characterized by tenderness, affection, mutual respect, and trust with and toward another. Undoubtedly, the capacity for love and affiliation presupposes the capacity for trust, for hope, for will, for purpose, and for fidelity—all qualities resulting from the successful resolution of those critical junctures encountered throughout the life stages thus far. In the absence of such qualities, the

---

65. F. L. Gross, *Introducing Erik Erikson: An Invitation to His Thinking* (Lanham, MD: University Press of America, 1987), 39.

66. The Living End, "I Can't Give You What I Haven't Got," *EMI Music Publishing*, 2004. Lyrics available from *http://www.lyricstime.com/living-end-i-can-t-give-you-what-i-haven-t-got-lyrics.html*.

young adult may be unwillingly or unable to negotiate the give-and-take and selflessness that such intimate relationships often involve and necessitate. Fear of rejection and of the ego pain associated with it, coupled with the mistrust that it breeds, often leads to a sense of *isolation* that militates against the very relationality necessary for the emergence of one's fully flourishing personhood.

Stage Seven: Middle-Aged Adult: 35–65 Years: Generativity vs. Stagnation

Erikson's stage seven of personhood development encompasses the central tasks of productive work and raising a family. The work envisioned by Erikson is not primarily self-serving but, rather, other-serving; it contributes to the improvement of society. The attention to one's family envisioned by Erikson is not primarily for the purpose of securing one's household or fulfilling one's parental needs, but also of securing the future and preparing the next generation to fulfill its role in the culture, the society, and the world. The essential relationships that impact this stage of life, therefore, are those shared with colleagues, with a circle of friends, with the local and church communities, and, once again, with one's family—at a far different stage of personal development, however, than when last family relationships played an essential role. During this time, adults establish themselves within stable relationships with friends and, often, with a spouse; begin to have and raise children; and become involved in civic and community organizations and activities. If adults in their middle years of life successfully negotiate the many and varied demands upon them, they develop and act with a capacity for *generativity* and the *qualities of productivity and care.*

Generativity is the sense that one is contributing to the wider scheme of life, is productive in a sphere and for a cause larger than oneself, and is preparing and guiding the next generation to be socially responsible adults one day. Productivity and care is demonstrated by the ability to make a difference in the community and in the lives of those they love. Adults who struggle with or even fail to meet these responsibilities or nurture these capacities are often left with a sense of *stagnation*. Focused more on one's own needs than that of family or society or engulfed by the present without regard for the future, these adults grapple with the meaning and purpose of their lives and lack stable and fulfilling relationships with family or friends. Simply put, their sense of themselves as fully functioning and fully flourishing persons is at risk, which does not bode well as they enter the final stage of life.

Stage Eight: Late Adult: 65 Years–Death: Integrity vs. Despair

As adults enter into the latter years of life, further shifts in family, friendship, and functioning occur. For many, these are the retirement years, which provide the opportunity for reflection and retrospection on one's life project. If, on balance, older adults look back on their lives with contentment, they experience *integrity*, a sense of authenticity and of congruence between the values that they have held dear and the life that they have lived well. Characteristic of such adults is the *quality of wisdom* so frequently associated with old age. Such wisdom represents the confluence of knowledge and experience used to improve and enhance well-being of self and others; with self-knowledge and candor toward self and others; and with consistency between one's actions and one's ethical beliefs. [67]

If, however, at this stage of life, the individual reflects back on a life deemed unproductive and unfulfilling, the outcome may well be a state of *despair*. When goals go unaccomplished and when an absence of meaning pervades the life one lived, the result may be depression, hopelessness, and fear as death looms ahead. Careful attention to the critical movements of Erikson's eight stages of psychosocial development clearly reveals the emergent nature of this process as each stage is interdependent. From the appropriate resolution of each crisis emerges the capacity to meet and engage the next developmental task until the person in his or her fullness emerges in the serenity of a life well lived. Ideally, the elder person constituted by integrity and personified by wisdom represents the epitome of the relation of emergence.

---

67. Andrew C. Harter, "8," in *Character Strengths and Virtues: A Handbook and Classification*, ed. Christopher Peterson and Martin E. P. Seligman (Oxford: Oxford University Press, 2004), 181–96.

SUMMARY

This chapter has explored the remarkable array of relations that constitutes the human person from conception to death and beyond in the memories of others. It began with the philosophical considerations that viewed the person first as a series of relations within developing consciousness; then as relations among consecutive memories nonetheless conceived as a unity; and ultimately as the relation between the mind and body. Moving from these philosophical insights, the chapter examined the question of the influence of nature and nurture on human personhood and concluded that both are necessary relations in personal development. In the relation of origin called nature, personhood is constituted through heritable characteristics and embodiment; in the relation of effect called nurture, human personhood is constituted through the influences of environment and social locations, both for good and ill. Finally, the relation of emergence traced the constitution of personhood through Erik Erikson's eight stages of psychosocial development and noted the critical interrelation of each stage with all the others. As chapter 2 demonstrated through scientific insights that being is relation in the cosmos, this chapter demonstrated through the behavioral and social sciences that being is relation in the human person. In chapter 4, theological and religious insights demonstrate that relation constitutes even divine being itself.

FOR FURTHER READING

Erikson, Erik. *Childhood and Society*. New York: Norton, 1950.

Hui, Edwin. *At the Beginning of Life: Dilemmas in Theological Bioethics*. Downers Grove, IL: InterVarsity Press, 2002.

Macmurray, John. *Persons in Relation*. New York: Harper Brothers, 1961.

Chapter 4

DIVINE BEING AS RELATION

"Despite their orthodox confession of the Trinity, Christians are, in their practical life, almost mere "monotheists". . . . The venerable classical doctrine . . . is thought to be . . . a collection of pious speculations . . . [put] together in a system about which we cannot help wondering whether God has really revealed to us such abstruse things in a manner which is so obscure and needs so many complicated explanations."[1]

INTRODUCTION

Contrary to this evaluation of belief in God as Trinity that was given by theologian Karl Rahner in the late-twentieth century, the doctrine of the Trinity has captured the theological energies and imaginations of Catholic, Orthodox, and Protestant scholars and persons of faith since the third century CE and continued to occupy a critical place in Christian thought until the eighteenth century. Twentieth-century theologian Elizabeth Johnson relates a vignette attributed to

---

1. Karl Rahner, *The Trinity*, trans. Joseph Donceel (New York: Herder and Herder, 1970), 10, 11, 14, 39, 40.

fourth-century Orthodox theologian Gregory of Nyssa. As Johnson tells it,

> In the late fourth century . . . contemporaries, high and low, seriously engaged the question of how to speak about God. Their issue, in a culture awash with Greek philosophical notions, was whether Jesus Christ was truly divine or simply a creature subordinate to God the Father. The question engaged not only theologians or bishops but just about everybody. "Even the baker," wrote Gregory, "does not cease from discussing this, for if you ask the price of bread he will tell you that the Father is greater and the Son subject to him."[2]

Nevertheless, as exemplified by the 1831 publication of *The Christian Faith*, by Friedrich Schleiermacher, in which he discussed the Trinity in an appendix,[3] the doctrine of Trinity was either ignored, relegated to secondary status, indicted as unscriptural and irrational, or subjected to concerted anti-Trinitarian onslaughts from the period of the Reformation onward. These onslaughts arose from biblically based criticism, from the disciplines of philosophy and science, and even from theology itself, spurred on by thought movements such as rationalism, naturalism, and empiricism.[4] While developments in the latter part of the twentieth century brought about renewed interest in the doctrine—and symbols of Trinity abound in worship—the concept of God as Trinity too often continues to be regarded as a merely speculative symbol that has no practical consequence.

In contrast to such common disregard, however, contemporary theological writings on God as Trinity bring to the fore the fundamental connections with and radical implications of the life of the

---

2. Elizabeth A. Johnson, "A Theological Case for God-She: Expanding the Treasury of Metaphor," *Commonweal* (January 29, 1993); available from *http://findarticles. com/p/articles/ mi_m1252/is_n2_v120 /ai_13370402/.* Internal quote from Gregory of Nyssa, *"De deitate Filii et Spiritu sancti,"* in *Patrologiae cursus completus, Series graeca,* in 161 volumes, ed. Jacques-Paul Migne (Turnholti, Belgium: Brepols, 1977), 46.557.

3. Friedrich Schleiermacher, *The Christian Faith,* trans. and eds. H. R. Macintosh and J. S. Stewart (Edinburgh: Clark, 1948).

4. Claude Welch, *In This Name: The Doctrine of the Trinity in Contemporary Theology* (New York: Scribner, 1952), vii, viii.

Trinity for the life of the human community and the evolving cosmos.[5] The main objective of this chapter is to consider the triune life of God in terms of the relations of origin, emergence, and effect that have been shown to constitute the being of the cosmos and the being of the human person. Before moving to these categories, the chapter begins with a brief summary of the rise of Trinitarian doctrine rooted in the Gospel narratives and in the metaphysical perspectives of the theologies in the Roman West and the Greek East. Within this context, it explores key questions and controversies that arose in response to these earliest attempts to articulate the mystery of the Triune God, the God who Christians claim is One God in three Divine Persons. In the process, this historical section highlights several key theological concepts used to address these controversial issues to both positive and negative effect. Ultimately, the chapter retrieves this classical terminology in dialogue with the scriptural tradition to propose that divine being as Trinity has consistently been understood in terms of relations, a fact that has significant ramifications for the cosmic and human community.

THE RISE OF TRINITARIAN THEOLOGY

The doctrine of the Trinity summarizes the central Christian affirmations about God that are grounded in the religious experience of the first community of Christians. These experiences are narrated in the Christian Gospels and shape the questions and circumstances that gave rise to the Epistles. Although the Christian scriptures are "permeated with the thought, now latent, now manifest, of the three Divine persons," most scholars find only elemental Trinitarianism in the Christian scriptures.[6] As a result, the specific term *trinity* does

---

5. See, for example, Denis Edwards, *The God of Evolution: A Trinitarian Theology* (Mahwah, NJ: Paulist, 1999); John Haught, *God after Darwin: A Theology of Evolution* (Boulder, CO: Westview, 2000); Johnson, *Quest for the Living God*; Catherine Mowry LaCugna, *God for Us: The Trinity and Christian Life* (San Francisco: Harper San Francisco, 1991); Sallie McFague, *The Body of God: An Ecological Theology* (Minneapolis: Fortress, 1993); Peacocke, *Theology for a Scientific Age* and Gloria L. Schaab, *The Creative Suffering of the Triune God: An Evolutionary Theology* (New York: Oxford University Press, 2007), among others.

6. Felix Klein, *The Doctrine of the Trinity*, trans. Daniel Sullivan (New York: Kennedy, 1940), 54.

not appear in the New Testament. The earliest use of the term was by Theophilus of Antioch circa 180 CE as *trias* and by Tertullian and Origen in the third century as *trinitas*.[7]

Despite the lack of specific terminology, the religious testimony of Christianity as recorded in the Gospels and Epistles clearly witnesses that God revealed Godself to Christians as Creator, Father, and Judge; as Lord, in the person of Jesus Christ, who lived among humans and was present in their midst as the Resurrected One; and as Holy Spirit, the power of new life and impetus in history for the coming of the Kingdom of God.[8] However, because of the distinctive belief in monotheism, rooted in their Jewish history of faith, the Christian community soon raised the question of how to reconcile its professed belief in the oneness of God with the threefold nature of their religious experience of God as Father, Son, and Holy Spirit.

In the first two centuries, different answers often stood in juxtaposition to one another, focused on either Christological (the nature of Jesus Christ) or pneumatological (the nature of the Holy Spirit) issues. They were shaped by each community's experience of the historical and risen Jesus and the power of the Holy Spirit, by the development in Christological and pneumatological insights stemming from prayer, reflection, and worship, and by the influence of the Neoplatonic philosophical worldview with its hierarchical dualisms and its substance ontology. While the questions and insights that arose generally focused on the persons of Christ Jesus and the Spirit, they inevitably affected the development of the theology of God as Trinity.

---

7. G. H. Joyce, "The Blessed Trinity," *Catholic Encyclopedia Online*, available from *http://www.newadvent.org/cathen/l5047a.html:1*.

8. Throughout this book, the author is committed to the use of inclusive language for cosmic, human, and divine being. This chapter continues the use of such inclusive nouns and pronouns for the Divine *except* in material that is directly quoted from or based on primary sources. If all noninclusive nouns and pronouns were corrected or noted within such material, the preponderance of insertions and *sic* notations would be prohibitive in view of the prevalence of noninclusive nouns and pronouns for the human person and for the Christian Triune God within the scriptures and the classical theological tradition.

Emerging Controversies

As Christianity grew beyond the apostolic age, its early questions turned into controversies concerning the beliefs it professed about Christ and the Holy Spirit. Arius the Antiochene voiced one of the earliest and most significant controversies about the nature of Christ. His school of thought placed strong emphasis upon the historicity of Jesus and had an equally intense interest in maintaining the oneness of God. For Arius, the "oneness of essence" of the Son with the Father contradicted belief in the oneness of God. Arius claimed that this would make the Son "second God, under God the Father,"[9] which contradicted monotheism. Similar to the objections Arius raised about Jesus were those that Macedonius I of Constantinople and his followers posed about the Spirit. This group, known as *pneumatomachoi* or *pneumatomachians* ("opponents of the Spirit"), did not believe that the Holy Spirit shared the same nature or substance as the Father and the Son. Rather, they asserted that the Holy Spirit was a creature of the Son, a servant of the Father and the Son, and thus subordinate to the Father and the Son. Ultimately, Athanasius, bishop of Alexandria, and Basil the Great, bishop of Caesarea, refuted the claims of Arius and the teachings of the *pneumatomachoi.*[10] Athanasius' reasoning influenced subsequent creedal statements concerning the doctrine of Trinity. In 325 CE, the Council of Nicaea definitively proclaimed the divinity of the Father, Son, and Holy Spirit as one God in three equal persons. In 381 CE, the Council of Constantinople amplified the Nicene Creed in asserting that the Holy Spirit is the Third Person of the Trinity, "who with the Father and the Son is worshipped and glorified."[11]

As challenges to the divinity of Christ and the Holy Spirit swirled, so disputes about Trinitarian orthodoxy continued to arise under a variety of guises and with a variety of names. These challenges to orthodoxy, called "heresies," included Sabellianism (belief that the eternal Being of God existed in three forms), monophysitism

9. "Trinity: Arius and the Nicene Creed," *Interactive Bible;* available from *http://www.bible.ca/trinity/trinity-history-arius.htm.*

10. "Macedonianism," *Encyclopædia Britannica Online,* Encyclopædia Britannica, 2011; available from *http://www.britannica.com/EBchecked/topic/354332/Macedonianism.*

11. James E. Kiefer, "The Filioque Clause," *Internet Christian Library;* available from *http://www.iclnet.org/pub/resources/text/history/creed.filioque.txt.*

(belief in three separate Gods), adoptionism (belief that Jesus Christ was a man who, for his great virtue and merit, was adopted into the Godhead), psilanthropism (belief that Jesus Christ was only a man, not God in any sense), and pneumatomachianism (the denial of the Godhead of the Holy Spirit). Regardless of their guises and their names, however, most of these challenges struggle with three temptations seemingly inherent in the Trinitarian mystery: the temptations to tritheism, to subordinationism, and to modalism. Tritheism contradicts the doctrine of monotheism. Subordinationism contradicts the doctrine of the equality of the Divine Persons. Modalism contradicts the doctrine of the three Divine Persons are truly distinct, one from another, and not merely aspects or "modes" of being in God.

Theological Responses

With every contradiction or challenge posed, theologians and teachers in the early church such as Tertullian, Athanasius of Alexandria, Basil of Caesarea, and Cyril stepped up to clarify orthodox interpretations of the Trinitarian mystery. The definitive response to these earliest disputes was set forth by the Council of Nicaea in 325 CE and augmented by the Council of Constantinople in 381 CE. Together, these councils refuted the controversies concerning the divinity of Christ and the Holy Spirit and asserted the authoritative beliefs of Christianity in their formulation of the Nicene-Constantinopolitan Creed.[12]

With these conciliar responses, Trinitarian terminology was given "technical precision," especially regarding ideas such as the "consubstantiality" of the Father, Son, and Spirit. Based on the substance ontology examined in chapter 1 of this book, *consubstantiality* means, "the Persons of the Trinity shared the same nature or essence." Each and all are of the same Godhead; each and all are divine. However, some of this technical terminology precipitated a confusion all its own. A case in point involved the use of the Greek terms *ousia*, or *essence*, and *hypostasis*, or *substance*, for the One and the Three in God as Trinity. These two Greek terms mean fundamentally the same

---

12. For a common articulation of the Nicene-Constantinopolitan Creed, see "The Nicene Creed (381 CE)," *ICLnet* (*Internet Christian Library*); available from *http://www.iclnet.org/pub/resources /text/history/nicene381.html*.

thing. Nonetheless, they were being used to distinguish the essence of the One in God from that of the Three in God. This use of the terms led to no end of confusion in theological circles. Ultimately, theologians resolved the confusion by declaration, settling upon the use of *ousia* for the One Nature or Essence of God and *hypostases* for the Three Persons in God. However, this declaration did not occur before *ousia* was erroneously translated into Latin as *persona* (or *subsistentia*). As a result, the term *person* was introduced into Trinitarian theology to the lasting chagrin of theologians throughout the ages.

Augustine, bishop of Hippo and noted theologian, bemoaned the use of the term *persons* as designating the Three in Trinity. Nonetheless, in his masterwork, *On the Trinity*, Augustine defends the use of the term *person* "because with us the usage has already obtained," that is, because theologians, teachers of the faith, and the community of believers alike had accepted a common understanding of the term as it applied to the Trinity.[13] In addition to common assent to the term, however, Augustine advanced an additional reason for continuing to use *person* that had a practical, pastoral, and even mystical basis. While Augustine realized that the Trinity is a mystery that can never be fully understood or expressed, he, nonetheless, recognized the necessity of being able to speak of that which is so central to the faith of Christians. Hence, Augustine embraced the term despite its inaccuracy, acknowledging that "the formula 'three persons' has been coined, not in order to give a complete explanation by means of it, but in order that we might not be obliged to remain silent."[14] As late as the eleventh century, theologian Anselm of Canterbury likewise remarked about both the mystery and impropriety of the term *person* in a famous quote in which he calls the Three in the One God "*tres nescio quid.*" As Anselm explains it, there is "a unity [in the Trinity] because of the unity of essence," however, there is "a trinity, because of the three *I know not what* (*trinitatem propter tres nescio quid*)."[15]

---

13. Augustine of Hippo, *On The Trinity*, in *A Select Library of The Nicene and Post-Nicene Fathers of The Christian Church*, Vol. 3, ed. Philip Schaff (Buffalo: The Christian Literature Company, 1887), 5:9.

14. Ibid., 5:10.

15. Anselm of Canterbury, quoted by Dennis K. P. Ngien, "The *Filioque* Clause in the Teaching of Anselm of Canterbury—Part I"; available from *http://www.church society.org/churchman/ documents/cman_118_2_ngien1.pdf: 107*

In the centuries that followed, more technical terminology would develop. In response to a veritable onslaught of Christological, pneumatological, and theological controversies in the early centuries of Christianity, both Roman Western and Greek Eastern theologians responded by advancing ever more highly speculative claims about the inner and outer life of the Trinity based upon the philosophical worldview that prevailed in their times. However, they began from two different starting points.

On the one hand, Western theologians began with the question, "How can the One be Three?" In their attempt to answer this question, theologians in the West proposed speculative concepts about the inner life of the Trinity. These included the "notions" of paternity and sonship, the "processions" of the Son and of the Spirit, the "missions" of incarnation and sanctification, and the doctrine of appropriation. While each of these concepts was fundamentally rooted in the ground of relationality, the speculative complexity that grew out of it often obscured this simple source with a tangle of terminology.

On the other hand, Eastern theologians began with a different question: "How can the Three be One?" Beginning with God's self-revelation in history as Father, Son, and Spirit, Greek theologians used the terms *hypostasis* to speak of the three Divine Persons, *ousia* to speak of the divine essence they shared, and *perichoresis* to speak of the basis of the unity. Their use of the term *perichoresis*, which literally means "to move or dance around," imaged the oneness of the three Persons not as a static reality but as a dynamic community characterized by interpermeation and interdependence of the three Persons in love.

These attempts at theological precision, however, came at a pastoral price. Rather than clarifying many questions for the community of faith, the sophisticated Trinitarian formulations eventually "relegated [the Divine Persons] to an intradivine realm locked up in itself, hidden from view" across a vast "ontological chasm." As a result, the Father, Son, and Spirit of the Gospels "faded into the background," precipitating what theologian Catherine LaCugna called "the defeat of the Trinity."[16] Rather than recognizing this dilemma, however, theologians continued to use the theological vocabulary

---

16. LaCugna, *God for Us*, 9.

and formulations of these earliest centuries of the Christian era to shape the majority of their Trinitarian constructions in the West and East for centuries to come. In so doing, they often ignored the sole dynamic that can both unite and differentiate the Trinitarian Persons—the dynamic of relation.

The Turn to Relation

The complexity and strangeness of many of the theological terms used to talk about the life of the Trinity often provoke the wonderment expressed by Karl Rahner in the quote that opens this chapter. Like Rahner, people of faith as well as students of theology may shake their heads "wondering whether God has really revealed to us such abstruse things in a manner which is so obscure and needs so many complicated explanations." Nonetheless, beneath this abstruse and seeming anachronistic terminology lies the very dynamic that forms the thesis of this book. All the language of paternity, sonship, generation, spiration, and consubstantiation—as well as the language of creation, incarnation, and sanctification through grace—is about *relation.* As it unfolds, therefore, this chapter explores the claim that classical terms such as *procession, mission, perichoresis,* and *person,* which have been used to express the mystery of Trinity for many centuries, can validly be understood within the evolutionary categories of relation of origin, relation of effect, and relation of emergence defined by this text.

There are two overarching concepts that represent commonly accepted ways of referring to God as Trinity. The terms are *Economic Trinity* and *Immanent Trinity.* The Trinity manifested within history and experienced by the Christian community has been termed the *Economic Trinity.* This name derives from the Greek word *oikonomia,* meaning, literally, "management of a household." Thus, to speak of the Trinity within the "economy" is to speak of the Trinity in terms of the way in which God exercises "management of God's household or God's creation" within historical time. The term *Economic Trinity,* therefore, refers to the Triune God who has revealed and communicated Godself in history through Jesus the Christ and the Holy Spirit. The narrative of the Economic Trinity is principally found in the scriptures of the Christian tradition, especially in the Gospels. Here, the first intimations of God as Trinity are revealed through the teaching, actions, ministry, and experiences of Jesus of Nazareth.[17]

Conversely, *Immanent Trinity* is the term that theologians have used to refer to the internal life that the three Divine Persons of the Trinity enjoy within and among themselves. This internal life of the Trinity, by definition, exists in a realm that transcends time, space, and human experience. Because of this, the assertions made about the Divine Persons and the dynamics of their life together in transcendence are, of course, not subject to empirical proof. They derive rather from metaphysical principles that largely have their basis in Platonic and Aristotelian philosophical thought. This very approach to Trinitarian theology has drawn criticism as being nonbiblical and has reinforced the conception that the Trinity has little practical consequence in the lives of Christians.

Nonetheless, it is important to remember that these two conceptions of Trinity have an intrinsic link, namely, that one would not be able to speak of the divine life within the Trinitarian *mystery* had God not revealed Godself as Trinity in cosmic and human *history*. This realization led to a famous axiom articulated by theologian Karl Rahner who stated quite simply that "The 'economic' Trinity is the 'immanent' Trinity and the 'immanent' Trinity is the 'economic' Trinity."[18] Through this axiom, Rahner expressed profound truths, two of which bear noting here.

First, the axiom asserts the truth that speech about God as Trinity *begins* in the economy and *ends* in the economy. This means that authentic speech about God as Trinity must be rooted in Christianity's historical experience of Jesus Christ and the Spirit as the starting point for any claims about divine *mystery*. However, the theological process cannot stop at the claim itself. Any claim about the Trinitarian *mystery* must then return to be validated by *history*, not only in

---

17. Notable in these narratives are passages referring to God as Father in juxtaposition to Jesus as Son (e.g., Matthew 11:27; Mark 13:32; Luke 10:22; John 5:19–45); to the presence and action of the Holy Spirit in Jesus' life and ministry and in relation to the Father (e.g., Matthew 3:11; Mark 3:29; Luke 1:15–67; John 14:26), and finally to the Trinitarian formulation as a whole (Matthew 28:19).

18. Rahner, *The Trinity*, 22.

the revelation of God in Jesus Christ and the Spirit *but also* in the joys and hopes, the suffering and grief, in every age of the human and cosmic condition. In the twenty-first century, moreover, the insights of evolutionary science and quantum physics shape that human and cosmic history. Hence, claims made about God can authentically arise from the dialogue between faith and science within the "economy" and return to that dialogue for validation.

Second, the axiom affirms the truth that

> God really exists as these revelatory events [of the economy] have disclosed. We are not duped. . . . The God whom Israel knows as creator and liberator, whom Christians know and experience through the Messiah, Jesus, who . . . was raised by the Spirit on the third day, the same Spirit who is present now in the world—this is who God really is when no one is looking.[19]

Thus, the axiom known as Rahner's Rule, succinctly expresses a "crucial understanding basic to all trinitarian theology."[20] The understanding is this: the Triune God exists eternally in *mystery* in the very personal distinctions experienced through God's self-revelation in *history*.

RELATION OF ORIGIN: THE PROCESSIONS

Against the all-too-brief history of Trinitarian theology and language as a backdrop, this section explores the contours of these theological concepts and the language used to express them in the context of being-as-relation. The first relation examined is the relation of origin, explored in dialogue with the classical Trinitarian concept of "processions."

---

19. Johnson, *Quest for the Living God*, 210.
20. Ibid.

Relation of Origin in the West

As already noted, theologians from the Western Latin schools of theology began their inquiry into the mystery of Trinity by asking the question, "How can One God exist as Three Divine Persons and yet not be three Gods?" Foundational among these thinkers was fifth-century theologian and bishop Augustine of Hippo, whose thought was not only influenced by the beliefs and traditions of Christianity but also by the philosophy of Plato. Plato taught that there was a single transcendent source of all being, which he termed the *One*. According to Plato, the One is the Source of Being and life, but is nonetheless beyond all being. The One is the ontological foundation of all existence, yet is beyond everything that exists. Therefore, the "One" remains absolutely transcendent and nothing can be said of it except that it is "One."

Because Christianity's vision of God was monotheistic—the belief that there is only one God and that God is One and not many—Augustine saw the similarity between this Platonic concept of the One and Christian monotheism. Nonetheless, Christianity also professed that this One Source of Being existed as three Divine Persons. Augustine reasoned that if the Gospels clearly witness to God's self-revelation in history as Father, Son, and Spirit, and there is in fact only one God, then the manifestation of God as Trinity in history must reflect the very nature of God as Trinity in mystery. Therefore, to speak about Trinity authentically within both a Platonic and Christian worldview, Augustine realized that he had to clearly demonstrate how the One could be Three and yet remain One.

It is important to recall that Augustine did his theological reflection within the philosophical context of substance ontology. This presented a theoretical difficulty for him in trying to understand the inner life of the Trinity in relational terms of *Father*, *Son*, and *Spirit*. In substance ontology, "relation" was one of the ten accidents and, therefore, not intrinsic to one's substance. Accidents, moreover, were changeable, and Augustine's concept of God held that God is unchangeable (immutable). However, Augustine realized that the only way to speak of Three Persons as One God was to demonstrate their integral relation to one another. He had to reinterpret the concept of relation as it applied to the Trinity.

Rather than interpreting relation as an accident in the Being of the Trinity, Augustine interpreted relation as "subsistent within" the Being of the Trinity. If their relations are "subsistent," the Persons of the Trinity do not *have* relations, but in fact *are* relations and these relations do not simply *exist in* but are *identical to* the divine substance, that is, to God's own self. Thus, Augustine moved from the ontological category of substance to that of relationality as "the inner structure of an 'essence' that remains one."[21] Augustine's interpretation set the tone for subsequent Western theology by demonstrating that what constitutes the Trinitarian Persons *as* persons are the relations that they *are* to one another. Thus,

> The three divine persons are mutually distinct only in and through their *relations of origin*. The internal relation between (*sic*) the three persons form their sole distinguishing feature. We can and should, for instance . . . [hold] that whatever we say about the Father we can also say about the Son except that he is the Father. . . . Thus the (subsistent) relations account for what differentiates (and unites) the one trinitarian reality.[22]

Alternatively, as the venerable theologian Thomas Aquinas would say centuries later, "Distinction in God arises only through relation of origin."[23]

In order to demonstrate the processes that constituted these relations of origin, Augustine turned to theological anthropology, which is the understanding of the human person in the context of relationship with God. Basing its claim on the book of Genesis, theological anthropology maintains that humans are made in the image and likeness of God and reflect in a limited way the attributes of the Divine. Because of this, Augustine reasoned that if humans are created in the image and likeness of God, then the Being of the Trinity could be further understood by examining the capacities of humans. Using this line of thought, Augustine developed an analogy

---

21. Ibid., 57.

22. Gerald O'Collins, *The Tripersonal God: Understanding and Interpreting the Trinity* (New York: Paulist, 1999), 178, emphasis added.

23. Aquinas, *ST*, Ia.29.4.

between the thought processes of the human mind and Persons of the Trinity.[24] The concept that resulted came to be known as the "psychological analogy of the Trinity." It served for centuries as the most widely accepted basis for theological insight into the processions that constituted the inner life of the Trinity.

How did the processes of human consciousness demonstrate the relational processes within the Trinity? Consider the analogy based on memory (*memoria sui*), knowledge (*intelligentia sui*), and love (*voluntas sui*) of God in the human mind.[25] The first thing to notice is the word *sui*, meaning *of one's own*. Next, *memoria*, or *memory*, does not refer to a recollection but to *self-consciousness* or, better, *self-presence*. Combining these two as the basis for the analogy enabled Augustine to say that "each of these activities is identical with the one self which is acting and yet relationally distinct from the other two activities."[26]

Therefore, the process that Augustine points out is this: the mind, which is conscious of or present to itself (*memoria sui*), in turn knows itself (*intelligentia sui*) and thus loves itself (*voluntas sui*). For Augustine, these are not three separate steps or acts within human consciousness; self-presence, self-knowledge, and self-love are essentially *one act* but in *three* distinguishable constituents. Note, however, that, while remaining one act—self-knowledge, which is an expression of self-presence, and self-love, which results from self-presence actualized as self-knowledge—both *proceed from* self-consciousness rather than the other way around.

Now shift this analogically to the inner life of the Trinity. God is conscious of and present to Godself (self-presence) and, thus, knows

---

24. Of course, no analogy is perfect. However, the use of analogy is necessary if we are to be able to say anything about the mystery of God. Thomas Aquinas clearly articulated this belief in the theory of the analogy of being. The theory states that there exists a correspondence or analogy between natural order and God because God created the cosmos and its creatures. Because something of a creator is always revealed in a creation, one can draw inferences about God from the objects and relationships of the cosmic and human existence God created.

25. Translated from the Latin, these refer to the memory of oneself, the knowledge of oneself, and love of oneself, although Augustine and others after him use the word *voluntas*, meaning "volition or will." This understanding becomes important in Aquinas who defines love not as affect or emotion, which Greek philosophy asserted is not an attribute of God, to love as an act of will.

26. William Hill, *The Three-Personed God: The Trinity as the Mystery of Salvation* (Washington, DC: Catholic University of America Press), 56.

Godself (self-knowledge) and loves Godself (self-love). Analogous to the human mind, in One God, the processes of self-presence, self-knowledge, and self-love are essentially *one act* but in *three* distinguishable constituents. While remaining one act, divine self-knowledge, as an expression of self-presence, and divine self-love, as the result of self-presence actualized as self-knowledge, both *proceed from* self-consciousness rather than the other way around.

What remained for Augustine was to apply this analogy to the constituent relationality of the Trinity as personally revealed in the economy of history. Augustine associated the three constituents of memory, knowledge, and love to the three Persons of the Trinity in this way. The Father is God's presence to Godself, the Son is God's knowledge of Godself, and the Spirit is God's love of Godself. While remaining One God, the self-present Father expresses self-knowledge as the Son, which results in self-love between the Father and the Son as Spirit. While remaining One God, the Son proceeds from the Father and the Spirit proceeds from the Father and the Son, and not the other way around. The dynamism through which the Son and the Spirit proceed from the Father came to be called the "processions." To accent the essential relationality in the Trinity that the processions express, the procession of the Son from the Father was termed *begottenness*, meaning, "to procreate or generate an offspring," like a son from a father. By the same token, the procession of the Spirit from the Father and the Son was termed *spiration*, referring to the "breath" of life and love they share. However, because this relationality is one act that equally and eternally involves the Father, the Son, and the Spirit, this analogy contains no threat of tritheism, of subordinationism, or of modalism. Thus, as the Nicene Creed proclaims,

> We believe in one God, the Father, the Almighty, maker of heaven and earth. . . . We believe in one Lord, Jesus Christ, the only son of God . . . begotten, not made, one in being with the Father. . . . We believe in the Holy Spirit . . . who proceeds from the Father and the Son and with the Father and Son is worshipped and glorified.[27]

---

27. "The Nicene Creed," *ICLnet*, adapted for language.

Relation of Origin in the East

Eastern Christianity also emphasized the relation of origin in the Trinity, but began with the question, "How can the Three be One?" Because of this, it took as its point of departure the mystery of three distinct Persons in the Trinity in contrast to the Western starting point of the unity of nature. Greek theologians such as the Cappadocians Basil the Great (330–379), Gregory of Nyssa (c. 330–395), and Gregory of Nazianzus (329–389) began with the self-revelation of God as three Persons to which the Gospels witnessed and then set about to reason how these three *hypostases* could be one *ousia*. Contrary to Western thought, the Cappadocians did not envision any *ousia* (essence)—divine or otherwise—as being separable from a *hypostasis* (existent). Unlike Western theologians, they could not fathom speculating about a divine nature unrelated to its existing in some form. For the Cappadocians, therefore, the three *hypostases*—Father, Son, and Spirit—were assured through revelation. What was not evident, however, was how these three *hypostases* shared the same *ousia* and, thus, were One God. To answer this question, Eastern theology also turned to relations of origin.

Like its Western counterpart, the relation of origin began with the Father and proceeded with the Son and Spirit. However, the Eastern use of relation had some subtle theological differences. Because the divine *ousia* could not be spoken of apart from a divine *hypostasis*—in other words, divine nature could not be spoken of as separate from the Divine Persons who hypostasized that nature—Greek theology applied the term *Theos* or *God* principally to the Person of the Father, rather than to a divine nature that subsumed it. As a result, Greek theologians saw the Father as the source and origin of the intradivine relations. Like the Western formulation, the Son proceeded from the Father as eternally begotten, and the Spirit proceeded from the Father *through* the Son as the "breath of the Son."[28]

---

28. Note here the difference between the Western and Eastern formulations of the processions. Western theology states that "the Spirit proceeds from the Father *and the Son* (*Filioque*)," whereas Eastern theology states that "the Spirit proceeds from the Father *through the Son* (*ex Patre per Filium*)." The difference in the two not only had ramifications for the status of the Holy Spirit in relation to the Father and particularly to the Son but was also at the root of a Trinitarian controversy between Western and Eastern Christianity that was only resolved in the twentieth century!

Two Greek theological concepts explained the unity of the Father, the Son, and the Spirit. The first is a unique form of relationality captured by the concept of *perichoresis*, which comes from two Greek words *peri* and *choreio*, meaning "to move around" or "to dance around." Theologically, it was used to refer to the dynamic interpermeation of the three Persons of the Trinity, one in another while yet retaining their uniqueness of person. As described by church historian Philip Schaff, *perichoresis* refers to "the peculiarity of the relations of the Three Divine Persons . . . , their Indwelling in each other, the fact that, while they are distinct they yet are in one another, the Coinherence which implies their equal and identical Godhead."[29]

The second concept is the doctrine of recapitulation, which is properly considered a relation of origin. According to this doctrine, the Son and the Spirit proceed from the Father, are not separated from the Father, and are both contained in the Father. Hence, the Father is the source of their oneness with each other and, of course, with the Father as well. This interpretation understands the Son as the Power or Wisdom of the Father and the Spirit as the Holiness of the Father. Together, the Son and Spirit are the *dynameis*, or "dynamism," of the Father and subsist as relations in the Father who, as the Godhead, extends divine existence. This union is so complete that, in the words of Gregory of Nazianzus, "No sooner do I conceive of the One than I am illumined by the splendor of the Three; no sooner do I distinguish them than I am carried back to the One. . . . When I contemplate the Three together, I see but one torch, and cannot divide or measure out the undivided light."[30]

Hence, whether one approaches the question from the East or the West, from the One or the Three, what constitutes the One God in Three Divine Persons is relation, beginning with a relation of origin. From each perspective, this origin traces itself to the First Person of the Trinity, the Father from whom the Son and the Spirit proceed eternally, equally, and dynamically. This relationality, moreover, is

---

29. Philip Schaff, "Hilary of Poitiers, John of Damascus," n. 1569, in *A Select Library of the Nicene and Post-Nicene Fathers of the Christian Church*; available from *http://www.ccel.org/ccel/schaff/ npnf209.txt.*

30. Quoted by F. Scott Petersen in "Perichoresis," *Ars Theologica: An Intersection of Theology, Poetry, Art, and Music*; available from *http://arstheologica.blogspot. com/2005/12/perichoresis.html.*

not what the Trinitarian Persons *have*, but what the Trinitarian Persons *are*. "Quite simply," William Hill maintains, "God is . . . self-related . . . [and] the relationality is not something 'within' God but is rather itself constitutive of Divinity."[31]

RELATIONS OF EMERGENCE: THE MISSIONS

As the previous section demonstrates, theologians in the East and West spent a good deal of philosophical time and energy in their search for intelligible ways of speaking about how One God could be Three Persons within the mystery of intradivine life. However, it is important to recall that the source of the question did not arise from philosophical inquiry, but from the testimony of the disciples of Christ whose personal experiences and ongoing witness led to the striking claim that the God whom they had professed as One had revealed Godself as Three Persons through the life and teaching of Jesus of Nazareth. Had there been no Jesus of Nazareth whose words, deeds, death, and Resurrection led to the conviction that he was truly the Son of the God he called Father in the power of the Holy Spirit, such theological and philosophical speculation would have been unnecessary. Some may argue that God may have followed a different course in the span of history through which to reveal Godself as Trinity; nonetheless, such a point is moot. The only verifiable point is this: were it not for the self-revelation of the Triune God through Jesus of Nazareth in history, there is no cause for speculation about a triune nature in the God of mystery.

Because of the historical revelation in the person of Jesus of Nazareth, however, further theological speculation ensued to explain the relation between the Immanent Trinity who, despite all explanations, yet dwelled in mystery and the Economic Trinity experienced and proclaimed in history. If the dynamic of processions rationally accounted for the internal relations among the Divine Persons, what dynamic accounted for the *external emergence* of these Divine Persons in cosmic and human time and space? Why might such relations be called emergence? *Emergence* refers to novel forms of life

---

31. Hill, *The Three-Personed God*, 60.

that emerge or develop from prior forms of life but are not reducible or explainable in terms of the form that preceded them. Emergents require new language and concepts capable of describing them accurately in new and nonreductionist ways. At the same time, a link must be maintained between the preceding form and the emergent that is actualized in surprising new forms. In the context of classical Trinitarian theology, the concept of emergence affirms that the Economic Trinity emerged in history from the Immanent Trinity. However, this emergence took so novel a form that speech about the Economic Trinity requires a new vocabulary, one that maintains the link between the Immanent and Economic Trinity but that testifies to the reality of the Divine becoming human, of the eternal Word-made-flesh, of the immaterial God-made-matter in cosmic history.

Despite the extensive reflection and wisdom that Augustine manifested in his discussion of the intradivine life of the Trinitarian Persons, he himself signaled the notional priority of the Economic Trinity by reflecting on the historical emergence of the Son and the Spirit in his book *On the Trinity* before considering the processions. He termed this emergence of the Son and the Spirit into history *the missions*. The word *mission* is derived from the Latin *missio* and *mittere*, meaning "to be sent"; thus, it describes what Augustine understood to be the functions and purposes of the Son and Spirit within history, the reasons why each was sent. According to Augustine, the mission of the Son is incarnation by which he assumes human nature and is literally incorporated into the created world. The mission of the Holy Spirit is sanctification and transformation, wherein the Spirit is sent as the effective means by which all creation becomes receptive to God's gift of self in love.[32]

Nevertheless, while Augustine dealt with them separately in his text, he saw an inextricable continuity between the eternal processions and missions in time. This continuity occurred as a kind of going forth and returning, between eternity and time. Theologian Fred R. Sanders described this dynamic interrelation this way:

> The Son is the one who is sent by the Father (his mission in the economy), just as he is the one who eternally comes forth from the Father (his eternal begetting). . . . [This

---

32. Welch, *In This Name*, 117–18.

dynamic] can be generalized to the Spirit as well.
. . . Economic mission reveals immanent procession, and
immanent procession is elongated or extended to become
economic mission.[33]

For his part, Aquinas later stated the interrelationship between mission and procession in his *Summa Theologiae*: "Mission includes an eternal procession, but also adds something else, namely an effect in time."[34] Thus, the Son and the Spirit acquired new relations with creation by means of these missions and, in so doing, further constituted the relational unity and diversity of the Persons in the Trinity.

How do the missions as a relation of emergence constitute the Being of the Trinity? With the emergence of the Divine into history, humanity comes to a fuller knowledge of God because God has chosen to reveal eternal Being to and through the confines of time and space. Moreover, through the divine missions, God reveals Godself not only as three distinct Persons but also as self-communicating, sending the very Word and Wisdom of God to dwell in time in ways heretofore unknown.

Incarnation: The Mission of the Son

In the life, teaching, and ministry of Jesus of Nazareth, the understanding of the personal nature of God deepened and the promise of personal relationship with God intensified. Jesus of Nazareth was a devout Jew, schooled in the language, beliefs, and traditions of the Jewish culture and religion. He believed in one God, studied the Torah, recited the *Shema*, celebrated the Sabbath and the Passover, sang the Psalms, heeded the prophets, preached like a rabbi, and taught his disciples the Great Commandments of the Law: "You shall love the Lord your God with all your heart, and with all your soul, and with all your might" (Deuteronomy 6:5) and "You shall love your neighbor as yourself" (Leviticus 19:18). Nevertheless, Jesus experienced a unique relationship with the God of Israel, the intimate relationship between a father and a son. Jesus called the Most

---

33. Fred R. Sanders, *The Image of the Immanent Trinity: Rahner's Rule and the Theological Interpretation of Scripture* (New York: Peter Lang, 2005), 37.

34. Aquinas, *ST*, Ia.43.2.

High God 'Abba, Father,' and taught his followers to use his relationship with God as a model for their own (Matthew 6:9–13). Because
of this revelation, a new understanding of the transcendent God
emerged and with it a further constitution of divine being. The mission of the Son further revealed God in a personal way as Father not
only to Jesus but also to all who followed him.

However, these disciples not only encountered the living God in
a qualitatively new and personal relationship as the one whom Jesus
called Father; they also recognized and proclaimed that, in their relationship with Jesus, they encountered the living God in human flesh.
This encounter came, moreover, through Jesus' wholehearted embrace
of human experience in its fullness; Jesus revealed through his human
nature the depth and breadth of divine love and compassion. He
incarnated this divine love and compassion as he companioned tax
collectors and sinners whom others rejected and put human needs
before Sabbath laws. He forgave those who had broken relationship
with God and the community and healed those suffering from illness
and deformity. Jesus proclaimed the Kingdom of God using a different vision of those who were truly blessed: the poor in spirit, those
who mourn, the meek, those who hunger and thirst for righteousness, the merciful, the single-hearted, the peacemakers, and those persecuted for righteousness' sake. In Jesus, God entered into solidarity
"with all those who suffer and are lost in this violent world, thereby
opening up the promise of new life."[35] This solidarity threatened both
religious and political authorities, which tried to silence God's Word-
made-flesh through crucifixion and death. Nevertheless, Jesus was
raised to new life in the power of the Holy Spirit. Furthermore, Jesus
assured his disciples of God's ongoing revelation through the Holy
Spirit that the Father would send (John 14:25–26). As a mission of
the Trinity, the Incarnation provided a multifaceted revelation that
constituted the meaning, nature, and attributes not only of the person
of Jesus of Nazareth but also of the Triune God whom he proclaimed
in his person, his actions, and his teachings. The mission of the Son,
therefore, clearly communicates the relationality of Divine Being as
hope to those who suffer, as promise to those who wait, as forgiveness

---

35. Elizabeth A. Johnson, "Banquet of the Creed," Yves Congar Award Lecture,
January 14, 2008, Barry University, Miami Shores, FL; available at *http://www.barry.
edu/theologyphilosophy/News/ eJohnson.htm.*

to those who sin, as compassion for those oppressed, as providence for those who are poor, as welcome for those outcast, as light to those in darkness, and as fullness of life for those who believe.

Pentecost: Mission of the Holy Spirit

From the earliest attempts at Trinitarian proclamation, questions were raised about the person of the Holy Spirit in the life of the Trinity. Is the Holy Spirit the Spirit of God spoken of in the Hebrew scriptures as the "mighty wind" who hovered over the waters of creation (Genesis 1:2), as the one poured out over all humankind as proclaimed in the book of Joel (3:1–2), and as the Spirit sent forth to renew the face of the earth (Psalms 104:30)? Is the Holy Spirit the Spirit of God in the Gospels who overshadowed Mary at her annunciation (Luke 1:35), who descended upon Jesus in the form of a dove at his baptism (Mark 1:10; Matthew 3:16; Luke 3:22), who drove Jesus into the desert after his baptism (Mark 1:12; Matthew 4:1; Luke 4:1), in whom Jesus prayed and rejoiced (Luke 10:21), who distributes spiritual gifts for the benefit of the community (1 Corinthians 12:4–11), and in whom we are sanctified (2 Thessalonians 2:13–14)? Or is the Holy Spirit the Spirit of Jesus whom Jesus breathed upon the disciples after the Resurrection (John 20:21–3), who enables us to cry out, "Abba, Father" (Galatians 4:6), and who makes it possible for believers to belong to God (Romans 8:9)? Are these one and the same Holy Spirit? Is it the same Holy Spirit at work in creation, in incarnation, in grace, and in salvation?

The conclusion of those who posed the question was "yes." It is the same Holy Spirit who "can come mightily upon a human being" (Judges 14:6; 1 Samuel 16:13) and "clothe" (equip) that person for powerful works (Judges 6:34ff). The very same Spirit also enables humans to perform supernatural deeds, such as the physical salvation of Israel by the judges (Judges 3:10, 6:34) or visions by the prophets (Ezekiel 3:12, 8:3, 11:1).[36] The same Holy Spirit who anoints charismatic leaders such as Gideon (3:10), Jephthah (6:34), and Samson (13:25, 14:6, 19) in the book of Judges is the Holy Spirit who anoints the Messiah in the books of the prophets. The prophet Isaiah speaks

---

36. Veli-Matti Kärkkäinen, *Pneumatology: The Holy Spirit in Ecumenical, International, and Contextual Perspectives* (Grand Rapids, MI: Baker Academic, 2002), 27.

of the Messiah who is "ordained and empowered by the Spirit (11:1–8)" and who accomplishes the salvation of the Jews and the Gentiles in the power of the Spirit (42:1–4, 49:1–6). The outpouring of God's Spirit brings about justice and peace (Isaiah 32:15–20), healing and restoration (Ezekiel 11:19ff, 18:31, 36:36ff), and the new creation (Ezekiel 37:1–4). And the same Spirit fills the prophet-messiah Jesus of Nazareth (Luke 4:18–19) in whose ministry of justice and healing the reign of God breaks forth for the oppressed and afflicted. If it is the same Holy Spirit, however, how can one speak of the emergence or mission of the Holy Spirit in new and surprising ways? What distinguishes the Trinitarian Person of the Holy Spirit from the Spirit of the Divine who animated, vivified, and inspired the leaders and prophets of Israel? As theologian Gerald O'Collins states,

> What kind or amount of personal characteristics should lead to the conclusion that we face an ontologically distinct person? What indicates that we encounter not simply a new mode of divine action in salvation history but a distinct, *personal* presence? . . . [What] leads believers to move beyond Jewish ideas and recognize within God not only a distinct divine Son but also a distinct divine Spirit?[37]

While some, like O'Collins, point to the "conspicuously personal effects" that the Holy Spirit has in the ministry of Jesus of Nazareth,[38] such indications do not present compelling evidence for a unique personhood of the Holy Spirit as distinct from that of the Incarnate Son. The overshadowing of the Holy Spirit in the conception of Jesus (Luke 1:35), the impulse of the Spirit that drives Jesus into the desert (Mark 1:12; Matthew 4:1; Luke 4:1), the presence of the Spirit in the form of a dove at Jesus' baptism (Mark 1:10; Matthew 3:16; Luke 3:22) and in the form of a cloud at Jesus' transfiguration (Mark 9:1–8; Matthew 17:1–6; Luke 9:28–36), and the prohibitions about sins against the Holy Spirit (Mark 3:28–30; Matthew 12:30–32; Luke 12:8–10) give clearer support for this uniqueness, especially when there is reference to or manifestation of the Father or Son as well. Nonetheless, the question remains: How is

---

37. O'Collins, *The Tripersonal God*, 166–67.

38. Ibid., 167.

any one of these a proper "mission" or "sending" of the Holy Spirit in a way that fully constitutes the particular personhood of the Holy Spirit as distinct from the Incarnate Son who was sent? At what point does the Holy Spirit "emerge" in the Christian narratives in so novel a way as to constitute a unique and personal being and to necessitate a new way of speaking about the Holy Spirit?

To answer that question, one must attend to the words of Jesus himself. It is he who signals the emergence of the Spirit as a distinct person with a distinct mission. One of the first inklings of this new emergent comes through in the Gospel of John. In the midst of the "farewell discourses" of Jesus in John chapters 13–17, Jesus makes several references to the *Advocate*, or *Paraclete*, whom the Father will send. The term comes from the Greek word *parakletos*, which can be translated as *comforter*, *counselor*, *advocate*, or *defender*: "In the Gospel, the sense of Advocate, counsel, [is] one who pleads, convinces, convicts, who strengthens on the one hand and defends on the other."[39]

Consider the five ways in which Jesus speaks about the Holy Spirit in the Gospel of John—four that use the term *Advocate* and one that implies such a role.

- In John 14:16, Jesus tells his disciples: "I will ask the Father, and he will give you another Advocate to be with you always, the Spirit of truth, which the world cannot accept, because it neither sees nor knows it." By referring to the Holy Spirit as "another" Advocate, Jesus clearly distinguishes the Holy Spirit from himself, even as he implies that he himself was the first advocate.

- In John 14:26, Jesus elaborates: "The Advocate, the Holy Spirit that the Father will send in my name will teach you everything and remind you of all that I told you." Expanding the notion that he will ask the Father to send the Spirit of truth, Jesus further develops the character of the Spirit as a teacher in the Spirit's own right, even as he affirms that the Spirit reinforces what Jesus himself has taught.

- In John 15:26, Jesus attributes the sending of the Holy Spirit not only to the Father but also to the Son: "When the Advocate comes

---

39. "What Does it Mean that the Holy Spirit Is Our Paraclete?" in *GotQuestions. org: Bible Questions Answered*; available from *http://www.gotquestions.org/paraclete-Holy-Spirit.html*.

whom I will send you from the Father, the Spirit of truth that proceeds from the Father, he will testify to me." This corresponds to
the relational distinction of persons through the internal dynamic
of the Trinitarian processions. As Christians profess in the Nicene-
Constantipolitan Creed, the Holy Spirit is the one "who proceeds
from the Father and the Son." Moreover, the Spirit is now spoken of as a witness, one who testifies to what one has seen or
heard, which further emphasizes the distinction of persons.

* In John 16:7, Jesus definitively testifies to this distinction
  between the Spirit and himself: "I tell you the truth, it is better
  for you that I go. For if I do not go, the Advocate will not come
  to you. But if I go, I will send him to you." Two further insights
  about the Spirit emerge in this part of the discourse. On the
  one hand, the statement contends that the Son and the Spirit
  are mutually exclusive, for if the Son remains, the Spirit does
  not come. On the other hand, the sending of the Spirit is now
  exclusively attributed to the Son rather than to the Father or the
  Father and the Son together.

* In John 20:21–23, Jesus sends the Spirit in a different way: "Jesus
  breathed on [his disciples] and said to them, 'Receive the Holy
  Spirit. Whose sins you forgive are forgiven them, and whose sins
  you retain are retained.'" While this seems to indicate a mission
  of the Spirit with a broader purpose, it nonetheless implies that
  the Spirit serves to counsel the disciples in discerning the forgiveness of sins.

This series of Jesus' sayings concerning the Holy Spirit promises
something truly novel that requires a new way of viewing and speaking about the Holy Spirit. From this novelty emerges a new sense
of the Holy Spirit both in relation to the Father and the Son and in
relation to the nascent Christian community.

The promises to send the Spirit that surface in the farewell discourses in Gospel of John reflect an earlier narrative found in the
Acts of the Apostles.[40] Commonly considered a companion volume

---

40. Most scholars date the composition of the Gospel and Acts attributed to Luke
between 80–90 CE and date the Gospel attributed to John between 90–100 CE. That
the Gospel of John is situated between the Gospel of Luke and the Acts of the Apostles in the biblical canon may confuse the sequence of the Pentecost narrative and the
farewell discourses.

to the Gospel of Luke and attributed to the same author, Acts opens
with a promise of its own, one that reveals another characteristic of
the Holy Spirit to be sent. In Acts 1:8, before his ascension, Jesus
says to his disciples, "You will receive power when the Holy Spirit
comes upon you, and you will be my witnesses in Jerusalem, throughout Judea and Samaria, and to the ends of the earth." This description attributes a power to the Holy Spirit, a power that the Spirit
gives to the disciples to enable them to witness to the words and
deeds of Jesus, even as the Spirit witnesses to Christ. The fulfillment
of this promise comes in the second chapter of Acts, in the narrative
of Pentecost.

> When the time for Pentecost was fulfilled, they were all
> in one place together. And suddenly there came from the
> sky a noise like a strong driving wind, and it filled the
> entire house in which they were. Then there appeared to
> them tongues as of fire, which parted and came to rest on
> each one of them. And they were all filled with the Holy
> Spirit and began to speak in different tongues, as the Spirit
> enabled them to proclaim. (Acts 2:1–4)

This is a narrative full of symbolic language: the rushing wind signals a new and unexpected act of God within history (John 3:8);
the tongues of fire call to mind the fire of the presence of God in
the giving of the covenant on Sinai (Exodus 19:18). With fire, the
Christian community now must witness to a new covenant in the
power of the Spirit, one that reaches to all parts of the world, symbolized by the utterance in different tongues. How did this power
of the Spirit manifest itself through the disciples? It enabled them
to speak of the mighty deeds of God in language that those present
could understand despite the fact that they were Jews from many
disparate regions around Jerusalem (2:6–11). It empowered them to
testify fearlessly to the mighty deeds, wonders, and signs that God
had worked through Jesus (2:22), to proclaim his Resurrection from
the dead (2:32), and to call for repentance that those who listened
might have their sins forgiven and receive the Holy Spirit (2:38).

Many other insights into the personhood of the Holy Spirit
follow as the relation of effect further constitutes the distinctive
being of the Spirit in the community of the Trinity. Nonetheless,

the emergence of the Spirit through a defined mission within history furthers Christian understanding of this Third Trinitarian Person. Amplified beyond conceptions of inspiration, prophecy, renewal, and empowerment found in the Hebrew scriptures and the Nicene Creed, the previous biblical passages sharpen the contours of the Spirit in ways that reveal the Spirit's personal uniqueness and relationality within the Trinity. The Spirit emerges as (1) distinct from the Father and the Son, (2) as sent from both the Father and the Son, (3) as the Spirit of the Son as well as the Father, (4) as advocate and counselor to the disciples and the nascent Christian community, (5) as teacher of "everything," even beyond the revelation given by Jesus himself, (6) as active remembrance of all that Jesus taught, (7) as power of proclamation of the Risen Christ, and (8) as impetus for the spread of the Gospel to "make disciples of all nations" (Matthew 28:19). Clearly, this Holy Spirit is no longer an impersonal force or indiscernible from the Father and the Son. Remaining fully united with the Father and the Son, the Holy Spirit yet emerges in novel ways as fully personal and unique through the mission of the Spirit in history.

RELATION OF EFFECT: DOCTRINE OF APPROPRIATIONS

While relations of origin and emergence make a compelling argument for the constitutive nature of relationality in the immanent being of the Trinity, it remains to be seen how these categories correlate with the Christian experience of the Divine Persons in the economy of cosmic and human history. Faith witnesses to the reality that the Persons of the Trinity are not merely transcendent beings who enjoy an intrinsic and constitutive relationality in eternity, but are effective beings who exercise an ecstatic and constitutive relationality with the cosmos and its creatures. This is to say, the Persons of the Trinity were not revealed, recognized, and embraced because of their dynamic relationship to each other, no matter how intriguing and inspiring it might be. The Persons of the Trinity are revealed, recognized, and embraced first and foremost because of their salvific relationships to creation and its creatures disclosed in the life and ministry, death and Resurrection of Jesus the Christ and in the Holy Spirit given to continue and complete his mission.

Thus, it was through *relations of effect* that God as Trinity was first disclosed. These effects were communicated through the marvels of creation, through the efficacy of Christ's ministry, cross, and Resurrection, and through the Spirit's inspiration and liberation of creation and its creatures in history. Through these relations of effect, Christians came to embrace God not solely in their relations to one another as Father, Son, and Spirit, but in their effective relations to cosmic and humankind.

The Doctrine of Appropriations

When considering the effects of God as Trinity in history, Trinitarian theologians ascribe to the dictum, "*opera Trinitatis ex extra indivisa sunt*," that is, "the works of the Trinity outside itself are indivisible." Based on and preserving the essential unity of God, this statement means that every act of the Trinity in history is an act of the Trinity as a whole. Nonetheless, the experience of the community with Christ and the Spirit in the biblical witness attested to a different dynamic: specific actions were attributed to one or another of the Divine Persons. For example, the Christian witness ordinarily attributes creation to the Father who transcends history, although in the Nicene Creed all three Persons have something to do with the creation of life.[41] Christianity attributes redemption to the Son who became incarnate, died, and was raised in history, although it clearly acknowledges that the Father sent the Son (John 3:16; 1 John 4:10)[42] and the Son was raised in the power of the Spirit (Romans 1:4, 8:11). Finally, liberation, sanctification, fellowship, and prophetic witness are attributed to the Holy Spirit, although these attributes are clearly ascribed to the actions of the Father and the Son as well (Joel 2:29; Acts 2:17; 1 John 1:3).

---

41. In the Nicene Creed, Christians affirm their belief in "the Father Almighty, Maker of heaven and earth"; in the Son "through whom all things were made"; and in the Holy Spirit, "the Lord and Giver of life."

42. Isaiah 44:24 even states "Thus says the LORD, your *Redeemer*, and *the one who formed you* from the womb, 'I, the LORD, am *the maker of all things*, stretching out the heavens by myself and spreading out the earth all alone.'"

So, in the attempt to reconcile the One and the Three, Western theologians such as Hilary of Poitiers, Leo the Great, and Augustine proposed the doctrine of the appropriations. By this doctrine is understood "a mode of predication in which the properties and activities of God which are common to the Three Persons are attributed to an Individual Person . . . to make manifest the differences in the Divine *proprietates* [possessions or properties] and persons."[43] The point of this attribution is not simply to clarify what properties belong to whom, but to manifest the differences in their *persons*. Rather than simply describing particular differences in the activities of the persons, these differences constitute their personal uniqueness as well. Theologian William Hill aptly described this:

> What is in reality a common prerogative of the trinitarian members is predicated of one alone *to manifest his personal uniqueness* in the Godhead. But this cannot be done arbitrarily; some mysterious affinity between a person and an action *ad extra*, or an essential attribute, lies at the base of this kind of speech.[44]

From what does this "mysterious affinity" that Hill pointed out arise? From human relationship with and experience of God as told in the scriptures and throughout Christian history.

The Father: Creation and Vivification

In light of this unfolding relationship between the Persons of the Trinity and the Christian community, consider how the Nicene Creed not only asserts belief in the unity of the Triune God with its opening proclamation "We believe in one God" but then continues by distinguishing each member personally by means of the effects each Person has in the history of the cosmos and the history of salvation. This one God is "the Father, the Almighty, Maker of heaven and earth, of all that is seen and unseen," an assertion that echoes the earlier Apostles Creed, which calls the Father "the Creator of

---

43. Ludwig Ott, "The Appropriations," in *Fundamentals of Catholic Dogma*, trans. Patrick Lynch and ed. James Bastible (St. Louis, MO: Herder, 1962), 72.

44. Hill, *The Three-Personed God*, 283 (emphasis added).

heaven and earth." Such creedal statements identify the First Person of the Trinity with the Creator God of the book of Genesis who formed heaven and earth (1:1), who gives breath and spirit to those who walk in it (Isaiah 42:5), who forms mountains and creates the wind, who makes dawn into darkness and treads on the high places of the earth (Amos 4:13). These effects distinguish the essential Personhood of the Father as creative and sustaining of the cosmos and those who dwell within it. These attributes constitute that personal and unique identity as Creator, while in no way deny the indivisibility of the Trinity's work of creation.

The Son: Incarnation and Salvation

Creedal affirmations centered on the birth, life, death, and Resurrection of Jesus constitute more fully the Personhood of the Son. The statement about Christ found in the Creed is undoubtedly the fullest proclamation concerning the Trinitarian Persons since it derives in large measure from the biblical witness. It begins, nevertheless, in the philosophical speculations that refuted to the earliest Christological heresies: "We believe in one Lord, Jesus Christ, the only Son of God, eternally begotten of the Father, God from God, Light from Light, true God from true God, begotten, not made, one in being with the Father. Through Him all things were made." Implied in this first statement are answers to the questions raised by the Christological controversies, which also had an impact on Trinitarian beliefs. Is the Son created or uncreated, and what is the Son's role in creation (Arianism)? How can the One God be two persons, let alone three (tritheism)? Is the Son of the same (*homoousíos*) or similar (*homoiousíos*) substance as the Father? Is the Son equal or inferior to the Father in divinity (subordinationism)? Is the Son eternally God or elevated as a reward for his fidelity to the Father (adoptionism)? The responses to these questions framed in the Creed came not only from the theological insights of the early church fathers but also from the scriptures.[45] Of particular importance in the scriptural corpus were

---

45. These included Polycarp (70–155 CE), bishop of Smyrna; Justin the Martyr (100–165 CE), Irenaeus (115–190 CE), bishop of Lyons, and others. See M. Slick, "Early Trinitarian Quotes," *Christina Apologetics and Research Ministry (CARM)*; available from *http://carm.org/early-trinitarian-quotes*.

the prologue to the Gospel of John (1:1–2, 9)[46] and the Letter of
Paul to the Philippians (2:5–11).[47]

All four Gospel narratives, along with the Epistles, provide the
foundation for this further development of the meaning of the person of Jesus the Son through the effects of history. These effects
include his conception, his birth, his suffering, death, and Resurrection, and his return as judge of the living and the dead. The Nicene
Creed continues: "For us and our salvation He came down from
heaven (John 1:1–5, 14): by the power of the Holy Spirit (Luke
1:35), He was born of the Virgin Mary (Matthew 1:16, 25; Luke
1:31–32), and became man. For our sake, He was crucified under
Pontius Pilate (Mark 15:1–15; Matthew 27:1–26; Luke 23:1–24;
John 19:1–22); He suffered, died, and was buried (Mark 15:16–47;
Matthew 27:27–66; Luke 23:26–56; John 19:23–42). On the third
day, He rose again in fulfillment of the scriptures (Mark 16:1–8;
Matthew 28:1–10; Luke 24:1–53; John 20:1–29): He ascended into
heaven (Acts 1:3–11) and is seated at the right hand of the Father
(Matthew 25:31; Hebrews 1:1–3, 13–14; 8:1–2, 10:11–14; 12:1–2).
He will come again in glory to judge the living and the dead (Mat-
thew 24:27–31, 25:31–46; 1 Thessalonians 4:16–17; Revelation 1:
17–18, 4: 1–11), and his kingdom will have no end (Luke 1:33;
Hebrews 1:8–9)."

Creedal statements such as these clearly appropriate to the Sec-
ond Person of the Trinity the identity of self-expressive Word of
God who became incarnate in history (John 1:14; 1 Timothy 3:16).
The appropriation of these effects to the Son has significant impact
in constituting the personhood of the Son. To no other Person of the
Trinity is the effect of incarnation attributed, even as the scriptures

---

46. "In the beginning was the Word, and the Word was with God, and the Word
was God. He was with God in the beginning. . . . The true light, which enlightens
everyone, was coming into the world."

47. "Have among yourselves the same attitude that is also yours in Christ Jesus,
who, though he was in the form of God, did not regard equality with God something to be grasped. Rather, he emptied himself, taking the form of a slave, coming
in human likeness; and found human in appearance, he humbled himself, becoming
obedient to death, even death on a cross. Because of this, God greatly exalted him and
bestowed on him the name that is above every name, that at the name of Jesus every
knee should bend, of those in heaven and on earth and under the earth, and every
tongue confess that Jesus Christ is Lord, to the glory of God the Father."

decisively witness to the indivisibility of the action of the Father and the Holy Spirit (Mark 1:8, 10; Matthew 1:18, 20; Luke 1:35, 3:22, 10:21; John 3:31–34, *inter alia*) in his conception, incarnation, birth, and ministry. At the same time, moreover, the effects of his suffering, death, and Resurrection uniquely constituted his personhood as Savior and Redeemer (John 14:6–7; Acts 4:12, 20:28; Romans 5:8; Ephesians 1:20, 2:8; Hebrews 9:26–28; 2 Timothy 1:10; 1 Peter 2:24, *inter alia*).

These salvific effects are ritually celebrated during the Easter Vigil, notably through the proclamation of the Exsultet, a hymn composed circa sixth century CE and preserved in various translations. One particular translation declares in part,

> Rejoice, O Mother Church! Exult in glory!
> The risen Savior shines upon you!
> Let this place resound with joy,
> echoing the mighty song of all God's people!
> . . . .
>
> For Christ has ransomed us with his blood,
> and paid for us the price of Adam's sin
> to our eternal Father!
> . . . .
>
> This is the night when Christians everywhere,
>   washed clean of sin
>   and freed from all defilement,
>   are restored to grace and grow together in holiness.
> This is the night when Jesus Christ
>   broke the chains of death
>   and rose triumphant from the grave.
> What good would life have been to us,
> had Christ not come as our Redeemer?
> Father, how wonderful your care for us!
> How boundless your merciful love!
>   To ransom a slave
>   you gave away your Son.
> . . . .

> The power of this holy night
> dispels all evil, washes guilt away,
> restores lost innocence,
> brings mourners joy;
>> it casts out hatred, brings us peace, and humbles
>> earthly pride.[48]

Once again, while the Father and the Holy Spirit play a critical part in the salvific mystery of Jesus' death and Resurrection, the roles of savior and redeemer are clearly appropriated to the Second Person of the Trinity and are essential attributes of the Son's personal and unique identity.

The Holy Spirit: Revelation and Love

Regrettably, little is said about the Holy Spirit in the Nicene Creed in comparison to the proclamations concerning the First and Second Persons of the Trinity. As pointed out earlier, the Holy Spirit is acknowledged as "the Lord and Giver of Life," which affirms the general indivisibility of the creative and life-giving works of the Trinity. The unique affirmation made of the Spirit in the Creed is that the Holy Spirit has "spoken through the prophets." Nevertheless, the particularity of this assertion is somewhat mitigated by the recognition of the Son as the Word of God. One must, therefore, delve into the biblical witness and the Christian tradition to glean the effects that distinguish the Person of the Spirit. Many think that the most obvious distinction between the Spirit and the other Persons of the Trinity lies in the presumption that the Spirit is nonpersonal. This reality played no small part in conceiving the Holy Spirit "as a power [which] appeared graphically only in the form of the dove and thus receded, to a large extent, in the Trinitarian speculation."[49]

As seen through the lens of the relation of emergence, however, the Holy Spirit is truly manifest as a distinct and unique Person with attributes and agency that are efficacious not only for the believer and for the community in history but also for the inner life of the

---

48. *The Roman Missal*, English Translation Prepared by the International Commission on English in the Liturgy, (City: Press, 1973), 182–84. Used with permission.

49. "Christianity: The Holy Trinity," *Encyclopedia Britannica Online*.

Trinity *in se*. The biblical and classical traditions point to the efficacy of the Spirit for ongoing revelation and unitive love, effects that further constitute the Spirit's unique identity.

The first effect appropriated to the Spirit by the Johannine Jesus is ongoing revelation. This activity clearly follows from the mission of Holy Spirit as teacher and witness to the deeds, wonders, and signs that God had worked through Jesus Christ. Based on the way in which Jesus spoke of the mission of the Spirit in John's Gospel, it is apparent that the Spirit is sent to continue and to reinforce the revelation begun in Jesus' teaching ministry, to witness to Christ and Christ's teaching, to teach all things and to testify to what is true. The Acts of the Apostles and the Epistles further amplify the revelatory works appropriated to the Spirit. In the Acts of the Apostles, the Spirit frequently inspired revelatory utterances in crises (4:8, 13, 29–31; 13:9) and in teaching and testimony (5:32, 6:10, 18:25). Persons "filled with the Holy Spirit" proceed to offer daring proclamations and revelations and to "speak the word of God with boldness" (4:31). Likewise prompted by the Spirit, the elders of the community at the Council of Jerusalem decided not to impose the Law of Moses on Gentile Christians, laying upon them "no greater burden than [what is] essential" (15:1–30). In the Epistles, the Holy Spirit empowers believers to confess Jesus as Lord (1 Corinthians 12:3), designates apostles and prophets (Ephesians 3:5), and fills believers with firm conviction (1 Thessalonians 1:5).

The Spirit also shared revelations through inspiration and visions in the doctrinal and theological development of Christianity. In the third century, Cyprian, bishop of Carthage, reported having visions inspired by the Holy Spirit. Earlier in that century, the theologian Hippolytus credited the Holy Spirit with the refutation of heresies. Furthermore, priest and theologian Novatian proclaimed that the Holy Spirit "instructs the Church's teachers . . . inspires the Church's councils and dispenses other gifts of grace. In this way, he perfects and completes the Church of Christ everywhere and in all things."[50]

The second activity appropriated to the Holy Spirit is love, sometimes characterized as community or as *koinonia*, a Greek word meaning "communion by intimate participation." Each of these terms points to the reality that the Holy Spirit is the essential impetus for

---

50. Kärkkäinen, *Pneumatology*, 40.

intimate and loving interrelationship, not only in the immanent life of the Trinity but also in the mission of the Spirit in history.

From the writings of Augustine through those of Aquinas, and even in the work of theologians today, the conception of the Holy Spirit as the mutual love between the Father and the Son has been generally well accepted.[51] As explained in the words of Aquinas, "The Holy Spirit is called the bond between the Father and the Son, in that he is Love, since the Father loves the Son and the Son loves the Father by the one single love; thus, the name of the Holy Spirit as Love implies a relation of the Father to the Son, that is to say a relation of the one who loves to the beloved one."[52] Nonetheless, as Perfect Love, the Trinity does not—in fact *cannot*—reserve this love solely between the Lover and the Beloved. Thus was the claim of mystical theologian Richard St. Victor. To substantiate this claim, he developed the understanding of Love within the Trinity in a way that further distinguishes the uniqueness of the Holy Spirit.[53] St. Victor began with the model of Lover and Beloved as metaphors for the Father and the Son. However, St. Victor explicitly argued that love between two persons is less perfect than love shared among three "and that only when a third belongs to the circle of love is love perfected."[54] The Third Person who completes the circle and assures the perfect love of the Trinity is the Holy Spirit. Therefore, of necessity, "the Holy Spirit stands forth clearly as a *person* in Richard's work, co-equal with the Father and the Son."[55]

---

51. Cf. Augustine, *On the Trinity,* 15.5.29–31; Aquinas, *ST,* I:37.1; *SCG,* IV: 20–22; Joseph Ratzinger, "The Holy Spirit as Communio: Concerning the Relationship of Pneumatology and Spirituality in Augustine," *Communio* 25 (1998): 324–37; Stanley Grenz, "The Holy Spirit: Divine Love Guiding Us Home," *Ex Auditu* 12 (1996): 1–13; Robert W. Jenson, *The Triune God* (New York: Oxford, 1997), 146–61; Clark H. Pinnock, *Flame of Love: A Theology of the Holy Spirit* (Downers Grove: InterVarsity Press, 1996), 37–40; David Coffey, "The Holy Spirit as the Mutual Love of the Father and the Son," *Theological Studies* 51 (1990): 193–229.

52. Aquinas, *ST,* I:37.1.3.

53. Roger Olson and Christopher Alan Hall, *The Trinity* (Grand Rapids, MI: Eerdmans, 2002), 58–59.

54. Ibid., 59.

55. Paul Burgess, "Three Are the Perfection of Charity: The *De Trinitate* of Richard St. Victor" based on the work of Gervais Dumeige, *Richard de Saint-Victor et l'idée chrétienne de l'amour* (Paris: Presses Universitaires de France, 1952), 31; available from *http://www.paulburgess.org/ richard.html#fn89*, italics in the original.

The Holy Spirit's activity as Love does not only apply to the Spirit's activity within the inner life of the Trinity. This divine love overflows into history in the mission of the Holy Spirit. The Acts of the Apostles and the Epistles give other instances of the Spirit exercising the effect of love in the form of communion or *koinonia* within the Christian community. The Acts of the Apostles speaks of the Spirit as intimately and powerfully abiding within individuals and the community by virtue of baptism and the laying on of hands (4:31, 8:15–19, 10:44–47, 19:6). Through the revelation of the Spirit, the apostle Peter came to understand the breadth of God's loving embrace in Jesus Christ, realizing that "God is not one to show partiality, but in every nation the [one] who fears [God] and does what is right is welcome to [God]" (10:34). The Pauline letters repeatedly associate the Holy Spirit with salvation (Romans 8:9, 14–16; Galatians 4:6), justification (1 Corinthians 6:11; Galatians 3:14), and grace (Romans 3:24; 1 Corinthians 15:10; Galatians 1:15), all of which restore loving relationship between God and creation.

While this brief survey cannot exhaust the plethora of ways in which the Holy Spirit was spoken of in the earliest Christian tradition, the majority of the activities and effects appropriated to the Spirit can arguably be linked to the ongoing revelation and loving participation in the life of God and in the life of the cosmic and human community effected by the Spirit. Surely, the Holy Spirit is distinctively recognized as that unique Person who secures the dynamic relationality of the Trinity *ad intra* and of the Trinity with all creation *ad extra*.

SUMMARY

Undoubtedly much more could be said about the Triune God based on scripture, classical theology, creedal statements, and doctrine. It calls to mind the concluding line from the Gospel of John that states in retrospect, "There are also many other things that Jesus did, but if these were to be described individually, I do not think the whole world would contain the books that would be written" (21:25). The same could be said about the mystery of the Trinity discussed in retrospect throughout this chapter. However, even just a survey of the principal biblical, creedal, and classical traditions concerning the Trinity—examined here through the hermeneutical lens of a relational ontology of origin, effect, and emergence—demonstrates that there is an enduring tradition that holds that the very Being of the Triune God is a Being-in-Relation. Moreover, this divine Being-in-Relation is consistent with the three types of relation explored in the context of cosmic and human being.

The classical Trinitarian concept of "processions" articulated in the theologies of both the West and the East is consistent with the relation of origin. From both perspectives, this relation of origin traces itself to the First Person of the Trinity, from whom the Second and Third Persons proceed eternally, equally, and dynamically, demonstrating that relationality is not what the Trinity *have*, but what the Trinity is. The missions of the Son and Holy Spirit from the Father into history is consistent with the relation of emergence, revealing Godself not only as three distinct Persons but also as self-communicating, sending the Divine Word and Wisdom to dwell in time in ways heretofore unknown. Finally, relation of effect is demonstrated through the doctrine of appropriations, which clarifies not simply what capacities belong to each Person, but the differences in their Persons. Thus, rather than simply describing particular differences in their activities, the appropriations constitute their personal uniqueness as well.

At this stage in the text, it is important to recall from chapter 1 that Thomas Aquinas believed that the relational ontology of the Triune God provided the essential foundation of the relational ontology of cosmic and human being as well. This, as Aquinas explains, is because "all beings apart from God are not their own being, but are beings by *participation.* . . . All things which are diversified by the diverse participation of being . . . are caused by one First Being, Who possesses being most perfectly."[56] Clearly, if every being comes from God and participates in Being Itself *and* if Being Itself is essentially relational, then human and cosmic being is essentially relational as well. Beyond being an assertion peculiar to theology, chapters 2, 3 and 4 have demonstrated that this is a point on which the natural and physical sciences, the social and behavioral sciences, and the Christian biblical and theological traditions agree.

56. Aquinas, *ST*, I.44.1.

FOR FURTHER READING

Augustine of Hippo. *On the Trinity. In a Select Library of the Nicene and Post-Nicene Fathers of the Christian Church*, Vol. 3, edited by Philip Schaff. Buffalo: The Christian Literature Company, 1887.

Hill, William. *The Three-Personed God: The Trinity as the Mystery of Salvation*. Washington, DC: Catholic University of America Press, 1982.

LaCugna, Catherine Mowry. *God for Us: The Trinity and Christian Life*. San Francisco: Harper San Francisco, 1991.

Rahner, Karl. *The Trinity*. Translated by Joseph Donceel. New York: Herder and Herder, 1970.

Chapter 5

DIVINE AND COSMIC BEING
IN RELATION

"Without claiming to have a definition or exact description
of the divine being, one should be entitled to say that with
a given model of God one is making an ontological claim,
however tentative, about the reality of God even apart
from human experience."[1]

INTRODUCTION

Chapter 4 advanced the insights of Thomas Aquinas that "every
being in any way existing is from God" and that "all beings apart
from God are not their own being, but are beings by participation."[2] His insights allowed for the assertion that all being—divine,
cosmic, and human—is in essence relational either in itself or by
participation. This assertion, moreover, prompts the further claim
that, because the natures of divine, cosmic, and human beings are
essentially and intrinsically relational within themselves, it is entirely
appropriate to speak of essential and intrinsic relations between and

---

1. Joseph Bracken, "Images of God within Systematic Theology," *Theological Studies* 6:2 (June 2002): 362–73 at 365.

2. Aquinas, *ST*, I.44.1.

among them as well. The question is how best to do so. Chapter 5 engages this very question as it examines and assesses the various models of God-world relationship that have been proposed throughout the centuries. Each of these models reflects the philosophical worldview of those who proposed it. After considering the various models, this chapter then identifies the one most consistent with the evolutionary worldview predominant in this century and explores how such a model affects the Christian vision of and the religious language used to describe the Triune God in relation to the cosmos and its creatures.

OF ANALOGIES, MODELS, AND METAPHORS IN THEOLOGY

As one embarks on an exploration of models of God, it is particularly important to understand that any interpretations drawn from cosmic reality and applied to divine reality should be characterized by the scholarly tentativeness advised by Joseph Bracken in the opening quote of this chapter. In view of the ultimate mystery of God and the cosmos, one cannot speak naïvely as if a one-to-one correspondence exists between the finite meaning of one's words and the realities to which they refer. However, neither can one speak instrumentally as if one's words were simply useful fictions bearing no intrinsic connection to their referent. Concerning assertions about the Infinite Reality of God and the finite realities of the cosmos, one strives to demonstrate as clearly as possible that the realities to which one points truly exist, to signify those realities as accurately as possible through the language one chooses, and yet to accept that all human speech ultimately fails to encompass the mysteries of either God or creation.

To accomplish its scholarly tasks, therefore, theology employs figurative and imagistic language—the language of analogy, models, and metaphors—to articulate in terms accessible to human experience that which is beyond the fully communicable. Consider the various descriptions already used in this text and in the Christian tradition: God as Father, Creator, sovereign or king; Jesus as Word, Christ, Messiah, or redeemer; the Holy Spirit as ghost, comforter, advocate, or paraclete. Reflect on the God-world relationships as monarchical, organic, or emanationist, or as parent to child, lord to servant, hen to chick, or lover to beloved. Think about conceptual notions such as transcendence and immanence or ransom and redemption. All of these and more exemplify the often-unacknowledged dependence of theology upon analogy, model, and metaphor in its attempt to articulate something of Ultimate Reality *in se* and in relation to the cosmos.

Analogy

Theologically, the use of analogy is most often associated with the assertions of Thomas Aquinas. Aquinas claimed that words drawn from human experience to express the divine attributes are used neither univocally nor equivocally but analogically. Based on the notion that created being participates in Being Itself as its principal Source and Cause, Aquinas wrote,

> Univocal predication is impossible between God and creatures. The reason of this is that every effect . . . receives the similitude of the agent not in its full degree, but in a measure that falls short. . . . Neither, on the other hand, are names applied to God and creatures in a purely equivocal sense . . . because if that were so, it follows that from creatures nothing could be known or demonstrated about God at all. . . . Therefore . . . these names are said of God and creatures in an analogous sense . . . according to the relation of a creature to God as its principle and cause. . . . For in analogies the idea is not . . . one and the same, yet it is not totally diverse . . . but . . . signifies various proportions to some one thing.[3]

Stated simply, because one can only speak of God in the concepts and parlance of human experience, such speech would be meaningless if it did not legitimately refer in some way to God. However, because of the ontological difference between God and creation, attributes based on finite experience do not literally correspond to the attributes of God (univocal). However, neither do these

3. Ibid., I.13.5.

attributes mean something entirely different when attributed to God (equivocal). Because God as Being Itself is the cause and source of finite being, the attributes of finite being participate in the attributes of Being Itself and thus may be applied to the Infinite God. Yet, they apply only in a proportional way because of the magnitude of difference between creation and its Source of life.

Take, for example, the attribute of God as "good." Persons who attribute goodness to God do so on the basis of their human experiences of goodness found in other persons and events. Moreover, people experience different degrees of goodness, if you will, in different situations and from different people. Nonetheless, no matter how good another person or situation is thought to be, those experiences of goodness are ultimately limited because they take place in finite persons and in finite situations. However, God is infinite, unlimited in nature and in being. Because of this, the attributes applied to God are equally unlimited in comprehension and in degree. When persons say that God is good, the limits of human experience dictate that the attribute good does not exactly match the human experience of goodness. It is not univocal. Nevertheless, neither is experience of human goodness completely different from that of divine goodness. It is not equivocal. So how does one describe the relation between goodness experienced in finite creatures and goodness experienced in God? One does so on the basis of analogy, affirming that "good" applies to both creatures and to God but in vastly different degrees.

Metaphor

While an analogy operates with a difference of degree, a metaphor "is a word or phrase used *in*appropriately. It belongs properly in one context, but is being used in another."[4] According to Protestant theologian Sallie McFague, "What a metaphor expresses cannot be said directly or apart from it, for if it could be, one would have said it directly. . . . [A metaphor] is an attempt to say something about the unfamiliar in terms of the familiar, an attempt to speak about what

4. Sallie McFague, *Models of God: Theology for an Ecological Nuclear Age* (Philadelphia: Fortress, 1987), 33.

we do not know in terms of what we do know."[5] Linguistically, the metaphor is related to a simile, which makes a comparison with the use of *like* or *as*, but in the metaphor the distinction is implied, rather than explicit. The Psalms, for instance, are replete with examples of metaphorical language applied to God. They assert that God is a rock, a fortress, a shepherd, a warrior, and the like. That God is *like* each of these, but is *not literally* so is implied. While the metaphor and the analogy are based on different principles, the propriety of using metaphor in speech about God echoes the rationale for using analogy: Because of the ultimate mystery of God and the cosmos, metaphor articulates that which is beyond the fully communicable in terms accessible to human experience. However, unlike analogy, "metaphor always has the character of 'is' and 'is not': an assertion is made but as a likely account rather than a definition."[6]

Models

Finally, models in theology represent more overarching paradigms. In the words of McFague, "A model is a metaphor that has gained sufficient stability and scope so as to present a pattern for relatively comprehensive and coherent explanation."[7] In other words, it has staying power. When used in theological discourse, however, a model should not be regarded as "a literal picture of reality, yet neither should it be treated as a useful fiction."[8] Models are symbolic representations of realities that are not directly accessible. Such realities include not only the mystery of God, which exceeds human comprehension but also constituents and interactions studied by the sciences that are beyond literal description. These include theological models, such as that of God as Father or king, and scientific models, such as the Big Bang or the double helix. Because of their ability to signify realities beyond comprehension by the finite mind, theologians consider models essential and permanent features of the discourse of the discipline. As constructive and imaginative expressions of reality,

---

5. Ibid.

6. Ibid.

7. Ibid., 34.

8. Ian Barbour, *Myths, Models and Paradigms* (London: SCM, 1974), 69.

models reflect networks of relationships, structures, and processes in the world, thus fostering discovery and opening the unintelligible to intelligibility. According to philosophical theologian Janet Soskice, models "are allowable, their vagueness valuable, and their relational structure useful to theoretical accounts . . . , [because] one can refer to . . . little understood features . . . without laying claim to an unrevisable description of them."[9]

Sallie McFague points to the image of God as Father as an "excellent example" of a theological model, demonstrating the qualities of a model that Soskice points out. Clearly, using the term *father* for God suggests a broad, familiar, and intricate relational structure through which one can infer any number of attributes and activities of the Divine. As an ideal father, God is strong, provident, loving, and protective, like the father described in the Lukan parable of the prodigal son (15:11–32). As the parable implies, if God is modeled as father, then humans can envision themselves as God's children. Furthermore, if God is like the father in this parable, then sin is a rebellion against paternal authority, like that of each of the sons in turn. The return of the prodigal son models both divine forgiveness and human redemption as the once rebellious child is embraced as beloved offspring.

As Soskice indicates, this model of God as Father, particularly in the context of a broader narrative, clarifies and highlights particular features of God and the God-world relationship that may otherwise prove incomprehensible. It implies significant aspects of God's relationship to humans and reveals characteristics of the Divine that might not have been imagined. For example, some people image God as a judge who keeps a tally of their transgressions and waits to pronounce judgment on those who have sinned. A model that presents an alternative image of God as unconditionally loving, patient, forgiving is invaluable to them. This demonstrates another characteristic of models in religious traditions. Like the model of God as Father, religious models are often relational in nature and have a strong affective function that evokes emotion, inspires involvement, and stirs commitment. Ongoing human experience makes a model

---

9. Janet M. Soskice, *Metaphor and Religious Language* (Oxford: Oxford University, 1984), 210–11.

such as God as Father a revisable one, particularly if the relationship between the believer and his or her father undergoes positive or negative change. Nonetheless, because theological models often draw from the most significant of human experiences, believers "respond to models . . . [and] they believe them in some way to depict states and relations of a transcendent kind," that is, of the nature of God and the God-world relation.[10]

Speaking Rightly of God

Mystery confronts the seeker of the essential and the real. Ultimately, if the Essential and the Real who is sought is God, then as Augustine cautioned, "If you think you have understood"—if you suppose that you have more than limited and revisable knowledge—"then what you have understood is not God."[11] Nevertheless, "In spite of everything,"—in spite of the limitations of human speech, the finitude of human comprehension, the boundaries of human experience, and the inscrutable Being of the Divine—"we go on saying 'God.'"[12] Moreover, we do so because the Divine Mystery, which the human experiences and immeasurably values, must be expressible in some speech. The difficulty arises in the tension between the experience of the Divine and that human capacity to articulate that experience, influenced by social, cultural, personal, religious, and semantic factors. These constraints on theological language do not, however, call for silence. Rather, they call for humility born from realizing that, while the finite reality and Infinite Reality of which theology speaks are essentially mysteries, they are, nonetheless, mysteries that continually communicate themselves and are infinitely accessible to believers in every age.

Hence, an appropriate understanding of analogy, metaphor, and model proves critical to the task this chapter and those that follow undertake. These chapters present names for and models of God and God-world relationships that claim to refer to both cosmic and divine realities *without* claiming to be the final, total, or unalterable word on the topic. Like any other theological enterprise, the analogies,

---

10. Soskice, *Metaphor*, 176.

11. Augustine, *Sermo* 52, c. 6, n. 16: PL 38:360, in "Creeds, Trinity, and Providence," *Catechism of the Catholic Church*; available from *http://www.illinoisknights.org*.

12. Rowan Williams, "Trinity and Revelation," *Modern Theology* 2 (1986): 197.

metaphors, and models are drawn from finite reality. Because of this, they are necessarily shaped and unavoidably constrained by the time, space, and material limits of the experiences that shape the language being used. The images, therefore, represent a distinct worldview, employ a specific vocabulary, and draw upon particular examples that are limited by the social and personal context of the theologian. Nonetheless, the questions that analogies, models, and metaphors seek to answer are the same ones that have grasped theologians in every time: What language authentically and meaningfully describes God and the God-world relationship in this day and age?

MODELS OF GOD-WORLD RELATIONSHIP

Based upon biblical, philosophical, and theological insights, various scholars have explored and analyzed an array of images and models of God-world relationship that have expressed Christian belief and experience throughout the centuries. Because of their reflection, they have advanced four main models of God-world relationship: deism, pantheism, theism, and panentheism. Because such models reflect networks, structures, and processes that foster intelligibility about the world, about God, and about the relationship between the world and God, each has a different capacity to cohere with and to express fully the particular concepts that frame the discussions and the aims of this text. A particular model must cohere with and must be able to express three concepts:

- First, the Christian understanding of God as Trinity (described in chapter 4)
- Second, the evolutionary view of the cosmos as revealed by the sciences (described in chapter 2)
- Third, the radical relationality characteristic of divine, cosmic, and human being intrinsically and extrinsically (demonstrated throughout this book)

Any model unable to meet these three conditions is not sufficiently viable and expansive enough to communicate the relational under-standing of God and God-world relationship required for creation, incarnation, and grace in an evolving cosmos.

Deism

As a religious and philosophical belief, *deism* accepts the reality of God as a "Supreme Architect" whose existence is discernible through reason brought to bear on that which is observable in nature. The deist model of God arose during the period of the Enlightenment. Sufficiency of reason supplanted the need for revelation, and natural theology superseded evidence from scripture. According to deism, God created a law-abiding universe that God then left to run on its own. Thus, "the Deist maintained that God endowed the world at creation with self-sustaining and self-acting powers and then abandoned it to the operation of these powers acting as second causes."[13]

Because this paradigm stresses the unequivocal transcendence of God and allows no interaction or involvement between God and the world, the God of deism was a "Cosmic Designer . . . impersonal and remote—not a God who cares for individuals . . . or a Being to whom prayer would be appropriate." Beyond being "a hypothesis for the origin of the world," therefore, the deist God is essentially "irrelevant to daily life."[14]

Hence, regarding the criteria listed previously, deism is inconsistent with the radical and constitutive relationality within and between divine, human, and cosmic being. Moreover, it fails to allow for God's incarnate, immanent, and enduring presence and action within the world, which is the essence of God as Trinity. Finally, its excessive emphasis on divine transcendence and on original creation contradicts the notion of ongoing creativity demanded by an evolutionary worldview.

Pantheism

The philosophical converse of deism is pantheism, which derives its name from the Greek words *pan* (all) + *theos* (God), interpreted as meaning "all is God." This paradigm identifies God with the totality of nature, with the laws of nature, or as the world soul inherent in

---

13. John Orr, *English Deism: Its Roots and Its Fruits*. Grand Rapids, MI: Eerdmans, 1934), 13.

14. Ian Barbour, *Religion and Science: Historical and Contemporary Issues* (New York: HarperCollins, 1997), 36–37.

nature. It holds that "Nature is divine (God) and we humans are part of the One, interconnected whole." As described by ancient philosopher Zeno of Citium in the third century BCE, pantheists believe that "God is not separate from the world; He is the soul of the world, and each of us contains a part of the Divine Fire. All things are parts of one single system, which is called Nature; the individual life is good when it is in harmony with Nature."[15] In contrast to deism, therefore, this paradigm—often imaged as "the world as God's body"—stresses the immanence of God in the universe, a universe that God in no way transcends. In his assessment of pantheism from a philosophical perspective, David Pailin writes that, in classical pantheism, "the divine being is constituted by the sum total of all that truly is" and is completely receptive to all cosmic events. As a result, classical pantheism "involves a denial of God's genuine independence of the world."[16]

Based on the criteria by which each model is to be evaluated, pantheism is insufficient for the aims of this project. It denies the essential and constitutive relationality within and between cosmic and divine being by identifying the two and obscuring the ontological distinction between them. In so doing, it rejects the essential and constitutive relationality of the Persons of the Trinity with each other and with the cosmos. As a result, pantheism fundamentally limits cosmic creativity to the workings of the cosmos itself by concealing any evidence of the creative activity of the Divine. Finally, it robs divine incarnation and immanence of their uniqueness by making each of these relations indistinguishable from the materiality and processes of the cosmos itself.

Theism

The God-world model of theism is the model to which classical Christianity most closely adheres. Theism views God as a personal and purposeful eternal Being who both transcends the world and yet is immanent within it. This paradigm theoretically incorporates both

---

15. Zeno of Citium, in "Pantheism," *Open-Site Free Internet Encyclopedia*; available from *http://open-site.org/Society/Philosophy/Religion/Pantheism*.

16. David Pailin, *God and the Processes of Reality* (New York: Routledge: 1989), 77.

the transcendent and immanent aspects of God. However, the possibility of true relationality between God and the cosmos in theism is mitigated in two ways.

First, because it presumes Greek philosophical concepts, classical theism asserts that while God can affect, cause change, and transform the universe, often through its own creatures, the universe cannot affect God. If God were to be affected, changed, or transformed by another, God's perfection could be at risk. This is because, according to the Greek philosophy that undergirds classical theism, perfection consists in the fact that a being is unchangeable (immutable) and unable to be affected by another outside itself (impassible). This now leads to a second assertion. The fact that God is immutable and impassible means that God bears no real relation to the world. This is because in Greek philosophy "relation" was an attribute of a being or substance that could be changed or affected by another. Therefore, if God in divine perfection cannot be changed or affected by another, then "relation" cannot be an attribute of God. Therefore, while the universe has a real relation to God, that is, the universe can be changed and affected by God, there is, as Aquinas wrote in the *Summa Theologiae*, "no real relation in God to the creature."[17]

How can this be the case? Think, for example, of the Washington Monument or some other such imposing structure. On any given day, hundreds of people circle that monument. As people move around it, their spatial relation to the monument changes. Some people are behind it, some in front of it, others on either side of it, some even within it. In this process, each person has a real and changeable relation to the monument. Yet while the spatial relation between each person and the monument is real and changeable, the spatial relation of the monument to each person remains unchanged. The monument itself never moves! It is immutable and unaffected.

---

17. Aquinas, *ST*, Ia. 28. 1. Aquinas explains in more detail: "Since therefore God is outside the whole order of creation, and all creatures are ordered to Him, and not conversely, it is manifest that creatures are really related to God Himself; whereas in God there is no real relation to creatures, but a relation only in idea, inasmuch as creatures are referred to Him. Thus there is nothing to prevent these names which import relation to the creature from being predicated of God temporally, not by reason of any change in Him, but by reason of the change of the creature; as a column is on the right of an animal, without change in itself, but by change in the animal." (*ST*, Ia. 13. 7)

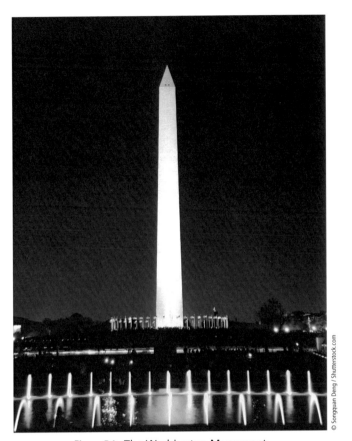

Figure 5.1: The Washington Monument

Its spatial orientation and relation to the onlookers, to the landscape, to compass directions is constant. The north face never revolves to face the south; its east face never turns to the west. Therefore, in Aquinas's frame of reference, the monument is not "related" to its surroundings. Although this understanding preserves freedom and autonomy of both the cosmos and the Divine, it severely limits any true mutuality or reciprocity between them.[18] In classical theism, God depends in no way upon the world God created. Rather, God is perfect, absolute, necessary, and unaffected.

18. Pailin, *God and the Processes of Reality*, 78.

While theism has proven compatible with the understanding of God as Trinity and can accommodate the notion of ongoing creativity in the cosmos through secondary causality—the concept that God acts in the world through what God has created—it does so at the cost of three critical elements of full relationality between God and the cosmos. First, in theism, relationality is unidirectional; God affects the cosmos, but the cosmos does not affect God. The cosmos has a real relation to God, but God has no real relation to the cosmos. This hardly reflects an authentic relationality between divine and cosmic being. Second, theism emphasizes divine transcendence and diminishes divine immanence or relegates it to particular people and places. Moreover, it reduces divine incarnation to an exceptional event within the normal course of God-world relation. Third, creativity is viewed through the lens of the event of original creation, leaving continuous creation as interventionist rather than as a capacity inbuilt by the Creator into creation itself.

Panentheism

The fourth model is panentheism. Typically, *panentheism* is defined as "the belief that the Being of God includes and penetrates the whole universe, so that every part of it exists in Him but (as against pantheism) that His Being is more than, and is not exhausted by, the universe."[19] This model has particular capacities that make it persuasive in a Christian evolutionary worldview. First, it balances the aspects of divine transcendence and divine immanence by envisioning God in the world and the world in God without identifying the world with God or God with the world. Second, it maintains the ontological distinction between Creator and creature because it is grounded in a relational ontology, which distinguishes beings on the basis of relation, not substance. Third, it envisions a truly intimate God-world relationship in which God both affects and is affected by the world and in which the world truly participates in the Being of God.[20] Finally, it incorporates a critical form of God-world relationality demanded by Christian belief in the Incarnation of God

19. F. L. Cross and E. A. Livingstone, eds., "Panentheism," in *Oxford Dictionary of the Christian Church*, 2nd edition (Oxford: Oxford University, 1983), 1027.

20. Barbour, *Religion and Science*, 329–32, 357–60.

in Christ, that of divine incarnation, which is not as clearly accommodated in the emphatic transcendence of deism, the exclusive immanence of pantheism, or in the lack of real relation between the cosmos and God of theism.

A panentheistic paradigm models the ontological relationality of the humanity and divinity of Christ in an intimate and essential way. In substance ontology, belief that Jesus Christ is truly divine and truly human is fraught with philosophical difficulty because a spiritual substance (divine nature) cannot be united with a material substance (human nature) and remains ontologically unchanged. This philosophical obstacle was dogmatically removed by the Council of Chalcedon in 451 CE, which proclaimed by fiat that the spiritual and material natures were truly united in the one person of Jesus Christ without the ontological change to either nature. Thus, the creed of Chalcedon states that the person of Jesus Christ is

> recognized in two natures, without confusion, without change, without division, without separation; the distinction of natures being in no way annulled by the union, but rather the characteristics of each nature being preserved and coming together to form one person and subsistence.[21]

Unlike deism, theism, or pantheism, panentheism images the reality that Chalcedon spoke about in an explicit and enduring way. In the panentheistic model, the Being of God is perennially in union with material being without loss of the divine nature, and material being is perennially in union with divine being without loss of material nature. Because panentheism presumes a relational ontology, the union between the Divine and the cosmos endures in an analogous fashion and is describable in analogous terms as Chalcedon uses of the Incarnation. In panentheism, God and matter are intimately and enduringly united "in two natures, without confusion, without change, without division, without separation; the distinction of natures being in no way annulled by the union, but rather the characteristics of each nature being preserved."[22] Moreover, in the fullness of time, this

---

21. "The Definition of the Council of Chalcedon (451 CE)," *Center for Reformed Theology and Apologetics*; available from *http://www.reformed.org/documents/index. html?mainframe=http:// www.reformed.org/documents/chalcedon.html.*

22. Ibid.

subsistent relation between God and matter represented in panentheism comes to explicit and unique expression in the union between divinity and humanity in the person of Jesus Christ.

Because of these important capacities, many scholars view panentheism as a middle way between classical theism, with its inordinate emphasis on the transcendence of God with regard to the cosmos, and pantheism, with its excessive identification of God with the cosmos. As a middle way, panentheism first "affirms . . . that God is so immanent within the world that this divine interpenetration means that [God is within] all things . . . while . . . affirming . . . that God transcends the realm of finite realities."[23] Moreover, panentheism also maintains that "everything finite must somehow be contained within the infinite reality of God and be sustained by the divine power of being *even as it retains its own existence as a subsistent finite reality.*"[24] Hence, as Pailin concludes, "panentheism is not a new position but a new appreciation of the proper conceptual structure of a dominant tradition of religious faith in God," a tradition that seeks to hold in balance the transcendence, immanence, and incarnation of God in relation to the world.[25]

Because no theological model bounded by finite time, space, and language can adequately express the infinite mystery of God, like the other models of the God-world relationship discussed in this chapter, the model of panentheism has its limitations. Some criticize this model for blurring the distinction between the eternal Being of God and God in relation to creation. Others suggest that it undermines divine freedom and sovereignty by making the attributes and actions of God dependent on finite being. Still others contend that speaking of God in terms of God's relation to the cosmos reduces God simply to an entity or a function within the cosmos and its processes, and risks identifying God with the world.

However, if one is careful to navigate these risks, the philosophical concept of panentheism does have the unique capacity to draw together and balance both the attributes of God preserved in other

---

23. Curtis L. Thompson, "From Presupposing Pantheism's Power to Potentiating Panentheism's Personality: Seeking Parallels between Kierkegaard's and Martensen's Theological Anthropologies." *Journal of Religion* 82:2 (April 2002): 225–51 at 234.

24. Bracken, "Images of God within Systematic Theology," 367, italics added.

25. Pailin, *God and the Processes of Reality*, 81.

models of God-world relation and the elements of scientific and theological thought. As the later chapters of this book demonstrate, this paradigm effectively integrates into one cohesive model the Christian concept of God as Trinity in transcendent, incarnate, and immanent relation to the world and the evolutionary and quantum insights disclosed through the sciences. Although one must use the model of panentheism fully cognizant that "'words strain, crack and sometimes break, under the burden' of trying to speak in the least misleading way possible about the divine nature,"[26] the panentheistic model of God-world relationship has the remarkable capacity to entwine manifold theological and scientific strands of argument intelligibly and productively. This is especially true as a model for the world's relation to the Triune God.

Envisioning a Panentheistic Model of God-World Relationship

If one were to try to visualize a panentheistic model of God-world relationship, what might it look like? What relationship within human experience might symbolize it effectively? The essential notion in panentheism is that "there is no 'place outside' the infinite God in which what is created could exist. God creates all-that-is *within* Godself."[27] Now, if one were to imagine a being within whom and through whom another distinct being is created and sustained, what image comes to mind? Search as one might among traditional theological images of God-world relationship—images that predominately reflect a patriarchal imagination and symbol-system—it is difficult to find a model that adequately communicates the understanding of the permeation of God in the cosmos and the cosmos within God in ontologically distinctive, yet internal ways. Traditional Western models of God-world relation often place "too much stress

---

26. Peacocke, *Creation and the World of Science*, 199. Enclosed quote from T. S. Eliot, "Burnt Norton V," from *Four Quartets. Art of Europe;* available from *http://www. artofeurope.com.*

27. Arthur Peacocke, "Articulating God's Presence in and to the World Unveiled by the Sciences," in *In Whom We Live and Move and Have Our Being: Panentheistic Reflections on God's Presence in a Scientific World,* ed. Philip Clayton and Arthur Peacocke (Grand Rapids, MI: Eerdmans, 2004), 147, italics in the original.

on the externality of the process—God . . . [is] regarded as creating rather in the way the male fertilizes the female from outside."[28]

In response to this tradition, however, Anglican scientist-theologian Arthur Peacocke and Catholic feminist theologian Elizabeth Johnson both suggest a pregnant mother as a particularly fruitful image for such a being within whom and through whom another distinct being is created and sustained. Consider what Johnson wrote about the panentheistic model in terms of female procreation:

> To be so structured that you have room inside yourself for another to dwell is quintessentially a female experience. To have another actually living and moving and having being in yourself is likewise the province of women. . . . This reality is the paradigm without equal for the panentheistic notion of the coinherence of God and the world. To see the world dwelling in God is to play variation on the theme of women's bodiliness and experience of pregnancy, labor and giving birth . . . as suitable metaphor for the divine.[29]

Clearly, only the female of the species can bear within herself an other with whom she is intimately and reciprocally related; an other who is essentially free, distinct, and autonomous subject; an other within whom her life and spirit are immanent, and yet beyond whom her life and being are transcendent; an other in whose struggle for life she passionately participates in anxious waiting, in anguished cries, and in exultation as a new creation bursts forth. While such an image might seem strange to Christians raised on traditional images of God as Father and Son and disembodied images of God as Spirit, might this imaginative shift in image from a male to a female and from a spiritual to an embodied relation between God and the world meaningfully exemplify the Trinity's intimate relation to the cosmos in a panentheistic worldview? Might one claim with Arthur Peacocke that, in the divine womb, "God, according to panentheism, creates a world other than Godself and 'within herself' (we find ourselves

28. Arthur Peacocke, *Paths from Science towards God: The End of All Our Exploring* (Oxford: Oneworld, 2001), 139. *Paths from Science.*

29. Elizabeth A. Johnson, *She Who Is: The Mystery of God in Feminist Theological Discourse* (New York: Crossroads, 1992), 234–35.

saying for the most appropriate image)—yet another reminder of the need to escape from the limitations of male-dominated language about God."[30]

The question remains as to whether this approach coheres with the being of God as Trinity. From the perspective of relational ontology, the model of a mother with child demonstrates how, in the words of Acts 17:28, a being lives and moves and has its own unique being within another being and yet remains ontologically distinct and unique. The mother and the child remain ontologically distinct and unique on the basis of relation; while intimately related to one another, the mother is not the child and the child is not the mother. In fact, relationally, the mother transcends the being of the child, and the child is incarnate within the mother. However, the mother is more than transcendent in relation to the child; an aspect of her being is also immanent within the child. Her very lifeblood courses through the child within her, carrying the nutrients that nourish and strengthen the growth, the development, and the well-being of the incarnate child in her womb.

Envisioning the pregnant mother and child in the variety of relationships between and within one another—transcendent, incarnate, and immanent relations—undeniably provides a plausible way of modeling the relationship between the Trinity and the cosmos in which "the Being of God includes and penetrates the whole universe, so that every part of it exists in [God] but (as against pantheism) that [God's] Being is more than, and is not exhausted by, the universe."[31] Such a model serves well in demonstrating the following:

- how God can be viewed in the Trinity of transcendent, incarnate, and immanent relationship with creation
- how each of the three relations is unique and personal
- how these relations imply relations of origin, emergence, and effect
- how these relations conceivably coincide with the Christian doctrines of creation, incarnation, and grace as intimate and enduing relations between the Trinity and the cosmos

---

30. Peacocke, *Paths from Science*, 139.
31. Cross and Livingstone, "Panentheism," 1027.

As compelling as it might seem from the foregoing description, the analogy between the panentheistic model of God-world relationship and the mother pregnant with child should not be taken literally, as is the case with any other of the spatial or embodied models of the God-world relationship that are more familiar to believers or more firmly entrenched in the Christian tradition. The intention in proposing it, however, is to enable one to envision what a panentheistic model of God-world relationship "looks like" through a familiar analogy and to see how this model might function theologically and spiritually. Let us now consider more closely how effectively the panentheistic model coheres with Christian Trinitarian theology and in an evolutionary worldview.

RE-VISIONING TRINITARIAN RELATION IN A PANENTHEISTIC MODEL

Christian theology has not historically drawn on a panentheistic formulation of the concept of God as Trinity to hold together the variety of ways the Trinity relates *ad intra* and *ad extra*. As chapter 4 revealed, the tradition has opted for more speculative and philosophical constructions of God-world relations, such as procession, missions, appropriations, and the like. However, many contemporary Protestant theologians (for example, Arthur Peacocke, Sallie McFague, and Jürgen Moltmann) and Catholic theologians (including Joseph Bracken, John Haught, Walter Kasper, Catherine LaCugna, Denis Edwards, and Teilhard de Chardin) have pointed out the inadequacy of Western classical theism in conceptualizing the Trinity in authentic and intimate relation to the cosmos. This inadequacy stems in part from its insistence on utilizing substance ontology to speak of the nature of being. As a result, it continues to describe the ontological distinction between the Creator and creation in terms of discrete "substances." Because different substances cannot be internally present to each other, the created realm has been conceived not only as "outside" of God but also as opposed to God. Thus, God's ongoing influence in history and on creation could only be conceived in terms of interventions from outside the world. Peacocke accurately presented the problem confronting those attempting to represent the God-world relationship in ways as constitutive, intimate, and enduring as the relations that constitute God and the world themselves:

> It has become increasingly difficult to express the way in which God is present to the world in terms of 'substances', which by definition cannot be internally present to each other. . . . We therefore need a new model for expressing the closeness of God's presence to the finite natural events, entities, structures and processes and we need it to be as close as possible to imagine, without dissolving, the distinction between Creator and what is created.[32]

In response to the problem presented by substance ontology, these theologians have shifted to the realm of relational ontology to discover the "new model" they were seeking. Echoing themes that have run through this book thus far, Walter Cardinal Kasper asserted that "the ultimate and highest reality is not substance but relation."[33] Australian theologian Denis Edwards has written similarly, suggesting "reality . . . is more a network of relationships than a world of substances."[34] The late Catherine LaCugna, in her book G*od for Us: The Trinity and Christian Life,* concluded from the ontological traditions of Greek and Latin theology that "*personhood is the meaning of being.* To define what something is, we must ask who it is or how it is related. . . . We need now to specify the ontology appropriate to this insight, namely an ontology of relation or communion."[35] Ultimately, LaCugna expressed a conclusion thoroughly consistent with this investigation so far: "A relational ontology understands both God and the creature to exist and meet as persons in communion . . . God's To-Be is To-Be-in-relationship, and God's being-in-relationship-to-us *is* what God is."[36]

---

32. Peacocke, *Paths from Science*, 138.

33. Kasper, *The God of Jesus Christ*, 156.

34. Denis Edwards, "The Discovery of Chaos and the Retrieval of the Trinity," in *Chaos and Complexity: Scientific Perspectives on Divine Action*, ed. Robert J. Russell, Nancey C. Murphy, and Arthur R. Peacocke (Berkeley: Center for Theology & the Natural Sciences, 1995), 60.

35. Catherine M. LaCugna, *God for Us: The Trinity and Christian Life* (San Francisco: Harper Collins, 1991), 248–249 (italics in the original).

36. Ibid., 250 (italics in the original).

Hence, if "God's To-Be is To-Be-in-relationship, and God's being-in-relationship-to-us *is* what God is," can the panentheistic model adequately communicate that essential Being-in-Relation within God and between God and the cosmos in a Christian context? With many contemporary theologians, this book says yes.[37] Moreover, contrary to other models of God-world relation, panentheism demonstrates that it can not only express the intimate and internal relationality of God and the cosmos but also balance many beliefs about God and the cosmos that are significant to Christians. As subsequent chapters demonstrate, beliefs about God held in balance by panentheism include understanding God as Trinity in transcendent, incarnate, and immanent relation to creation; as Creator and Source of cosmic being; as necessary and free; as omnipotent and omniscient; and as attentive, compassionate, and responsive to the cosmos. Beliefs about the cosmos held in balance by panentheism include understanding the cosmos as beloved creation of God; as bearing inbuilt propensities for growth and development; as finite and contingent; as full of potential and radically free; as embodied and inspirited; and as historical and self-transcendent.

Several consequences flow from appropriating the panentheistic model as this book moves toward envisioning creation, incarnation, and grace as intimate and enduring relations between God and the cosmos. First, if, as suggested previously, God as Trinity is ontologically understood in terms of particular relations to the cosmos—relations that have been designated as transcendent, incarnate, and immanent in keeping with the Christian tradition and with panentheism—classical distinctions between knowing who God is *in se* and who God is in relation to creation are resolved. Therefore, rather than an understanding of God that relies on philosophical speculation about the inner life of the Trinity, knowledge of God is inferred from the way God is experienced in relation to the cosmos and its creatures. One could articulate this by restating Rahner's Rule in relational terms: "The Trinity in relation to creation

---

37. In his essay "Naming a Quiet Revolution: The Panentheistic Turn in Modern Theology," in *In Whom We Live and Move and Have Our Being: Panentheistic Reflections on God's Presence in a Scientific World,* ed. Philip Clayton and Arthur Peacocke (Grand Rapids, MI: Eerdmans, 2004): 1–15, Michael Brierley lists more than 70 theologians, philosophers, and movements associated with panentheism.

is the Trinity in relation *in se* and the Trinity in relation *in se* is the Trinity in relation to creation." Secondly, if God as Trinity is ontologically understood as Being-in-Transcendent-Incarnate-and-Immanent-Relation to the cosmos, then no aspect of God as Trinity is detached from the God-cosmos relationship. Hence, all events in the life of the cosmos—events of birth and death, of joy and pain, of comfort and suffering, of peace and war, of growth and diminishment, of well-being and woe—are events in the life of God, who responds no differently *ad intra* as opposed *ad extra*. Finally, if God *is* how God *relates* to the cosmos and its creatures, then attributes of God must be inferable from the experience of God communicated through the cosmos. Thus, however inadequate and faltering they may be, images for the Divine drawn from the cosmic and human experience of God remain appropriate means by which to express the triune mystery of God, trusting that "All that is created is embraced by the inner unity of the divine life of the Creator—Transcendent, Incarnate, and Immanent."[38]

RE-VISIONING TRINITARIAN ACTION IN A PANENTHEISTIC MODEL

In his book *Religion and Science*, Ian Barbour affirmed that the model of God to which one ascribes has implications for the way one envisions divine action or agency toward the world. Although some of the terminology that Barbour uses reflects the language of God-world relationship used previously, his ways of referring to theologies, models of God, and modes of agency are uniquely his own. Barbour's clarity in demonstrating the connection among each theology, model, and mode of action is illuminative for the task of revisioning divine agency in a panentheistic model of God as Trinity that the following chapters undertake.

---

38. Arthur Peacocke, "The New Biology and Nature, Man and God," in *The Experiment of Life: Proceedings of the 1981 William Temple Centenary Conference*, ed. F. Kenneth Hare (Toronto: University of Toronto, 1983), 35.

Barbour's Models of Divine Relation and Divine Agency

Barbour correlates nine theological schools of thought with the dominant model of God-world relation and mode of divine agency associated with each.[39] Classical theology aligns with a monarchical model of God-world relation with a mode of agency characterized by omnipotence, omniscience, and immutable sovereignty. Deist theology envisions the God-world relationship through the analogy of the Clockmaker and a clock. God acts as the Designer of a law-abiding world. A theistic model of God-world relation, which Barbour terms the Neo-Thomist model, is analogous to the relation between a Workman and a tool, in which God as primary cause (the Workman) acts in the world through secondary causes (the tools).

In dialogue with contemporary science, Barbour next proposes a quantum theology in which God is Determiner of the World's Indeterminacies. In accord with the Heisenberg Principle, events in a quantum universe are not predictable in advance; the best one can hope for is a range of possible outcomes to a particular situation. Hence, the role of the Divine in such a universe is to be the Actualizer of Potentialities. The Divine acts by selecting a particular potentiality from the range of possibilities at any given time and actualizing that potentiality as a particular outcome.

Barbour returns to a more traditional school of thought with the Word or Logos theology. The dominant God-world relation in this theology is that of Speaker to hearer. In keeping with this model, God acts in the world as Communicator of Information through which patterns of events take shape, divine intentions and purposes are made known, and novel structures are conceived and organized. This information is freely communicated without a pre-determined plan or outcome. Hence, cosmic and human freedom and agency is preserved. A less traditional form of this theology, what Barbour calls linguistic theology, is actualized in the relation between an Agent and an action. It envisions events in the world as divine actions, as communications of divine intentions, which nonetheless require interpretation to discern the purposes of the Divine in a particular experience.

---

39. Barbour, *Religion and Science*, 305–25.

Another theology Barbour considers is kenotic or self-emptying theology. This theology implies a God-world relation modeled
on that of a Parent and child. While the Divine remains essentially
omnipotent, the love of the Parent for the child calls for voluntary
self-limitation and vulnerability. Because authentic love is always
accompanied by freedom and detachment in order that the child
may mature to full flourishing, it necessarily entails vulnerability and
risk. Nonetheless, it is a vulnerability and risk full of fidelity, patience,
and enduring presence. Barbour next proposes an embodiment theology, which construes the God-world relation as a Person-body
relation. In this model, the universe is conceived as the body of God,
and thus, God knows and responds to events in the cosmos as a person knows and responds to the events within one's body. Barbour is
quick to point out that proponents of this model do not subscribe to
a mind/body or spirit/body dualism; nonetheless, they do discern a
level of self-consciousness and self-awareness that distinguishes one's
personhood from one's embodiment. Finally, Barbour discusses a
process model of theology, which envisions the Divine as the Leader
of a Community. Consistent with the principles of process theology,
God acts as a Creative Participant in the cosmic community—luring,
drawing, teaching, and persuading the community of cosmic beings,
individually and collectively, toward new and fuller life.

Divine Relation and Agency in Trinitarian Panentheism

In keeping with Barbour's valid insight that the model of God to
which one ascribes has implications for the way one envisions divine
action or agency toward the world, the revisioning of Trinity within
a panentheistic model of God-world relation calls for a re-vision of
how the Trinity acts in the world within a panentheistic model as well.

How might Barbour's systematic analysis of the connections
among theology, divine-world relation, and divine agency influence
such a movement from ontology to agency in this present study? To
define the parameters established thus far, the theology is Christian
Trinitarian and the model of God-world relation is panentheism. Both
Trinity and panentheism are grounded in a relational ontology, as are
the cosmos and its creatures with which the Trinity relates. A logical line of thought suggests that a relational theology grounded in a

relational ontology and expressed in a relational model of God and
world calls for a mode of agency that is relational as well. Nonetheless, consistent with how panentheism was appropriated as a model
of God-world relation, the mode of divine agency selected must fulfill certain conditions. These conditions include coherence with the
Christian understanding of God as Trinity, consistency with the evolutionary worldview observed by the sciences, and expression of the radical relationality that characterize cosmic, human, and divine being.

A point of departure is the principal ways the Christian tradition says that the Trinity has ostensibly acted in or on the world. As
demonstrated in chapter 4, the three most central God-world interactions in the tradition are creation, incarnation, and grace. Each of
these ways of acting in or on the world has traditionally been appropriated to one of the Persons of the Trinity: creation to the Father,
incarnation to the Son, and grace to the Holy Spirit.

As pointed out, however, Christianity has traditionally viewed
and described these divine actions as isolated or occasional interventions that sometimes disrupted the course of nature or of human
events. The act of creation has generally been thought of as a singular occurrence that happened at a moment forever past; the cosmos
came into being from nothing through the word of a lone Creator.
The event of the Incarnation, in which the Word of God became
flesh in Jesus of Nazareth, is proclaimed as a once-and-for-all phenomenon that lasted some thirty years more than 2,000 years ago.
Finally, although grace is still seen as operative in the midst of life,
it is most often understood as a discrete thing that God gives, rather
than as a way God relates to the world.

Nevertheless, the natural and physical sciences, the social and
behavioral sciences, and the Christian tradition have revealed that
nothing about the cosmos, the person, or the Divine is isolated,
singular, once-and-for-all, or discrete. All being at the very core of
Being is relational! Hence, if what one *is* is essentially relational, then
as a consequence, what one *does* must be essentially relational because
one can only act in accord with one's essential nature. A relational
ontology demands a relational agency.

Hence, fidelity to the relational ontology of the Trinity, the cosmos, and the human person calls for a reinterpretation of the divine
activities of creation, incarnation, and grace in terms of essential and

particular relations between the Triune God and cosmic and human being—relations most appropriately expressed through a panentheistic paradigm. This is a cosmos envisioned by the natural and physical sciences as a web of interrelations evolving within, between, and among beings in kaleidoscopic complexity. This is a humanity that the social and behavioral sciences see as inextricably interconnected, evolving in consciousness and personhood through global networks and interactions. This is a Triune God whom Christian theology calls Love, whose very nature is self-giving and self-communicating and in whose very Being all being participates.

SUMMARY

This present chapter began with the assertion that, because the nature of divine, cosmic, and human beings is essentially and intrinsically relational, it is entirely appropriate to speak of fundamental and integral relations between and among them as well. It went on to examine the power and limits of human language that one must inevitably use in articulating the mystery of God. It pointed out that, as one embarks on an exploration of models of God, it is particularly important to understand that any interpretations drawn from created reality and applied to divine reality should be characterized by the scholarly tentativeness. Such tentativeness signals the realization that one cannot speak as if one-to-one correspondence exists between finite words and infinite reality. However, neither can one speak as if these words bore no intrinsic connection to that reality. Because of this, theology has recourse to the figurative and imagistic language of analogy, models, and metaphors to articulate the attributes of divine mystery in terms accessible to human experience. While the fullness of the Infinite Reality of which theology speaks is essentially inexpressible, it is, nonetheless, a Reality that continually self-communicates to believers in every age.

In addition to attempting to express the attributes of Infinite Reality *in se*, theology and philosophy have also attempted to propose ways in which Infinite Reality relates and interacts with the finite realities of cosmic and human life. This chapter discussed four principal models through which this has been done. The first is deism, which accepts the reality of God as a "Supreme Architect" whose existence is discernible through reason brought to bear on the observable in nature. The second is its converse, pantheism, which identifies God with the totality of nature, with the laws of nature, or as the world soul inherent in nature. The third is the model of theism, which views God as a personal and purposeful eternal Being who both transcends the world and yet is immanent within it. The fourth and final model discussed in this chapter was panentheism, the belief that the Being of God includes and penetrates the whole universe, so that every part of it exists in God, but that Divine Being is more than, and is not exhausted by, the universe.

The model of panentheism that this chapter envisions as compatible with the relational, evolutionary, and Christian worldview grounds the proposals of this text. Panentheism has the capacity to balance divine transcendence and immanence, to maintain the ontological distinction between Creator and creature, to provide for a truly intimate, affective, and participative God-world relationship, and to include the God-world relationality demanded by Christian belief in the Incarnation and in the Being of God as Trinity. Moreover, within an ontology of relation, the model of panentheism serves well in demonstrating how God can be viewed in transcendent, incarnate, and immanent relationship with creation. It also supplies the paradigm through which each Trinitarian Person-as-Relation is constituted as unique and personal. Finally, panentheism assimilates the relations of origin, emergence, and effect in such a way as to validate their coincidence with the Christian doctrines of creation, incarnation, and grace.

Hence, informed by the relational ontology of divine, cosmic, and human being, the relational panentheistic paradigm of God-world relation, and the demand for a relational agency consistent with each, the chapters that follow propose a reinterpretation of divine creation, incarnation, and grace—frequently interpreted as discrete and occasional acts—as more fittingly understood as intimate and enduring relations between God and the evolving cosmos. In doing so, it sets forth a view of the Christian God as intimately and ceaselessly present and active in the evolving history of the cosmos. This is a God nearer to us than we are to ourselves, a God of relation dynamically engaged in the full flourishing of creation and its creatures.

FOR FURTHER READING

Barbour, Ian. *Myths, Models, and Paradigms.* London: SCM, 1974.

Johnson, Elizabeth A. *She Who Is: The Mystery of God in Feminist Theological Discourse.* New York: Crossroads, 1992.

McFague, Sallie. *Models of God: Theology for an Ecological Nuclear Age.* Philadelphia: Fortress, 1987.

Introduction to

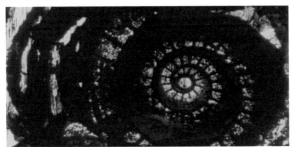

PART II

T he first part of this book set forth the concept of relational ontology and the way it manifests itself in cosmic, human, and divine being through relations of origin, effect, and emergence.

By design, the chapters on the cosmos and the human person focused primarily on philosophy and on the natural, physical, behavioral, and social sciences to substantiate their claims about the relational nature of all reality. With chapter 4, on divine being, however, the line of thought took a decided turn toward the theological and now continues on that line for the remainder of this exploration. On this path, concepts from the earlier chapters on cosmic, human, and divine being return in an expanded and developed form in dialogue with Christian doctrine and the Triune Christian God. As a result, the cosmic, human, and Divine interact in perhaps new and surprising ways, deepening and amplifying the grasp of—and the mystery of—relation within and between God and the world, relations that the Christian tradition terms *creation*, *incarnation*, and *grace*.

Chapters 6 through 8 unfold in five movements. Each chapter begins with a summary of the traditional Christian doctrines on creation, incarnation, and grace, respectively. Secondly, each introduces and explores the salient element of evolutionary theory associated with that doctrine. The third section of the chapters reinterprets the traditional doctrine in terms of a God-world relation derived from the insights of evolutionary theory and Christian theology. The fourth movement discusses how this doctrinal reinterpretation revises traditional images of God. Finally, the fifth section seeks resonances of the particular evolutionary relation in the biblical, ecclesial, liturgical, and theological traditions of Christianity.

The first aspect of God-world relation considered is cosmic being in dialogue with the Christian doctrine of creation as a *relation of origin*. This perspective envisions God as the continuous Creator of the evolving cosmos, in, with, and through the very evolutionary processes and structures of the cosmos itself. The second aspect of God-world relation considered is human being in dialogue with the Christian doctrine of incarnation as a *relation of emergence*. This perspective envisions God as not only incarnate Word-made-flesh in the unique person of Jesus of Nazareth but also as incarnate and enduring Word-made-matter, continuously revealing Godself in enduring and ontological relation to cosmos as a whole. The third aspect of God-world relation considered is cosmic being in dialogue with the Christian doctrine of grace as a *relation of effect*. This perspective envisions God as the transcendent and transformative impulse and power, spurring and urging both natural and human beings along their journey of self-transcendence toward fullness of union with God.

Chapter 6

CREATION AS RELATION IN AN EVOLVING COSMOS

> "The postulate of God as Creator of all-that-is is not,
> in its most profound form, a statement about what happened
> at a particular point in time. To speak of God as Creator is a
> postulate about a perennial or 'eternal'—that is to say,
> timeless—relation of God to the world."[1]

INTRODUCTION

By all accounts, the starting point for a Christian doctrine of creation is in the Hebrew scriptures. While the principal focus is on the Genesis account in the beginning of the Bible, the Hebrew and Christian scriptures contain more than a dozen passages that give a variety of meanings and nuances to the creedal phrase, "the Maker [Creator] of heaven and earth." Some of these passages speak of God as the one "who created the heavens and stretched them out, who spreads out the earth with its crops, who gives breath to its people and spirit to those who walk on it" (Isaiah 42:5); who fashions the cosmos as a potter models clay (Isaiah 45:9; Jeremiah 18:1–6; Romans

---

1. Arthur R. Peacocke, *God and the New Biology* (San Francisco: Harper & Row, 1986), 95. *God and the New Biology.*

9:20–21); whose fingers shape the heavens (Psalms 8:4) and whose wisdom wrought Earth and its creatures (Psalms 104). God the Creator "founded the earth . . . determined its size . . . stretched out the measuring line for it . . . and laid the cornerstone" (Jeremiah 38:4–6). More marvelous still, when God simply "spoke, it came to be, commanded, it stood in place" (Psalms 33:9). In the Gospels and Epistles, this Divine Word through whom the universe came into being is identified with the Divine Word that became flesh in Christ. John's Gospel proclaims that through this Word of God, "All things came to be . . . and without him nothing came to be" (1:3). Moreover, the Letter to the Hebrews affirms that "the universe was ordered by the word of God" (11:3) and 2 Peter adds that "earth was formed out of water and through water by the word of God" (3:5). Premier among the biblical narratives that allude to the creative activity of the Divine, however, is the story of creation recounted in the epic poetry of Genesis 1:1—2:3.

THEOLOGY AND DOCTRINE OF CREATION
Genesis 1:1—2:3

In his discussion of the Genesis creation narrative, theologian James Wiseman points out that, although Genesis 1:1 has frequently been translated "In the beginning God created the heavens and earth," biblical scholars such as Richard Clifford and Roland Murphy dispute the accuracy of that translation. They assert that the verse (1:1–2a) is better rendered as "When God began to create heaven and earth—earth being formless and void." Likewise, E. A. Speiser: "When God set about to create heaven and earth—the world being then a formless waste." Although a question about the translation of the text remains, there is no question about the actor or the action in the text. The scriptures use the Hebrew verb *bara'*, translated as *create*, only when God is the subject. When the human—and sometimes God—"makes" an object, the verb used is *'asah*. This verb selection for the divine activity in Genesis makes clear that when God is said to "create," something qualitatively different is going on.[2]

---

2. James Wiseman, *Theology and Modern Science: Quest for Coherence* (New York: Continuum, 2002), 37–38.

To some, the disagreements about translation among biblical scholars may seem of little consequence. Nonetheless, the alternative renderings have called into question a metaphysical principle held from ancient times. This principle is articulated in two particular scripture verses and holds that "God did not make [the heaven and the earth and all that is in them] out of existing things" (2 Maccabees 7:28) and that "what is visible came into being through the invisible" (Hebrews 11:3). Although these verses, like many others, are open to multiple interpretations, the convictions articulated in them are two-fold: first, the universe had a temporal beginning, and, second, in the beginning, God created all that is *ex nihilo*, out of nothing.

Creatio ex Nihilo

What is at stake in the doctrine of *creatio ex nihilo*? Theologically, this doctrine preserves the unique eternality and sovereignty of God. Metaphysically, it rules out the possibility that matter was likewise a fundamental, primary, and eternal principle. The issue is this: If matter were uncreated like God, then matter shares ontological primacy and equality with God. Thus, God would no longer be one who "creates" (*bara'*) in a wholly unique way, but simply one who "makes" (*'asah*) from existing materials as any human artisan might. As Theophilus, patriarch of Antioch, argued in the second century CE,

> If God is uncreated and matter is uncreated, then . . . God is no longer the Creator of all things. . . . What great thing would it be if God made the world out of existing matter? Even a human artist, when he obtains materials from some-one, makes of it whatever he pleases. But the power of God is made evident in this, that [God] makes out of what does *not* exist whatever [God] pleases, and the giving of life and movement belongs to none other, but to God alone.[3]

Consistent with such an assertion is the thought of second-century Christian theologian Irenaeus of Lyons. He emphasized that the capacity to create *ex nihilo* was an ontological statement about the very nature of God, of such significance as to distinguish human

---

3. Theophilus of Antioch, *Ad Autolycum* 2, 4, in *The Faith of the Early Fathers*, vol. 1, trans. W. A. Jurgens (Collegeville, MN: Liturgical Press, 1970), 75.

being from Divine Being: "Humans . . . are not able to make something from nothing. . . . God, however, is greater than humans first
of all in this: that when nothing existed beforehand, [God] called
into existence the very material for . . . creation."[4]

Affirming the insights of these second-century theologians,
Augustine of Hippo in the fourth century and Bonaventure in the
thirteenth century contended that one could prove the temporal
beginning of matter through philosophical reasoning. For his part,
however, Thomas Aquinas asserted that creation and *creatio ex nihilo*
by God was an article of belief, not demonstrable by proof. The
novitas mundi, newness of the world, Aquinas maintained, could be
known only through divine revelation and apprehended only through
faith. As he stated in the *Summa Theologiae*, "By faith alone do we
hold, and by no demonstration can it be proved, that the world did
not always exist."[5]

Whether demonstrable by proof or an article of belief, the
doctrine of *creatio ex nihilo* nonetheless echoed down the centuries
with the same resonances of ontological distinction and ontological
dependence struck by these earlier theologians. In the last century,
professor of theology Keith Ward of Oxford continued to assert,
"The doctrine of creation *ex nihilo* simply maintains . . . that the
universe is other than God and wholly dependent upon God for its
existence."[6] In his book *God in Creation*, theologian Jürgen Moltmann crafts a similar explanation:

> Wherever and whatever God creates is without any precon-
> ditions. There is no external necessity which occasions his
> creativity, and no inner compulsion which could determine
> it. Nor is there any primordial matter whose potentiality is
> pre-given to his creative activity, and which would set him
> material limits.[7]

---

4. Irenaeus of Lyons, *Adversus haereses* 2, 10, 4, in *The Faith of the Early Father*, 87.

5. Aquinas, *ST*, I.46.2.

6. Keith Ward, "God as a Principle of Cosmological Explanation," in *Quantum
Cosmology and the Laws of Nature: Scientific Perspectives on Divine Action*, 2nd ed., eds.
Robert John Russell, Nancey Murphy, and C. J. Isham (Berkeley, CA: Center for The-
ology and the Natural Sciences, 1996), 248–49.

7. Jürgen Moltmann, *God in Creation*, trans. Margaret Kohl (Minneapolis: Fortress, 1993), 74.

While the particular how and when of *creatio ex nihilo* may remain unresolved, this theological notion clearly claims that, if God had not acted to bring the universe into being freely and unconditionally, what Moltmann calls *creatio e libertate Dei*, and if God had not sustained the existence given it in like manner, "there would be only nothing."[8]

Creation as Relation

While the centuries between patristic and contemporary theology have not brought significant changes to the concept of *creatio ex nihilo*, there has been development in the understanding of the theological meaning of creation itself. The tendency to identify the notion of creation solely with the singular divine act of *creatio ex nihilo* has, according to twentieth-century theologian William Carroll, resulted in a "fundamental confusion . . . about what creation is." Carroll contends that narrowing the notion of creation to one extraordinary act of *creatio ex nihilo* truncates the meaning of the concept. However, if understood as a metaphysical and theological concept, rather than as a particular act, then the concept of creation "affirms that all that is, in whatever way or ways it is, depends upon God as cause."[9] In other words, the most basic sense of the cosmos as "creation" is not about *temporal* origination, but about ontological dependence upon God, a primal dependence that physicist and theologian Robert John Russell terms "ontological origination."[10]

In his writings, Jesuit philosopher Frederick Copleston contends that even Aquinas's understanding of God as First Cause did not denote a temporal sequence, but an ontological hierarchy of causal activity. For Aquinas, the sequence of causality is "not a lineal or horizontal series, so to speak, but a vertical hierarchy, in which a

---

8. Ted Peters, "On Creating the Cosmos," in *Physics, Philosophy, and Theology: A Common Quest for Understanding*, 3rd ed., eds. Robert John Russell, William R. Stoeger, and George V. Coyne (Vatican City: Vatican Observatory Foundation, 1997), 288.

9. William Carroll, "As It Was in the Beginning," *Notre Dame Magazine*, available from *http://magazine.nd.edu/news/15913-as-it-was-in-the-beginning/*.

10. Robert John Russell, "Finite Creation without a Beginning: The Doctrine of Creation in Relation to Big Bang and Quantum Cosmologies," in *Quantum Cosmology*, 294.

lower member depends here and now on the present causal activity of the member above it." With reference to God as First Cause, therefore, "the word 'first' does not mean first in the temporal order but supreme or first in the ontological order,"[11] that is, as ground, or source, of being. Such a perspective views creation less as a transcendent, discrete act at a time long past than as an ongoing relation of being between God and the world. In the case of creation "in the beginning," it denotes that this ongoing relation of being is, moreover, a primordial relationship, akin to the relation of origin described in this text.

Scientist-theologian Arthur Peacocke echoes this understanding of creation as a relation of ontological dependence, of cosmic contingency, and of divine necessity: "The principle stress in the Judeo-Christian doctrine of creation . . . is on the dependence and contingency of all entities, and events, other than God himself: it is about a personal relationship between God and the world and not about the beginning of the Earth, or the whole universe, at a point in time."[12] Therefore, rather than understanding creation as a singular event, effected by a sole Creator at a moment long past, Peacocke asserts that "the postulate of God as Creator of all-that-is . . . is a postulate about a perennial or 'eternal' . . . relation of God to the world, a relation that involves differentiation and interaction."[13] Moreover, this perennial or eternal relation is quite suitably modeled by a panentheistic paradigm. Within this model—in which the Being of God includes, indwells, and yet transcends the whole universe—the creative relation of God as the original ground and source of cosmic being is rightfully termed *transcendent*, because the cosmos, like a child in the mother's womb, depends on a being beyond itself for its very existence. In keeping with the principles of relational ontology, the relation of divine transcendence differentiates the Being of God from that of the cosmos. God as the ground of cosmic being subsumes and yet exceeds the being of the universe. Hence, God is not one ordinary cause or entity among others in the

---

11. Frederick C. Copleston, *Aquinas* (Baltimore, MD: Penguin Books, 1961), 118–20.

12. Peacocke, *Creation and the World of Science*, 78. *Creation and the World of Science.*

13. Peacocke, *God and the New Biology*, 95.

complex causality and structure of the cosmos and is understood as ontologically "other than" the cosmos.[14]

At the same time, the panentheistic model also differentiates the ontology of the cosmos from that of God because cosmic being is dependent and contingent upon the creative and sustaining Being of God.[15] So, does this mean that the perennial and enduring relation of creation is rightly appropriated to God in divine transcendence? Because God is the Source and Ground as well as the Matrix of cosmic existence, is the relation of creation in the panentheistic model appropriate to God as Mother, or, in the traditional model, as Father? Before answering that question and appropriating creation as a transcendent relation between God and the cosmos, it is important to see what evolutionary theory adds to an understanding of creation and how it influences thinking about the God-world relation of creation.

EVOLUTIONARY PERSPECTIVES ON THE COSMOS AS CREATION

As introduced in chapter 2, the scientific description of the cosmos as creation begins at a time nearly 14 billion years ago. When no more than a fraction of a second old, the cosmos took the form of a compressed fireball, a "primeval, unimaginably condensed mass of fundamental particles and energy," consisting of the most basic subatomic elements of matter-energy-space-time.[16] At a particular moment, which scientists term "t=0," all elements of matter, energy, space, and time that would ever exist erupted as a single quantum gift of existence from what scientists term the Big Bang, but which Brian Swimme and Thomas Berry characterize as "the primordial flaring forth."[17] From original unity came diversity. From primeval darkness

---

14. Arthur Peacocke, "Chance and Law in Irreversible Thermodynamics, Theoretical Biology, and Theology," in *Chaos and Complexity: Scientific Perspectives on Divine Action*, eds. Robert J. Russell, Nancey Murphy, and Arthur Peacocke (Vatican City State: Vatican Observatory Foundation, 1995), 138.

15. Peacocke, *Creation and the World of Science*, 77–78.

16. Peacocke, "Theology and Science Today," 30.

17. Brian Swimme and Thomas Berry, *The Universe Story: From the Primordial Flaring Forth to the Ecozoic Era—A Celebration of the Unfolding of the Cosmos* (San Francisco: HarperSanFrancisco, 1994), 7.

came light. From conditions "scarcely present in the early stages of the universe's history" came "conditions of chemical composition and temperature and radiation, permitting, through the interplay of chance and necessity, the coming into being of replicating molecules and life. . . . Thus evolution began on planet Earth."[18]

Beyond the questions that surround the Big Bang theory of the origin of the cosmos, there also exists considerable debate as to how the earliest structures that could be called "living" came into existence and developed the ability to replicate themselves. Some in philosophy have postulated a metaphysical drive that brings emergent forms into existence, especially when such forms are living. This postulate, called *vitalism*, contends that the initial emergence of life forms on Earth cannot be explained in solely materialistic terms reducible to physics and chemistry. It must be attributed to a vital principle, an energy, or force *extrinsic* to creation that causes life to begin. Principal proponents of vitalism included French philosopher Henri Bergson and German philosopher Hans A. E. Driesch, as well as Jesuit philosopher and paleontologist Pierre Teilhard de Chardin. Teilhard hypothesized that a spark of divine life was present throughout the evolutionary process, forming and informing the process as much as the physical forces. This divine spark of life is present as two forms of energy within the organism. One might think of these as potential types of energy like chemical, mechanical, and nuclear stored in an organism. Teilhard postulated that all living beings had two forces of energy within them: radial energy and tangential energy. These energies existed in different proportions to each other in an organism or system. Where tangential energy proves the stronger of the two—for example, in nonhuman forms of life such as plants and animals—the evolutionary process operates within the natural laws of chance and necessity in the direction of biological development and emergence. When radial energy prevails, as it does in human persons, the supernatural forces of divine creativity and consciousness direct the course of evolution toward greater intellectual and spiritual complexity.[19]

---

18. Polkinghorne, *One World*, 56.

19. Pierre Teilhard de Chardin, *The Phenomenon of Man*, trans. Bernard Wall (New York: Harper and Row, 1959), 53–77, 141–90.

Another prominent approach to the question of the emergence of life, of novel forms, and of greater complexity in the universe asserts that such innovation and intricacy require the concept of intelligent design and, for some, of an Intelligent Designer. *Intelligent design* refers to the assumption that the incredible novelty, complexity, and intricacies of cosmic life could not have simply emerged from the natural or coincidental dynamism present in the universe. Rather, a particular being, principle, or mechanism must exist that purposefully and explicitly set the parameters and/or conditions for the emergence of life and novel forms in the universe. Moreover, such design is not only purposeful and explicit but also intelligent as revealed in the marvelous intelligibility and fit observable in the cosmic order.

Few who observe the workings of the universe would deny the profound rationality expressed through the inherent orderliness and precision of the structures and processes of the cosmos.[20] As Albert Einstein claimed, "The eternal mystery of the world is its comprehensibility."[21] For some, the Intelligent Designer represents a personalization of such rationality in the universe, the one "who not only conceives of but actually makes each [entity] . . . separately and individually all at once."[22] Some scientists such as Gunther S. Stent have also equated such rationality with God. According to Peacocke, Stent believed that "'God' is the single principle that regulates everything and makes science possible."[23]

However, consensus is elusive when it comes to thinking on cosmic intelligibility and emergence in terms of intelligent design or an Intelligent Designer. Some thinkers do suggest that the intrinsic rationality of the cosmos supports a deistic or theistic interpretation of creation by an Intelligent Designer. In contrast, others claim that it renders the notion of a deity unnecessary, because it implies that the universe itself possesses the organizational and regulatory principles needed for the beginning and emergence of life. A third group contends that the reality of intrinsic cosmic intelligibility is irrelevant

---

20. Peacocke, *Theology for a Scientific Age*, 103–104.

21. Albert Einstein, *Out of My Later Years* (Westport, CT: Greenwood, 1970), 61.

22. Peacocke, *Paths from Science*, 69.

23. Peacocke, *God and the New Biology*, 60.

to any argument concerning either the divine design of the universe or the existence of an Intelligent Designer.[24] Finally, there are those such as Arthur Peacocke who not only believe that the notion of intelligent design springs from the "false supposition that molecular systems could not self-organize into such cycles." He also concludes that, in addition to its *intelligent* design, an evolutionary account of the cosmos includes "what might objectively be called the notable *imperfections* of 'design' in the features of many living organisms."[25]

Without resorting to reductionism, vitalism, or intelligent design, most scientists maintain that the emergence of cosmic life can be explained from the natural laws and regularities operating in the universe. Biochemists such as Ilya Prigogine and Gregoire Nicolis have demonstrated that fluctuations within certain living systems and organisms produce changes in the structure of the organism or system. In their studies, they found a class of systems with what they called "dissipative structures." These structures enable organisms or systems to maintain themselves in a state of order, although far from equilibrium. They found that when fluctuations in a system are amplified to a particular frequency, the entire system undergoes structural change. It becomes a newly ordered state with the capacity to take in energy and matter from the outside to maintain its novel form. They reasoned that a similar process of order-through-fluctuation made the conditions for the initial emergence of living organisms, as well as for their ongoing development, highly probable.[26]

Biophysical chemist Manfred Eigen and his colleagues in Göttingen, Germany, researched the effect of the interplay of chance and law on the emergence and development of macromolecules.[27] Using game theory, the study of how interactions among agents or participants in a situation produce outcomes, Eigen and Ruthild Winkler

---

24. See Michael J. Behe, *Darwin's Black Box: The Biochemical Challenge to Evolution* (New York: Touchstone Books, 1996); William Dembski, *The Design Inference: Eliminating Chance through Small Probabilities* (Cambridge: Cambridge University, 1999); and Kenneth E. Himma, "Design Arguments for the Existence of God, *The Internet Encyclopedia of Philosophy*, available from *http://www.iep.utm.edu/d/design.htm.*

25. Peacocke, *Paths from Science*, 69, italics added.

26. Ilya Prigogine and Gregoire Nicolis, "Biological Order, Structure and Instabilities," *Quarterly Review of Biophysics* 4 (1971): 107–48.

27. Manfred Eigen and Ruthild Winkler, *The Laws of the Game: How the Principles of Nature Govern Chance*, trans. Robert Kimber (New York: Knopf, 1981).

established with some precision what combination of law and chance would permit a population of information-carrying macromolecules to develop into a dominant species with the capacity for further evolution. They were led to conclude that

> the evolution of life, if it is based on a derivable physical principle [i.e., from an existing source], must be considered an *inevitable* process despite its indeterminate course . . . it is not only inevitable "in principle" but also sufficiently probable within a realistic span of time. It requires appropriate environmental conditions . . . and their maintenance. These conditions have existed on Earth.[28]

Therefore, supported by research such as this, evolutionary theory concludes that the process of the evolution of life "cosmologically, inorganically, geologically, [and] biologically" involves "a continuous, almost kaleidoscopic, recombination of the component units of the universe into an increasing diversity of forms."[29] In the course of this continuous recombination of existing units, the evolutionary process of the universe depends on certain factors that manifest particular characteristics.

Continuity and Natural Law

The universe manifests a characteristic *continuity of development* from one organized form to another. At each level of development, the cosmos gradually unfolds over great expanses of time the potential implicit in it from its very beginning as a compressed fireball. The continuity from the inorganic sphere through the biological sphere to the ecological sphere and so on depends on *natural laws* that guide the rates and possibilities of cosmic change and, hence, explain the transitions from one form to another.[30] However, ongoing scientific experimentation, observation, and research revealed that natural law was not the only factor operative in the evolutionary process.

---

28. Manfred Eigen, "*Molekulare Selbstorganisation und Evolution*," *Naturwissenschaften* 58, no. 10 (1971): 519. Trans. Arthur Peacocke, italics in the original.

29. Peacocke, "God as the Creator of the World of Science," 103.

30. Peacocke, *Science and the Christian Experiment* (Oxford: Oxford University Press, 1971), 82.

Emergence and Creativity

As the universe continued to evolve, its natural processes produced organisms of increasing uniqueness and particularity, yielding a splendid diversity of forms appropriate to particular environments. As described in previous chapters, these new forms were evidence of *emergence*—organisms and systems not fully explainable in terms of the components that constituted them and preceded them. As a result, scientists concluded that the evolutionary process demonstrated more than just continuity and regularity. The novel and unpredictable forms that developed through the process convinced scientists that the cosmos also displayed inherent *creativity*, as the potentialities of one level of molecular organization became actualized in new forms over great expanses of time.[31]

Chance and Indeterminacy

As discussed in chapter 2, the unpredictability of emergent outcomes and forms through the evolutionary process led scientists to conjecture that this process unfolded not only through the guidance of natural laws but also through the impact of chance occurrence. As chapter 2 explained, the attribution of chance applies to three scientific circumstances: (1) chance as scientific ignorance, (2) chance as a result of the intersection of two unrelated causal chains, and (3) chance as a manifestation of uncertainty at the quantum level. In the process of evolution, all three understandings of chance apply. Ignorance of parameters and quantum uncertainty are both operative in, for example, the mutation of the genetic material DNA. Frequently, scientists can neither identify or pinpoint the cause of genetic mutation nor anticipate the form and consequence that the mutation exhibits. This indeterminacy lasts until the mutation manifests itself at the macro level, at which point it displays regularity of development through the guidance of natural law. Hence, chance introduces an element of unpredictability into the equation at the molecular level but obeys the rules of the game at the level of populations.

---

31. Ibid., 77–88.

Because of the unpredictability of chance in the creative processes of the cosmos, some theorists see chance and the indeterminacy it produces as a form of "freedom" inherent in the cosmic organism. Physicist-theologian John Polkinghorne has given this propensity of the cosmos a name, calling it "free process" and paralleling it with the free will exercised by humans. According to Polkinghorne,

> In the great act of creation . . . God allows the physical world to be itself . . . in that independence which is Love's gift of freedom to the one beloved. The world is endowed in its fundamental constitution with . . . potentiality which makes it capable of fruitful evolution. The exploration and realization of that potentiality is achieved by the universe through the continual interplay of chance and necessity within its unfolding process. The cosmos is given the opportunity to be itself.[32]

From this perspective, God accords cosmic processes the same value and reverence that God accords to human choices. As a result, "the open flexibility of the world's processes affords the means by which the universe explores its potentialities, humankind exercises its will, and God interacts with . . . creation."[33] Nonetheless, this divine letting-go in love and freedom has particular consequences for the cosmos and its creatures, both human and nonhuman. On the positive side, the free process of creation in chance and law and the free will of humanity in choice and conscience are the basis for the inherent creativity of the natural and human order and serve as the means by which the cosmos and humanity unfold the wide-range of potentialities within living and conscious beings. Nonetheless, cosmic free process and human free will have a downside. Both the indeterminate interaction between chance and law and the unpredictable judgment of humans produce unforeseeable events in nature and in human life that cut short the life and growth of nonhuman and human creatures and work at cross-purposes with the creative movements of God.

---

32. John Polkinghorne, *Science and Providence: God's Interaction with the World* (Philadelphia: Templeton, 2005), 77.

33. Ibid., 78.

Consequences of Cosmic Creativity

As the scientific evidence from evolutionary cosmology and biology has demonstrated, creation is not something done once for all. It continues through the free process of cosmic being and through the free will of its human creatures. While free process produces a kaleidoscopic variety of cosmic life and well-being, it also spawns what humans often conceive as *natural evil*. This term describes events such as earthquakes, floods, tsunamis, and the like, as well as the biological breakdown of living organisms in diminishment and death. Moreover, while the human exercise of free will enables persons to act with purpose and direction, in sensitivity and love, and through self-transcendence and self-actualization, free will also give humans the capacity to inflict *moral evil* on one another, on creation, and on its creatures. "For humanity is free to go against the grain of creative processes, to reject God's creative intentions, to mar God's creation, and to bring into existence disharmonies uniquely of its own"; humanity has the capacity to make creation, its creatures, and even God suffer "in an especially distinctive way."[34]

Because of the divine choice to create the cosmos in this way—in autonomy and freedom, through chance within law, and indeterminate in principle—the continuing creation of the cosmos and its creatures results in a coincidence of opposites. Free process and free will not only occasion the emergence of new life forms but also the inevitably costly process of diminishment and death. They produce not only the kaleidoscopic fecundity that delights both creatures and Creator but also the calamitous events of pain and suffering. They create not only serendipitous moments of joy and well-being but also events that cause the destruction and extinction of cosmic and human life. Moreover, evolutionary theory contends that it was, in fact, the free process of self-creativity through chance and law in the cosmos that resulted in the emergence of free persons, humans who "are not the mere 'plaything of the gods,' or of God," but who are sharers in the "costly process of bringing forth the new."[35]

---

34. Ibid., 39.

35. Arthur Peacocke, "The Cost of New Life," in *The Work of Love: Creation as Kenosis*, edited by John Polkinghorne (Grand Rapids, MI: Eerdmans, 2001), 21–42 at 37.

INTERPRETING CREATION IN AN EVOLVING COSMOS

Observations such as these from the natural and physical sciences disclose that the concept of creation in an evolving universe cannot be limited to originating, sustaining, and preserving the cosmos. Evolutionary cosmology and biology have discovered a creative dynamism in the cosmos that has been ongoing since the origin of the universe and that has exercised its creativity in and through the very stuff of the material world. Because of these scientific findings, it has become evident that the theological notion of *creatio ex nihilo* as traditionally interpreted is a limited and, therefore, inadequate representation of the fullness of creative relation between God and the cosmos. Although *creatio ex nihilo* obviously preserves the transcendent differentiation of God from the universe and the dependence and contingency of the universe on God, it cannot accommodate the ongoing creativity of the cosmos, in which "the cosmos . . . sustained and held in being by God is a cosmos which has always been in the process of producing new emergent forms of matter."[36] Hence, static conceptions of God's differentiated relation to the cosmos, such as those of creative origination and faithful preservation, have to be augmented and nuanced by a notion of dynamic and continuous interaction between God and world. "For if the emergence of new forms of matter in the world is in some way an activity of God, then it must be regarded as his perennial activity and not something already completed," once and for all time.[37]

Theologically, this dynamic interaction between God as Creator and the cosmos as creation has been termed *creatio continua*. It arises from the understanding that the stuff of the world has an inbuilt creativity that makes the process of creation ongoing and incessant. Moreover, *if* God is understood as Creator and *if* the process of creation has been ongoing throughout cosmic history, into the present and the cosmic future, *then* the ceaseless creative processes revealed by the physical and biological sciences *must* be interpreted as the creative activity of God's very Self. In other words, "the stuff and

---

36. Peacocke, *Creation and the World of Science*, 79.

37. Peacocke, *Science and the Christian Experiment*, 123.

processes of the world as we know it are . . . an expression of God in his modality *as* Creator."[38] If valid, then this interpretation necessitates a radical understanding of God as continuous and immanent Creator in relation to the cosmos, as one who exercises divine creativity "in, with, and under the very processes of the natural world from the 'hot, big, bang' to humanity."[39] This immanent creativity of God in the cosmos is not about Thomistic primary and secondary causality. Rather, the creative dynamism of the cosmos is *itself* God's creative action; the creative processes of the universe are manifestations of the Divine as continuous Creator.

This perspective understands God as *semper Creator*, "creating now and continuously in and through the inherent, inbuilt creativity of the natural order—a creativity that is itself God in the process of creating."[40] God is not conceived as a separate or wholly transcendent Creator dwelling in serene detachment from the cosmos. Neither is God a "God-of-the-gaps" who creates in sporadic or interventionist ways. This God is continuous Creator, directly involved in the continuing processes of the cosmos through intimate and enduring relationship.

Hence, coupling the theological concepts of God as immanent continuous Creator with that of God as Ground of cosmic being suggests that the creative relationship of God to the world must always be expressed as a twofold understanding. First, God's relationship to the cosmos must be understood both in terms of initial creativity (*creatio ex nihilo*) and in terms of ongoing cosmic creativity (*creatio continua*), such that "the natural causal creative nexus of events *is* itself God's creative action."[41] Through the theological claim of *creatio ex nihilo*, one affirms that all of creation has its common source in God; through the claim of *creatio continua*, one also acknowledges that the creative intentions and activities of God perpetually participate in the evolutionary unfolding of the cosmos through all eons of cosmic history. *Creatio ex nihilo* suggests that God alone directly produced the conditions for the entire physical universe out of Godself

---

38. Peacocke, "Theology and Science Today," 35, italics in the original.

39. Peacocke, *God and the New Biology*, 95–96.

40. Ibid., 95.

41. Peacocke, "Theology and Science Today," 34, italics in the original.

with no mediation or dependence on other entities or forces. *Creatio continua* supplements this understanding by affirming that the ongoing creativity of God is also indirect and mediated through the entities, structures, and processes of the cosmos itself.[42] Ultimately, "If the world is in any sense what God has created and that through which he acts and expresses his inner being [in the creative processes of the world and uniquely in human consciousness,]then there is a sense in which God is never absent from his world."[43] This insight concerning God as Creator finds its utmost expression in the panentheistic model of the God-world relationship in which "God is either in everything created from the beginning to the end, at all times and in all places, or [God] is not there at all."[44]

Thus, within the panentheistic paradigm, the reinterpretation of a doctrine of creation must combine the understanding of God as original Creator who is the transcendent ground of being for *creatio ex nihilo* with the understanding of God as continuous Creator who is the immanent ground of being for *creatio continua*. To do so, God as ground of being must be understood as implying both transcendent and immanent relation. An insight of Jesuit theologian Joseph Bracken can illuminate this understanding. In his writing, Bracken discusses two different senses of the term *ground*.[45] The first sense of *ground* is as "external cause," which applies to God as transcendent Creator in the act of *creatio ex nihilo*. The second sense of *ground* is as "internal principle of existence and activity." This sense is applicable to God as immanent Creator in the act of *creatio continua*. As Bracken explains the distinction,

> Ground as an external cause is reflected in the Thomistic God-world relationship since God as the transcendent Ground of creation stands apart from creation as the finite effect of God's infinite creative activity. . . . Ground as the internal principle of existence and activity for an entity

---

42. Philip Clayton, *God and Contemporary Science* (Edinburgh: Edinburgh University, 1997), 21–24.

43. Peacocke, "Chance and Law," 139.

44. Peacocke, *God and the New Biology*, 96.

45. See Joseph Bracken, *The Divine Matrix* (Herefordshire, UK: Gracewing, 1995), 38–51 for a full exposition.

206 TRINITY IN RELATION

[is] that which makes the entity to be what it is. . . . If we apply this . . . to the God-world relationship, it follows that the ground of creation must be ultimately derivative from the ground of the divine being, namely, the divine act of being.[46]

A close reading of the second interpretation of ground as internal principle of existence has distinct resonance with Aquinas's notion of participation discussed earlier in this text. In Aquinas's train of thought, if God is Being Itself, then all creatures who have being must necessarily participate in God. Hence, the internal principle or ground of all existents that have being derives from Being Itself, that is, from "the divine act of being."

If God as Creator is both transcendent ground of being, effecting and embracing the cosmos in all its potentiality, and immanent ground of being, permeating and indwelling the cosmos and its creatures and influencing events and behaviors from the quantum to the human level, then "there is no aspect of space or time or matter or energy including ourselves to which God is not present."[47] In this intimate relationship characterized by divine, cosmic, and human freedom, the Creator and the created retain their inherent capacities to act, to receive, and to respond creatively and without coercion. No violence is done to the essential freedom and autonomy of either the Creator or creation. As indicated previously, this freedom and autonomy on the cosmic and human level is certainly the source of life, novelty, and emergence; nonetheless, it also produces mutations, disasters, and transgressions that militate against cosmic and human life and well-being. Beyond its impact on the cosmos and its creatures, however, this creaturely freedom also has ramifications for the creative agency of God. If the cosmos and its creatures, human and nonhuman alike, are truly free and autonomous, then both human and nonhuman creation has the capacity to affect, to divert, and even to constrain the intentions and activities of its immanent Creator. Hence, an evolutionary worldview not only calls

---

46. Joseph Bracken, "Trinity: Economic and Immanent," *Horizons* 25:1 (1998): 7–22 at 20. Bracken acknowledges his debt to F. W. J. Schelling, Martin Heidegger, and Paul Tillich for their contributions to the fuller understanding of the term.

47. Peacocke, "Theology and Science Today," 35.

for a reinterpretation of the creative relation of God to the cosmos from transcendent to immanent Creator but also a reinterpretation of attributes of the Creator as well.

INTERPRETING THE DIVINE THROUGH AN EVOLUTIONARY VIEW OF CREATION

As previously described, the evolutionary processes identified by the sciences, including natural law, emergence, and chance, manifest themselves within the evolving cosmos as continuity, creativity, and indeterminacy. Observing the interactions among these factors in cosmic creativity, especially those involving chance and indeterminacy, led some scientists to posit a type of inherent "freedom" that constituted the being of the cosmos—a freedom analogous to that of its human creatures. As theologians have reflected on these evolutionary insights, some have raised questions about the consequences the evolutionary processes might have for the Divine in relation to such a cosmos, particularly with regard to the qualities traditionally attributed to the Divine. The reality that cosmic agency (through free process) and human agency (through free will) can affect, divert, or constrain divine freedom to create seems to impinge on some of the attributes classically ascribed to God. In addition to the significant shift in understanding—from God as transcendent to God as immanent Creator in the cosmos—does cosmic creativity through free process and free will impact the traditional understanding of Divine Being as well?

God as Source of Law and Chance

From a scientific standpoint, the remarkable diversity in the cosmos derives from the creative interplay of chance occurrences at the multiple levels of the universe that ultimately operate within the law-like framework of natural systems. Chance operates unpredictably yet purposively within the framework of law, eliciting the possibilities that the cosmos possessed from its beginning. If, however, the operations of both chance and law are inherent capacities of the cosmos and the cosmos is truly the result of free, intentional, and loving choice of the Creator, then both law and chance must be regarded as God-endowed features of the cosmos and as consistent with God's purposes for it. This leads to the inference that God is not only the ultimate and necessary ground of the lawful order of the cosmos but also is the ultimate and necessary source of chance, which produces the diversity and novelty of the cosmos. If God is immanent and continuous Creator in, with, and through the creative properties of the cosmos, the continuous constitution of the cosmos through the interplay of chance and law may indicate both the divine intention and the divine means through which God-as-Creator actualizes matter-energy within space-time.

God as Self-Limited in Omnipotence

Giving existence to the cosmos *ex nihilo* certainly implies the omnipotence of God as understood in the classical tradition. Nonetheless, the scientific evidence of the creative and unpredictable role of chance, of "cosmic freedom," in the evolution of the cosmos seems to call this attribute into question. If the tradition is to maintain divine omnipotence, then one could infer that God must impose some form of self-restraint upon divine omnipotence. As Arthur Peacocke describes this possibility, "In order to achieve his purposes, [God] has allowed his inherent omnipotence . . . to be modified, restricted, and curtailed by the very open-endedness that he has bestowed upon creation," particularly related to the exercise of cosmic and human freedom.[48] Elaborating this idea, theologian Lucien Richard proposes, "In creating, God limits self and allows a cosmos to emerge with its own autonomy. God . . . makes room for human freedom and autonomy to emerge and for a natural order to be characterized by open-endedness and flexibility."[49]

The inference of divine self-limitation leads to the insight that God intends the universe to be an arena of improvisation of chance within law, a creation made to make itself and to realize its potentialities through processes of self-exploration in autonomy and freedom. However, neither the divine intent nor the evolutionary process

---

48. Peacocke, *Theology for a Scientific Age*, 121.

49. Lucien Richard, *Christ the Self-Emptying God* (New York: Paulist, 1997), 136.

comes without cost, as "evolution unavoidably makes 'mistakes,' enters blind alleys, and produces much suffering."[50] In such a universe, God truly acts transcendently and immanently but does not coerce and does not overrule. Rather, in such a universe, God purposefully and lovingly guides its creative processes but respects the integrity of free process and preserves the autonomy of cosmic being.[51]

The concept of God's self-limitation of omnipotence, therefore, strikes a balance between the freedom and autonomy of the Creator and of the created. While this balance undoubtedly preserves the integrity of the inherent creativity of the universe, it does so at the risk of outcomes detrimental to the life and well-being of nonhuman and human creation alike. From a theological standpoint, the self-limitation of God's omnipotence seems to require a modification of the classical understanding of the very nature of God in relation to the cosmos. However, some Christian theologians suggest that rather than signaling the need for a modified Christian God-image, such divine self-limitation is actually a definitive demonstration of the most distinctive attribute of the Christian God, that of self-giving, self-emptying Love.

God as Vulnerable Love

If the nature of God is Love, then, fidelity to this divine nature suggests that God must act in a manner consistent with God's nature as Love. If in God's nature as Love, God created both the cosmos and humanity as free and autonomous, then God has chosen not to exercise coercive power over the cosmos and its creatures. Moreover, if one considers such loving self-limitation as analogous to the loving limitation of human relationships—relationships between lovers or friends or parents and children—one must conjecture that the divine choice to limit Godself in power and to expose Godself to constraint is immensely costly to God. As with parents who want the best for their children and yet also desire their children's growth in autonomy and freedom, divine self-limitation in love continually places the

---

50. Ron Highfield, "Divine Self-Limitation in the Theology of Jürgen Moltmann: A Critical Appraisal," *Christian Scholar's Review* 32, no. 1 (2002): 63.

51. Polkinghorne, *Science and Providence*, 95.

divine purposes for the cosmos at risk, a risk that entails frustration, pain, suffering, and death in the cosmos.

Because of this, some theologians believe that these costs and risks borne by God constitute a form of divine vulnerability to the very processes that God constituted. In this vulnerability, God opens Godself to and involves Godself in the pleasures and pains, joys and sufferings, and life and death that occur at all levels of the cosmos. Moreover, in accord with the panentheistic model and the relational nature of the Christian God, this vulnerability is borne in a triune manner. God in transcendent relation encompasses and embraces the cosmos within the divine being itself; God in Incarnate relation embodies divine vulnerability by becoming one with the cosmos in its costly being and becoming; and God in immanent relation labors, creates, and transforms the cosmos from within.

God as Suffering Creator

God's intimate presence and action in the creative processes of the cosmos—which are themselves pervaded by pain, suffering, and death—inevitably imply not only divine vulnerability but also God's own costly suffering within these processes themselves. This stands in opposition to another classical divine attribute, that of impassibility or the inability to suffer. Drawing on the Greek notion that perfection requires immutability, that is, the inability to change or to be affected by external forces, the Christian tradition has long held that divine immutability also entailed divine impassibility. The reasoning behind this is that the ability to suffer implies the ability to be affected by another. However, in view of the pain, suffering, and death that both pervades and results from the processes of cosmic creation, "for any concept of God to be morally acceptable and coherent . . . we cannot but tentatively propose that *God* suffers in, with, and under the creative processes of the world with their costly unfolding in time."[52]

This assertion adds a further richness and dimension to the Christian affirmation of God as Love. Not only does God self-offer and self-empty in love for the created other, but also, as a consequence

---

52. Peacocke, "The Cost of New Life," 37, italics in the original.

of divine love, God suffers the natural evils of the world along with a suffering creation. The inevitable conclusion of such observations is that "love and self-sacrifice are . . . seen as inherent in the divine nature and expressed in the whole process of creation."[53] In addition to the suffering that comes from intimate relation to and presence within a cosmos fraught with pain and death in its very processes of creativity and emergence, there is another form of suffering that is associated with experiences and events that obstruct such creativity and the emergence of life in the cosmos and in its creatures. They are events of oppression and exploitation, of violence and injustice, and of destruction and despoliation. This suffering is not one in union with another's. Rather, it is a primal and immediate suffering that wells up whenever the full flourishing of the cosmos and its creatures is at risk of frustration or demise. This is a suffering that can be described as protopathy and defined as a primary suffering that is immediately produced, not one that is consequent of or produced by another's suffering.[54]

Protopathy is the particular kind of suffering of the God who is immanent within the cosmic processes. This is the suffering of the God who experiences with unparalleled immediacy the events within creation and its history that militate against that movement toward the new creation in which life and right relations within the universe come to fulfillment in the reign of God. This primal suffering, moreover, is one that reverberates with the righteous rage, resolute resistance, and ethical activity of God in opposition to all that hinders the creativity of the cosmos and everything that spawns the senseless suffering inflicted against its communion of life. This is a God who "keeps vigil through endless hours of pain . . . [and whose] grief awakens protest." Nonetheless, this is a suffering alive with promise for a future full of hope because it "works not just to console those who are suffering, but to strengthen those bowed by sorrow to . . . resist. If God grieves with them in the midst of disaster, then there may yet be a way forward."[55]

---

53. Ibid., 41.

54. "Protopathy," *The Oxford English Dictionary Online*; available from *http://dictionary.oed.com*.

55. Johnson, *She Who Is*, 260–61.

CREATION IN AN EVOLVING COSMOS: RESONANCES IN THE TRADITION

The evolutionary worldview outlined in both this chapter and in chapter 2 makes clear that creation of and in the cosmos consists of more than a singular, original event *ex nihilo* or a series of episodic interventions effected by a transcendent Creator. Creation of and in an evolving cosmos is an enduring and continuous relation between the Creator God immanent in the cosmos and its creatures who continuously creates in and through the evolutionary processes of the cosmos itself. Thus, evolving creation proceeds through the immanent vitality of the Divine, active in the very being, structures, and processes of the universe itself.

As discussed in chapter 4, the Divine Person recognized as immanent in the cosmos and in its creatures, acknowledged as Giver of Life, and reverenced as living and active Presence who vivifies, quickens, transforms, and renews creation throughout the Christian tradition is the Person of the Holy Spirit. In addition to this Christian proclamation, *Holy Spirit* is also the name that this text has given to the immanent relation of God to the cosmos in the panentheistic model of God-world relation. Thus, even as it affirms the concept of *creatio ex nihilo* as validly transcendent in nature, the line of thought pursued in this chapter in dialogue with an evolutionary worldview considers this appropriation inadequate and puts forth a different one. In an evolving cosmos, which burst forth because of a vitality deep within its primordial elements, creation was, is, and continues to be aroused, sustained, and spurred on by an immanent Creator. Therefore, the perennial and enduring relation of creation is most suitably appropriated to God the Holy Spirit, immanent Creator of an evolving universe. For, as theologian Walter Cardinal Kasper writes,

> [The] Spirit is . . . the source of movement and life in the created world. Whenever something new arises, whenever life is awakened and reality ecstatically reaches beyond itself, in all seeking and striving, in every ferment and birth, and even more in the beauty of creation, something of the being and activity of God's Spirit is manifested.[56]

---

56. Kasper, *The God of Jesus Christ*, 227.

Mindful that scripture and Christian tradition classically appropriated the work of cosmic creation to "the Father Almighty, Maker of
heaven and earth," there are, nonetheless, resonances of *Creator Spiritus* in the biblical, liturgical, and ecclesial tradition of Christianity, as
well as in contemporary Christian theology.

Biblical, Religious, and Liturgical Resonances

The primary biblical reference that asserts the creative power of the
Spirit of God is found in Genesis 1:2 in which the *ruah* hovers over
the chaos. The word *ruah* can be variously translated as "breath,"
"wind" or "spirit." Nevertheless, many Christian thinkers lean toward
understanding it as the Spirit of God. If this is the case, then, according to Franciscan friar Jack Wintz, "What this primal image suggests to us perhaps is that the foremost role or activity of God's Spirit
is . . . to draw forth from the chaotic waters an orderly genesis of
new life."[57] Later in the book of Job, Elihu contends, "The spirit of
God has made me; the breath of the Almighty gives me life" (Job
33:4), and Psalms 104 proclaims, "When you send your Spirit, they
are created, and you renew the face of the earth" (104:30). It is the
Spirit as well who vivifies the dry bones over which Ezekiel proph-
esied, saying, "From the four winds come, O Spirit, and breathe into
these slain that they may come to life . . . and the Spirit came into
them; they came alive" (37:9–10). The word of the Lord goes on in
this prophecy to promise, "when I open your graves and have you
rise from them, O my people. . . . I will put my spirit in you that
you may live" (37:13–14). This life-giving dynamic foreshadows the
action of the Spirit in Christ's Resurrection and in the lives of believers. As the Letter to the Romans declares, "If the Spirit of [God]
who raised Jesus from the dead is living in you, [God] who raised
Christ from the dead will also give life to your mortal bodies through
[God's] Spirit, who lives in you" (8:11).

In an intriguing extension of the presence and action of the
Spirit in creation, professor of religion Mark Wallace points out that
the Bible is replete with images of the Spirit that are specifically

---

57. Jack Wintz, OFM, "The Holy Spirit: Life-Giver," *AmericanCatholic.org*, available from *http://www.americancatholic.org/e-News/FriarJack/fj042804.asp#F1*.

connected to or drawn from nature. "Far from being ghostly and bodiless," Wallace asserts, "the Spirit reveals herself in the biblical literature as an earthly *life-form* who labors to create, sustain, and renew humankind and otherkind in solidarity with one another."[58] These images include water, light, dove, mother, fire, breath, and wind. In addition to characterizing the Spirit as the animating breath of life (Genesis 1:2; Psalms 104:29–30), Wallace identifies several other pneumatological activities imaged through natural phenomenon. He calls attention to the Spirit as the healing wind that enveloped Gideon in Judges 6:34, as the impetus of rebirth in John 3:6, and as the wind and fire that swept over the disciples at Pentecost (Acts 2:1–4). Wallace highlights the presence of the Spirit as living water (John 7:37–38), as a purgative fire (Matthew 3:11–12), and as a dove hovering over Jesus at his baptism (Matthew 3:16; John 1:32). Because of such imagery and its effects, Wallace contends that the Spirit is "a wild and insurgent natural force who engenders life and healing throughout the biotic order."[59]

Christian liturgical and ecclesial writings also testify to the Holy Spirit as the immanent giver and sustainer of life. The Nicene Creed affirms belief in the Holy Spirit as "the Giver of life." The Byzantine liturgy of the Orthodox Church prays, "It belongs to the Holy Spirit to rule, sanctify and animate creation. . . . Power over life pertains to the Spirit."[60] In a ninth-century hymn still widely used in the Christian Church, the Holy Spirit is named "*Creator Spiritus.*"[61] Furthermore, in the encyclical *Divinum Illud Munus*, written in 1897, Pope Leo XIII called the Holy Spirit "the ultimate cause of all things,"[62] while in *Dominum et vivificantem*, Pope John Paul II asserts that the life-giving power of the Holy Spirit extends not

---

58. Mark Wallace, "The Green Face of God: Christianity in an Age of Ecocide," *Cross Currents* 50:3 (Fall 2000): 310–31 at 316.

59. Ibid.

60. John Paul II, "The Holy Spirit Acts in All Creation and History," Papal General Audience, August 19, 1998, *L'Osservatore Romano*; available from *http://conservation.catholic.org/ holy_spirit_acts_in_all_creation.htm.*

61. *"Veni, Creator Spiritus,"* *Thesaurus Precum Latinarum*; available from *http:// www.preces-latinae.org/thesaurus/Hymni/VeniCreator.html.*

62. Leo XIII, *Divinum Illud Munus*: On the Holy Spirit, May 9, 1897; *Libreria Editrice Vaticana;* available from *http://www.vatican.va/holy_father/leo_xiii/encyclicals/ documents/hf_l-xiii_enc_09051897_divinum-illud-munus_en.html.*

only to natural life but also to the gift of eternal life. He wrote that the Church "has proclaimed since the earliest centuries her faith in the Holy Spirit, as the giver of life, the one in whom the inscrutable Triune God communicates himself to human beings, constituting in them the source of eternal life."[63]

Contemporary Theological Resonances

In addition to the biblical, religious, and liturgical resonances of *Creator Spiritus*, a number of contemporary theologians have set forth pneumatologies that accent the role of Spirit as Creator in an evolving universe. Therefore, the final section of this chapter draws attention to the contributions of four theologians whose works underscore and enhance the line of thought developed in this text: Presbyterian theologian Mark I. Wallace, Catholic theologians Elizabeth A. Johnson and Denis Edwards, and Evangelical theologian Jürgen Moltmann.

Mark I. Wallace: "The Green Face of God"

In his essay, "The Green Face of God," Mark Wallace not only highlights biblical resonances of the Spirit as Creator but also sets the creative activity of the Holy Spirit squarely in a Trinitarian theological context. "God as Trinity," he writes, "is set forth in the Father/Mother God's creation of the biosphere, the Son's reconciliation of all beings to himself, and the Spirit's gift of life to every member of the created order who rely on her beneficence for daily sustenance."[64] Wallace points out that, historically, the Holy Spirit has always been associated with both God and creation. Within God, the Spirit is the bond of love and reciprocity within the Trinity. Within creation, however, the Spirit has been acknowledged as the "breath of God who indwells and sustains the cosmos."[65] Because Wallace maintains that this latter role has time and again been underplayed, he sets out to reinstate

---

63. John Paul II, *Dominum et vivificantem: On the Holy Spirit in the Life of the Church and the World*, May 18, 1986; *Libreria Editrice Vaticana;* available from *http://www.vatican.va/holy_father/john_paul_ii/encyclicals/documents/hf_jpii_enc_18051986_dominum-et-vivificantem_en.html.*

64. Wallace, "The Green Face of God," 317. See also Mark I. Wallace, *Fragments of Spirit: Nature, Violence, and the Renewal of Creation* (New York: Continuum, 1996).

65. Ibid., 318.

the Spirit's "cosmic identity as the divine breath who interanimates all other lifeforms" by shifting from a theocentric and anthropocentric emphasis to a biocentric model of the Spirit in creation.

In order to do so, Wallace emphasizes what he terms the coinherence of the Spirit and the natural world through which the Spirit indwells creation as both a vivifying and unifying presence. The way Wallace speaks about this indwelling clearly resonates with relational ontology as well as with the panentheistic model of God in divine immanence proposed in this text. In Wallace's ecological pneumatology, the Spirit and earth "internally condition and permeate one another . . . without collapsing into undifferentiated sameness or equivalence . . . [or] confusion of the two." Hence, the Spirit and earth are inseparable and yet distinguishable because "the Spirit is the unseen power who vivifies and sustains all living things while the earth is the visible agent of the life that pulsates through creation."[66]

This interpermeation of Spirit and creation, nevertheless, leads Wallace to a conclusion about the Divine consistent with the one reached earlier in this chapter. Wallace foresees that, in the mutual indwelling of Spirit and creation, the "Spirit is vulnerable to serious loss and trauma insofar as the earth is abused and spoiled."[67] This is, however, a risk taken in freedom and not necessity by the Spirit, even though earth's despoliation threatens to "do irreparable harm to the Love and Mystery we call God."[68] Nonetheless, even as the Spirit agonizes over the violence done to the cosmos, the Spirit continues to abide with creation, to groan within creation (Romans 8:18–39), and to plead with humankind on behalf of creation to stop the havoc being wreaked on otherkind in the cosmic order.

Elizabeth Johnson: Creator Spirit in the Evolving World

Like Mark Wallace, Elizabeth Johnson enters her investigation of the Creator Spirit in the evolving world through an ecological context. In her book, *Quest for the Living God*, Johnson describes this context as one both of wonder and of waste. While humankind stands in wonder at the workings of the universe discovered

---

66. Ibid., 319.

67. Ibid., 320.

68. Ibid.

and described by the sciences, it also grieves over the despoliation humans have wrought on creation. This paradoxical situation, nonetheless, has led people of faith to refocus on the presence and action of the Creator Spirit in the natural world.

Lamenting the fact that Christians have not been well served by the study of the Holy Spirit in Western theology, Johnson calls for an ecological theology attentive to both the natural world and the Spirit of the living God who "pervades the material world with graceful vigor . . . [as] the source, sustainer, and goal of the whole shebang."[69] Evolutionary theory discloses that the material world that the Spirit pervades is full of wonder: it is old, incomprehensibly large, complexly interconnected, and profoundly dynamic. At the same time, the world that evokes so much wonder is being laid waste by overconsumption, overpopulation, exploitation of resources, and burgeoning pollution. Hence, this wondrous *and* wasteful world demands a vision of Spirit in the world that is both consistent with its ongoing creativity and responsive to its ecological devastation.

In exploring the divine presence of *Creator Spiritus*, Johnson focuses on three rubrics. The divine presence is continuous, cruciform, and promissory. Johnson appropriates the panentheistic model to image the *continuous* presence of the Spirit in the cosmos, which gives the world a sacramental character. Thus, "matter bears the mark of the sacred" and mediates the presence of God in and through its materiality. At the same time, the Spirit "moves over the void, breathes into the chaos, quickens, warms, sets free, blesses, and continuously creates the world, empowering its evolutionary advance."[70]

In addition to being continuous, the divine presence is also *cruciform*, filled with pain, suffering, and death from the free process of a creative cosmos. However, as proposed earlier in this chapter, the Creator Spirit abides in compassion and solidarity with all living beings, groaning in labor with all creation, bringing new life from suffering and death.[71] This enduring hope of new life, moreover,

---

69. Johnson, *Quest for the Living God*, 183. Johnson's other works on the topic include *She Who Is: The Mystery of God in Feminist Theological Discourse* (New York: Crossroad, 1993) and *Women, Earth, and Creator Spirit*: Madeleva Lecture in Spirituality (Mahwah, NJ: Paulist, 1993).

70. Ibid., 189.

71. Ibid., 189–90.

characterizes divine presence as abiding in the mode of *promise*. Because of the kaleidoscopic complexity and fecundity that emerges from evolutionary creativity, "the universe is seeded with promise, pregnant with surprise." The Creator Spirit has continuously bubbled up like a "wellspring of novelty" throughout evolutionary history, persistently opening the cosmos to the future with possibility and hope. In so doing, the Creator Spirit fulfills the Word of God spoken through revelation, "Behold, I make all things new" (21:5).[72]

Jürgen Moltmann: God in Creation—Creation in the Spirit

In his essay, "Spirit and Creation," theologian and biochemist Sjoerd L. Bonting contends that "Jürgen Moltmann gives the Spirit a near monopoly in creation."[73] Moltmann, in his opus *God in Creation*, seems to validate this assessment in the following claim: "Everything that is, exists and lives in the unceasing inflow of the energies and potentialities of the cosmic Spirit."[74] Thus, the Creator does not simply "confront" creation in divine transcendence, but enters into it in divine immanence.

Moltmann focuses on Psalm 104 to biblically ground his interpretations. Based on this psalm, Moltmann conceives of the relationship of the Spirit (*ruach*) to creation as threefold: creation is formed (*bara'*) in the Spirit, exists in the Spirit, and is renewed (*hadash*) in the Spirit.[75] From this foundation, Moltmann unfolds his notion of creation in the Spirit through many of the same relational and theological dynamics used throughout this text. He points to the scientific insights that the entities, structures, and systems of the world cannot be reduced to elementary particles or to fundamental components in a mechanistic model. Rather, the sciences have demonstrated that relationship is the primal constituent of creation. Hence, "nothing in the world exists, lives, and moves *of itself*. Everything exists, lives, and moves *in others*, in one another, with one another, for

---

72. Ibid., 191.

73. Sjoerd L. Bonting, "Spirit and Creation," *Zygon* 41:3 (2006): 713–26 at 720.

74. Moltmann, *God in Creation*, 9. Moltmann's other works on the topic include *The Trinity and the Kingdom of God: The Doctrine of God* (Minneapolis: Fortress, 1993) and *The Spirit of Life: A Universal Affirmation* (Minneapolis: Fortress, 2001).

75. *Ruach* is a variant form of *ruah*, previously defined in this text as "breath," "wind," or "spirit."

one another, in the cosmic interrelations of the divine Spirit."[76] As Moltmann delves more deeply into the relational nature of cosmic being, he extrapolates its implications for the nature of divine being in ways consistent with those of chapter 4 of this book. If creation is constituted by fundamental relations and the Spirit as God is the necessary Being from whom and in whom creation lives and moves and has its being, two things follow: The first is that the essential being of the Spirit as God is constituted by relation and the second is that the Spirit's immanent presence in creation is constituted by relation as well. Thus, the relational presence of the Creator Spirit in the cosmos "must be viewed as an intricate web of unilateral, reciprocal, and many-sided relationships."[77] Divine actions such as making, preserving, and perfecting certainly reflect the unilateral nature of the Spirit's cosmic activities; nonetheless, God-world relations such as indwelling, participating, accompanying, and enduring are relations of mutuality and "describe a cosmic community of living between God the Spirit and all . . . created beings."[78]

However, Moltmann recognizes with others in this chapter that these mutual relations are not without cost. Reflecting a panentheistic perspective, Moltmann points out that "the evolutions and the catastrophes of the universe are also the movements and experiences of the Spirit of creation."[79] Like Wallace, Moltmann turns to the Epistle to the Romans as evidence that, in response to the fits and starts of cosmic creativity, the Divine Spirit "sighs" when world processes meet with futility. However, the Spirit ceaselessly provides the dynamism for continuing creation, moving it toward self-transcendence in the emergence of new and abundant life.

Denis Edwards: Holy Spirit as Immanent Life-Giver

Among the many other theologians whose work resonates with the conclusions of this chapter, the last but not least to be considered here is Denis Edwards. His book *Breath of Life: Theology of the Creator Spirit* represents a next step in the development of his thought

76. Ibid., 11, italics in the original.
77. Ibid., 14.
78. Ibid.
79. Ibid., 16.

220 TRINITY IN RELATION

concerning the relations between the Trinity and the evolving cosmos.[80] In his pneumatology, Edwards explores the relation of the Spirit to the universe, to humans, to the Christ event, and to the Church. Of significance to this discussion, however, are his insights on the theology of the Creator Spirit.

Like this investigation, Edwards situates his theology of Creator Spirit in an evolutionary worldview, in relational ontology, and in "a particular form of panentheism."[81] Within this context, Edwards sees the distinctive and proper role of the Spirit in creation as "The Immanent One who creates through bringing each creature into dynamic relationship with the divine communion."[82] In concepts discussed throughout this study, the Spirit is neither a physical force nor a form of vitalism for Edwards. Rather, Edwards speaks of the Spirit in thoroughly relational terms as the personal presence of God in a relationship of ongoing creation. As such, the Spirit is the one who "goes 'out' to what is not divine and enables it to exist by participation in the divine persons."[83] Moreover, the Spirit not only provides the impetus to bring creation into relation with the Trinity but also the power through which creatures enact and engage in their own patterns of relationship at all levels of cosmic existence.

In a fashion similar to that of this chapter, Edwards explores what this immanent relation between the Spirit and creation implies for God and the God-world relationship.[84] Pointing out the beauty and harmony of nature as well as its harshness and death, Edwards first turns to the implications of such a worldview for the Christian conception of God. His first movement is a redefinition of divine power

---

80. Denis Edwards, *Breath of Life: Theology of the Creator Spirit* (Maryknoll, NY: Orbis, 2004). Edwards' other works include *God of Evolution: A Trinitarian Theology* (New York: Paulist, 1999) and *Jesus and the Cosmos* (New York: Paulist, 1991).

81. Edwards delineates six characteristics of his form of panentheism that are essentially consistent with this study: (1) it is trinitarian; (2) it understands God as wholly other than creatures and, because of this, as radically interior to them; (3) its spatial image of all-things-in-God is an appropriate but limited analogy; (4) it conceives of the Creator as enabling creaturely autonomy and integrity; (5) it sees creation as a free act of self-limitation; and (6) it understands creation as a relation that has an impact on God as well as creatures. Edwards, *Breath of Life*, 140–42.

82. Ibid., 117.

83. Ibid., 120.

84. Ibid., 105–16.

as the power to love. Because "the only source for a fully Christian understanding of divine power is found in the cross and resurrection of Jesus," Edwards contends that the paschal mystery reveals divine power as self-emptying and limitless love that, nonetheless, brings life from death and victory from defeat. While it "involves boundless generosity . . . and the capacity to bring life out of a violent death," such divine love also implies "incomprehensible vulnerability, [and] free self-limitation."[85]

The life, death, and Resurrection of Jesus, therefore, do not reveal a God who does or commands whatever God desires regardless of the consequences. Rather, the Christ event discloses a God of kenotic, vulnerable, and self-limiting love. According to Edwards, it is this kind of love that the Creator Spirit communicates in immanent relation to creation. In self-limiting, vulnerable love, the Spirit respects "the proper nature and autonomy" of the creatures and creative processes of the cosmos and does not intervene to counteract the free process or the free will of the cosmos and its creatures. Even at the risk of suffering, death, and diversion from divine desires, such a view of divine power suggests that the Creator Spirit "may not be free to overturn the proper unfolding and emergence of creation."[86]

As all creation groans in its birthing pangs of coming to completion (Romans 8:19–27), the Creator Spirit groans within as well. The Spirit groans with creation in its sufferings like a mother who labors as her child grows to full term. In addition to the image of a mother who "empowers creation from within," Edwards also envisions this presence of the Spirit as a "midwife who helps creation in its travail as it brings the new to birth."[87] Edwards further extends this analogy in his conception of the Spirit as the faithful companion who accompanies, delights in, suffers with, and promises each creature eschatological communion with God. This is the ultimate conclusion drawn from a doctrine of creation that conceives of the Creator Spirit immanent within the cosmos as it both bursts forth in new and emergent life and struggles for survival and growth. Realization of this presence, Edwards concludes, leads to worship and

85. Ibid., 107.
86. Ibid., 110.
87. Ibid., 112.

thanksgiving. As bread and wine, oil and water, fire and ash through the blessing of the Spirit become sign and sacrament of divine presence in created matter, all creation anticipates "the final communion of all things in God."[88]

SUMMARY

The following summary statements emphasize the major points of this chapter's reinterpretation of God as Creator and creation as relation in an evolving cosmos:

1. Evolutionary cosmology and biology have discovered a creative dynamism in the cosmos that has been ongoing since the origin of the universe and that has exercised its creativity in and through the very stuff of the material world.

2. God's relationship to the cosmos must be understood both in terms of initial creativity (*creatio ex nihilo*) and in terms of ongoing cosmic creativity (*creatio continua*).

3. If God is understood as Creator and if the process of creation has been ongoing throughout cosmic history, the creative processes of the universe are manifestations of the Divine as continuous Creator, directly involved in the continuing processes of the cosmos through intimate and enduring relationship.

4. Consistent with the immanence of such creativity, the Christian tradition and panentheistic model of God-world relationship point to the perennial and enduring relation of creation as most suitably appropriated to God the Holy Spirit, immanent Creator of an evolving universe.

5. Evolutionary theory also indicates that ongoing cosmic creativity takes place through the interplay of the dynamics of both law and chance, manifested as both continuity and indeterminacy. Some theorists see chance and the indeterminacy it produces as a form of "freedom" inherent in the cosmic organism. This has been called "free process" and seen as parallel with free will exercised by humans.

---

88. Ibid., 116.

6. If, however, these operations of both chance and law are inherent capacities of the cosmos and the cosmos is truly the result of free, intentional, and loving choice of the Creator, this leads to the inference that God is not only the ground of the lawful order of the cosmos but also the source of chance, which produces the diversity and novelty of the cosmos.

7. Cosmic creativity through free process and free will, however, necessarily impact the traditional understanding of divine omnipotence. One then infers that God must impose some form of self-restraint upon divine omnipotence, allowing it to be modified, restricted, and curtailed by the very freedom and love that God has for creation and its creatures.

8. Divine self-limitation in love, nevertheless, entails the cost of placing the divine purposes for the cosmos at risk and thus constitutes a form of divine vulnerability to the very processes that God constituted.

9. Moreover, if God is intimately present and active in the creative processes of the cosmos that are pervaded by pain, suffering, and death, this implies not only divine vulnerability but also God's own costly suffering within these processes. Moreover, God also suffers whenever the full flourishing of the cosmos and its creatures is at risk of frustration or demise. This primal and immediate suffering called protopathy is produced from within and is not the result of another's suffering.

10. However, divine protopathy is a suffering full of promise as it consoles and strengthens the suffering to resist, giving the cosmos a future full of hope and a way forward.

FOR FURTHER READING

Edwards, Denis. *Breath of Life: Theology of the Creator Spirit*. Maryknoll, NY: Orbis, 2004.

Swimme, Brian, and Thomas Berry. *The Universe Story: From the Primordial Flaring Forth to the Ecozoic Era—A Celebration of the Unfolding of the Cosmos*. San Francisco: HarperSanFrancisco, 1994.

Wiseman, James. *Theology and Modern Science: Quest for Coherence*. New York: Continuum, 2002.

Chapter 7

INCARNATION AS RELATION IN AN EVOLVING COSMOS

"The very nature of being human is to exist as *imago mundi,*
a reflection of embodiment of the biophysical world. . . .
We are . . . representatives of Earth, interdependent parts
of nature—and this totality is what God became immersed
in through . . . the Incarnation."[1]

INTRODUCTION

The doctrine of the Incarnation states the Christian belief that the Second Person of the Trinity, the Divine Son and Divine Word, became flesh and "assumed a human nature."[2] By this belief, Christianity holds that, in and through the Incarnation, the divine nature of the eternal Son was perfectly united with the human nature of the historical man Jesus of Nazareth in one person, a reality called the hypostatic union. Based on the scriptures and on theological

---

1. James Nash, *Loving Nature: Ecological Integrity and Christian Responsibility* (Nashville, TN: Abingdon, 1999), 108–9.

2. *Catechism of the Catholic Church*, no. 461; available from *http://www.scborromeo. org/ccc/p122 a3p1.htm#II.*

reflection, the tradition teaches that the Incarnation took place for four reasons.[3]

First, the Word became flesh to save humanity from sin and to reconcile humanity with God. The meaning of this divine providence is described by Cappadocian bishop and saint Gregory of Nyssa: "Sick, our nature demanded to be healed; fallen, to be raised up; dead, to rise again. . . . Closed in the darkness, it was necessary to bring us the light; captives, we awaited a Savior; prisoners, help; slaves, a liberator."[4] Second, the Word became flesh in order to reveal the love of God. The first Letter of John attests to this: "In this the love of God was made manifest among us, that God sent his only Son into the world, so that we might live through him" (1 John 4:9). Third, the Word became flesh to model the holiness that humans are called to follow, so that as Jesus has done for others, Christians also should do (cf. John 13:15, 14:6). Finally, the Word became flesh so that humans may become "partakers in the divine nature" (2 Peter 1:4). As Athanasius of Alexandria taught, "For the Son of God became [hu]man so that we might become God."[5] Just as the reasons for the Incarnation are rooted in the scriptures and tradition, so too is the meaning of the Incarnation, the union of the truly human and the truly divine in Jesus Christ.

THE DOCTRINE OF INCARNATION IN THE CHRISTIAN TRADITION

Biblical References

The biblical foundation for the doctrine of the Incarnation centers on two key passages, the earlier from the Letter of Paul to the Philippians and the latter from the Gospel of John. While other verses in the scriptures allude to or corroborate the declarations in these two primary passages, the texts of Philippians 2:5–8 and of John 1:14

---

3. Ibid., § 457–460.

4. Gregory of Nyssa, *Oratio catechetica* 15, in *Patrologiae Cursus Completus, Series Graeca*, ed. J. P. Migne (Paris: Migne, 1857–1866), 45, 48B.

5. Athanasius, *De incarnatione*, 54:3, in *Patrologiae Cursus Completus, Series Graeca* 25, 192B.

226 TRINITY IN RELATION

form the starting points from which theological reflection on the mystery of the Incarnation begins.

Philippians 2:6–11: "He emptied himself"

The biblical verses from Philippians focus on the dynamics of the Incarnation. Composed and edited some 30 years after the death of Jesus and, thus, prior to the first Gospel, Paul's Letter to the Philippians contains one of the earliest testaments to the community's reflections on the identity of Christ Jesus. This passage in Philippians is generally considered an existing hymn in tribute to Christ that Paul then cites in his letter. Scholars who hold this perspective assert that the hymn was used in early Christian liturgy to proclaim the movement of kenosis through which Christ assumed humanity in the Incarnation.[6]

Kenosis comes from the Greek word *kénōsisi*, meaning "emptying." As a theological term in Christianity, it describes the decision and action of the eternal Son of God, Second Person of the Trinity, to divest himself of the attributes of divinity and to be born in humanity. In the passage from Philippians, Paul uses the word *ekénōsen* (2:7) to describe the Son's *self*-emptying:

> Christ Jesus, though in the form of God, did not regard equality with God something to be grasped. Rather, *he emptied himself*, taking the form of a slave, coming in human likeness; and found human in appearance, he humbled himself, becoming obedient to death, even death on a cross. (Philippians 2:5–8, emphasis added)

In these verses, the subject who acts is the Son. Though sent by the Father, the Son freely chooses to enter fully into the human condition. Refusing to cling to equality with God, the Son elects to empty himself, to be born in human likeness, to take the form of a slave, and to humble himself even unto death. However, this hymn's apparent clarity in expressing the decision and dynamic of kenosis in

---

6. Leander Keck, "The Letter of Paul to the Philippians," in *The Interpreter's One-Volume Commentary on the Bible*, ed. Charles M. Layton (Nashville, TN: Abingdon, 1971), 849f. Not all scholars agree with Keck's interpretation. Some interpret the hymn as exhorting the community to model the humility of Jesus; others see it as describing Christ's death and Resurrection.

Christ did not result in a similar degree of clarity about the meaning and the ramifications of Incarnation for the person of Jesus.

This lack of clarity provoked numerous questions: "Was Jesus truly human or did he only appear human? Did Jesus Christ retain two natures or did one absorb the other? How can a divine nature and a human nature truly unite and yet remain truly divine and truly human? If Christ exists in two natures, how can he be one person? What becomes of his divine attributes when the Son assumed human nature and to Jesus' human attributes when assumed by divine nature? Was Christ always divine or did he become divine? What does it mean for humanity that God assumed human nature? What does it mean for the Divine that Jesus was proclaimed Son of God?" These questions, in varied forms, precipitated both controversies and creeds about the relation between the divine and human natures in Christ and between the two natures and the one person of Christ.

John 1:14: "The Word became flesh"

In possibly the most succinct articulation of Incarnation, John 1:14 states forthrightly, "the Word became flesh and made his dwelling among us, and we saw his glory, the glory as of the Father's only Son, full of grace and truth." A reading of the fuller text of the prologue of John, moreover, elucidates who this Word is. The opening verses of John chapter 1 clearly articulate the nature and power of this Word: "In the beginning was the Word, and the Word was with God, and the Word was God. He was in the beginning with God. All things came to be through him, and without him nothing came to be "(John 1:1–4). While this obviously resonates with the opening verses of the book of Genesis, this Word of God implies something more complex than the *dabar* (word) of God spoken at creation. The term that the Gospel of John uses for this Word is *Logos*.

Throughout the history that led to the time when the Gospel was written, *logos* had a complexity of definitions and inferences in common Greek usage. These included *word, maxim, promise, speech, reason, analogy, narrative,* and more.[7] In the context of Greek

---

7. "*Logos,*" in Henry George Liddell and Robert Scott, *An Intermediate Greek-English Lexicon*; available from *http://www.perseus.tufts.edu/hopper/text?doc=Perseus%3Atext%3A1999.04.0058%3Aentry%3Dlo%2Fgos.*

philosophy, however, the term *logos* referred to something more specific. *Logos* was the organizing principle of the cosmos that gave the universe order, form, and significance.[8] The term first gained this specificity in the work of the philosopher Heraclitus, who used it to draw an analogy between the rationality of the cosmos and human reasoning. However, philosophically, *logos* exceeded human reason; it possessed an existence peculiarly its own and gave existence to other than itself. Reflecting this meaning, Stoicism saw *logos* as "an active rational and spiritual principle that permeated all reality."[9]

While scriptural use of *logos* resonates with many of these understandings, its biblical meaning was more directly shaped by Philo of Alexandria, a Hellenistic Jewish philosopher who lived at the turn of the first millennium. For Philo, *logos* referred to an intermediate divine being or Demiurge who bridged the gulf between God as spiritual and world as material.[10] He considered *logos* primary among such intermediaries, "the first-born of God [who] was both immanent in the world and at the same time the transcendent divine mind."[11] *Logos* acted as the agent of cosmic creation and continued to work on behalf of God in the physical world.[12] Philo also considered *Logos* as the means through which the human mind apprehends God.[13]

Connections can plainly be made between the understanding of *Logos* in Philo and the Christian understanding of the Word-made-flesh in Jesus. *Logos* in John possesses divinity (John 1:1), humanity (John 1:14), and creativity (John 1:3). Through the *Logos*, humanity apprehends God (John 1:18) and receives enlightenment (John 1:4), grace, and truth (John 1:14). In the Letter to the Colossians, *logos*-made-flesh in Christ is "the image of the invisible God,

---

8. "Logos," *Encyclopædia Britannica. Encyclopædia Britannica Online*; available from *http://www.britannica.com/EBchecked/topic/346460/logos*.

9. Ibid.

10. "Philo Judaeus," in *The Cambridge Dictionary of Philosophy*, 2nd Edition, ed. Robert Audi (Cambridge, UK: Cambridge University Press, 1999).

11. "Logos," *Encyclopædia Britannica.*

12. Frederick Copleston, *A History of Philosophy*, Vol. 1 (New York: Continuum, 2003), 458–62.

13. "Logos," *Encyclopædia Britannica.*

the firstborn of all creation" (1:15), before all else that is and "in all things . . . preeminent" (1:18). As the ordering principle of creation, "all things hold together" in *Logos* (Colossians 1:17). Finally, in the Letter to Ephesians, through *Logos*-made-flesh, God "has made known to us the mystery" (Ephesians 1:9) of what God intends for creation—to order all things in Christ in the fullness of time (1:10).

Incarnation as Relation

Chapter 4 discussed various disputes sparked by the proclamation of God as Trinity. Central to these controversies was how to define the nature of the Son and Word-made-flesh in Jesus Christ. These challenges, however, merely scratched the surface of more probing questions centering on the reality of Incarnation itself. The sections that follow describe some of the core controversies surrounding the relation between the natures and the person of Christ and the creeds that defined orthodox belief in the Incarnation as relation.

Controversies Challenging Divinity

Many of the disputes over the meaning of the Incarnation took issue with the true humanity of Christ. However, the earliest questions concerned the true divinity of Christ. Such was the case with Arianism, the Trinitarian heresy that disputed the uncreated nature of the Son. In addition to Arianism was the challenge of adoptionism.

Adoptionism held that Jesus was born solely as a human and was divinized through adoption by God either at the time of Jesus' baptism or at the Resurrection. It sprung from the desire of early Christians to reconcile the proclamation of Jesus as the Son of God with the unequivocal monotheism of their Jewish heritage. Adoptionism attracted a variety of proponents throughout the first several centuries of Christianity. Second-century Christian writer Theodotus of Byzantium asserted that Jesus' adoption as the Son of God was effected by the descent of the Spirit at his baptism.

The writings of the "Shepherd of Hermas" contain visions, mandates, and parables and are attributed to a former slave. They suggest that Jesus' divinization occurred after "the career of this flesh" had ended: "When then [this flesh] had lived honorably in chastity, and had labored with the Spirit, and had cooperated with it in everything . . . He *chose it as a partner* with the Holy Spirit. . . . [and] *took the son as adviser* . . . that this flesh . . . might have . . . the reward for its service."[14] Paul of Samosata, bishop of Antioch, taught that, "The Savior became holy and just; and by struggle and hard work overcame the sins of our forefather. By these means, he succeeded in perfecting himself, and was through his moral excellence united with God."[15] In 325 CE, the Council of Nicaea condemned the heresy of adoptionism (along with Arianism), proclaiming that the Son is "begotten, not made, being of one substance with the Father."

Controversies Challenging Humanity

Subsequent challenges contested the full humanity of the Son. Primary among these were Docetism, Apollinarianism, Nestorianism, and Eutychianism.

Docetism arose within a group of early followers of Christ called the gnostics. The gnostics (Greek *gnosis* means knowledge) held a dualistic vision of the universe. They considered matter illusory and inherently evil and believed in spirit as the solely true reality and ontologically superior. Their core beliefs about matter and spirit led them to reject the belief that God had truly assumed flesh. They proposed a line of thought known as Docetism (Greek *dokeo* means to seem), which taught that Jesus did not truly possess a physical body but only "seemed" to do so. Moreover, because his body was an illusion, so also was his crucifixion. Because this heresy was prevalent during the time when some Christian epistles were being composed, its teaching is refuted in them. The First Letter of John declares "By this you know the Spirit of God: every spirit that confesses that Jesus Christ has come in the flesh is from God" (1 John 4:2–3). John's Second Letter is like it: "For many deceivers have gone out into the world, those who do not acknowledge Jesus Christ as coming in the flesh" (2 John 7). Because the heresy endured, theologians such as Ignatius of Antioch, Irenaeus, and Hippolytus preached against Docetism into the third century. The Council of Chalcedon in 451 CE ultimately

---

14. The Shepherd of Hermas, 6[59]:5–7, *Early Christian Writings*; available from *http://www.earlychristianwritings.com/text/shepherd-lightfoot.html*.

15. "Adoptionism," *The New World Encyclopedia*; available from *http://www.new worldencyclopedia.org/entry/Adoptionism#cite_note-2*.

condemned this heresy and affirmed Jesus Christ as "consubstantial with us . . . in all things like unto us."[16]

Apollinarianism receives its name from Apollinaris the Younger, fourth-century bishop of Laodicea. It is a form of *monophysitism* (Greek *mono* means one; *physis* means nature), the belief that Jesus Christ had one nature only. In different forms, it contends that the human Jesus is truly the Divine Son of God in one person, but that his divine nature either supersedes, substitutes for, or mixes with his human nature. To Apollinaris, the belief that Christ was fully divine *and* fully human implied two logical impossibilities: either that Christ was two persons or that two wholes could be one. To preserve the fullness of the divine nature, Apollinaris taught that Christ possessed a human body and soul, but *not* a human mind. He posited that the Divine *Logos* took the place of the human mind in Jesus, so that "the two [natures] were merged in one nature in Christ."[17] This solution preserved the full divinity of Christ but at the expense of full humanity and full redemption.

Theologians such as Athanasius and Gregory of Nazianzus opposed the thought of Apollinaris. Gregory of Nazianzus stated, "If anyone has put their trust in [Christ] as a human being lacking a human mind, they are themselves mindless and not worthy of salvation. *For what has not been assumed has not been redeemed*; it is what is united to his divinity that is saved."[18] Athanasius taught that Christ is "of a reasonable soul and human flesh subsisting."[19] The Council of Constantinople condemned this heresy in 381 CE and taught that Christ was fully human with "a soul, and body, and intellect."[20]

Nestorianism takes its name from Nestorius, fifth-century Patriarch of Constantinople. Emphasizing the full reality of the divine

---

16. "The Chalcedonian Creed," *Early Church Texts*; available from *http://www.early churchtexts.com/public/chalcedonian_definition.htm*.

17. "The Apollinarian Heresy," *Christian Classics Ethereal Library*; available from *http://www.ccel. org/ccel/schaff/hcc3.iii.xii.xx.html*.

18. Gregory of Nazianzus, quoted in "Apollinarianism," *Religions of the West*, Jacqueline Mariña; available from *http://web.ics.purdue.edu/~marinaj/apollina.htm*, italics added.

19. "Athanasian Creed," *Christian Classics Ethereal Library*; available from *http:// www.ccel.org/creeds/athanasian.creed.html*.

20. "Documents from the First Council of Constantinople," *Internet History Sourcebooks Project*; available from *http://www.fordham.edu/halsall/basis/const1.txt*.

and human natures in Christ, Nestorius struggled with expressing the union of these natures in one person. The issue for Nestorius focused on calling Mary, mother of Jesus, *theotokos*, a Greek term meaning "Bearer of God." Seeking to preserve the union *and* distinction of natures in the Incarnation, Nestorius taught that the title *theotokos* should be avoided as it seemed to preference Christ's divine nature and to obscure Christ's human nature. Rather than *theotokos*, Nestorius taught that Mary should be called *Christotokos*, Mother of Christ.

This controversy was not actually about the motherhood of Mary, but about the person of Christ. Critics said that if Mary is called Mother of *God*, the status of Christ's human nature is diminished; if called Mother of *Jesus*, the status of Christ's divine nature is diminished. In 431 CE, the Council of Ephesus reaffirmed the hypostatic union of the divine and human natures in Christ by calling Mary *theotokos*. This teaching was stated in a letter sent by Cyril of Alexandria to Nestorius: "We confess the Word to have been made one with the flesh *hypostatically*. . . . Therefore, because the holy virgin bore in the flesh God who was united hypostatically with the flesh . . . we call her mother of God."[21]

Eutychianism, finally, is a form of monophysitism attributed to Eutyches, fifth-century priest and abbot of Constantinople. He taught in opposition to the Nestorian claim that Christ, in possessing two natures, could be conceived of as two persons. Nonetheless, orthodox Christianity also objected to Eutyches' response to Nestorius. To affirm that Jesus Christ is in fact one person, Eutyches taught that the divine and human natures of Christ became fused into one hybrid nature. This ensured that Christ was one person with one primarily divine nature. Eutyches claimed, "I confess that our Lord was of two natures, before the union [i.e., the Incarnation]; but after the union, I acknowledge one nature."[22] Although given the opportunity to repudiate his false teaching of one nature in Christ, Eutyches continued to preach his position. The Council of Chalcedon condemned his monophysitism in 451 CE.

---

21. "Third Letter of Cyril to Nestorius," *Papal Encyclicals Online*; available from *http://www.papalencyclicals.net/Councils/ecum03.htm#Third%20letter%20of%20 Cyril%20to%20Nestorius*, italics in the original.

22. Ibid.

Creed of Chalcedon

The Council of Chalcedon definitively set forth the orthodox belief concerning the Incarnation in 451 CE, although several prior councils produced creedal statements concerning the nature and person of Jesus Christ. Against Arianism, the Council of Nicaea in 325 CE pronounced that Jesus Christ was true God, "being of one substance with the Father" and against Docetism, it taught that the Son "was made man."[23] Against Apollinarianism, the Council of Constantinople in 381 CE proclaimed that Jesus Christ was "begotten of his Father before all worlds."[24] Against Nestorianism, the Council of Ephesus in 431 CE confirmed that the "Word . . . has been united . . . with the flesh and is one Christ . . . God and man together."[25] All of these Councils defined relations constituted by the Incarnation: between the Father and the Son, between the eternal Son and the historical Jesus, between the two natures of Christ, and between the natures and person of Christ. However, Chalcedon gave the definitive teaching on Incarnation.

Chalcedon proclaimed the meaning of the Incarnation in terms of the relation between the divine and human natures, united in and giving identity to the one person of Christ. In so doing, it proclaimed that Christ is *who* he is because of the relation between these natures. What defines the person and meaning of Christ in a unique and inimitable way is that the fullness of his divine nature is indissolubly united to the fullness of his humanity. History has shown that anytime Jesus' human nature was subordinated to his divine nature or his divinity was denied because of his humanity, the true personhood of Jesus was distorted and his meaning confused. The deepest reality of who Jesus is as a person is only expressed by keeping both his divine and human nature in equal and indivisible relation with each other. Moreover, this ontological relation between the divine and human in Christ was necessary, because it was the

---

23. "The Nicene Creed," in "The Seven Ecumenical Councils," *Christian Classics Ethereal Library*; available from *http://www.ccel.org/ccel/schaff/npnf214.vii.iii.html*.

24. "The Holy Creed," in "The Seven Ecumenical Councils," *Christian Classics Ethereal Library*; available from *http://www.ccel.org/ccel/schaff/npnf214.ix.iii.html*.

25. "The Council of Ephesus—431 A.D.," *Eternal Word Television Network*; available from *http://www.ewtn.com/ library/COUNCILS/EPHESUS.HTM*.

precondition for his redemptive mission. Only if Jesus is human, like those he came to redeem from sin, and divine, like the One offended by sin, could he gain salvation for humanity. Thus, against all heresies to the contrary [*inserted in brackets in quotation*], the Council of Chalcedon proclaimed:

> Following the saintly fathers, we all with one voice teach the confession of one and the same Son, our Lord Jesus Christ: the same perfect in divinity and perfect in humanity, the same truly God and truly man, of a rational soul and a body [*contra Apollinarianism*]; consubstantial with the Father as regards his divinity [*contra Arianism*], and the same consubstantial with us as regards his humanity [*contra Docetism*] . . . in two natures which undergo no confusion, no change, no division, no separation; at no point was the difference between the natures taken away through the union, but the property of both natures is preserved and comes together into a single person [*contra Eutychianism*] . . . not parted or divided into two persons [*contra Nestorianism*], but one and the same only-begotten Son, God, Word, Lord Jesus Christ.[26]

This creed would forever influence the ways theologians and believers alike understood the meaning and purpose of Christ. Its affirmations provide a context for the following sections, which focus on the Incarnation in dialogue with evolution. How does humanity's place in the evolutionary scheme of things inform what it means to say that God became human flesh in the person of Jesus Christ? How does God's self-communication through the Word-made-flesh at a unique moment in history shed light on the self-revelation of God throughout all of history? How might emergence in the cosmos illuminate the personhood of Jesus, and with it, the potential inherent in all humanity and in the cosmos itself?

---

26. "Dogmatic Definition of the Council of Chalcedon, 451," *Eternal Word Television Network*; available from *http://www.ewtn.com/faith/teachings/incac2.htm.*

EVOLUTIONARY PERSPECTIVES ON HUMAN BEING

Chapter 3 of this book, "Human Being as Relation," introduced the notion that human beings are part and parcel of the evolving cosmos. Generated through the inherent structures, processes, matter, and energy of the universe, humans, like all creatures of the cosmos, are the product of the interplay of law and chance, of the phenomenon of emergence, and of innumerable cause-and-effect interactions. This chapter takes up the topic of humans as *natural* beings, constituted by and enmeshed in the fabric of life unfolding in the cosmos. As opposed to conceiving of the human as an exceptional addendum to an otherwise naturally evolving cosmos, the natural and physical sciences provide evidence that "the emergence of new functions and capabilities [in humans are] consequent upon that growth in complexity which characterizes the evolution of biological systems" as a whole.[27]

The Evolutionary Family Tree

The history of nature, stretching back some 14 billion years, is a matrix of evolving forms, dynamic in character, always in process, and manifesting both unity and diversity. As chapter 2 explained, all the elements of the cosmos that would ever exist erupted from what has been called the "Big Bang" or "the primordial flaring forth." From this initial event, replicating molecules occurred and life came into being. Thus, evolution began and continues through a "recombination of the component units of the universe into an increasing diversity of forms."[28]

The "being" of the world is always a "becoming" as matter-energy-space-time emerges toward greater diversity and complexity while retaining an essential unity and simplicity. This unity and simplicity is rooted in a single origin and a common ancestry, which makes each cosmic entity ontologically related to all others over eons of time, expanses of space, modifications in matter, and

---

27. Peacocke, *Theology for a Scientific Age*, 219.
28. Peacocke, "God as the Creator of the World of Science," 103.

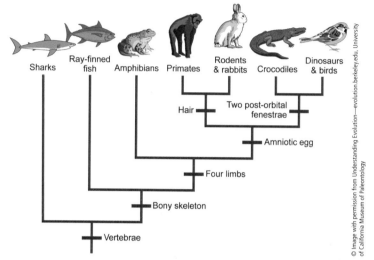

Figure 7.1: The Branching Tree of Evolution

transformations of energy. Diversity thrives through unity, and unity bonds diversity, as evolution produces a pattern of relationships among species akin to a kind of family tree.

Trends in the Evolutionary Process

The branching of this family tree demonstrates the trend toward increasing complexity of organic structures that pervades the evolutionary process from its earliest stages. Observing this phenomenon, scientists such as paleontologist George Simpson have posited other trends in biological evolution that seem dependent on this ongoing process of complexification. These trends include the emergence of consciousness, sentience, and subjectivity, reaching unparalleled levels in the emergence of humans.[29]

Complexity and Emergent Consciousness and Sentience

The coincidence of complexity and consciousness occupied the thought of Jesuit paleontologist Teilhard de Chardin, who developed

---

29. George G. Simpson, *The Meaning of Evolution: A Study of the History of Life and its Significance for Man* (London: Oxford University Press, 1950), 248–60.

what he termed the law of complexity-consciousness. According to Teilhard, scientific observations revealed that evidence of life in organic matter correlated with an increase in molecular complexity from the infinitesimal to the immense and from the simple to the complex. The movement from unicellular life to multicellular life, to vertebrates and invertebrates, to dinosaurs and mammals, to the early hominid, and to modern humans surely displayed this increase in complexity. He further observed that as living organisms increased in complexity, they also tended to display increased consciousness and mental capacity as well. Connecting this dynamic of complexification to the phenomenon of emergence, moreover, biophysicist Bernd-Olaf Küppers writes,

> The main idea behind these concepts can be summarized by the general claim that, if a material system reaches a certain level of complexity, manifested in a high degree of relatedness of its components, then genuinely novel properties and processes may emerge, which cannot be explained by the material properties of the components themselves.[30]

Certainly, if the variables of complexity and consciousness became factors in the assessment of evolutionary trends for other scientists as they did for Teilhard, then the human person would surely qualify as the most complex and conscious of all creatures. With the development of sensory organs and nervous systems, sentience combined with complex consciousness to increase human capacity for information gathering through sensory stimuli. This enabled humans to adjust to and control their environments in very practical ways. It also led to a greater capacity for analysis and prediction based on information from its environment and thus the greater capacity for survival of the organism.

Emergent Subjectivity and the Anthropic Principle

There is no question that on the criteria of consciousness and sensitivity to the environment, humans reach an evolutionary height

---

30. Bernd-Olaf Küppers, "Understanding Complexity," in *Chaos and Complexity*, eds. Robert John Russell, Nancey Murphy, and Arthur R. Peacocke (Vatican City: Vatican Observatory, 1995), 94.

unrivaled by other species both in kind and in degree. Observations along these lines and of the physical constants of the universe conducive to the emergence of the human person led scientists to what has been termed the *anthropic principle* in biological evolution. First proposed by physicist Brandon Carter, the anthropic principle suggests that the physical constants of the universe seem "finely tuned" to the emergence of human intelligent life.[31] If the values of these constants had been even slightly different in the process of evolution, the principle suggests, life as it now exists would not have emerged. Some examples:

- If the gravitational constant were slightly larger, stars would have burned too hot and too quickly to support life; if it were slightly smaller, the process of nuclear fusion would not have initiated. Either way, no life forms would have been possible.[32]
- If the cosmic expansion rate happened to be slightly greater than the present value, life-supporting galaxies would have been unable to form; if it were slightly smaller, the early universe would have collapsed on itself shortly after the Big Bang. Either way, no life forms would have been possible.
- If the uncertainty magnitude in the Heisenberg Uncertainty Principle were smaller, oxygen transport to body cells would be too small and, if it were larger, oxygen transport to body cells would be too great. Either way, certain life-essential elements would be unstable; no life forms would have been possible.[33]

Carter articulated the anthropic principle in both weak and strong forms. In its weak form, the anthropic principle simply states that any theory of the universe must be consistent with the presence of its human observers in this time and place within the universe. Nevertheless, its strong form asserts that the universe *must* have

---

31. Brandon Carter, "Large Number Coincidences and the Anthropic Principle in Cosmology," in *Confrontation of Cosmological Theories with Observational Data*, ed. M. Longair (Boston: D. Reidel, 1974).

32. Michael A. Corey, "Anthropic Principle," *Encyclopedia of Science and Religion*; available from *http://www.enotes.com/science-religion-encyclopedia/anthropic-principle*.

33. Hugh Ross, "Design Evidences in the Cosmos (1998)," *Reasons to Believe: Integrating Faith and Science*; available from *http://www.reasons.org/design-evidences-cosmos-1998*.

properties that allow the development of life in its history. Two significant difficulties derive from this latter form of the principle. First, the strong anthropic principle is tantamount to saying that a particular being, principle, or mechanism *purposefully* set the parameters of the universe for the emergence of intelligent life. This principle seems to imply the notion of "intelligent design"—the theory that the universe cannot have arisen through the operation of chance or through the process of natural selection that much of evolutionary science affirms. Rather, "intelligent design" contends that the intricacies of its entities and structures as well as its particular trajectory must have been designed and created by some intelligent being. Second, the strong anthropic principle appears to suggest that this human emergence was inevitable. This implies a sort of inbuilt trajectory toward humanity that much of evolutionary theory would deny.

Whether it signifies intelligent design in the cosmos or not, the anthropic principle decidedly affirms the integral place of the human in the universe. First, the universe, from its own essential stuff and through its own inherent processes, has engendered a distinctive emergent entity, the human person. Second, because humans emerged from the stuff and through the processes of the cosmos, each human person unequivocally shares the common origin, ancestry, and ontology of the cosmos and is knit into the past, present, and future fabric of the universe. Third, because, as an emergent in the cosmos, humans manifest consciousness, sentience, and self-consciousness, this means that consciousness is an inherent potential of the cosmos itself. Therefore, the inherent consciousness of the cosmos is actualized in the human part of it.

Hence, the anthropic principle relates the essential structure of the universe to the emergence of human existence. Moreover, whether or not it supports the universe as intelligently designed, the anthropic principle does say something about the Source of a cosmos that seems fine-tuned to the emergence of relational subjectivity. It suggests that to produce a relational subject, the Source must be a relational subject as well. A first reason for this suggestion is the contention in the first part of this text that the basis for the relational structure of the universe and its inhabitants is the relational nature of the Triune God who created it. A second reason for this, according to theologian Paul Tillich, is that the personal, which this text has demonstrated is both relational and subjective, cannot come from what is "lower than the personal, from the realm of things or sub-personal living beings."[34] A third reason, put quite simply, is that one cannot give what one does not possess. The Source of the relational, the personal, the subjective must be at least relational, personal, and subjective in itself. If this is true, then not only is the human person ontologically related to the cosmos but is also ontologically related to its Source as well. The Incarnation makes this abundantly clear.

INTERPRETING INCARNATION IN AN EVOLVING COSMOS

Evolution serves as a wide-angle lens through which to envision and interpret the Incarnation. Christianity has ordinarily focused on Incarnation as a discrete, unique, and unrepeatable event in the history of the God-world relationship. Nonetheless, an evolution-ary exploration of the human person within the web of cosmic life expands the meaning of Incarnation for both God and the cosmos from a singular event to an enduring relation. Best characterized as a relation of emergence, Incarnation symbolizes and portends novel forms of being and relation for the cosmos, for humanity, and for God. Taking an approach similar to ascending and descending Christology,[35] this chapter explores two relations of emergence: one

---

34. Paul Tillich, *Theology of Culture* (New York: Oxford University Press, 1959), 131.

35. Approaches to Christology, "the study of Christ," can be categorized into two types: descending Christology and ascending Christology. *Descending Christology* starts its reflections with the preexistent Son of God, the Second Person of the Trinity in relation to the Father and the Holy Spirit. This method then "descends" through the event of the Incarnation to the person of Jesus Christ understood as the Word-of-God-made-flesh. This approach accentuates the divinity of Christ and focuses upon the uniqueness of the Incarnation in the one person of Jesus Christ. *Ascending Chris-tology* begins with a focus on the human person of Jesus of Nazareth. Envisioning Jesus as a fully human being living in a particular social and cultural location and historical period, ascending Christology tends to rely on historical-critical study of the scriptures. It then "ascends" through reflection on Jesus' singular relationship with God, his Abba, to recognize how that unique relationship shaped his self-understand-ing, ministry, and choices, even to the cross. This approach emphasizes Jesus' solidarity with humanity and gives insight into how Jesus fit into his milieu, how he was influ-enced by his Jewish heritage, and what brought about tensions between him and the political and religious authorities of his time.

that begins with the human nature of Christ in the context of life in the cosmos and another that starts with the divine nature of Christ in the context of life in God.

Incarnation as Emergence and Cosmos

The evolutionary section of this chapter introduced the notion that humans are an essential and emergent part of the evolving cosmos. Generated from the inherent matter and energy of the universe throughout time and space, humans emerged in cosmic history through the same processes of law and chance and of cause and effect through which all natural beings arise. What is critical to remember is that two fundamental realities constitute every emergent entity. The first reality is that an emergent is a novel form of life that develops from more elemental forms of life but is not fully explainable in terms of the forms that preceded it. Therefore, new vocabulary and concepts are required in order to describe the emergent accurately in nonreductionist ways. The second is that the emergent, while not reducible to them, bears an inherent ontological relation to its preceding forms. This means that the emergent actualizes the potential of earlier levels of existence in itself.

How does envisioning the reality of the Incarnation within the evolutionary dynamic of human emergence influence the interpretation of Incarnation? From an evolutionary perspective, Jesus Christ represents a new emergent in cosmic history. In its teaching on Incarnation, the creed of Chalcedon proclaimed that Jesus Christ, the Son and Word of God, was "consubstantial with us as regards his humanity." As fully human, then, Jesus bears an inherent ontological relation to all the cosmic, natural, and human forms that preceded him in the evolutionary unfolding of life. However, the union of his human nature with his divine nature makes Jesus an emergent, a novel form of human life that cannot be reduced to or fully explained in terms of the forms that preceded him. Nonetheless, he is not independent of them.

In an evolving cosmos, therefore, the Incarnation produces a new emergent who clearly requires new concepts and vocabulary to describe him, concepts such as hypostatic union, consubstantial, and Word-made-flesh. In his emergence as a human, Jesus actualized in and through the Incarnation the potential inherent in the earlier life forms that preceded him in the expanse of evolutionary existence. Moreover, as Denis Edwards points out, "In this one product of evolutionary history, the cosmos accepts God in a definitive and absolute way."[36]

How does one characterize the cosmic potential actualized in Jesus Christ through the Incarnation? According to the way the tradition describes Incarnation, the potential of the cosmos actualized in Jesus is the union of creation, present in his human nature, with its Creator, present in his divine nature. In his emergence in cosmic history, Jesus "has made known to us . . . [God's] plan for the fullness of times, to sum up all things in Christ, in heaven and on earth" (Ephesians 1:9–10). Thus, "the Christ-mystery . . . pertains to the very nature of the cosmos as God intended it."[37] What is this intention? Simply this: that the cosmos emerge into union with God as its evolutionary goal and completion.

The Incarnation, therefore, represents both fulfillment and promise for the cosmos. It is a sign of both the already and the not yet in cosmic history. From one perspective, the Incarnation represents the fulfillment of cosmic history. The union of the human and divine that constitutes the person of Christ symbolizes the union between the cosmos come to full stature and its Creator. While this union with the Divine is already fully actualized in Jesus, it is not yet a *fait accompli* for all creation. Creation is ongoing and unfinished; it waits in eager expectation and groans in the pains of coming to birth (Romans 8:19, 22). In the fits and starts, the wrong turns and dead ends, the trials and errors of evolution, creation is still groping toward the harmony and wholeness of the reign of God. Thus, the Incarnation is also a sign of promise for the cosmos. Portending a future full of hope, it foreshadows the potential in the cosmos and its creatures, which will be actualized in the expanse of evolutionary time when divine, human, and cosmic being "all reach unity . . . and become mature, attaining to the whole measure of the fullness of Christ" (Ephesians 4:13) in the reign of God.

---

36. Denis Edwards, *Jesus and the Evolving Cosmos* (Eugene, OR: Wipf and Stock, 2004), 66.

37. Zachary Hayes, OFM, "Christology-Cosmology," *Spirit and Life* 7 (1997): 48.

Incarnation as Emergence and God

The interpretation of Incarnation as a relation of emergence that begins with the human nature of Jesus of Nazareth culminates in the good news of fulfillment and promise for the cosmos as a whole. In this ascending approach, the Incarnation symbolizes the evolution of the cosmos toward union with God in the fullness of time. If one were to begin with the divine nature of Jesus of Nazareth, what might Incarnation as emergence symbolize for God? Chapter 4 of this text laid some of the groundwork for responding to this question. In that chapter, Incarnation was identified as the relation of emergence in the Trinity and this relation was connected to what the tradition terms the Mission of the Son into history. As a Trinitarian Mission, the Incarnation constituted the person of the Son-made-flesh in Jesus of Nazareth who revealed the Triune God. Does the interpretation of Incarnation as emergence have any other consequences for the Christian understanding of God? Put another way, does a descending approach to Incarnation as emergence reveal anything more about God and the God-world relation?

Recall that emergence results from the evolution of a novel form of life, which can be neither reduced to nor explained by its preceding forms, yet is not independent of the potential inherent in such forms. When applied to God, a question may arise: If emergence is about evolution of potential and evolution of potential implies change, then does the Incarnation as emergence signify change and potential in God? The answer is both yes *and* no.

Incarnation and Change in God

Operating within a different theological model and ontology than this text, theologian Karl Rahner addresses this question of Incarnation and change in God in his essay "On the Theology of the Incarnation."[38] Rahner begins with the statement and question at hand, "The Word of God has *become* man: this is the assertion which we are trying to understand better. We take the word 'become'. Can God 'become' anything?"[39] Rahner admits that the classical tradition

---

38. Karl Rahner, "On the Theology of the Incarnation," in *Theological Investigations*, Vol. IV, trans. Kevin Smith (New York: Crossroad, 1982), 105–20.

39. Ibid., 112, italics in the original.

of philosophy and theology "begins to blink and stutter" at such a question.[40] Nonetheless, rooting himself in the classical tradition of divine immutability, yet maintaining that in the event of the Incarnation the very Word of God *becomes* flesh, Rahner proposes the following: God "who is unchangeable in himself can *himself* become subject to change in *something else*."[41] Rahner explains his proposal in a very long footnote to his essay. He admits that one could simply say that the change has taken place on the human side of the event. Rahner is concerned, however, that such a statement risks missing the most important point: "that God *himself* has become flesh."[42] Pointing out that the key to "the mystery of the Incarnation [lies] in God himself," Rahner states, "Though unchangeable 'in himself', [God] can become something 'in another'. . . . But we cannot and may not think of either as prior to the other."[43]

To support this, Rahner considers the example of how the One and the Three exist in the Trinity simultaneously with neither the unity nor the diversity before the other. He then claims that the same "coincidence of opposites" is evident in the Incarnation and immutability. Even as the One is Three and the Three are One simultaneously, God, who is unchangeable, can truly *become* something in the other without violating the immutability of divine nature. As in the Trinity, opposites coincide. In the event of the Incarnation, God is both infinite and finite, both Creator and creation, both eternal and in time, both Being and becoming—indeed, both perfection and paradox. However, this coincidence of opposites in God "is not a sign of deficiency, but the height of his perfection, which would be less if in addition to being infinite, he could not become less than he (always) is. This we can and must affirm."[44]

Incarnation and Potential in God

Taking a leaf from Rahner's book, then, one can say that a similar coincidence of opposites exists when Incarnation is a relation of

---

40. Ibid., 113.

41. Ibid., italics in the original.

42. Ibid., n. 3, italics in the original.

43. Ibid., 114, n. 3.

44. Ibid.

emergence in God: the coincidence of actuality and potentiality. As a relation of emergence in God, Incarnation is enduring; it is constitutive of who God is in Godself. This means that the relation is an actuality within the Trinity. When the relation of Incarnation becomes actualized historically in Jesus Christ, one could say, with Rahner, that there is no change in the being of God because the relation already exists in God. The change is in the being of "another," the cosmos. Moreover, Incarnation does not even change the essential nature of the cosmos. As a relation of emergence in the cosmos, Incarnation is intrinsic to the evolving cosmos and constitutive of its nature as evolving.

However, while this might answer the question of whether there is change in God, it does not address the issue of *potentiality* in God. As a relation of emergence or Mission in the Trinity, Incarnation clearly implies potentiality in God. Translating this into a theological version of the anthropic principle, Incarnation as emergence and Mission suggests that the being of God in eternity is fine-tuned for the emergence of the Word-made-flesh in time. What is potential in God—namely, the potential for the Word to become flesh—becomes actualized in the Jesus of Nazareth. In so doing, the Incarnation actualizes a coincidence of opposites in the human being of Jesus of Nazareth as it did in the being of God: Jesus is divine and human, continuous and novel, derivative and other, actualization and potential.

Following a descending Christology, Jesus of Nazareth as divine is continuous with God, but as human is radically novel. His divine nature derives from God, but his human nature is ontologically other. As divine, he is the actualization of God; as human, he is full of potential. In an ascending Christology, the assertions are reversed. As human, Jesus is continuous with the cosmos, but as divine is radically novel. His human nature derives from the cosmos, but as divine he is ontologically other. As human, Jesus represents the potential of the evolving cosmos, but as God, he is fullness of being. Interpreted through the evolutionary lens of emergence, in the Incarnation, Jesus Christ is both actuality and potentiality, both unchanged and novel, both immortal and mortal, both divine *and* human. However, he is such, in the words of Chalcedon, without confusion and with the attributes of both natures preserved.

If this is the case, then what does Incarnation as emergence mean for the life of the Trinity? If one takes seriously that emergence actualizes a potential that already exists in that from which it emerges, Incarnation as emergence implies that human and cosmic life exist as potential within the very life of God. All the being and becoming, continuity and change, inevitability and unpredictability, life and death, joy and suffering of the cosmos and its creatures have their place within the life of the Divine who is the Ground and Source of their being. Conversely, if an emergent is the actualization of what is potential in its nature, the Incarnation signifies that divinity has not only become actualized in Jesus of Nazareth but also by extension of his humanity, in the very fabric of the cosmos itself.

This is a preeminent example of the coincidence of opposites. However, as Rahner contends, it is not a sign of deficiency but the height of perfection. In the Incarnation, divine potential becomes something in "an other." This novel "other" requires new vocabulary and concepts for the Divine but without change to the divine nature that preceded it. Is this not consistent with the relation of emergence? This novel "other" has an intrinsic relation to the natures from which it emerged. Does this not affirm the ontology of enduring relation between the cosmos and its Creator? This novel "other" retains diversity in and through its relation of unity. Is this not akin to the God-world relationship modeled in panentheism? In the final analysis, can this not be essentially stated in words infused with the spirit of Chalcedon? In Incarnation, divine, cosmic, and human being subsist in both unity and diversity, as both Uncreated and created, at no point is the difference between the natures taken away through the union, but the property of both natures preserved together in the single person, the Son, the Word, the Lord Jesus Christ.

INTERPRETING THE DIVINE THROUGH EVOLUTIONARY INCARNATION

Like the evolutionary understanding of creation discussed in chapter 6, an evolutionary understanding of Incarnation has ramifications for the Divine as well as for the evolving cosmos and emergent humanity. These ramifications are reinforced by the two biblical foundations for Incarnation examined in the beginning of this chapter: (1) the Christian hymn in the Letter of Paul to the Philippians, which declared that the Son who was in the form of God did not cling to divinity but emptied himself to embrace humanity in its fullness and (2) the prologue of the Gospel of John, which proclaimed that the Word who is God became flesh and pitched his tent within the cosmos. Each points to aspects of the God-world relation illuminated by an evolutionary perspective on Incarnation: divine suffering and divine self-revelation.

Divine Suffering in the Kenosis of the Son

Clearly, the understanding of divine self-emptying into and through the Incarnation provides another way to envision the suffering of the Divine within the history of a suffering cosmos. In the Incarnation, "the suffering of God, which we could infer only tentatively in the processes of creation, is in Jesus the Christ concentrated into a point of intensity and transparency that reveals it as expressive of the perennial relation of God to the creation."[45] Because, in the Incarnation, the fully Divine Son emptied himself and became flesh in the fully human Jesus, God's very self participated in human being and becoming and so had firsthand experience of cosmic pain, suffering, and death in the suffering and death of Christ. Furthermore, if Incarnation as relation constitutes the very Being of God, the actualization of that relation in cosmic matter and history means that the Being of God is forever woven into the fabric of that matter and history and continues to share in the sufferings of creation ontologically and experientially. As God in Jesus "is the same yesterday, today, and forever" (Hebrews 13:8) and Jesus was "despised and rejected" (Isaiah 53:3), so God "yesterday, today, and forever" is a bearer of sorrows and acquainted with grief (Isaiah 53:4).

From an evolutionary perspective, therefore, the Incarnation of the Son of God not only manifested but also involved the Divine in the life of the cosmos and its creatures intimately, immediately, and inextricably. In the One who did not cling to equality with God but emptied himself to take the form of those enslaved by oppression

---

45. Peacocke, "The Cost of New Life," 42.

and marginalization, God has forever entered into the fate of the afflicted, suffering their pain and death and groaning with their anguish (Matthew 10:40; Mark 9:37). The experience of this kind of divine suffering can be characterized as *empathy*, which connotes a type of suffering that is incarnate, rooted in and shaped by one's own present or past experience of suffering. Because suffering has been woven into the fabric of one's own life, the empathetic sufferer has a capacity for understanding and a sensitivity to the feelings, thoughts, and experiences of another, to the extent of vicariously identifying and experiencing them as one's own. Thus, empathy is a suffering uniquely attributable to God-Incarnate, who has experiential knowledge of affliction, rejection, and exile both through the history of Jesus and in the history of creation in which Incarnation made God a participant.

However, the history of God incarnate in the cosmos is not without hope. The Gospels testify to the liberating action of Jesus on behalf of the suffering and the oppressed. The Resurrection of Jesus symbolizes that suffering and death can be transformed through the salvific presence and power of the God. This is not a salvation for humans alone, but for the cosmos, of which humanity is an integral part. While God's self-limited power did not prevent the evil endured by the Incarnate One, neither was he overcome by such evil. Rather, the vivifying love of God moved through suffering and death toward life, liberation, and transformation. This is the good news of salvation and the hope for liberation inherent in belief in God-Incarnate.

Beyond divine suffering, the Resurrection of Jesus Christ highlights an evolutionary reality. Dimly reflecting the creativity that raised Jesus from death, the evolutionary process itself demonstrates that the potential for new life always proceeds in some way from the suffering, death, and destruction that attend evolutionary creativity. Hence, both the Resurrection of the Incarnate One and the evolutionary process reveal that pain, suffering, and death exist within the creative embrace of God. In the embrace of God, life is changed not ended, bringing forth from the events of cosmic history new and emergent modes of life.

Divine Revelation in the Word-Made-Matter

Paralleling the hymn in Philippians, the prologue to John's Gospel proclaims that "the form of God" (Philippians 2:6) who became flesh and dwelt in history was the Divine Word. In so doing, the Johannine tradition amplified the biblical testimony to God as essentially self-communicating, which stretches back to "the beginning when God created the heavens and the earth" through the Divine Word. This sacred Genesis narrative reveals that all of creation is the self-expression of God and that everything has the capacity to reveal the Living God. Thus, as Franciscan theologian Zachary Hayes writes, "One must conclude that the cosmos itself is the first and primal revelation of God through the divine Word."[46]

Through the history of Christianity, however, the cosmic expanse of this divine self-communication has often become narrowed and concentrated in the Word-made-flesh, Jesus Christ. Rather than interpreting the Word-made-flesh as a symbol of the revelatory potential of the cosmos, Christianity has depreciated divine self-revelation through the cosmos and centralized authentic revelation in the teachings of Jesus Christ. An exception is found in the concept of the sacramental principle, "the profound sense that the invisible divine presence is disclosed through created realities that function as symbols."[47] Providing a foundation for sacramental theology as well as for the dynamic of general revelation,[48] this principle affirms that "The essence of a sacrament is the capacity to reveal . . . God, by . . . being thoroughly itself. . . . By its nature, a sacrament requires that it be appreciated for what it is and not as a tool to an end."[49]

The meaning of the sacramental principle hinges on the understanding that a sacrament is a symbol and a symbol is more than a

---

46. Hayes, "Christology-Cosmology," 51.

47. Thomas P. Rausch and Catherine E. Clifford, *Catholicism in the Third Millennium* (Collegeville, MN: Liturgical Press, 2003), 85.

48. "General revelation, mediated through nature . . . has been understood as a universal witness to God's existence and character." See A. Bruce A. Demarest, *General Revelation: Historical Views and Contemporary Issues* (Grand Rapids, MI: Zondervan, 1982) 14.

49. Michael J. Himes and Kenneth R. Himes, "The Sacrament of Creation: Toward an Environmental Theology," *Commonweal* 117 (1990): 45–46.

sign. A sign has no internal connection with what it points to; its meaning is based on human convention. People encounter many signs each day that hold conventional meaning. Think of a traffic light. Drivers know that red means "stop"; green, "go"; and yellow, "caution" not because of any inherent connection between the colors and their meanings, but because those connections were established by a particular society. Members agree to abide by those meanings or suffer a traffic ticket!

A symbol, on the other hand, mediates something other than itself and has an intrinsic relation to what it symbolizes. It is "a word or image that participates in the reality being signified, opens it up to some understanding, yet never exhausts it completely."[50] The understanding that a symbol participates in the reality signified refers to the teaching of Aquinas discussed earlier in this text. Aquinas taught that a relationship of participation exists between God and creation. All that has being participates in God who is Being Itself. This allows for an analogy of being between natural being and God where the natural world can serve as a symbol of God and mediate God to humans. As a result,

> . . . the cosmos is a symbol system in which something of the mystery of the divine is communicated to those capable of reading the symbols. . . . This sense of the sacramental is radicalized in the Christian perception of Christ. The human reality of Jesus is the most focused statement of what God is about with the world more generally.[51]

While participation in divine being and thus the sacramental principle comes to full focus in the Incarnation (with Jesus himself as the preeminent sacrament of God), this preeminence should serve to validate rather than derogate divine revelation through the sacrament of creation. An evolutionary viewpoint makes clear that the precondition for the possibility of the Word becoming *flesh* in Jesus Christ was that the Word became *matter* in creation. A material world from which humanity emerged must necessarily have existed

---

50. Elizabeth A. Johnson, "To Let the Symbol Sing Again," *Theology Today* 54 (1997): 300.

51. Hayes, "Christology-Cosmology," 54.

in order for the Divine to assume humanity in it. If the cosmos itself never existed or if humans had never evolved and emerged from the very stuff of that cosmos, then there would be no place, no matter, no natural or human being in and through which Jesus could become flesh. If *full humanity* unites with divinity in the Incarnation, then it does so within the very materiality that the cosmos as creation has possessed all along. Creation, therefore, is not simply the stage on which the Word eventually becomes flesh; it provides the very condition for its happening at all. Moreover, as this text has pointed out, all that is created communicates something of the nature, attributes, and intentions of its Creator, a reality analogically expressed in the biblical revelation of creation through the Divine Word. Thus, when the Word of God reaches full expression and revelation in Jesus Christ, it does so as part of the universe that has disclosed God's nature, attributes, and purposes all along.

In an evolutionary worldview, the divine self-communication that comes to its fullness in the person of Jesus does so because the potential for divine revelation exists in the very being and matter of the cosmos. This means that the capacity to mediate divine revelation has existed and continues to exist in all of cosmic being albeit in varying degrees. Therefore, those who profess belief in the Word of God through whom all things came to be—the Word of God who was made flesh in Jesus of Nazareth—must attend to the Word of God continuously spoken and made matter in the cosmos and its creatures.

Bearing an intrinsic relation to cosmic history, the history of human experience also mediates God's self-communication. Examples overflow in the Jewish and Christian scriptures. The story of God-world relationship is told through those who grow wheat and weeds, who seek fine pearls and choice land, who bake with yeast and sow with seed. God is revealed in human analogies as a father who provides and protects; a mother who cries out in labor, gives birth, and nurses her young; and a parent who teaches a child to walk. God speaks through the widow petitioning for a cause that is just and the vineyard owner faulted for generosity, through the shepherd seeking lost sheep and the woman searching for the lost coin. God continues to communicate a self-revelatory Word in encounters with people today through personal prayer and in communities of faith, in creation and its creatures. Surely, "the word of God is living and effective" (Hebrews 4:12) and proclaims union of the cosmic and divine as the fulfillment of its potential.

INCARNATION IN AN EVOLVING COSMOS: RESONANCES IN THE TRADITION

Biblical, Religious, and Liturgical Resonances

A search of the scriptures reveals that the principal ways the Incarnation connects to the history of the cosmos and humanity is in the context of creation and redemption. With regard to creation, the Word-made-flesh is the one through whom all things came to be (John 1:3). He is the Son through whom God created the universe and whose word sustains all things in being (Hebrews 1:2–3). This is echoed in 1 Corinthians, which connects God's creative work to that of Christ. Like the Creator "from whom all things are and for whom we exist," Christ is the Lord "through whom all things are and through whom we exist" (1 Corinthians 8:6). The Letter to the Colossians concurs, affirming that all things were created by and for Christ (Colossians 1:16). However, it also sees Christ's connection to the cosmos, proclaiming him "the firstborn of all creation" (1:15).

The redemptive work of the Incarnation also has a cosmic context. Not only does Christ reconcile humanity to God through the cross but also all things on Earth and in heaven (Colossians 1:20). This occurs because, in God's plan for the fullness of time, "all things in heaven and things on earth" are united in Christ (Ephesians 1:10). Creation receives new life in his person (1 Corinthians 15:22), and Christ fulfills all things (Ephesians 4:10). The groaning of creation for fulfillment, moreover, parallels the yearning of the children of God.

> Creation awaits with eager expectation . . . [to] be set free from slavery to corruption and share in the glorious freedom of the children of God. We know that all creation is groaning in labor pains even until now; and not only that, but we ourselves, who have the first fruits of the Spirit, we also groan within ourselves as we wait for . . . the redemption of our bodies. (Romans 8:19–23)

Thus, as theologian Zachary Hayes states, "The biblical tradition has long been convinced that the destiny of humanity is intertwined with that of the cosmos."[52]

The biblical tradition has, of course, been appropriated into the Christian tradition and uniquely so into the Catholic tradition. Summing up the message of Romans, the *Catechism of the Catholic Church* concludes: "Revelation affirms the profound common destiny" of the cosmos and humanity. It maintains, "The visible universe, then, is itself destined to be transformed," sharing the glorification of the risen Christ.[53] Because of this, "the mystery of Christ casts conclusive light on the mystery of creation and reveals the end for which 'in the beginning God created the heavens and the earth:' from the beginning, God envisaged the glory of the new creation in Christ."[54] Hence, in the Incarnation, "human history and indeed all creation are 'set forth' and transcendently fulfilled."[55]

This line of thought has also been pursued in papal writings. In his World Day of Peace message in 1990, Pope John Paul II applied biblical revelation to the ecological crisis. He proclaimed that the commitment of believers to the cosmos "stems directly from their belief in God the Creator . . . and from the certainty of having been redeemed by Christ. Respect for life and for the dignity of the human person extends also to the rest of creation, which is called to join [humanity] in praising God."[56] In his 2011 homily for the celebration of the Easter Vigil, Pope Benedict XVI preached the good news that "In the resurrection [of Christ], creation has been fulfilled. The world had changed. . . . A new form of life had been inaugurated, a new dimension of creation."[57] Eastern Orthodox theologians

---

52. Ibid., 52.

53. *Catechism of the Catholic Church*, nos. 1046, 1047.

54. Ibid., 280.

55. Ibid., 668.

56. Pope John Paul II, "The Ecological Crisis: A Common Responsibility," Message of His Holiness for the Celebration of the World Day of Peace," January 1, 1990, *Libreria Editrice Vaticana*; available from *http://www.vatican.va/holy_father/ john_paul_ii/messages/peace/documents/hf_jpii_mes_19891208_xxiii-world-day-for-peace_en.html*, § 16.

57. Pope Benedict XVI, "Easter Vigil: Homily of His Holiness Benedict XVI," April 23, 2011, *Libreria Editrice Vaticana*; available from *http://www.vatican.va/holy_father/benedict_xvi/homilies/2011/documents/hf_benxvi_hom_20110423_veglia-pasquale_en.html*.

also speak of "the unity of heaven and earth . . . personified in Jesus Christ as the eternal creator who assumed creation."[58] This is articulated in the "double movement theory," which teaches that "through the Divine *Logos* the Creator moves toward creation and through its *logoi* [natural laws] creation moves toward its Creator. . . . to participate in God's uncreated energies; that is, to be deified or to attain to its perfection."[59]

The interplay between the Incarnation and the cosmos reveals itself liturgically in Christian sacramental life. As discussed above, the premise of sacramentality is the God who is by nature self-communicating and who shares Being with all that possess being. Thus, the sacramental life of the Church invites believers into the "exuberant wealth of symbolic expression" that proliferates in religious traditions. In the sacraments of Baptism, Eucharist, and Confirmation, for example, God expresses divine presence and love through water and flame, through bread and wine, and through oils and the laying on of hands. The sacramentals of incense and candles remind the senses of the nearness of God and draw believers into prayer. Such sacramental symbols reveal a profound truth: "As creatures, corporeal beings in space, time, and cultural context, we relate to God through created things."[60] That mode of relation, moreover, goes both ways, as God continuously chooses to relate to the cosmos and its creatures through "corporeal beings," both in creation and in Incarnation.

Contemporary Theological Resonances

In addition to the biblical, religious, and liturgical resonances, theological resonances come from contemporary theologians with an evolutionary approach to Incarnation. Therefore, this final section draws attention to the contributions of three theologians whose

---

58. John Chryssavgis, "Christian Orthodoxy"; available from *http://www.clas.ufl. edu/users/ bron/PDF--Christianity/Chryssavgis--Christian%20Orthodoxy.pdf*.

59. Paul Negrut, "The Eastern Orthodox Church," *Christian Research Journal*, 20: 3 (1998); available from *http://www.equip.org/articles/the-eastern-orthodox-church*.

60. Monika K. Hellwig, "What Can the Roman Catholic Tradition Contribute to Christian Higher Education?" in *Models for Christian Higher Education: Strategies for Survival and Success in the Twenty-First Century*, eds. Richard T. Hughes and William B. Adrian (Grand Rapids, MI: Eerdmans, 1997), 17.

works underscore and enhance the line of thought developed in this chapter: Protestant theologian Sallie McFague, Lutheran theologian Norman Habel, and Catholic theologian Karl Rahner.

Sallie McFague: The Christic Paradigm

In her book *The Body of God*, Sallie McFague reflects on the mystery of the Incarnation and proposes the following thought experiment: "Were we to imagine 'the Word made flesh' as not limited to Jesus of Nazareth but as the body of the universe," McFague asks, "might we not have . . . an awesome metaphor for both divine nearness *and* divine glory?"[61] In keeping with this metaphor, God is immanently present in and through all bodies, but transcends any one particular expression of that presence. The Divine, therefore, is "radically and concretely embodied . . . in the concrete embodiments, that constitute the universe."[62] While McFague contends that, in this metaphor, "God is not reduced to the world," it clearly "puts God 'at risk'" in the exigencies suffered by the cosmos and its inhabitants. God is "made vulnerable" by God's immanence in the materiality of the world. Thus, "In the metaphor of the universe as the self-expression of God—God's incarnation—the notions of vulnerability, shared responsibility, and risk are inevitable."[63] From McFague's incarnational viewpoint, "at one level our model [of God's Word-made-matter] . . . moves us in the direction of contemplating the glory and grandeur of divine creation . . . at another level it moves us in the direction of compassionate identification with and service to the fragile, suffering, oppressed bodies that surround us."[64]

Because the doctrine of the Incarnation shapes the fundamental structure of Christian belief, McFague considers Christianity uniquely suited to embrace the metaphor of the world as the incarnation of the Divine Word. McFague terms the shape and scope of this metaphor "the Christic paradigm." Based upon the life, ministry, death, and Resurrection of Jesus of Nazareth, the Christic paradigm

61. McFague, *Body of God*, 131.

62. Ibid., 155.

63. McFague, *Models of God*, 72.

64. McFague, *Body of God*, 135.

suggests that the direction of creation, like the mission of Jesus of Nazareth, is toward fullness of life and inclusive love for all, especially the needy and vulnerable. Nonetheless, McFague's understanding of the needy and vulnerable is cosmic in scope. In an ecological age, McFague contends, those who constitute the oppressed, the needy, and the outcast of the world must include the "new poor" of non-human beings and the environment itself that continuously mediates the self-communication of God in history. The Christic paradigm motivates Christians to live in right relationship with the larger whole of which humans *and* God are a part and to do so with an expanded understanding of the teaching of the Matthean Jesus, "whatever you do to the least of mine you do to me" (Matthew 25:40).

Norman Habel: Deep Incarnation

Drawing on the work of Lutheran theologian Niels Gregersen, Norman Habel, professor of Hebrew Scripture, sought to explore the theology of creation in the context of worship. Reflecting on the liturgy of the Word and the Creed, Habel offered "A Theology of Deep Incarnation and Reconciliation," which examines the relationship between Christ and creation. He asked the questions, "Who is the Christ we worship? A spiritual being detached from Earth, residing in heaven and liberated from the burden of the material world? Or a living presence who is somehow revealed in, with and under the substances from which all creatures emerge?"[65] His response to these questions is rooted in several affirmations: (1) that the Gospel is a message intended for all creation, (2) that in deep incarnation God joins the biological web of life, (3) that Jesus Christ is the crucified God who suffers in and with creation, and (4) that the risen Jesus is the Cosmic Christ who reconciles and restores all of creation.

Of particular interest is his use of the term *deep incarnation*, which Habel acquired from theologian Niels Gregersen. According to Gregersen, in an evolutionary context, "the incarnation of God in Christ can be understood as a radical or 'deep' incarnation, that is,

---

65. Norman Habel, "A Theology of Deep Incarnation and Reconciliation," *The Season of Creation*; available from *http://seasonofcreation.com/theology/theology-a-theology-of-deep-incarnation-and-reconciliation/*. Unless otherwise noted, all quotations that follow are taken from this site.

an incarnation into the very tissue of biological existence, the system of nature."[66] In his theological writing, Habel described deep incarnation as God's joining the web of cosmic life through which God becomes part of the biology of Earth. "The incarnation means that the Creator becomes a creature, the God whose presence permeates Earth becomes a human born of Earth." Because of this, God is revealed in all of creation and most definitively in Jesus Christ.

In so doing, Habel asserts, God not only becomes incarnate in a Galilean Jew but also in all of humanity. Thus, a deeper dimension of the Divine is revealed. However, Habel also contends that the Incarnation reveals a deeper dimension of creation as well. Speaking from an evolutionary-environmental context, Habel poses the following:

> If we recognise Earth as a living organism, can we also say that God became 'incarnate' in Earth? Does Jesus the creature represent all creation? The answer . . . is yes! Jesus, as animated dust from the ground, is that piece of Earth where God's presence is concentrated in the incarnation. God becomes flesh, clay, Earth.

Habel focuses the concept of deep incarnation on the suffering of God in the event of the cross. In keeping with his Lutheran heritage, he envisions God hidden in the scandal of the cross as well as in the glory of creation. Through the cross, God reveals to the eyes of faith that the Divine suffers with God's people and with creation: "the God whose presence fills Earth is the suffering God known to us at Calvary." With the cross as representative of the travail of Earth, Habel goes on to assert, "In Christ, Earth too suffers and bears the cross. The land too is crucified with the incarnate God."

In contrast to a number of theologians whom he cites, Habel cautions against too hasty a movement toward Resurrection in this theological model, insisting that only through the cross does God liberate Earth. Nonetheless, he acknowledges that ultimately the Crucified Christ becomes the Cosmic Christ who restores and revitalizes creation in himself. Through the Resurrection, therefore, "The God who becomes part of the biology of Earth is also the God who

---

66. Niels Gregersen, "The Cross of Christ in an Evolutionary World," *Dialog: A Journal of Theology* 40 (2001): 205.

fills this Earth with new life, a deep biology." In the rising of Christ, creation arises, and as it does so, it reveals "the fullness of God's Wisdom, the cosmic force that restores and holds all things together in the universe."[67]

Karl Rahner: Christology within an Evolutionary View of the World

In contrast to the focus on Incarnation and suffering set forth by the preceding theologians, Karl Rahner takes an evolutionary view of Incarnation in a different direction: that of self-transcendence. His aim is to show "an intrinsic affinity and the possibility of a reciprocal correlation" between Christology and an evolutionary view of the world without reducing it to a "necessary and intrinsic element" in that worldview. In other words, Rahner does not want to reduce the meaning of the Incarnation to a merely natural event that can be fully explained in evolutionary terms or that can be arrived at through human reason. Rather, he wants to preserve the mystery of the Incarnation revealed uniquely in the scriptures and affirm the necessity of faith for belief in Christ.[68]

It is important to note that Rahner's concept of self-transcendence bears a fundamental relationship to the evolutionary dynamic of emergence this text has used to discuss Incarnation. As Rahner describes it, self-transcendence occurs when "something which existed earlier really surpasses itself in order . . . to become something different and to preserve itself."[69] This definition includes all the elements essential to an emergent: prior existence that surpasses itself to become something different while preserving its connection to that which preexisted it. Thus, "the lower form prepares for and is a prelude to this self-transcendence in the unfolding of its own reality and order."[70]

In his interpretation of Rahner's Christology of self-transcendence in an evolving cosmos, Edwards proposes that, for Rahner, Jesus represents three interrelated dynamics: (1) the self-transcendence of the

---

67. Habel, "A Theology of Deep Incarnation and Reconciliation."

68. Karl Rahner, *Foundations of Christian Faith*, trans. William Dych (New York: Crossroad, 1985), 179.

69. Ibid., 186.

70. Ibid.

cosmos toward God, (2) the self-communication of God to the cosmos, and (3) the link between the self-communication of God to all people and God's self-revelation in Christ.[71] Certainly, these three dynamics resonate with points taken throughout this chapter. However, this final section centers on the dynamic that "whole process of the world's self-transcendence into God" is embodied in the person and life of Jesus Christ.[72] According to Edwards, since Rahner views cosmic history as a movement of self-transcendence into God, Jesus' obedience to the intention of God for his life can be understood as "the 'yes' to God's self-communication that the whole cosmos has been moving toward throughout its history."[73]

Like this chapter, Rahner understands creation and Incarnation as two related aspects of God's self-communication in history. As such, "creation and incarnation [are] not two disparate and juxtaposed acts of God" with two different initiatives and two different ends. Rather, they are "two moments and two phases of the *one* process of God's self-giving and self-expression"[74] with the single end of self-transcendence into the immediacy of God. For the cosmos, therefore, Incarnation symbolizes the ultimate culmination of a movement that Rahner sees as intrinsic to the nature of matter: the evolution of matter toward spirit, that is, union with God.

Hence, one cannot regard the Incarnation of the Logos as "simply a higher realization of God's self-communication which leaves the rest of the world behind."[75] Incarnation exists as a "*relationship* of mutual conditioning"[76] between the realities of God and the world that represents the "climax in the development of the world towards which the whole world is directed."[77] Rahner also emphasizes the fact that the Incarnation not only represents God's definitive self-communication *to* the cosmos but also the definitive acceptance of this self-communication *by* the cosmos in Jesus Christ. These two

71. Edwards, *Jesus and the Evolving Cosmos*, 65.

72. Ibid., 66.

73. Ibid., 67.

74. Rahner, *Foundation of Christian Faith*, 197

75. Ibid., 200.

76. Ibid., italics added.

77. Ibid., 199.

movements "constitute a unity" that is "definitive and irrevocable."[78] As Edwards summarizes it, in the Incarnation, "we find God giving God's self to the world irreversibly. We also find a part of the world, a human being, the product of evolutionary history, accepting the self-giving God without reservation."[79]

SUMMARY

The following summary statements emphasize the major points of this chapter's interpretation of Incarnation as relation in an evolving cosmos:

1. The doctrine of the Incarnation holds that the divine nature of the eternal Son was perfectly united with the human nature of the historical man Jesus of Nazareth in one person, which is termed the *hypostatic union*.

2. The biblical foundation for the doctrine of the Incarnation centers on two key passages: Philippians 2:5–8 and John 1:14.

3. Philippians 2:5–8 proclaims the movement of kenosis or self-emptying through which Christ divested himself of the attributes of divinity and assumed humanity in the Incarnation.

4. John 1:14 proclaims, "the Word became flesh and made his dwelling among us." The term that the Gospel of John used for this Word was *Logos*, understood as divine being who bridged the gulf between God as spiritual and world as material.

5. Many controversies arose concerning the meaning and implications of the Incarnation; these included challenges to Christ's full divinity and to his full humanity.

6. The Council of Chalcedon in 451 CE issued the definitive statement of belief concerning the Incarnation asserting the ontological relation between the divine and human natures in the one person of Christ.

---

78. Karl Rahner, "Christology in the Setting of Modern Man's Understanding of Himself and of His World," *Theological Investigations XI* (London: Darton, Longman, and Todd, 1974), 226–27.

79. Edwards, *Jesus and the Evolving Cosmos*, 74.

7. From a cosmic perspective, Incarnation can be viewed as producing a new emergent who actualizes the potential inherent in the cosmic life forms that preceded him: the potential for the union of creation with its Creator as its goal and fulfillment.

8. From a divine perspective, Incarnation can be viewed as the emergence of God through which divinity becomes actualized not only in Jesus of Nazareth but also in the very fabric of the cosmos itself.

9. The Incarnation symbolizes both fulfillment and promise for the cosmos. As fulfillment, the union of human and divine in Christ represents the union between the cosmos and its Creator. As promise, the union actualized in Jesus is not yet a *fait accompli* for creation, still groping toward the reign of God.

10. The Incarnation symbolizes both the suffering and the self-revelation of God. In the Incarnation, God became part of the fabric of cosmic history and continues to share in the sufferings of creation ontologically and experientially. In the Incarnation, divine self-revelation in the Word-made-flesh Jesus Christ epitomizes God's self-communication throughout history in Word of God-made-matter in creation.

FOR FURTHER READING

Delio, Ilia. *Christ in Evolution*. Maryknoll, NY: Orbis, 2008.

Edwards, Denis. *Jesus and the Evolving Cosmos*. Eugene, OR: Wipf and Stock, 2004.

Rahner, Karl. *Foundations of Christian Faith*. Trans. William Dych. New York: Crossroad, 1985.

Chapter 8

GRACE AS RELATION IN AN EVOLVING COSMOS

"Grace always involves relationships. The word "grace" . . .
points to the relationship between God and the world."[1]

INTRODUCTION

This chapter on grace completes the triad of relations proposed as
constitutive of cosmic, human, and divine being in relation. Chapters
6 and 7 have explored the Christian doctrines of creation and incarnation through the lens of evolutionary theory; chapter 8 now looks
at grace as a relation in an evolutionary worldview. As the biblical
and theological insights discussed here will demonstrate, grace is an
efficacious relation that invites and impels cosmic and human beings
to evolve and to become, to seek and to live, toward the fullness of
being into which God draws them. Moreover, grace is a transcendent
relation, calling cosmic and human beings beyond their past and
present, beyond their frailty and finitude, into a future full of hope.
Thus, grace has a particular affinity with God in transcendent relation to the cosmos, understood as the divine Father-Mother-Matrix.

---

1. Elizabeth Dreyer, *Manifestations of Grace* (Collegeville, MN: Liturgical Press,
1990), 21.

Because grace is the energy of self-transcendence, the power that "is able to accomplish far more than all we ask or imagine" (Ephesians 3:20), the nature of this relation is conceived as a *relation of effect.*

THEOLOGY OF GRACE

Venturing into an examination of the theology and doctrine of grace is a labyrinthine experience. While the notion of grace is ubiquitous in the Christian tradition, this ubiquity makes an examination of grace complex. As theologian Roger Haight comments, "Grace means many different things to different Christians; it corresponds to many different Christian experiences and understandings."[2] Moreover, these meanings and experiences vary among different Christian denominations.

The *Catechism of the Catholic Church* states that "Grace is *favor*, the free and undeserved help that God gives us to respond to [God's] call to become children of God . . . , partakers of the divine nature and of eternal life."[3] Moreover, the goal of this favor is "*participation in the life of God.* It introduces us into the intimacy of Trinitarian life."[4] Eastern Orthodoxy understands grace as "a communication of the divine energies" for the purpose of *theosis* or divinization, that is, participation in the life of God.[5] Lutheranism classically defines grace as "the free and undeserved favor of God, whereby without any merit or worthiness on our part, he declares sinners righteous and just in his sight for the sake of the all-sufficient life, suffering, death and resurrection of His Son Jesus Christ."[6] The followers of John Calvin view grace as an attribute of God, "which emphasizes

---

2. Roger Haight, SJ, *The Experience and Language of Grace* (Mahwah, NJ: Paulist, 1979), 6.

3. *Catechism of the Catholic Church*, no. 1996.

4. Ibid., no. 1997, italics in the original.

5. Aristotle Papanikolaou, "Grace of God in the Eastern Orthodox Tradition," in *The Cambridge Dictionary of Christianity*, ed. Daniel Patte (New York: Cambridge University Press, 2010), 478.

6. Daniel Preus, "The Lutheran Identity Crisis: With Emphasis on the Doctrine of Justification," *Issues, Etc.*; available from *http://www.mtio.com/articles/aissar58.htm*, italics in the original.

the fact of His infinitely glorious perfection." God reveals this attribute "towards and in" God's people as "undeserved, unmerited favor which God is pleased to work in us for Jesus' sake." Moreover, the gift of grace is not static; rather, "this grace of God is grace that *works* . . . , that is *power*. It fashions and forms [God's] people according to God's own design."[7]

Linking grace exclusively to any one meaning, experience, or connection is to do injustice to the expansive reality of grace. Hence, if one were to define *grace* it is vital that the definition be broad enough in scope and inclusive enough in compass to subsume the variety of experiences and understandings of grace rife within the tradition.

Despite the diversity of these perspectives on grace, "in all of them, there should be some inner core that remains the same,"[8] if indeed they refer to a single concept. This text suggests an inner core among these varied descriptions that has two dimensions. The first dimension of that core reveals that grace signifies *relationship*—the relationship between God, the cosmos, and its creatures. The second dimension reveals that grace signifies a particular kind of relationship—an *efficacious* relationship—between God and creation. Thus, as an efficacious relationship, grace at its innermost core constitutes what this text has called a *relation of effect*.

Biblical References

The etymology of the word *grace* has its roots in the Latin word *grātia* and its derivative *grātus*; its literal meanings include "favor," "kindness," "esteem," and "approval." However, the original scriptures employed the language of Hebrew and Greek rather than Latin. In addition, each used a variety of terms that are, nonetheless, translated as or associated with the word *grace* in English. Specific examples demonstrate that no matter which term is used, each is multivalent in nature and meaning.

---

7. Gise J. Van Baren, "Irresistible Grace," in *The Five Points of Calvinism* by Herman Hanko, Homer Hoeksema, and Gise J. Van Baren (Grandville, MI: Reformed Free Publishing Association, 1976); available from *http://www.prca.org/fivepoints/chapter4.html*.

8. Haight, The Experience and Language of Grace, 6.

Hebrew Scriptures

The Hebrew scriptures associate the divine relationship of grace with unmerited favor from God and do so in words that derive from three roots: *hesed*, "faithful love"; *rhm (raham, rahamin)*, "mercy, compassion, or compassionate"; and *hnn (hen, hanan)*, "favor, gracious, or graciousness."[9] While the ways these roots designate grace appear to overlap, biblical scholars have discerned different connotations based on the specific use of these words in the scriptures.

The divine grace expressed by the concept of *hesed* has a number of different but related translations. Some texts render it "faithful love;" others, "steadfast love;" still others, "loving kindness" or "kindness." Regardless of the translation, *hesed* indicates an *effective* relationship of grace demonstrated by "an action by God (rather than simply an attitude) that fulfills an essential need that humans cannot meet by themselves."[10] Examples are found in Isaiah, which recounts the "kindnesses of the Lord" and "the good things [God] has done" (63:7), and in the book of the prophet Hosea, which affirms God's steadfast love for Israel that called the chosen people out of bondage in Egypt (11:1).

The root *rhm (raham, rahamin)* is used in the Hebrew scriptures when grace "expresses the benevolence of a superior toward a weak or needy [individual who is in an] inferior [position]."[11] The book of Deuteronomy assures Israel of this kind of divine grace when it proclaims that "the LORD, your God, is a merciful God, [who] will not abandon and destroy you" (4:31). The prophet Isaiah echoes this assurance when he announces to the chosen people that God desires to have mercy on them and rises to show compassion (30:18).

Finally, *hnn (hen, hanan)* as favor or graciousness "refers to a type of relationship that God has with humans and that humans can also have with others." In this case, "grace is the action of freely and unilaterally offering an undeserved gift or favor" that cannot be

---

9. Spellings beyond the root vary because Hebrew uses only consonants in its root words. Hence, *rhm* may be rendered *raham* or *rahum* or *rahem*, yet each is translated as *compassion* in English.

10. Daniel Patte and Eugene TeSelle, "Grace in the Western tradition," in *The Cambridge Dictionary of Christianity*, ed. Daniel Patte (New York: Cambridge University Press, 2010), 478.

11. Ibid.

coerced.[12] This sense is conveyed in multiple Psalms that seek divine favor (25:16, 86:16, 119:32) and in passages requesting that God "be gracious" to another (Numbers 6:25).

Christian Testament

The word most frequently used in the Christian Testament for *grace* is the Greek term *charis*, which literally means "goodwill, loving-kindness, favor, and benefit." Its meaning corresponds to each of the three terms used in the Hebrew scriptures: *charis* refers to God's acts of faithful love, of mercy, and of graciousness. It was often used as an introductory or final greeting in the Epistles; it expressed the atmosphere or condition desired for the early Church and for its members.[13] Biblical scholar John McKenzie notes the efficacious and relational character of *charis/grace* as a gift "given, [and] received, a reality in the Christian and in the world in which the Christian lives."[14]

McKenzie identifies several uses of *charis* in the Christian Testament: (1) the goodwill of God in the general and specific sense, (2) the saving will of God in principle and in effect, (3) the Gospel itself, and (4) the principle of Christian life and action.[15] *Charis* as the *goodwill of God* came upon Jesus at his baptism when the voice pronounced Jesus as the Son in whom God is well pleased (Luke 2:40). The disciples ask that the goodwill of God be with Paul and Barnabas in their missionary travels (Acts 14:26, 15:40). *The saving will of God* manifested through the life and death of Jesus Christ (Ephesians 1:6; Romans 2:24–25a) produces righteousness (Romans 3:24; Titus 3:7), spiritual riches (2 Corinthians 8:9), and faith and love (1 Timothy 1:14). *Charis* applies as well to the good news of *the Gospel* in which the Christian should stand (1 Peter 5:12), endure (Acts 14: 43), and grow (2 Peter 3:18). As a result, *charis* also serves as *the principle of Christian life and action*. It gave Stephen the power to speak (Acts 6:8) and Paul his power to preach (Romans 12:3;

---

12. Ibid.

13. John McKenzie, "Grace," in *The Dictionary of the Bible* (New York: Touchstone, 1995), 324.

14. Ibid., 325.

15. Ibid., 324–25.

1 Corinthians 3:10; Ephesians 3:7). It is also a gift that Paul can share with others (Ephesians 3:2; Philippians 1:7). Those who partake of this grace find their good works multiplied (2 Corinthians 8:1), gain strength to resist temptation (2 Corinthians 12:9), and possess a sure guide for their conduct (2 Corinthians 1:12). Therefore, as in the Hebrew scriptures, grace in the Christian Testament is efficacious and relational: "The Christian, while . . . absolutely a recipient of grace, is not an inert recipient; the saving good will of God enables [one] to hear the Gospel, to believe it, to become one with Jesus Christ and to live in union with Christ."[16]

Grace as Relation

These resonances between the understanding of God's grace in the Hebrew and Christian scriptures have given rise to a number of different interpretations of the nature and effects of grace throughout the centuries. "While all three connotations . . . are found in all [Christian] traditions, in each instance one or another is given primary emphasis."[17] Demonstrating these different emphases are four theologies of grace in the tradition: the theologies of Augustine of Hippo, Thomas Aquinas, Martin Luther, and Eastern Orthodoxy.

Augustine of Hippo

Augustine of Hippo's conviction concerning grace derived from three sources: his life experience, the teaching of scripture, and his opposition to the writings of Pelagius. Furthermore, like other theologies of grace both before and after him, Augustine's understanding of grace was juxtaposed to his understanding of sin. The necessity of grace stems from the sin of Adam in which all humans partake; the nature of grace is God's assistance to avoid evil and do good; and the effects of grace are freedom from enslavement to sin and reformation in the image of God in which humans are born.

While grace was the element that formed Augustine's theological development, the element that fomented his theology of grace was the teaching of Pelagius, a fifth-century British monk. In

16. Ibid., 325.
17. Patte and TeSelle, "Grace," 479.

essence, Pelagianism taught that the fall of Adam did not corrupt human nature with original sin or moral weakness and that humans have the ability to fulfill the commands of God through free will without divine grace. In opposition to these teachings, Augustine emphasized that original sin affected all humans, that free will was enslaved to disordered affections, and that grace alone frees the will to obey God.

Augustine was all too familiar with the inclinations and effects of sin on the human from his experience of a dissolute life. For Augustine, his own struggle characterized the human condition. Endowed with free will and divine aid, the first humans, nevertheless, chose to sin. This "original sin" corrupted human nature and affected the exercise of free will, now wounded, enslaved, and incapable of choosing to do good. According to Augustine, the grace of God frees humans from this enslavement; that alone can free the will from its bondage to sin.

Augustine likened grace to the law of God written within human hearts, which both liberates human will and kindles one's desire to turn to God and choose the good that God desires. However, this does not mean that human nature is no longer corrupted; rather, humanity remains always dependent upon the God's infinite mercy and undeserved favor. The grace of God, however, does not absolve humans of responsibility for their salvation. Each person must cooperate with the grace God has given through the exercise of the will, for although "'the will . . . alone does not suffice if the mercy of God be not also present'. . . . neither does the mercy of God alone suffice if the will . . . is not also active."[18]

Thomas Aquinas

Thomas Aquinas's theology of grace also begins with a consideration of the ontology of humans before and after original sin but arrives at a rather different conclusion about human nature than does Augustine. Aquinas did not conceive of sin as irreparably destroying the image and likeness of God in human nature. Nonetheless, he did recognize that sin weakened the capacity of human nature to choose the good and to avoid evil and the need for grace to restore and direct

---

18. Mary T. Clark, *Augustine* (New York: Continuum, 2000), 46; internal quote from Augustine, *Enchiridion ad Laurentium de fide, spe, caritate,* 32.

human nature to its truest end, the beatific (blessed) vision of God as Godself. Thus, while humans can still attain to natural good, they "cannot achieve the whole good natural to [them]."[19] Because the beatific vision is a supernatural orientation, humans always needed grace to attain it. However, having sinned, humans need this grace all the more, first to be healed of the effects of sin and then to attain supernatural good. Because of this, Aquinas taught that grace "builds on nature." Grace "is like a second nature to us, an ultimate principle within us elevating us to perform those operations and actions which lead us to our final goal, the vision of God."[20]

Grace for Aquinas has five effects: "first, that the soul is healed; second, that it wills what is good; third, that it carries out what it wills; fourth, that it perseveres in good; and fifth, that it attains to glory."[21] Aquinas relates these five effects in a causal sequence. Each grace causes an effect; however, the effect then becomes the cause for the next effective grace. The point is simply this: grace by its nature is characterized as an ongoing relation of cause and effect. More-over, this relation is enduring and unremitting as each effect of grace becomes a cause of grace in its turn.

Martin Luther

Like Augustine of Hippo, Martin Luther's theology of grace has its roots in personal experience, study of scripture, and disputation. In Luther's case, it was his concern for salvation, his biblical studies, and his controversy with the Catholic Church over indulgences and justification. His consonance with Augustine, however, also reflects that Luther himself was an Augustinian monk before his Ninety-Five Theses and subsequent writings resulted in his excommunica-tion from the Catholic Church. Luther's teachings and convictions are ordinarily credited with precipitating the Protestant Reformation and his theology formed the basis of the Augsburg Confession, the definitive statement of Lutheran religious belief.

---

19. Aquinas, *ST*, II.109.2.

20. Michael Lapierre, "Grace in Thomas Aquinas;" available from *http://www.catholic-church.org/grace/western/scholars/lap1.htm*.

21. Aquinas, *ST*, II.111.3.

The Letter of Paul to the Romans and Paul's concept of God's righteousness particularly influenced Luther. In his reading of Paul, Luther came to understand this righteousness not as divine judgment but as divine grace. Only through this grace, were humans justified and not by their works of penance or of charity. Luther's thinking on grace and justification caused him to take issue with the Catholic Church's practice of granting indulgences, the remission of temporal punishment due to sin that has been forgiven.[22] It is important to understand, however, that his objection to indulgences was rooted in Luther's understanding of human nature and justification.

For Luther, sin is not a temporary breach between humanity and God; sin is an essential state of "alienation from God. . . . one's *basic condition* as turned from God toward one's self."[23] If the nature of sin is ontological estrangement, then only the divine initiative of the gift of grace toward the sinner could heal this separation from God. Luther taught that God had taken the initiative to bridge the estrangement in Christ. Luther believed that humans were *simul iustus et peccator* (at once righteous and sinful). One did not gain righteousness through good works or the intercession of saints; rather, a person is justified through God's grace merited through Christ alone.

Based on human merit, therefore, a Christian is essentially sinful.[24] These understandings are expressed in Luther's famous five *solas* ("only" or "alone"): *sola scriptura* (scripture alone), *sola fide* (faith alone), *sola gratia* (grace alone), *solus Christus* (Christ alone), and *soli Deo Gloria* (glory to God alone). For Luther, "God only through Christ only . . . by grace only, received by faith only, disclosed in scripture only saves sinful humanity."[25] All the advantages of grace come "at no cost or labor on our part, but not without cost and labor on the part of Christ." [26]

---

22. See *Catechism of the Catholic Church*, no. 1471.

23. "Indulgences," *Catholic Encyclopedia*, available from *http://www.newadvent.org/cathen/07783a.htm*.

24. David M. Whitford, "Martin Luther (1483–1546)," *Internet Encyclopedia of Philosophy*; available from *http://www.iep.utm.edu/luther/*.

25. Ibid.

26. Martin Luther, "Second Christmas Sermon; Titus 3:4–8: A Sermon by Martin Luther; taken from his Church Postil of 1522," *Our Redeemer Lutheran Church*; available from *http://www.orlutheran.com/ html/mlseti03.html*.

Eastern Orthodoxy

Consistent with its view of divine-human communion as "the ultimate goal of Christian life," Eastern Orthodoxy envisions grace as "a communication of the divine energies, in which one participates" in the movement toward *theosis* or divinization.[27] These divine energies proceed from the essence of the Triune God, which in itself is unknowable. However, while distinguishing the energies and essence, participation in the divine energies is truly participation in the divine nature.[28]

According to Orthodox theologian Aristotle Papanikolaou, the concept of grace as the self-communication of divine energies derives from the event of the Incarnation.[29] Through the grace of the Incarnation, humans "participate in the divine nature, without our essence becoming thereby the essence of God. In deification [*theosis*] we are by grace . . . all that God is by nature."[30] Moreover, because "[t]he act of creation established a relationship between the divine energies and that which is not God,"[31] participation in these energies is not reserved to humans alone; rather, their salvific effects extend to the entire cosmos.[32] Grace is also communicated by the Holy Spirit through ascetic practices and through the sacraments of the Church, especially Baptism and Chrismation. The Holy Spirit bestows "the common energy of the Holy Trinity which is divine grace."[33] Moreover, this divine grace "is everywhere-present and fills all things *directly*," inspiring all creation "toward another better, albeit invisible and mysterious world."[34]

27. Aristotle Papanikolaou, "Grace of God in the Eastern Orthodox Tradition," in *The Cambridge Dictionary of Christianity*, ed. Daniel Patte (New York: Cambridge University Press, 2010), 478.

28. Vladimir Lossky, *The Mystical Theology of the Eastern Church* (London: James Clark and Co., 1957), 86.

29. Papanikolaou, "Grace of God in the Eastern Orthodox Tradition," 478.

30. Lossky, *Mystical Theology*, 87.

31. Ibid., 88.

32. Archbishop Demetrios Trakatellis, "Orthodox Churches, Eastern," in *The Cambridge Dictionary of Christianity*, ed. Daniel Patte (New York: Cambridge University Press, 2010), 894.

33. Lossky, *Mystical Theology*, 170–71.

34. Saint Theophan the Recluse, *The Path to Salvation*, trans. Seraphim Rose (Platina, CA: St. Herman of Alaska Brotherhood, 1996), 110.

EVOLUTIONARY PERSPECTIVES ON CAUSALITY AND ITS EFFECTS

Chapter 2 demonstrated how many of the entities, structures, and events experienced in the world result from specific causal relationships. These cause-and-effect relationships constitute a *relation of effect*. As used in this text, a relation of effect is one that exists among the essential elements of a particular entity such that the entity is a unique outcome of the operative relationships among its elements. Chapter 2 also explored the wide variety of causal relationships studied by different scientific disciplines at the macro and micro levels of existence.

Thus, along with the relations of origin and emergence, the relation of effect plays a key role in the ongoing evolution of the universe. It underlies the continuity that follows from natural law; it integrates chance occurrences into the broader matrix of cosmic existence. It impacts the play of particles and the actualization of outcomes at the subatomic level. These observations have led many scientists to consider cause and effect in the cosmos as proceeding from the "bottom-up" or from "part-to-whole," such that the properties, events, and behaviors of the parts of the cosmos influence the properties and behaviors of the cosmos as a whole.

Take for example the 9.0 magnitude earthquake that devastated Japan in 2011. Not only did it have disastrous effects on the people and infrastructure of Japan but also it affected the properties and behaviors of Earth itself. It shortened Earth's day by 1.8 microseconds, shifted Earth's axis by 6.5 inches, and moved the main island of Japan by almost 8 feet. However, these shifts in planetary properties are not unusual. Earthquakes, atmospheric winds, and ocean currents frequently change Earth's rotation, affect the length of the day, and alter the position of Earth's axis.[35]

In addition to the "bottom-up" or "part-to-whole" effect demonstrated in evolutionary processes, scientists have also observed that systems as a whole can exert influence on their component parts. In these instances, the relation of effect proceeds from top-down or

---

35. Doyle Rice, "NASA: Japan Quake Shortened Earth's Day, Shifted Axis," *USA TODAY*, March 15, 2011; available from *http://content.usatoday.com/communities/sciencefair/post/2011/03/japan-earthquake-shifted-earth-axis-shorter-day-nasa/1*.

from whole-to-part. How has this effect operated in the universe? Is the universe open to such whole-part interaction? To answer these questions, a brief overview of the concept of "system" proves helpful.

Systems

A system is a set of interdependent components that forms an integrated whole and maintains its existence through the mutual interaction of its parts. In the cosmos, tissues and organs, life forms and their environments, businesses and organizations, cities and nations, planets and stars, the Milky Way galaxy and others like it, all constitute systems. Each of these systems is defined by boundaries, with anything outside a defined system called its surroundings or environment.

The science of physics characterizes systems as open, closed, or isolated. The classification is based upon the nature of their boundaries and the state of the system itself. The state of a system is often discussed in terms of the laws of thermodynamics,[36] the division of physics concerned with the conversion of energy. The most significant of these laws for the current discussion are the first and second laws of thermodynamics. Stated simply, the first law of thermodynamics states that the total amount of energy of all kinds in a closed system remains constant; it can neither be created nor destroyed. The second law of thermodynamics states that entropy or unusable energy in a closed system increases over time; as entropy increases, randomness and chaos also increase within the system. As demonstrated by these definitions, these two laws apply most specifically to systems considered isolated or closed.

An isolated system can be contained within a larger system but has no communication with the outside system. Its boundaries are impermeable, and it cannot exchange either energy or matter. The most frequently cited example of an isolated system is a sealed and insulated thermos with either hot or cold liquid inside it. A closed system may also be part of a larger system, but it has limited interaction with it. The boundaries of a closed system are semi-permeable, which allows them to exchange energy but not matter with its

---

36. For a summary of the four basic laws of thermodynamics, see "Thermodynamics," *TheFreeDictionary*, available from *http://www.thefreedictionary.com/thermodynamics*.

environment. Thus, the system is relatively self-contained and self-maintaining; its total energy is fixed by boundary conditions; and it tends toward increased entropy.[37] Examples of a closed system include a greenhouse or an air conditioner; each exchanges energy in the form of heat or cold with its environment.

An open or dissipative system, on the other hand, is part of a larger system and is in intimate and interactive contact with it. It has permeable boundaries that can exchange both matter and energy with its environment and require interaction with its surrounding environment for the input of energy necessary to sustain vitality, development, processes, and order. As described by biologist Ludwig von Bertalanffy, an open system "maintains itself in a continuous inflow and outflow, a building up and breaking down of components, never being, so long as it is alive, in a state of chemical and thermodynamic equilibrium but maintained in a so-called steady state."[38]

The System of the Universe

Most of the systems examined by the sciences involve a defined region of the cosmos with real or theoretical boundaries that set the limits of their study. Scientists then measure the exchanges of energy or matter that occur between the system and its environment and so define the type of system being examined. However, having the universe itself as the system in question presents particular difficulties. How do scientists assess the status of the universe system? How do they define its boundaries? What kinds of transfers occur across its boundaries? Is the universe closed or open?

Questions about an open or closed universe can elicit two sets of responses: The first set involves speculation about the demise of the universe. The theory of demise associated with a closed universe indicates that the universe ends in the "Big Crunch" as gravity stops

---

37. *Entropy* is defined for a closed system as "a quantitative measure of the amount of thermal energy not available to do work" and as a "measure of the disorder or randomness." See *Entropy, The American Heritage Dictionary of the English Language,* 2009 (Boston: Houghton Mifflin, 2009); definition available from *TheFreeDictionary* at *http://www.thefreedictionary.com/entropy.*

38. Ludwig von Bertalanffy, *General Systems Theory: Foundations, Development, Applications* (New York: George Braziller, 1969); excerpts available from *http://www. panarchy.org/vonbertalanffy/ systems.1968.html.*

the ongoing expansion of the universe, and the universe collapses once again into a singularity. An open universe ends in either the "Big Freeze," in which the expansion of the universe results in so significant a diminishment of thermodynamic energy that it is unable to sustain life, or in the "Big Rip," in which the acceleration caused by dark energy[39] overcomes the effects of the gravitational and electromagnetic forces.

While the demise of the universe is of no small concern, this chapter asks a different kind of question that produces a second set of responses. It asks whether the universe is a closed or open system. Is the universe open to intimate exchange of energy with its surrounding environment (open), is it limited by boundary conditions (closed), or is the universe all there is (isolated)? Because it is empirically impossible to define the boundaries of the cosmic system, undisputed answers to such questions are largely unattainable. Nonetheless, thinkers from a variety of disciplines have weighed in on the issue.

The Universe as a Closed or Isolated System

When presented with the question of whether the universe is a closed, an isolated, or an open system, many speculate that the universe must be closed or isolated. Proponents of a closed or isolated universe argue "there is only one system, 'the Universe,' and all other systems are really just sub-systems of this larger system."[40] Another line of reasoning submits that, if open, the universe must demonstrate energy exchange with its environment and, they assert, the universe doesn't have an environment for such an exchange to occur. Others take an etymological approach and suggest that, because "the universe . . . is a term to describe the entire space-time continuum, including all of the energy stored in it," then, by definition it is an isolated system.[41]

---

39. Dark energy is a hypothetical form of energy that permeates space. It is the most accepted theory used to explain the accelerated rate at which the universe appears to be expanding. It is hypothesized to account for 75 percent of the total mass-energy of the universe. See P. J. E. Peebles and Bharat Ratra, "The Cosmological Constant and Dark Energy," *Reviews of Modern Physics* 75 (2003): 559–606.

40. Gene Bellinger, "Systems: A Journey along the Way," *Systems Thinking*; available from *http://www.systems-thinking.org/systems/systems.htm*.

41. "Second Law of Thermodynamics," *Rational Wiki*; available from *http://rationalwiki.org/ wiki/Second_law_of_thermodynamics*.

The physics of thermodynamics also provides a basis for concluding that the universe is a closed system. Biologist and systems researcher Stuart Kaufmann points out that beginning with the assumption of a closed universe that obeys the laws of thermodynamics is a logical point of departure. After all, "The theorists of thermodynamics and statistical mechanics have studied such systems for over 100 years. In contrast, remarkably little is known about the possible behaviors of open thermodynamic systems."[42] As an example of this approach, journalist David Mills writes that the first law of thermodynamics supports a closed system universe "since the total amount of energy within the universe remains constant."[43] Scientist Paul A. LaViolette indicates that the second law of thermodynamics concerning increasing disorder also "buttresses the closed system view" because cosmological observations reveal that the entropy of the physical universe only increases, never decreases.[44] Merging the two arguments, biologists Peter H. Raven, Ray Franklin Evert, and Susan E. Eichhorn conclude, "The matter and energy present in the universe at the time of the 'Big Bang' are all the matter and energy it will ever have. Moreover, after each and every energy exchange and transformation, the universe as a whole has less potential energy and more entropy than it did before. In this view, the universe is running down."[45]

The Universe as an Open or Dissipative System

While arguments based on the laws of thermodynamics seem persuasive, others contend that the evolving creativity, novelty, and complexity of the universe actually indicate that it does not fit the rules of a closed system. Contrary to the statement that the energy and matter at the Big Bang are all the energy and matter the universe will ever have,[46] arguments for an open system assert that cosmic

---

42. Stuart A. Kaufmann, *At Home in the Universe: The Search for Laws of Self-Organization and Complexity* (New York: Oxford University Press, 1996), 50.

43. David Mills, *Atheist Universe* (Berkeley, CA: Ulysses, 2006), 126.

44. Paul A. LaViolette, *Subquantum Kinetics: A Systems Approach to Physics and Cosmology* (Alexandria, VA: Starlane, 2003), 6.

45. Peter H. Raven, Ray Franklin Evert, and Susan E. Eichhorn, *Biology of Plants* (New York: W. H. Freeman and Co., 2005), 92.

46. Ibid.

dynamism affects levels of energy and entropy. In this dynamism, matter and energy constantly go in and out of existence in the universe, adding and subtracting rather than remaining static.[47]

Moreover, as Stuart Kaufmann indicates, "Open nonequilibrium systems obey very different rules from those of closed systems."[48] So, because an evolving universe is a prime example of an open system in nonequilibrium, it is critical to understand the rules that do apply.

Regarding the process of evolution, physicist Danah Zohar points out that, "creativity [in the cosmos] happens at far-from-equilibrium conditions."[49] Systems in nonequilibrium are those that are "changing or can be triggered to change over time, and are continuously and discontinuously subject to flux of matter and energy to and from other systems."[50] They hover between continuity and novelty, law and chance, probability and possibility, predictability and indeterminacy. In addition, rather than displaying the increasing disorder and disorganization, the structures and processes of the cosmos have shown an increase in novelty, organization, and complexity.

Because most systems in the process of such complexification are not in thermodynamic equilibrium, they "remain beyond the scope of currently known macroscopic thermodynamic methods."[51] In view of this evidence, the principles of classical physics often give way to those of quantum physics. Rather than requiring constancy of energy or increase of entropy, quantum theory "allows the possibility for matter and energy to become created, thereby increasing the matter/energy content of the universe and explaining the origin of the physical world within the universe's larger unseen environment."[52]

Evidence for these claims is found in the work of chemist Ilya Prigogine and physicist Gregoire Nicolis. They investigated how living organisms of greater novelty and complexity could come into

---

47. John Denker, *The Quantum God* (Bloomington, IN: iUniverse, 2010), 88.

48. Kaufmann, *At Home in the Universe*, 52.

49. Danah Zohar, *The Quantum Self* (New York: Harper Collins, 1990), 223.

50. "Non-equilibrium thermodynamics," *Wikipedia: The Free Encyclopedia*; available from *http://en.wikipedia.org/wiki/Non-equilibrium_thermodynamics*.

51. Ibid.

52. LaViolette, *Subquantum Kinetics*, 6.

278 TRINITY IN RELATION

existence in a universe that was supposedly tending toward increased entropy (disorder or disorganization). In their studies, they found a class of "dissipative" systems, that is, open systems operating far from thermodynamic equilibrium. Prigogine and Nicolis found that these systems had the capacity to maintain a state of order, even when the system itself was far from equilibrium.

Further investigation revealed that when disorder in a system is amplified to a particular rate, the whole system changes its structure. It becomes a newly ordered system with the capacity to take in energy and matter from the outside and to maintain its novel form. Examples of this phenomenon include rippled sand patterns from the ebb and flow of ocean waves, the formation of a school of fish from the meanderings of single swimmers, or the synchronous flashing of fireflies observed in Southeast Asia.[53] Prigogine and Nicolis reasoned that this capacity for order-through-fluctuations made the initial and ongoing emergence of living organisms probable. Consistent with this was their discovery of parallels "between dissipative structure formation and certain features occurring in the early stages of biogenesis and the subsequent evolution to higher forms,"[54] a finding that lent scientific support for the inherent evolutionary creativity of the universe.

Kaufmann points to the kinds of creativity that have occurred "far from equilibrium" in the dissipative, open system of the universe:

> The vast flowering of all life-forms over the past 3.45 billion years is merely a hint of the possible behaviors of open thermodynamic systems. So too is cosmogenesis itself, for the evolving universe since the Big Bang has yielded the formation of galactic and supragalactic structures on enormous scales. Those stellar structures and the nuclear processes within the stars, which have generated the atoms and molecules from which life itself arose, are open systems, driven by nonequilibrium processes. We have only begun to understand the awesome creative powers of nonequilibrium

---

53. Scott Camazine, "Self-organizing Systems;" available from *http://web.mac.com/camazine/Camazine/Self-organization_files/Self-organization.pdf*.

54. Ilya Prigogine and Gregoire Nicolis, "Biological Order, Structure and Instabilities," *Quarterly Review of Biophysics* 4 (1971): 107–148.

processes in the unfolding universe. We are all—complex atoms, Jupiter, spiral galaxies, warthog, and frog—the logical progeny of that creative power.[55]

In view of insights such as these from Prigogine, Nicolis, and Kaufmann, professor of physics Minas C. Kafatos and historian of science Robert Nadeau contend in their book *The Conscious Universe* that quantum theory holds the most promise for a complete description of the history of cosmic evolution.[56]

Envisioning the Universe as an Open System

In view of the preceding discussion about whether the universe is an isolated, closed, or open system, several factors converge to support the idea of the universe as an open system. The first is that evolutionary theory and quantum physics affirm the understanding of the universe as an open system that achieves order and novelty through fluctuation. Beyond this, however, additional grounds for affirmation lie in relational ontology and Trinitarian panentheism. The notion of the cosmos as an open system in intimate and interactive relation to other systems and to its environment—whatever that environment is conceived to be—is consistent with the fundamental premise of relational ontology, which holds that all being is intrinsically constituted by relation. Therefore, to opt for a view of the cosmos as a closed or isolated system essentially contradicts the very being-ness of the cosmos itself. Theologian Jürgen Moltmann expands on this idea when he writes: "All the systems of matter and life we know are open, complex systems. . . . Why should the universe as a whole, as the sum of its parts and individual systems, be a closed system? [Could we not] . . . infer from complex open systems a systematic openness of the whole that is not rounded off in an entirety[?]"[57]

In addition to the ontological grounds of the universe as an open system is the theological paradigm of Trinitarian panentheism,

---

55. Kaufmann, *At Home in the Universe*, 50–51.

56. Minas C. Kafatos and Robert Nadeau, *The Conscious Universe: Parts and Wholes in Physical Reality* (New York: Springer, 2000), 121.

57. Jürgen Moltmann, "Cosmos and Theosis," in *The Far-Future Universe: Eschatology from a Cosmic Perspective*, ed. George Francis Rayner Ellis (West Conshohocken, PA: Templeton Foundation, 2002), 263.

which images the Trinity in immanent, incarnate, and transcendent relation to the cosmos. In that model, the Being of God includes and yet transcends the being of the cosmos and the being of the cosmos exists within and participates in the Being of God. Following the scientific claim of the universe as an open system in receptive relation with its surrounding environment, the panentheistic paradigm makes a theological claim that the environment to which the universe is open and receptive is the very Being of God. Moreover, the panentheistic paradigm also indicates that the "observer" Who actualizes the events in the universe as a quantum system is the Triune God, "The Love that moves the sun and other stars,"[58] the One in whom the universe live and moves and has its being (Acts 17: 28).

Relations of Effect in the Open System of the Universe

The ubiquity of cause-and-effect relations within the system of the evolving cosmos gives much evidence for bottom-up or part-to-whole causality. The earthquake in Japan provides just one dramatic example of how the parts can affect the status of the whole. However, observations of self-organization in open systems continuously undergoing change and growth in a state of disequilibrium, like those studied by scientists such as Prigogine and Nicolis, give evidence that the converse is also true: the "whole" external environment in which a system exists has a relation of effect on its component parts. Philosopher Donald Campbell applied the interpretation of downward causation to the process of natural selection in the formation of jaw structures of worker termites and ants. In his study of how higher cultural values downwardly influence immediate humanitarian traits, psychologist Roger Sperry demonstrated that "downward causation" (whole-to-part influence) also applied to the realm of the behavioral and social sciences.[59]

---

58. "*L'Amor che move il sole e l'altre stele.*" Dante Alighieri, *Paradiso* xxx.iii. 139, *The Divine Comedy*; available from *http://www.everypoet.com/archive/poetry/dante/dante_x_33.htm*.

59. See Donald T. Campbell, "'Downward Causation' in Hierarchically Organized Systems," in *Studies in the Philosophy of Biology: Reduction and Related Problems*, eds. Francisco J. Ayala and Theodosius G. Dobzhansky (London: Macmillan, 1974) and Roger W. Sperry, *Science and Moral Priority* (Oxford: Blackwell, 1983).

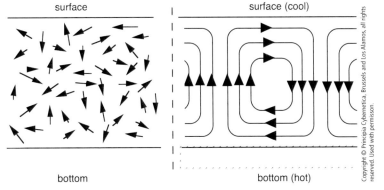

Figure 8.1: Movement of Liquid Molecules in the Bénard Phenomenon

A scientific example of the whole-to-part relation of effect is the Bénard phenomenon, which can be observed in liquid in an open container being heated by a hot plate from below. In this situation, the temperature of the water is uneven; the water at the bottom is heated, but the environment cools the water at the top. Warm water is lighter than cool water, so warm water moves toward the top and the cool water sinks. At first, this dual movement is disorganized. However, as Figure 8.1 shows, the cool and warm flows of water soon organize into a pattern with the warm flowing up one side of the pattern and the cool flowing down the other. As long as the environment of heat and cooling surrounding the water continues its effects, the parts of the system maintain their new organization.

Chapter 2 also presented an example of whole-to-part effect in an evolving universe. Recall the example of the peppered moth. While events at the genetic level played a role in the shift from a predominately light-winged population of moths to one with predominantly dark wings, it was actually the moth's relation to its shifting environment that effected the change in the observable population. The Industrial Revolution caused the effect of waste and pollution that produced the changed environment, which effected a change in the predatory habits of those who made meals out of the peppered-moth population. This change caused light-winged moths to be consumed in greater number than dark-winged ones, which then upped the percentage of dark-winged moths observed at the macro-level of the environment.

The list of such whole-part relations of effect is vast. The way the mind synchronizes the movement of the body in riding a bike, how an operating system coordinates the multiple programs and processes in a computer, and how a writer composes a theology text all demonstrate how the nature, intention, or function of a system as a whole has a relation of effect on given parts. However, testing how this whole-part relation applies to the parts of the cosmos as an open system and the "whole" of its surrounding environment as the Being of God presents the same significant obstacle that always arises in trying to speak of the mystery of God in relation to the cosmos. As it is not possible to examine directly the divine environment surrounding the cosmos, one must be content to extrapolate from the examples considered here to the whole-part relation of effect between the Triune God and the cosmos, the whole-part relation of effect called grace.

INTERPRETING GRACE IN AN EVOLVING COSMOS

The chapters 6 and 7 developed an understanding of the Christian God as the One Who in creation and incarnation lives and loves in intimate and enduring relation to the cosmos and its creatures. Chapter 6 identified the Holy Spirit as God in immanent relation to the cosmos who is the origin of its continuing fecundity. Chapter 7 identified Christ as God in incarnate relation to the cosmos who is the fulfillment and promise of its emergence toward union with God. This chapter envisions God as Father-Mother-Matrix in transcendent relation to the cosmos whose relation of grace empowers the cosmos and its creatures in emergence and self-transcendence toward union with God. Although this relation exists between God in divine transcendence and the cosmos, the intimate and enduring relation of grace precludes divine transcendence from implying either God's dwelling in serene detachment from the cosmos or God's acting as a "God-of-the-gaps" in sporadic or interventionist ways in cosmic existence. Using a panentheistic paradigm in dialogue with whole-part interaction, moreover, also precludes the objection that this effective relation violates the laws and regularities operative in the cosmos. As the "circumambient Reality in which the world persists and exists,"[60]

---

60. Peacocke, *Theology for a Scientific Age*, 158.

the Divine Matrix is that "System of systems,"[61] so to speak, in which the cosmos lives, moves, and has its being. Through grace, God permeates the universe as a whole to all levels of its constituent parts and can influence events and behaviors at all levels in a whole-part fashion.

In explaining panentheism, chapter 5 asserted that this model entails that "there is no 'place outside' the infinite God in which what is created could exist. God creates all-that-is *within* Godself."[62] Envisioning a being within whom and through whom another distinct being is created and sustained led to the image of a pregnant mother as a particularly fruitful way to conceive of a God within whom and through whom the distinct being of the universe is created and sustained. Nonetheless, the Christian tradition, in keeping with the example Jesus provided, has clearly preferred to speak of God as Father in transcendent relation to the cosmos. In the present context, however, the image of God the Father as the One in Whom the Incarnate One becomes flesh is analogically flawed as it does not convey an image analogous to human experience. Nonetheless, the image of God the Mother, while analogically effective for this purpose, has not gained sufficient sanction in the tradition. Therefore, this chapter uses the scientific term *matrix*, variously defined as "a situation or surrounding substance within which something else originates, develops, or is contained"; "the womb"; and "that which contains and gives shape or form to anything."[63] *Matrix* conveys the spatial image of that which surrounds or sustains another being, the relation of transcendence associated with both Father and Mother, and the scientific context of this project as a whole.[64]

---

61. Wiseman, *Theology and Modern Science*, 117.

62. Arthur Peacocke, "Articulating God's Presence in and to the World Unveiled by the Sciences," in *In Whom We Live and Move and Have Our Being: Panentheistic Reflections on God's Presence in a Scientific World,* eds. Philip Clayton and Arthur Peacocke (Grand Rapids, MI: Eerdmans, 2004), 147, italics in the original.

63. "Matrix," *FreeDictionary.com*, available from *http://www.thefreedictionary.com/matrix*.

64. Other contemporary theologians have used this terminology effectively to speak of the all-encompassing and transcendent presence of the Divine. For examples, *inter alia*, see Joseph Bracken, *The Divine Matrix: Creativity as Link between East and West* (Maryknoll, NY: Orbis, 1995); Rosemary Radford Ruether, *Sexism and God-Talk: Toward a Feminist Theology* (Boston: Beacon, 1983); and Gregg Braden, *The Divine Matrix: Bridging Time, Space, Miracles, and Belief* (Carlsbad, CA: Hay House, 2008).

Having made the decision about naming the God who enjoys this transcendent relation of effect called grace, the next step consists of identifying the nature, operation, and effect of grace in the cosmos. Two signposts guide this next step—creation and incarnation. First, that both creation and incarnation involved the self-communication of God in some way—expressed primordially through the cosmos and its creatures and preeminently in Jesus Christ—points to the need to identify the nature of grace as divine self-communication as well. Second, both these forms of divine self-communication had a mode of operation in the cosmos. Creation operated according to the interplay of chance and law in the course of the free process of the cosmos and the free will of humanity. Incarnation operated through the dynamic of emergence to actualize the potential inherent in the cosmos. This highlights the necessity of identifying the operation of grace within dynamics already at work in the cosmos. Third, both of these forms of divine self-communication had an observable manifestation in the history of the cosmos. Creation as a relation of origin took shape in history as the cosmos and its creatures. Incarnation as a relation of emergence became flesh in history in Jesus Christ, who was both the prolepsis and the promise of cosmic fulfillment. This indicates that manifestations of grace also need to be identified within the history of the cosmos. If grace is a relation of effect, what is its nature, how does it operate, and when does it make history?

The Nature of Grace: Divine Self-Communication

There is perhaps a no-more-appropriate writer on the nature of grace as divine self-communication than German theologian Karl Rahner. First, Rahner conceives of grace as the relationship between God and the world, a conception entirely consistent with the ontology and God-world paradigm that grounds this discussion. Second, based upon an understanding of incarnation and creation shared by this text, Rahner contends God is essentially self-communicating by nature and through grace. Therefore, Rahner asserts that what God communicates through this relationship of grace is God's own self to the cosmos and its creatures, an assertion consonant with the intimate and enduring nature of the relations affirmed in this study. Quite simply, God communicates Godself in freedom and love to an open and receptive cosmos in whole-part influence; the Giver is indeed the Gift in an enduring relation called grace.

While Rahner conceives of God "as the abiding and holy mystery, as the incomprehensible ground of [humanity's] transcendent existence," he insists that God is not simply infinitely distant. Rather, God "wants to be the God of absolute closeness in a true self-communication . . . in the spiritual depth of our existence as well as in the concreteness of our corporeal history."[65] Moreover, this true self-communication in absolute closeness is neither intermittent nor episodic; God does not draw near and then depart. Rather, the grace of God and God as grace is continually present to the cosmos, communicating the divine gift of self "even in situations in which the divine offer has not been accepted."[66]

Rahner makes this proviso because the gift of grace comes as offer, not as imposition. In his work on Rahner, Catholic theologian John Galvin discusses the fact that divine grace is present in three ways. First, it is present as "offer and appeal" to cosmic and human freedom without requiring any response on the part of creation.[67] Second, it may be present as offer that is accepted and, as such, becomes an efficacious event in the life of the cosmos and its creatures. Finally, the offer of grace may be present in a state of rejection in human and cosmic freedom. Nonetheless, "even in this instance, the offer does not vanish without a trace but remains," because the God Who makes the offer is the One Who fulfills the groaning of creation and the longing of the human heart.[68]

The understanding of grace as unconditional offer resonates with the conception of God as the Divine Matrix Who, as Giver and Gift together, envelops the cosmos with the grace of Divine Being. This grace-filled environment spawns the being of the cosmos and, in whole-part influence, nurtures and guides its growth. In an

---

65. Rahner, *Foundations of Christian Faith*, 137.

66. John Galvin, "The Invitation of Grace," in *A World of Grace: Introduction to the Themes and Foundations of Karl Rahner's Theology*, ed. Leo O'Donovan (New York: Crossroad, 1987), 67.

67. While Rahner most often discusses grace in terms of humanity's relationship with God and free choice to respond to God, this text sees fit to broaden its context to the cosmos as well.

68. Galvin, "The Invitation of Grace," 69.

ongoing exchange of energy and matter, the grace and favor of the Divine Matrix sustains the processes and structures of the cosmos and provides the milieu through which the cosmos can participate fully in the Being of grace itself. Though ever present to the cosmos with this offer of vitality, sustenance, flourishing, and fulfillment, the Divine Matrix nonetheless respects the freedom of the cosmos and its creatures to respond to the Giver and the Gift of life with acceptance, rejection, or ignorance. The fits and starts, the wrong turns and dead ends, the trials and errors of evolution testify that the cosmos and its creatures are not always receptive to this life-giving grace—to the ruin and devastation of its being! However, this Matrix of grace is ever present, ever energizing, and ever offering this communication of grace in the hope that all open themselves to receive it.

The Operation of Grace: The Strange Attractor

The understanding of the cosmos as an open system situated within the Divine Matrix Who interacts with the cosmos through the whole-part influence of grace leads to the question of how this graced influence operates. As discussed in the previous section, the open system of the evolving universe operates far from equilibrium and yet maintains and increases order, novelty, and complexity within its component parts. Therefore, a consideration of grace as a relation of effect in such a cosmos benefits from a theory consistent with the dynamic of order-through-fluctuation and self-organization-within-disequilibrium. The theory that suits this model is chaos theory and its concept of the strange attractor.

Chaos Theory and the Strange Attractor

As utilized in various branches of science, chaos theory applies to complex systems in which apparently random phenomena have an underlying order. Observations by chaos theorists of systems like the universe, which tend toward loss of energy and increased entropy (disorder), led to the discovery that these seemingly chaotic systems have in their midst a subtle pattern of order termed an "attractor." This attractor is a state of order toward which a dynamic system tends to evolve, regardless of the random or disordered condition of the system.[69] The attractor draws disparate events toward higher levels of organization and complexity, such that, in the midst of apparently chaotic and cohesionless events, unity in diversity emerges.

Meteorologist Edward Lorenz discovered one of the most famous of these attractors while working on the problem of weather prediction. As astrophysicist Larry Bradley tells the story,

> Edward Lorenz was a mathematician and meteorologist at the Massachusetts Institute of Technology who . . . set out to construct a mathematical model of the weather, namely a set of differential equations that represented changes in temperature, pressure, wind velocity [and the like]. . . . On a particular day . . . , Lorenz wanted to re-examine a sequence of data coming from his model. Instead of restarting the entire run, he decided to save time and restart the run from somewhere in the middle. Using data printouts, he entered the conditions at some point near the middle of the previous run, and re-started the model calculation. What he found was very unusual and unexpected. The data from the second run should have exactly matched the data from the first run. While they matched at first, the runs eventually began to diverge dramatically—the second run losing all resemblance to the first within a few "model" months.[70]

At first, Lorenz was at a loss to explain such a drastic difference. However, after reviewing the data he had entered for the abbreviated run, he noticed that, while he had entered numerical values from the printout rounded to three decimal places (e.g., .506), the computer utilized and stored values up to six decimal places (e.g., .506127). Lorenz had assumed that this difference was inconsequential; nonetheless, the outcome proved him wrong. What he found was that, as a nonlinear system,[71] weather was extremely sensitive to small

69. "Attractors," *TheFreeDictionary*; available from *http://www.thefreedictionary. com/attractor*.

70. Larry Bradley, "The Butterfly Effect," *Chaos and Fractals*; available from *http:// www.stsci.edu/~lbradley/seminar/butterfly.html*.

71. A nonlinear system is one that is sensitive to chance occurrences and has disproportionate cause and effect. Because of the influence of chance and the inherent unpredictability of events at the quantum level, most physical systems like the evolving universe itself are nonlinear and, therefore, resist strict predictability and determinism.

changes in initial conditions. Hence, even the truncation of data by three decimal places was enough to produce unexpected outcomes, that is, chaotic behavior.

Scientist that he was, Lorenz decided to retest this outcome using more simplified equations. He set up an experiment that subjected gas in a container to a heat source at the bottom. Lorenz then plotted the behavior produced by this dynamical, nonlinear system. Here is the pattern of behavior that emerged:

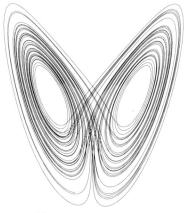

Figure 8.2: **The Lorenz Attractor (X–Z view)**

© George T. Yurkon. Used by permission.

This pattern that emerged came to be known as the Lorenz or the butterfly attractor. The name comes less from its shape than from the title given to a presentation by Lorenz in 1972, namely, "Does the flap of a butterfly's wings in Brazil set off a tornado in Texas?" The title and the presentation suggested that a butterfly's flapping wings could create alterations in the atmosphere that would produce or prevent the occurrence of a tornado in another location.

According to the theory, the butterfly's flapping produces an infinitesimal change in the initial condition of a weather system. This change at the micro-level of a system then produced a chain of events that results in alterations in the weather on the macro-level of a system. While the butterfly is not the direct cause of the tornado, the flap of its wings influences the initial conditions that result in tornado formation. In theory, without the flap, the tornado may never have come to exist. This phenomenon demonstrates two inter-related principles in chaos theory, which are displayed graphically by the Lorenz attractor.

On the one hand, the attractor shows that small variations in the initial conditions of a phenomenon can amplify over time and space and produce unpredictable and seemingly chaotic outcomes. This propensity for unpredictability is indicated by the divergence into the two patterns signified by the attractor's "wings." From an evolutionary perspective, this divergent patterning demonstrates how small genetic variations within a species can amplify to produce a new species over time. In an evolving universe, small differences magnify and reproduce in a pattern that diverges from the original pattern or species so that forecasting long-term outcomes becomes unlikely.

Nonetheless, the attractor also demonstrates that the outcome that appeared to be chaotic in comparison to expectations ultimately displays an underlying order within boundaries. While seemingly disorganized and chaotic in comparison to the patterns that were expected, over time the unpredicted outcome demonstrates a pattern of its own with the capacity to organize phenomena with similar behavior and characteristics. This propensity of organization-from-chaos is also displayed in the Lorenz attractor. It is demonstrated by the emergence of a well-defined alternate pattern or "wing" of the butterfly in tandem with the first. From an evolutionary perspective, the emergence of the parallel pattern represents the establishment and reproduction of the new species as a novel form over time. This novel form then becomes the pattern that signifies the species, a pattern that then subsumes like-featured forms into its dynamic organization.

The Lorenz attractor is just one example of several forms of attractors that chaos theorists have identified in dynamic systems like the cosmos. Theorists call these *strange attractors*, a term that means "an ordering principle that draws systems with similar conditions into a dynamic pattern." While basic to reality itself, strange attractors could not be observed until computers allowed scientists to study them. Moreover, although now recognized, the exact nature of the strange attractor is not yet clearly understood. "The strange attractor is both within the system and yet different from the system's usual pattern of behavior . . . it is unclear how it emerges. It arises spontaneously and gradually lures the system into new patterns of behavior without forcing the system to change radically."[72] Because of this, some "scientists have claimed that the appearance of the 'strange attractor' means that order is inherent in chaos because the 'attractor' itself is a novel pattern of order that arises spontaneously within a system. When systems are dislodged from a stable state . . . the strange attractor seems to 'spontaneously' appear."[73]

The strange attractor signifies that order can appear out of the chaos caused by changes in initial conditions in dynamic systems open to change. While ordinarily hidden from human observation, the strange attractor is nonetheless quite real. In the cosmos—dynamic, evolving, and open to change—they exist in unseen potentiality. Nevertheless, when a confluence of events, seemingly random or chaotic or far from equilibrium, is observed closely enough over time, one discovers the strange attractor, that subtle, discernible, and effective principle of relation that reveals and maintains their underlying order. This strange attractor provides an intriguing and appropriate way to image the cosmic operation of what Christians call grace.

Grace as a Strange Attractor

In an evolving universe in which natural, human, and cosmic systems are in dynamic and often chaotic flux, portending a future full of increasing disorder and ultimate death, the strange attractor is the pattern or "whole" that draws together the "parts" of law and chance, of continuity and novelty, and of consistency and indeterminacy to actualize the potential inherent in the cosmos. In like manner, grace is the "whole" of the Divine Matrix luring the "parts" of the universe toward greater harmony, unity, and complexity in interaction with the very processes of natural and human evolution itself.

In the midst of the chaos of conflict and division, self-centeredness and xenophobia, oppression and marginalization, the action of grace can cause a small and perhaps imperceptible change in the sensibilities of human persons, luring them beyond personal and social

---

72. Ilia Delio, *Franciscan Prayer* (Cincinnati, OH: St. Anthony Messenger Press, 2004), 41.

73. Ilia Delio, "Does God 'Act' in Creation? Part 3/3," *The Global Spiral*; available from *http://www.metanexus.net/magazine/tabid/68/id/7935/Default.aspx.*

fragmentation toward a pattern of solidarity and community. The action of grace through the natural environment of mountains and trees, lakes and streams, flora and fauna, sunrise and sunset changes human perceptions of the natural world, enabling the Divine Matrix to invite cosmic and human beings into a pattern of union with each another and with Being's own Self. In response to disaster and destruction, catastrophe and misfortune, decay and death, grace reorders the remnants of energy, matter, space, and time toward patterns of healing, vitality, and new forms of life. In each of these situations and at all levels of the universe, the action of grace of the Divine Matrix draws and integrates the disparate and random "parts" of cosmic life and pulls it forward into patterns of greater fecundity and complexity through the evolutionary processes themselves. From the seeming randomness of human and cosmic history, there emerges a graced order, a perceptible pattern that first orders and then continues to draw diversity into unity, death into life, and chaos into complexity. This is the action of grace, divine grace as the Strange Attractor.

How might this Divine Strange Attractor and the operations of grace be better understood? In his fanciful yet profound book, *The Universe Is a Green Dragon*,[74] mathematician and cosmologist Brian Swimme relates a fascinating conversation about the Strange Attractor between two speakers, "Youth," who represents the human species, and "Thomas," the late cosmologist and Earth scholar Thomas Berry. In this dialogue, Youth asks Thomas about the destiny of the cosmos, and Thomas responds that Youth's destiny is "To become love in human form. . . . The journey out of emptiness is the creation of love." Thomas goes on to explain:

> If we want to learn anything, we must start with the cosmos, the Earth, and life forms. Love begins as allurement—as attraction. . . . When we look at love from a cosmic perspective, we see attraction operating at every level. . . . Love begins there. To become fascinated, to feel allurement, is to step into a wild love affair on any level of life.

---

74. Brian Swimme, *The Universe Is a Green Dragon: A Cosmic Creation Story* (Rochester, VT: Bear & Co., 1984). The excerpts used in this section are drawn from *In Context: A Quarterly of Humane Sustainable Culture*, Context Institute; available from *http://www.context.org/ICLIB/IC12/Swimme.htm*.

What Thomas shares with Youth has profound meaning theologically. He says that the Strange Attractor, "the allurements filling the universe, of whatever complexity or order"—gravitation, electromagnetism, chemical bonds, ecosystems, culture, and the like—forms a cosmic matrix of relationality and love! Is this not what Christianity says about God and what this text has said about being itself at all levels? "God is love" (1 John 4:16)—truly the "The Love that moves the sun and other stars"—the Divine Matrix of grace in whom all live and move and have being. Without Love, the attraction and pattern that binds and draws the cosmos together and into its future, "The Earth would break apart . . . , all the minerals and chemical compounds dissolving, mountains evaporating like huge dark clouds under the noon sun. . . . all human groups would lose their binding energy. . . . Nothing left. No community of any sort. Just nothing."[75] Yet, the Strange Attractor of divine grace is the hidden pattern preventing this dissolution. God "who is over all and through all and in all" (Ephesians 4:6) is faithful and remains that abiding Divine Matrix of grace, the fullness of Love who fills all in all (Ephesians 1:23).

The Manifestation of Grace: Transcendence

The preceding sections spoke of divine grace as a hidden, mysterious Strange Attractor, as a Matrix of relationality drawing all things into union with one another and with itself. In the theological context, this Strange Attractor, this Matrix of dynamic unity within diversity, is the relation of effect called the grace of God. Clearly, the operation of grace as the Strange Attractor lures the cosmos and its creatures into union, novelty, and healing in the midst of influences and dynamics that thrust them otherwise. Moreover, it does so in different ways and with different results at various levels of the cosmos that it envelops as its Whole. Consistent with its being a transcendent relation between the Divine and the cosmos, the operation of grace functions at each level to draw that graced part of the cosmos beyond that which disorders and de-energizes into a form of life characterized by novelty, vibrancy, and complexity. However, like the

---

75. Ibid.

strange attractor of chaos theory, the operative and ordering presence of grace in the cosmos may often be hidden, mysterious, and undetected unless one cultivates the vision necessary to see the pattern underlying its effects.

Chapter 7 discussed this dynamic of transcendence in cosmic terms as emergence, pointing out how Karl Rahner's description of transcendence in his reflection on Christology with an evolutionary worldview correlates well with the dynamic of emergence. According to Rahner, transcendence in general occurs when "something which existed earlier really surpasses itself in order . . . to become something different and [yet] to preserve itself."[76] This definition includes all the elements essential to an emergent: prior existence that surpasses itself to become something different while preserving its connection to that which preexisted it. This chapter now adds to that notion by proposing that the impetus for cosmic emergence is the holistic influence of the Divine Matrix of grace upon the parts of the cosmos. It is the loving yet strange attractor of grace "that moves the sun and other stars," stirs being into becoming, lures the present toward the future, and actualizes the potential inherent in cosmic life. However, not only does this effect of grace manifest itself at the cosmic level; grace also draws life into transcendence, order, and novelty at the levels of persons and social systems as well.

Karl Rahner theorized that the self-communication of God as Grace draws humans into self-transcendence within oneself and in relation to other persons. Because Rahner held that the dynamic of self-transcendence constitutes an essential aspect of human nature, he maintained that humans are existentially ordered toward "the more": they question, desire, yearn, plan, hope, and search, always reaching out beyond their present experiences, always transgressing the limits of their existence. In Rahner's theology, the More toward Whom humans are ultimately ordered is the Infinite Horizon of God's own self. Thus, the dynamic impetus for any other form of transcendence in human existence is the God of grace, drawing humanity toward a final self-transcendence into union with the Divine Matrix itself.

Nonetheless, the impetus of grace toward transcending the self is also operative in interpersonal relationships. Rahner is fond of

---

76. Rahner, *Foundation of Christian Faith*, 186.

pointing out that love of God and love of neighbor are two sides of the same coin.[77] Hence, the dynamic of loving transcendence toward God is the flipside of loving transcendence toward others. In this context, the Strange Attractor of grace orders the human beyond self-centeredness toward other-centeredness, beyond selfish and self-serving inclinations toward compassion and right relationship with others. In a passage from his book, *Do You Believe in God?* Rahner gives this practical example of what such transcendence in grace looks like: "Have we ever made a sacrifice without receiving any thanks? Have we ever decided to do a thing simply for the sake of conscience? Have we ever tried to act purely for the love of God . . . when our act seemed a leap in the dark? If we can find such experiences in our life . . . then we have had that very experience of the Eternal."[78] And this experience of the Eternal is the transcendent experience of grace.

Grace not only orders human relationship with one another but also with the cosmos. As theologian Elizabeth Dreyer writes, "Grace can never thrive in isolation or solitariness. Indeed, one of its main functions is to connect [persons] . . . with the totality of reality."[79] Right relation with the cosmos in grace manifests itself in particular attitudes and actions toward the cosmos and its creatures. In her essay "God's Beloved Creation," Elizabeth Johnson proposes three attitudes that manifest graced relation with the cosmos: the contemplative, the ascetic, and the prophetic.[80] A contemplative attitude toward the environment invites persons to view the world lovingly, rather than with utilitarian arrogance. It calls one to appreciate the beauty of creation and to be awed by its mystery. An ascetic attitude encourages humans to practice discipline in using Earth's resources and to make ecologically and environmentally responsible choices. Finally, a prophetic attitude toward the cosmos recognizes the ongoing destruction of the cosmos as a sign of sinfulness and

---

77. See Karl Rahner, "Reflections on the Unity of the Love of Neighbor and the Love of God," *Theological Investigations,* Vol. 6, trans. Karl H. and Boniface Kruger (Baltimore: Helicon Press, 1969), 231–49.

78. Karl Rahner, *Do You Believe in God?*" in *Foundations of Theological Study: A Sourcebook*, ed. Richard Viladesau and Mark Massa (New York: Paulist, 1991), 27.

79. Dreyer, *Manifestations of Grace*, 22.

80. Elizabeth A. Johnson, "God's Beloved Creation," *America* 184:13 (2001): 8–12.

challenges persons to action for justice on behalf of Earth. This form of justice entails a conversion from anthropocentrism to ensure vibrant life in community for all and calls for political action and structural transformation to insure the vitality of the cosmos.

Hence, in an evolving cosmos, "human beings cannot be separated from the earth and the material world; their transformation is part of a transformation of the world."[81] When one is drawn beyond the self-concern and self-preservation that serve only to de-energize and disorder rather than to actualize one's emergence into greater consciousness and right relation with others and the cosmos, there is manifest the Strange Attractor of grace.

The transcendent attraction of grace is also effective at the level of social systems. In social systems, disorder and disintegration manifest themselves as conflict and division, xenophobia and exclusion, oppression and marginalization. Such disorders de-energize and destabilize families, neighborhoods, communities, societies, nations, and Earth itself. Nonetheless, the holistic attraction of grace upon these parts of the cosmos "changes . . . hearts: enemies begin to speak to one another, those who were estranged join hands in friendship, and nations seek the way of peace together." Grace is at work "when understanding puts an end to strife, when hatred is quenched by mercy, and vengeance gives way to forgiveness."[82]

The manifestation of graced transcendence at the level of social systems is often termed *liberation* and *transformation toward justice*. According to liberation theologian José Comblin, grace is "holiness and justice"[83] within the community and broader culture, "the soul" of the liberation movement, "the root of the liberation of the poor."[84] In the history of the poor and oppressed, grace "produces resistance, faith, hope." Moreover, in the midst of the chaos of poverty and oppression, "God's grace is the force that awakens, animates, and maintains the struggle of the oppressed, who are victims of injustice

---

81. José Comblin, "Grace," in *Mysterium Liberationis: Fundamental Concepts in Liberation Theology*, eds. Ignacio Ellacuría and Jon Sobrino (Maryknoll, NY: Orbis, 1993), 524.

82. "Eucharistic Prayer for Reconciliation II," *Basic Texts for the Roman Catholic Eucharist*; available from *http://catholic-resources.org/ChurchDocs/EPR1-2.htm*.

83. Comblin, "Grace," 526.

84. Ibid., 530.

and evil."[85] On the level of social systems, grace exerts a holistic effect on human existence, such that the history of the influence of God's grace is a history of liberation. Nonetheless, the grace that orders the whole of human history toward liberation depends upon the collaboration of the participants in that history, for grace is effective in society only as it is "operative in and through . . . human praxis as cooperation in God's transformation of the world."[86]

INTERPRETING THE DIVINE THROUGH AN EVOLUTIONARY VIEW OF GRACE

Like the evolutionary understanding of creation and incarnation, an evolutionary understanding of grace as a whole-part relation of effect has ramifications for the Divine, particularly with regard to divine suffering.

Divine Suffering

God's whole-part, circumambient interaction with the cosmos clearly addresses the means by which the Divine Matrix of grace influences creation. However, by following a fuller understanding of whole-part model, one finds that the movement of influence is not solely "whole-part" but is bidirectional. Even as science has demonstrated that a system-as-a-whole influences the constituent parts within its environment, it has also demonstrated that the constituent parts influence the system-as-a-whole. Thus, just as God the Divine Matrix genuinely influences events at all levels of created being in a whole-part fashion, so the actions and intentions of the parts of the cosmos also exert a part-whole effect on the Being of its Divine Matrix.

Because God is the Divine Matrix and the Strange Attractor, the environment of grace vivifying and transforming the cosmos in whole-part influence, then "every quark, every particle, every aspect

---

85. Ibid.

86. Mary Catherine Hilkert, *Naming Grace: Preaching and the Sacramental Imagination* (New York: Continuum, 2006), 41.

of matter and energy is connected to God's desire and hope for the world."[87] However, if this relation of effect is bidirectional then God does not remain isolated from the events of the cosmos. Rather, the Divine Matrix exists in intimate and enduring relation with these cosmic realities to the extent that these realities possess a relation of effect upon the Divine.

Because the cosmos retains autonomy and freedom in its relationship with its Divine Matrix, it is conceivable that God's capacity to influence the cosmos may encounter resistance and rejection in the exercise of free will and free process by the cosmos and its creatures. In the extreme, this cosmic and human freedom may hinder the participation of creation in the life-giving energies of Divine Grace that permeate the cosmos and, in so doing, even thwart or disrupt the unfolding of divine purpose and intention in the universe. Conversely, because the Divine remains free and autonomous, as well as in relation to creation, it is conceivable that God's love and justice restrains God from participating in those actions that oppose life and fecundity and promise death and devastation. Thus, one can never facilely attribute calamitous events and misfortunes to "God's will" or as "God's plan" for persons or for the universe.

Nonetheless, although refusing to provide energy and sustenance to such destructive tendencies, the Divine Matrix who surrounds, embraces, and sustains the very being of the cosmos within its own Being cannot remain unaffected by cosmic realities resulting in pain, death, suffering in God's beloved creation. In response to the travail of the cosmos, the Divine Matrix suffers in *sympathy*, "the quality or state of being . . . affected by the suffering or sorrow of another; a feeling of compassion or commiseration."[88] In the affliction of the cosmos and its creatures, the Divine Matrix moans with all creation as a mother who does not forget the child of her womb and whose senses reverberate with the prayers, intercessions, cries, and groanings of the universe and its creatures.[89]

---

87. Jeffrey C. Pugh, *Entertaining the Triune Mystery: God, Science, and the Space Between* (Harrisburg, PA: Trinity, 2003), 53.

88. "Sympathy," *The Oxford English Dictionary Online*; available from *http://dictionary.oed.com*.

89. Cf. Isaiah 49:15 (*NAB*).

Ceaselessly responding to all who are suffering and in need, the Divine Matrix continually permeates the chaos of the cosmos in all its pain and suffering with divine energy, drawing it toward order and new life. Eternally active in relation to creation, the Divine Matrix persistently pulses with the incessant offer and gift of grace. This never ceasing, always increasing, gift promises a future full of hope to those open and receptive to the divine love and attraction present in even the direst of circumstances. Even disordered and de-energizing events that arise in the course of cosmic evolution become the means through which the Divine Matrix intimately draws the cosmos and its creatures to self-transcendence toward union with the Source of their existence.

GRACE IN AN EVOLVING COSMOS: RESONANCES IN THE TRADITION

Biblical, Religious, and Liturgical Resonances

As the scriptures and the principal insights of the Christian tradition cited earlier indicate, grace is most frequently understood as the favor and love of God toward fragile and often sinful humans, enabling them to transcend suffering and death through new life in Christ and to order their lives toward God. Moreover, the Christian scriptures conceive of grace as the very atmosphere in which the early Church and its members must live. Those who dwell within this Matrix receive the capacity to transcend themselves to perform good works for others (2 Corinthians 8:1), to resist temptation (2 Corinthians 12:9), and to order their conduct around the example of Christ as a manifestation of grace (2 Corinthians 1:12).

This theme of self-transcendence continues into the theologies of grace of Augustine, Aquinas, Luther, and Eastern Orthodoxy and continues to religious traditions today. Because of the corruption of human nature caused by original sin, humanity lives in the chaos of disordered desires and disjointed relationships, to which grace alone can bring order and right relation. Yet, this grace is ever present, "a constant efflux from God," offering humans a way to pattern their lives toward the Good and the Gracious Goal of their being. As the *Catechism of the Catholic Church* states, "Grace is the free and undeserved help that God gives us to respond to [God's] call to become . . . partakers of the divine nature and of eternal life. . . . It introduces us into the intimacy of Trinitarian life."[90] This dynamic of graced self-transcendence is most explicitly expressed in Eastern Orthodoxy, which speaks of the divine energies that draw the cosmos and its creatures into the very life of God. These energies represent the grace of the Trinity, "that is everywhere-present and fills all things directly," the Matrix who is the dynamic pattern in which all being is formed and drawn "toward another better, albeit invisible and mysterious world."[91]

The recognition of the saving grace surrounding all of creation permeates devotional and inspirational Christian literature and song. Every Christian denomination acknowledges the "Amazing Grace" who saves and sets one free and Christian musicians sing of the grace that is "on me like water," the grace that "surrounds me like rivers deep."[92] Baptist pastor Rick Farmer exhorts his congregation that, "Grace surrounds us, overwhelms us, and guards us . . . without any desire to cease the gifts so faithfully delivered moment after moment after gracious moment. This is reality."[93] In his book *God Hides in Plain Sight: How to See the Sacred in a Chaotic World,* journalist Dean Nelson aptly summarized this wide-ranging appreciation of the graced environ in which the chaotic cosmos exists: "Something is constantly breaking through our dulled senses, telling us that we matter—that grace surrounds us. . . . Can we witness the holy within the finite? . . . If we're paying attention, we do."[94]

Liturgically, grace is most closely connected to the sacramental life of the Church. Its relationship with grace is articulated in the

---

90. *Catechism of the Catholic Church*, nos. 1996, 1997.

91. Theophan, *The Path to Salvation*, 110.

92. Ric Knott, "Grace"; lyrics available from *http://www.myspace.com/parachute-band/blog/ 483573591.*

93. Rick Farmer, "What Did David Discover on This Matter of God's Grace," *Grace Thoughts Continued,* Trinity Baptist Church, Marion, OH; available from *http://www.tbcmarion.org/pastors-blog/33-blog/86-grace-thoughts-continued.*

94. Dean Nelson, *God Hides in Plain Sight: How to See the Sacred in a Chaotic World* (Grand Rapids, MI: Brazos, 2009), 49, 24, 208.

definition of sacraments as "efficacious signs of grace" which "make present the graces proper to the sacrament" and "bear fruit in those who recieve them."[95] In dialogue with the analogy of grace as the Strange Attractor, this definition produces an intriguing resonance with some proposals in this chapter. As the Strange Attractor of grace is the hidden, imperceptible pattern giving deeper meaning to cosmic form and matter, so grace is the imperceptible pattern within the sacraments giving deeper meaning to the sacramental forms and matter. As the Strange Attractor of grace orders cosmic form and matter toward higher levels of existence, the grace of the sacraments orders believers toward union with the triune life of God. Finally, as the Strange Attractor of grace lures the cosmos and its creatures in self-transcendence toward justice and right relation, so the grace of the sacraments has the power to affect justice in those drawn into the dynamism of the Divine Matrix.

Contemporary Theological Resonances

In addition to the biblical, religious, and liturgical resonances, one finds theological resonances in the work of contemporary theologians who take an evolutionary approach to grace. Therefore, this final section draws attention to the contributions of theologians whose works enhance the line of thought developed in this chapter. It is interesting to note that, while using analogies discussed in this chapter, these theologians do not necessarily appropriate their God-world interactions to God in divine transcendence. Rather than being problematic, however, their application of similar models to different relations in the Trinity only serve to underscore the maxim "*opera Trinitatis ad extra indivisa sunt*" (the works of the Trinity in history are indivisible). This is evidenced in the proposals of Catholic theologian John Haught, scientist and Catholic theologian Ilia Delio, and Protestant theologian Peter C. Hodgson.

John Haught: The Informed Universe

John Haught develops his theology of the pervasive and effective relation of God to the universe from the perspective of an

---

95. *Catechism of the Catholic Church*, no. 1131.

"informed universe."[96] According to Haught, information is part and parcel of any contemporary view of the cosmos. Therefore, he proposes, the cosmos may be imaged analogically in computer terms and God's relation to the cosmos imaged as an input of communication termed *Information Incarnate*. This analogy, though contemporary, is consonant with traditions in both theology and cosmology. In religious traditions, the natural world has long been envisioned as a text rich in information about creation and its Creator. These traditions characterized God's "informing" presence as Word, Torah, Wisdom, or Teaching. In the information age, this analogy now reasserts itself as equally consonant with evolutionary information theory.

In this analogy, Haught images "God as self-giving love that seeks to 'inform' the world in a continually novel manner."[97] As such, God is neither manipulative nor coercive; rather, in the dynamic of loving and reciprocal relationship, God is gentle and persuasive in tolerance and self-restraint. A God imaged thus allows the cosmos to *become*, according to its emergent nature, rather than to *be* in an instantaneous act of creation. Unlike models that avoid "the dark and tragic side of nature's evolutionary creativity," the persuasive God of the information model welcomes the fits and starts of the creative process and embraces the chaos of creativity as sign of a cosmos creating itself in freedom and spontaneity.[98]

The informational model is based analogically on the hierarchical assembly of the circuitry, machinery, and programming of a computer. The highest level neither interferes with nor changes the principles governing the processes operative at the succeeding levels of the assembly. Rather, it "relies upon their predictable, invariant functioning according to fixed rules and natural laws" to produce an intelligible pattern of output.[99] The overarching meaning or purpose of the output is not found at the lower levels of operation but is discernible only at the highest level of input. However, because

---

96. John Haught, "The Informed Universe and the Existence of God," in *Existence of God: Essays from the Basic Issues Forum*, eds. John R. Jacobson and Robert Lloyd Mitchell (Lewiston, NY: Edwin Mellen, 1988).

97. Ibid., 224.

98. John Haught, "Science, Religion, and the Sacred Depths of Nature," *Quarterly Review* 21 (2001): 340.

99. Haught, "The Informed Universe," 231.

the communication depends upon the lower levels of processing, it is "vulnerable to any mechanical or electronic breakdowns that might occur at the subordinate levels," resulting in disruption or distortion of the information flow.[100]

The applicability of this model to the whole-part interaction between the Divine Matrix and the universe is clear. It suggests how the informing power of God, operative in transcendent relation to the cosmos, can influence the universe in noncoercive and non-manipulative ways. It accounts for the presence of suffering and evil in the cosmos as attributable to the noise and redundancy inherent in an "actual world . . . that emerges and persists out of . . . both order and chaos."[101] This analogy also responds to the objection of some in the sciences that claim that because a divine informational principle is undetectable at the lower levels of the hierarchy then it is nonexistent. However, Haught replies that this purposeful divine influence is discernible by those religious and spiritual traditions that have devised ways to "render our consciousness . . . 'adequate' to the higher . . . levels of reality."[102] According to Haught, this kind of awareness is named *faith*, a faith in "the ultimate incomprehensible level of reality . . . symbolized [as] . . . self-giving love (no other symbolization of God being worthy of defense)."[103]

Ilia Delio: Creation as Attraction

Beginning with the supposition that the "humility of divine love" is the condition making a self-organizing universe possible, the work of Ilia Delio calls for a shift in the Christian image of God as unconditionally omnipotent and omniscient to one whose power is "integrally related" to that self-emptying love.[104] Within the context of chaos and complexity, Delio affirms that God grants the universe the freedom to unfold in spontaneity and creativity. Nonetheless, she contends that the genuine, but finite, freedom of creation exists within

---

100. Ibid., 233.

101. Ibid., 240.

102. Ibid., 237.

103. Ibid.

104. Delio, "Does God 'Act' in Creation? Part 3/3." All quotations that follow in this section are taken from this essay unless otherwise indicated.

the infinite freedom of God. Hence, "the degree to which creation can become skewed due to a betrayal of freedom can never exceed God's will or love . . . [or] exist independently of that freedom which is its source." In view of this, how does God act in creation?

According to Delio, God's love is "the more that lures creation toward itself." To explain this, Delio utilizes the Trinitarian theology of Bonaventure. Bonaventure holds that the source of all creation is the relation between the Father and the Son or Word. As Word, the Son is the expression of the Father's ideas and thus serves as the exemplar for all creation. Moreover, the Father loves the Word and all creation in the Word. As all creation flows from the Word, in the fullness of time it returns to the Word as its fulfillment. In this way, "the fecundity of God's inner life . . . is the same fecundity that provides the diversity of creation." Hence, for Bonaventure, divine creation is essentially divine relation and, therefore, the search for how God "acts" in creation is enveloped "in the primordial mystery of trinitarian love."

However, Delio does not simply dispense with this mystery. Instead, she proposes, "If divine action is none other than the relationship between the Trinity and creation, we might say that the Trinity of love is always attracting creation as the beloved, as the Father attracts the Son in the eternal breath of the Spirit's love." Expressing this understanding in terms suited to her scientific background, Delio employs the analogy of the strange attractor. As the Strange Attractor, God lures creation toward "the more" or "the optimal good." Because its source lies within the life of the Trinity itself, creation is neither "in a state of equilibrium or at rest"; rather it is always "dynamically oriented toward the triune God." Thus, instead of understanding creation as a process of bringing new things into existence, creation as attraction implies a movement toward a "complexity of goodness or love," which comes to full fruition in reunion with God from Whom it flowed.

Peter C. Hodgson: God as the Strange Attractor

In his book *Winds of the Spirit*, theologian Peter C. Hodgson begins with the premise common to those engaged in the science-theology dialogue regarding the God-world relation: that God's interaction with the cosmic process must be conceived as continuous rather than sporadic and intrinsic rather than external. To express this divine-cosmic relationship, Hodgson proposes an understanding of God as the "personal spiritual *eros* that shapes and lures the world toward love and freedom . . . inwardly, evoking response, empowering power."[105] Hodgson develops his theology as a pneumatology, conceiving the Spirit of God as the "Creative and Alluring Cosmic Eros."[106] In so doing, Hodgson echoes Brian Swimme's understanding of cosmic attraction as the love that "lures, attracts, connects, empowers." He chooses the particular nature of love as erotic to signify that "God creates, desires, and allures the world in its vitality and materiality, while at the same time transfiguring that materiality into relationships of . . . mutuality [and] self-giving."[107] As erotic, this power of God is "primal energy" whose "fundamental quality is that of allurement, of drawing all things to itself and of sustaining and cherishing all things in relationship to it."[108]

Hodgson suggests that an appropriate term for the divine love and allurement permeating the cosmos is "the Strange Attractor" who is "not directly visible but appears in and through the turbulence and fluidity of countless dynamic events in natural and human history." While Hodgson acknowledges that appropriating this language to God is an act of faith that exceeds the limit of scientific theory, he nevertheless endorses this analogy as resonant with both science and with biblical images of divine presence and power. In particular, "God, the strange attractor, is like a mighty whirlwind," drawing all things to itself.[109]

Hodgson rounds out his analogy by examining the way God as the alluring and erotic Strange Attractor orders all things to a particular end. In the light of the Christ-event, Hodgson defines this end as "life-giving, love-enhancing, and liberative." Revealed as the Spirit of Christ, this Strange Attractor is not simply a force or power that has *eros*. Rather, this Spirit of Christ who animates and

105. Peter C. Hodgson, *Winds of the Spirit: A Constructive Christian Theology* (Louisville, KY: Westminster John Knox, 1994), 194.

106. Ibid., 195.

107. Ibid., 194.

108. Ibid., 195.

109. Ibid.

indwells all creation is a personal, relational presence Who is *Eros* itself. This perspective is consistent with the whole-part relation ascribed to the Divine Matrix as the One who vivifies and orders all things toward fullness of life and union with God. Nonetheless, in like fashion, Hodgson allows for the reality that the actualization of this divine allurement, always present and yet offered as gift, "depends on the contingency of each situation and the free play of conflicting forces." While the Divine is clearly a factor in the evolutionary unfolding of the cosmos in novelty and complexity, the free process and free will of the cosmos and its creatures means that God does not control the ultimate outcome. Rather, "God is at risk and suffers in the world but also rejoices in the emergence of everything that is good."[110]

SUMMARY

The following summary statements emphasize the major points of this chapter's interpretation of grace as relation in an evolving cosmos:

1. The Christian tradition defines grace as the free and undeserved favor that God gives to humans to respond to the divine call to participation in the life of God, the intimacy of Trinitarian life.

2. The meaning of grace in both the Hebrew and Christian scriptures refers to God's acts of faithful love, of mercy, and of graciousness. In the Christian Testament, grace is also understood as the saving will of God and the principle of Christian life and action.

3. These understandings of God's grace in scripture have given rise to a number of different interpretations of the nature and effects of grace throughout the centuries. Augustine of Hippo, Thomas Aquinas, Martin Luther, and Eastern Orthodoxy exemplify four basic movements in the Christian tradition concerning grace.

4. This chapter conceives of grace in an evolving universe as a relation of effect. In the cosmos, scientists have observed that relations of effect are bidirectional; they proceed from the

---

110. Ibid.

constituent "parts-to-the-whole" as well as from the "whole-to-the-parts." The direction of this relation often depends on whether the system being studied is a closed or open system.

5. Most of the systems examined by the sciences involve a defined region of the cosmos with real or theoretical boundaries that limit the area under study. However, when the system is the universe itself, scientists face particular difficulties in trying to assess the status of the universe as a whole.

6. Nonetheless, many scientists observe that the evolving universe behaves like an open system in dynamic fluctuation between continuity and novelty, law and chance, probability and possibility, predictability and indeterminacy. This observation is supported by the reality that, rather than displaying the increasing disorder and disorganization expected of a closed system, the cosmos has shown increasing novelty, organization, and complexity.

7. The notion of the cosmos as an open system is consistent with the paradigms of relational ontology and panentheism used in this text. In these paradigms, grace as a transcendent relation of effect is the "whole" luring the "parts" of the universe toward greater harmony, unity, and complexity in interaction with the processes of natural and human evolution itself.

8. In this paradigm, the nature of grace, like that of creation and incarnation, is divine self-communication. Its operation is analogous to what chaos theory calls the Strange Attractor, a hidden pattern of order that emerges in the organization of random events and continuously draws them toward novelty and complexity. In like manner, the operation of grace draws entities at each level of the cosmos beyond disorder and randomness into patterns of being characterized by novelty, vibrancy, and complexity. Consistent with the proposal that grace is a transcendent relation of effect, grace manifests itself as a form of transcendence at each level of cosmic life: from cosmic emergence, through other-centeredness, to social liberation and transformation.

9. Because the relation of effect in the cosmos is bidirectional, this affects the traditional interpretation of the Divine. In an

evolving cosmos, the Divine Matrix both affects events at all levels of created being in whole-part fashion and is affected by the events of the parts of the cosmos in part-whole fashion.

10. Although intimately affected by the cosmic realities of pain, death, and suffering in God's beloved creation, the Divine Matrix nonetheless faithfully embraces and continually permeates the chaos of the cosmos, ceaselessly drawing it toward loving relation in the pattern of divine life.

FOR FURTHER READING

Dreyer, Elizabeth. *Manifestations of Grace.* Collegeville, MN: Liturgical Press, 1990.

Haight, Roger. *The Experience and the Language of Grace.* Mahwah, NJ: Paulist, 1979.

Hodgson, Peter C. *Winds of the Spirit: A Constructive Christian Theology.* Louisville, KY: Westminster John Knox, 1994.

Chapter 9

LIVING IN TRINITARIAN RELATION

"What is the right way to speak about God? This is
a question of unsurpassed importance, for speech to and
about the mystery that surrounds . . . the universe itself is a
key activity of a community of faith. In that speech the symbol
of God functions as . . . the ultimate point of reference for
understanding experience, life, and the world."[1]

INTRODUCTION

Chapter 7 introduced the concept of symbol as that which mediates something other than itself and has an intrinsic relation to
what it symbolizes. It is "a word or image that participates in the
reality being signified, opens it up to some understanding, yet never
exhausts it completely."[2] That chapter pointed to symbols drawn
from creation or from the sacramental system of the Church. Yet,
the scope of symbols goes beyond the material or natural world and
includes concepts, languages, and systems. Furthermore, because they

---

1. Johnson, *She Who Is*, 3–4.

2. Johnson, "To Let the Symbol Sing Again," 300.

reach deeply into reality and yet never exhaust it, symbols expand human consciousness and trigger human imagination to conceive meanings and applications beyond what is evident to mere observation or experience.

Every chapter in this text has tried to stimulate consciousness and imagination by peering deeply into ideas to find unexpected insights and make novel connections between seemingly disparate concepts. In so doing, each has approached profound and weighty realities—the constitution of being, of the cosmos, and of personhood, as well as of the Trinity, and of creation, incarnation, and grace—as essentially *symbolic* in nature. However, referring to something as symbolic does *not* imply that it is not real. In fact, to engage anything as symbolic is to suggest that it has a depth of reality and significance that is not apparent on the level of mere words or propositions. Rather, a symbolic reality has multiple layers and contours that convey a depth of meaning that proves richer and more resonant than words can ever express.

Approaching Doctrine through Symbol

Why approach the doctrines of the Trinity, creation, incarnation, and grace through symbol? There are three fundamental reasons. The first is the essential ineffability of God and the God-world relation. As expressed in the words of Paul Tillich: "Nothing can be said about God as God which is not symbolic."[3] God as infinite, as ultimate, and as mystery can never be fully fathomed by the finite human mind or expressed through finite human speech. However, Christians have not always understood talk about the Triune God and God-world relationship in this way. With regard to the Trinity, Catholic theologian Elizabeth Johnson writes,

> Too often talk about the Trinity has been conducted in implicitly literal, descriptive language, as if we were peering into the divine mystery with a telescope. Who is processing from whom? And what are their relationships? In truth, however, this is a religious symbol that reveals its truth only

---

3. Paul Tillich, *Systematic Theology* (Chicago: University of Chicago, 1967), 239.

according to the power of symbol. . . . All religious speech is like this, like a finger pointing to the moon. . . . To equate the finger with the moon or to acknowledge the finger and not perceive the moon is to miss the point.[4]

Thus, the most that the finite human language can do is point toward the mystery of God and God-world relation in varied and fragmentary ways.

Secondly, although God utterly transcends limited human speech and categories, humans have profoundly tangible experiences of God. Within their finite existence, humans experience the genuine breaking in and through of the infinite God in cosmic creation and human history, particularly in that human history named Jesus the Christ. Moreover, because God knows, loves, and desires creation intimately and completely, God communicates the divine self in ways that creation is capable of receiving it. Thomas Aquinas fittingly expresses this: "God provides for all things according to their natures. It is natural for humans to attain knowledge through the use of sensible things, for all of our knowledge begins with sense experience."[5] And such sense experiences take shape in symbols for the Triune God in relation to the cosmos.

The final reason to approach doctrines through symbol lies in their capacity to transform human existence. Theologically, using symbols and symbol systems enables persons to move their engagement with beliefs, doctrines, and propositions from the intellectual level to the experiential level where they can deeply influence and transform individual and communal lives. By means of symbol, the mind not only apprehends words but the imagination contemplates, penetrates, and assimilates elements of reality that remain inaccessible to a purely intellectual mode of cognition. Furthermore, through symbol, the imagination can experience and communicate inner responses to symbolic realities by means of affections, dispositions, and insights expressible only by means of imagery and symbol. Hence, although always deficient and fragmentary, the use of symbol in theology has potency in religious and personal lives.

---

4. Johnson, "To Let the Symbol Sing Again," 304.

5. Aquinas, *ST*, I.9.

The Nature of Symbol

What does a symbol do that makes it so potent and transformative? Call to mind a particularly powerful visual symbol of Trinity or of the God-world relation or use one of the three below. These symbols of Trinity in relation to the cosmos suggest a variety of dynamic qualities that mere words could never express.

Lucas Cranach—1515–1518 CE
Trinity (Oil on Wood) Kunsthalle Bremen

© Kunsthalle Bremen—Der Kunstverein in Bremen

Andrei Rublev—1410 CE
The Holy Trinity (Wood and Tempura)
Tretyakov Gallery, Moscow

© Scala / Art Resource, NY

© Margie Thompson

Margie Thompson—2001 CE, *Trinita* (Oil on Wood) Mount St. Joseph, Philadelphia, PA

Figure 9.1: **Images of Trinity**

What does each communicate about God and the God-world relationship? Which invites the participation of the viewer? What thoughts does each evoke? What is the nature of the relationship expressed in each one? What does each inspire the viewer to do? When answers arise to any of these questions, then the nature and function of symbol is revealing itself.

The depiction of *Trinity*, by Lucas Cranach is largely focused through the areole of angels. His use of untamed landscape with architectural ruins, windswept trees, and effects of light and weather give his work emotional force; however, with no human figures or social references within it, Cranach's symbol seems to convey that this Trinity has no real relation to the world.

In the icon *Holy Trinity*, by Andrei Rublev, the three angels symbolize the Triune God as Persons equal in dignity and unique in diversity. Equality is imaged through the bodily and size similarity of the Three Persons. However, the symbolism found above each of their heads reinforces the diversity of Persons. The house above the figure on the left signifies the Father as the head of the household; the branch above the central figure signifies the tree of the cross on which the Son was crucified; and the wing arching above the figure on the right signifies the Holy Spirit as hovering over creation. Some see the figures as detached from the viewer, focused only within their own circles; others experience them as intimately inviting the viewer to occupy the space that opens out from the triad. Some interpret the scene as devoid of earthly life, energy, and love, while others speak of a profound intimacy, openness, and hospitality. As symbol, the God-world relationship depicted in this iconography is clearly open to interpretation!

Finally, the circular structure of the third piece, *Trinita*, represents the dynamic interrelationship of the Triune God with both the cosmos and humans. The image "symbolizes the primacy of relationship, a unity empowered by diversity, and an embrace of active, inclusive love."[6] The heart and wounded hands convey the vulnerability and tenderness of the Crucified and Incarnate One, while the flames communicate the fiery, energizing love of the Spirit.

---

6. Margie Thompson, "Reflections on *Trinita*," Deepening Day Gathering of the Sisters of Saint Joseph of Philadelphia, September 12, 2001, Chestnut Hill College, Philadelphia, Pennsylvania.

What do these reflections on the artistic symbols of Trinity disclose about the power of symbol? First, the symbol points beyond itself.[7] It reveals and proclaims a particular interpretation of the triune nature of God and the God-world relationship and moves the viewer beyond the symbol to the God symbolized. Second, the symbol gives rise to thought. It is pregnant with an abundance of meanings and allows a wealth of interpretations, each as personal and varied as those who experience and engage it.[8] Third, the symbol invites participation. It invites one to inhabit its environment, walk around and explore its nooks and niches, and discover its mysteries, possibilities, and values.[9] Finally, the symbol functions. In the oft-quoted words of Elizabeth Johnson, the way a community of faith shapes its symbolic language about God "implicitly represents what it takes to be the highest good, the profoundest truth, the most appealing beauty." The way the community symbolizes God, moreover, "powerfully molds the corporate identity of the community and directs its praxis. . . . [It] shapes the life orientation not only of the corporate faith community but in this matrix guides its individual members as well."[10]

Consciously or unconsciously, therefore, the symbols a community uses to envision God and the God-world relationship molds religious identity, highlights values, shapes choices, directs activities, and inspires particular types of relationships with God and with others.[11] Indeed, symbols are "a curious phenomenon"[12] that require a process of interpretation and do not yield their deeper significance through the mere perception of its visual sign. Nonetheless, they surrender their surplus of meaning and allurement to those who willingly engage the symbol and, in consequence, the mystery of the One symbolized.

---

7. Roger Haight, *Jesus, Symbol of God* (Maryknoll, NY: Orbis, 1999), 197.

8. Paul Ricoeur, *The Symbolism of Evil* (New York: Harper & Row, 1967), 347–48.

9. Paul Avis, *God and the Creative Imagination: Metaphor, Symbol, and Myth in Religion and Theology* (New York: Routledge, 1999), 106.

10. Johnson, *She Who Is*, 4.

11. Johnson, "To Let the Symbol Sing Again," 300.

12. David M. Rasmussen, *Symbol and Interpretation* (The Hague: Nijhoff, 1974), 1.

RELATION: THE SYMBOL THAT FUNCTIONS

The primary symbol this text has developed is relation. Chapter after chapter delved deeply into the various types of relation—as origin, emergence, and effect—and further still into how each of these relations played out in the cosmos, the human person, and the divine. Plumbing these depths through visual and linguistic images, each chapter tried to produce new attentiveness, perceptions, and insights that would enable persons to move their ideas, beliefs, and doctrines from the intellectual level to the experiential level where they can deeply influence and transform individual and communal lives. By means of the symbol of relation, this text explored layers and contours of familiar and traditional realities and proposed ways to image and engage their meanings in often unfamiliar and non-traditional terms.

This concluding chapter dives one final time into the depths of the relations that have been explored to examine the ramifications of understanding all of reality—from the quantum to the macro to the supernatural spheres—as essentially and existentially relational. What does it mean to live in a thoroughly relational universe? Why does it matter that humans are constituted by and for relation in the very depth of human nature? What does its intrinsic place within the very web of creation demand of humanity in relation to the cosmos? What practical difference does the triune reality of God make in life and relationships with the Divine and with one another? How does intimate and enduring relation with the God of infinite love stand as both promise and fulfillment in the midst of an evolving cosmos?

In response to such questions, this chapter examines four implications of how the essential relationality among cosmic, human, and divine being might function in practical, creative, and transformative ways to move the evolving cosmos toward a future full of hope in God. A relational and evolving universe demands a mode of living that (1) fosters nonhierarchical relationships of inclusivity, (2) recognizes and imitates divine solidarity with human suffering, (3) transforms ethical and political systems, and (4) embraces a diversity of images for Divine Being.

Fosters Nonhierarchical Relationships of Inclusivity

First, individuals and communities attempting to live in the relationality that constitutes the evolving universe foster nonhierarchical relationships of inclusivity in the image of the God, who is the
essence of nonhierarchical and inclusive relation itself. In so doing,
such persons and communities welcome a diversity of cosmic and
human life with the realization "that a universe containing every possible variety of creatures, from the highest to the lowest, is a richer
and far better universe than would be one consisting solely of the
highest kind of created being."[13] Each creature adds to the flourishing of all by offering what God has given to be developed and shared
for the good of the whole. In an analogous way, each person contributes his or her giftedness unlimited by gender, tradition, historicity,
or culture for the benefit of all.

This fullness of nonhierarchical inclusive relationality is perhaps nowhere better modeled than in the life and ministry of Jesus
of Nazareth. In his theological writing, liturgical theologian Regis
Duffy characterized Jesus as someone "on account of others," one
with God and one with the marginalized of his time.[14] This saving
work of Jesus is most clearly portrayed in his inclusive "table fellowship," his habit of eating and drinking with the sinner, marginalized,
and outcast of his time that drew the critique of religious leaders who
considered these persons unworthy of such hospitality. It is further
revealed in his awareness that his Father cares even for the lilies of
the field and the birds of the air (Matthew 6:26–30). What are the
consequences of his example for relations within and beyond the
Christian community, even to relations with the earth?

The table fellowship of Jesus throughout his life discloses first
and foremost that his table is "open to the forgotten and the mis-
begotten . . . who seek food in their hunger, consolation in their
pain, reconciliation in their alienation."[15] In his table fellowship with
the sinner, marginalized, and outcast, Jesus proclaimed the inbreaking

13. John Hick, *Evil and the God of Love* (San Francisco: Harper & Row, 1978), 72.

14. Regis Duffy, *Real Presence: Worship, Sacrament, and Commitment* (New York: Harper & Row, 1982), 138.

15. David N. Power, "A Prophetic Eucharist in a Prophetic Church," in *Eucharist: Toward the Third Millennium*, ed. Martin F. Connell (Collegeville, MN: Liturgical Press, 1997), 33.

of the Kingdom of God, and he embodied its reality in his actions. Jesus transgressed social barriers and extended an offer of intimate participation to those ordinarily excluded by social, cultural, or religious convention.[16] Based upon his manner "of inviting the outsider and the underdog to the table,"[17] Jesus constituted "a community of equals within the richness of diversity."[18]

This community abolished barriers, eradicated class distinctions, and reversed role expectations. Community replaced competition. Moreover, when Jesus called his disciples to live in remembrance of him, he challenged his followers to subvert the usual order of things, "to build . . . relationships of love and mutuality, not power and domination,"[19] and to assure that no person was isolated, marginalized, or ostracized by human judgment or social class. Jesus' challenge becomes especially necessary, states theologian David N. Power, "in times of social and cultural crisis and oppression." Periods of conflict and tyranny particularly challenge Christians to live as "an alternative community in which God's Spirit works, overcoming death-dealing forces abroad in the world."[20]

This stance of inclusivity, mutuality, and nonhierarchical relation, moreover, is not reserved solely to the human community, but also must extend to relation with the cosmos. Because of the common source and participation in God shared by human and cosmic being, a profound kinship exists among all members of creation. "Kin refers to those with whom we are related. . . . Kin have a common nature, origin, ancestor, spirit or quality. The relationship of kin is a given, implying specific ties and obligations."[21] Such kinship has the

---

16. William R. Crockett, *Eucharist: Symbol of Transformation* (New York: Pueblo, 1989), 252f.

17. John Howard Yoder, *For the Nations*, in Matthew Whelan, "The Responsible Body: A Eucharistic Community," *Cross Currents* 51:3 (2001): 366.

18. David N. Power, *The Eucharistic Mystery: Revitalizing the Tradition* (New York: Crossroad, 1992), 335.

19. Brian Wren, "Justice and Liberation in the Eucharist," *Christian Century* 103:28 (1986): 842.

20. Power, "A Prophetic Eucharist in a Prophetic Church," 28.

21. Norman Habel, David Rhoads, and Paul Santmire, "A Theology of Deep Incarnation and Reconciliation," in *A Theology for the Season of Creation*; available from *http://www.sjlc.org.au/rokdownloads/LCA_Wor_Res/index.html?season_of_creation__theology__.html*.

capacity to engender in humanity a spirit of humility and interdependence toward the cosmos.

Moreover, humanity's inherent kinship with and God's integral relation to the universe accentuates the intrinsic rather than instrumental value of the cosmos and makes plain that God's creative relation and intention extends not simply to the full flourishing of humanity but also to that of the natural world. Such kinship fosters ethical responses that protect, sustain, and enhance the cosmos and its creatures. Furthermore, it engages human persons as collaborators in the ongoing creativity of the Divine in relation to the entities and structures of the cosmos, both animate and inanimate alike. Clearly, these are values and actions in keeping with the love of a Divine Mother for the developing life within her, a love that demands abundance of life for her child and choices consistent with the kinship of all creation. While the "call for an inclusive society beyond oppressive divisions . . . is still far from realization,"[22] the constitutive relationality of cosmic, human, and divine being demonstrates the possibility of such a society and challenges Christians to imagine and incarnate a different way of being in relation to God, to one another, and to Earth.

Recognizes and Imitates Divine Solidarity with Human Suffering

In examining how the scientific view of the cosmos affects traditional interpretations of the Divine, the chapters on the relations of creation, incarnation, and grace each indicated that, in an evolutionary worldview, God clearly suffers in solidarity with the cosmos and its creatures. Each relation identified a particular mode of divine suffering with one of the Divine Persons.[23] The mode termed *protopathy* was associated with the Creator Spirit. Protopathy was a primal type of *suffering immanent in the cosmos* that reverberates with the righteous rage and resistance to everything that hinders the creativity

---

22. Enda McDonagh, "Fruit of the Earth—Work of Human Hands: A Prophetic Theology of Eucharist," in *The Candles Are Still Burning: Directions in Sacraments and Spirituality*, eds. Mary C. Grey and Danny Sullivan (Collegeville, MN: Liturgical Press, 1995), 28.

23. See chapters 6, 7, and 8 respectively for fuller explanations of these types of Divine suffering.

of the cosmos and spawns innocent suffering. The mode of suffering termed *empathy* was associated with the emergent Christ. This is a type of *suffering incarnate in the cosmos* shaped by Jesus' and, thus, God's participation in cosmic suffering and experience of affliction, rejection, and exile. Finally, the mode of suffering termed *sympathy* was associated with the Divine Matrix who embraces the cosmos within the Divine Being. This is a type of *suffering transcending the cosmos* in order to be the compassionate embrace that encircles and upholds the afflicted on the passage to healing and new life.

These modes of suffering, however, have more than theological validity. They also have a spiritual significance in a suffering and conflicted cosmos. Rather than asserting that suffering, disaster, or death results from the will or plan of God, distinguishing modes of suffering in the Triune God offers insights into how the Divine truly suffers with and for humanity and the cosmos. Through such insights, the afflicted first may find their own sufferings relieved by identifying them with the sufferings of God. In doing so through intercession, meditation, or contemplation, each individual may find his or her suffering alleviated or even eliminated. Moreover, having experienced the Divine suffering with and in them, those who have suffered may grow in their capacity to accompany others in suffering in the very ways modeled by the suffering God.

The following descriptions of the interaction between human and divine suffering suggest some ways that might come to pass. Clearly, they exhaust neither the range of human affliction nor the avenues of healing and liberation. They do, nonetheless, suggest how the differentiated suffering in God provides relief to those who suffer and models the solidarity in suffering to which inherent relationality calls each human.

Solidarity in Protopathy

When suffering results from the events that quash creativity and stymie emergence, healing and liberation come through a spirit of dynamic resistance to such oppression and an unrelenting urgency toward just and right relationship. These are the ones who suffer for righteousness' sake, who are persecuted for doing or seeking what is right and just (Matthew 5: 10–11). Impelled by the vision of human and cosmic flourishing, these persons experience protopathy—a primal and immediate anguish that wells up, under, and through events of injustice and exploitation, events of violence and discrimination, events of destruction and despoliation. They recognize that God immanent in the creative processes of the cosmos shares their own suffering for justice and liberation. Thus, those suffering futility and obstacles may find healing and liberation in the fact that the Creator God unceasingly moves the evolving cosmos through death and suffering toward new life and liberation. In the words of Elizabeth Johnson, "The power of this divine symbol works not just to console those who are suffering, but to strengthen those bowed by sorrow to hope and resist. If God grieves with them in the midst of disaster, then there may yet be a way forward."[24]

Solidarity in Empathy

In contrast to those whose anguish is relieved by knowing that God too suffers for the sake of justice and righteousness, others derive solace and strength in the sure knowledge that someone has experienced suffering akin to their own. Their liberation springs from the realization that they can identify their suffering with that of another—and that another identifies with them in their pain. This experience is reflected in the description of suffering as empathy, which connotes a type of suffering rooted in and shaped by present or past experience. Those seeking relief from suffering find consolation in God Incarnate in the cosmos, the God who, in Jesus the suffering servant, "was despised and rejected," a bearer of sorrows, and acquainted with grief (Isaiah 53:3–4). Because the Incarnate One shares natural being and experiences firsthand the ubiquity of pain, suffering, and death in the cosmos, the afflicted ones trust that God has known the rejection they have known, has borne the exile they have endured, has felt the forsakenness they have carried, and has yearned for the liberation for which they hope. Through this intimate, incarnate, and experiential knowledge of their affliction, God Incarnate shoulders the burdens of those who suffer and communicates to them that in the lowest and saddest times when they thought they were most alone, it was then that God carried them.[25]

---

24. Johnson, *She Who Is*, 260–61.

25. Adapted from Mary Stevenson, "Footprints in the Sand," *Poem4Today*; available from *http://www.poem4today.com/footprints-poem.html*.

Solidarity in Sympathy

Finally, others need only know that someone accompanies them in their suffering. They desire only the sympathy of another who provides solace and strength simply by being there. For them, the Divine Father-Mother-Matrix is a grace-filled companion readily offering a healing and consoling presence in time of need. They do not deem it necessary that God has physically occupied or endured the same anguish they bear themselves. The one thing necessary is that the Divine Embrace surrounds them and is available to them in their time of distress. Like the mother who does not forget the child of her womb (Isaiah 49:15) or the father who teaches his toddler to walk (Hosea 11:3), God need only draw near to the afflicted with love, raise them with a divine embrace, and supply sustenance and support on their passage through hardship to healing and through trial to new life.

Transforms Ethical and Political Systems

While solidarity with the suffering Triune God promises consolation, hope, and liberation to individuals, the relational symbol of Trinity demands a communal response in keeping with the inherent relation that each person bears to other people and to the cosmos. The God who suffers in the intimate relations of creation, incarnation, and grace challenges humans to reach beyond themselves toward others in need and to adopt a pattern of community modeled by the relations of the Trinity. Such a pattern of communal life may require the same solidarity in suffering between human and cosmic beings as that described between human and divine beings. Nonetheless, the relational symbol of Trinity calls humanity to work toward eliminating the kinds of suffering inflicted by personal, social, and systemic sinfulness by constructing ethical and political systems that forestall such suffering by their very nature.

Think of the state of the world over the past century. Let the following litany seep into consciousness: Auschwitz, Hiroshima, Rwanda, September 11, Iraq, Darfur, Tsunami, Katrina, Somalia. These allusions and others like them provoke images of staggering atrocities, unmitigated violence, incalculable destruction, and inexpressible terror. In addition to these unparalleled events, Earth's inhabitants live each day in the shadow of daunting and destructive realities: Weapons of mass destruction threaten the international community. Nationalistic genocide and terroristic suicide threaten the emotional and physical well-being and survival of millions. Poverty, starvation, and AIDS decimate human bodies. Global, urban, and domestic violence cut short promising lives. Racism, sexism, and classism stunt human potential. Political divisiveness and rancor stun human sensibilities. Natural disasters, exploitation, and abuse devastate and despoil Earth's ecosphere and atmosphere. While the reality of suffering has demanded a response in every age, the global scope and impact of suffering and death in this past century have driven this need for a response to an acute pitch. Atrocities committed in multinational and multicultural conflicts, through disordered human relations and by environmental devastation relentlessly provoke the question, "How am I—how are we—to respond?"

The relationality that constitutes divine, cosmic, and human beings precludes the response of burying one's head in one's hands and simply bemoaning the situation or burying one's head in the sand and simply ignoring it. Each human is an intrinsic part of the web of all life. Each human is kin not only to every other human but also to every creature in the cosmos. Thus, each human bears a responsibility to constitute his or her local and global relations in ways that mirror the Trinitarian relations in whose image each is made. This is precisely the point made by professor of theology and religious studies Kieran Scott when he states that living in a Trinitarian way is a twofold proposition comprised of both orthodoxy (correct believing) and orthopraxy (right practice). According to Scott, the doctrine of Trinity serves "as the theological criterion to measure the faithfulness of the practices" of the human community and, therefore, possesses "far-reaching consequences for Christian living."[26]

For these reasons, it is critical to link Trinitarian orthodoxy with Trinitarian orthopraxy such that "living out the doctrine amounts to living God's life with one another . . . [in] every dimension of life where God and creature live with one another."[27] Scott contends that living in this way calls for transformation ethically and politically.

---

26. Kieran Scott, "Practicing the Trinity in the Local Church: The Symbol as Icon and Lure," *Review and Expositor* 99:3 (2002): 429.

27. Ibid., 438.

Ethical Transformation

As the theological basis for Christian ethics, the doctrine of Trinity inspires a relatedness characterized by genuine mutuality, radical equality, and respect for diversity in a mutual exchange of love. In so doing, it calls Christians to raise a "prophetic protest" against the individualism and utilitarianism rampant in the world today. In the light of the Trinitarian relationality that serves as the model for all cosmic and human relationality, the "solitary, impersonal, self-centered life" is unnatural while a communal and self-giving life expresses the fullness of one's being. Thus, "Whatever promotes communion amid diversity and strife . . . , whatever cultivates habitual practices of compassion and care, whatever frees us from narcissism and making idols of things" forms the foundation of Trinitarian living.[28]

Scott indicates, however, that an ethical life modeled on Trinitarian relationality is not generic but must be further shaped by the life and ministry of Jesus of Nazareth. Echoing a theme discussed earlier in this chapter, Scott points out that living in the image of Trinity means that Christian solidarity must incarnate that of Christ. His solidarity was "with the slave, the sinner, the poor, the marginalized, and with the least of persons" and his ethical stance was "inclusive of every human concern and commitment."[29] Certainly, one should not use a relational Trinitarian ethic uncritically to validate a particular personal, social, or political ideology. Nonetheless, it does call people of faith to recognize that the Christian doctrine of God entails a social mission that initiates a transformed world order. Hence, Trinitarian relationality arouses an ethic in which economic and political decision making is informed by regard for the poor, the oppressed, and the marginalized and inspires a vision that refocuses discussion of human rights, sexual ethics, and ecological relations. "The needs of the poor take priority over the desires of the rich; the rights of workers over the maximization of profits; the preservation of the environment over uncontrolled industrial expansion; production to meet social needs over production for military purposes."[30]

---

28. Ibid., 439.

29. Ibid.

30. Pope John Paul II, "Address on Christian Unity in a Technological Age" (Toronto, Canada, 1984)," *Origins* 14:16 (October 4, 1984): 248.

Political Transformation

While acknowledging that the doctrine of Trinity itself derived from a patriarchal culture, Scott suggests that effective reinterpretation of the doctrine in terms of its essential relationality "allows it to function as a protest against patriarchal governance" in all its manifestations. Scott focuses his commentary on church governance; nonetheless, his intuitions regarding ecclesial structures suggest how a revitalized understanding of Trinitarian orthopraxy can transform political and social systems as well. The primary insight Scott offers centers on the reality that love and communion among equal persons constitute Trinitarian relationality. In the Trinity, "there is no domination and subordination, no first and last . . . no hierarchy nor inequality, neither division nor competition."[31] Rather, the life of the Trinity is unity in diversity sustained through love.

Hence, all communities—and the Christian community in particular—are challenged to mirror the inclusivity and reciprocity modeled in the Trinity. The symbol of Trinitarian relation, Scott contends, functions to evoke a community that is "a kinship of sisterhood and brotherhood, equal partners in mutual relations."[32] All patterns of relation that alienate, dominate, and divide or that shore up oppressive political or patriarchal power structures must be reordered according to the emancipatory relationality of Trinitarian life. In such a life, power is shared, elitism is dismantled, discrimination is eliminated, and competition is neutralized. When the relations shaping political and social structures mirror those of Trinitarian relationality, a "domain of inclusiveness, interdependence, and cooperation"[33] can arise to serve as a "prophetic counter-cultural presence" in the midst of a suffering world.[34] In light of such inclusiveness and interdependence, the words of the U.S. bishops' pastoral *Economic Justice for All* echo all the more clearly twenty-five years after they were first written:

> The "option for the poor" is not an adversarial slogan that
> pits one group or class against another. Rather it states that

---

31. Scott, "Practicing Trinity," 441.

32. Ibid., 441.

33. LaCugna, *God for Us*, 402.

34. Scott, "Practicing Trinity," 442.

the deprivation and powerlessness of the poor wounds the whole community. The extent of their suffering is a measure of how far we are from being a true community of persons.[35]

Embraces a Diversity of Images of Divine Being

Finally, individuals and communities endeavoring to live in the relationality that constitutes the evolving universe embrace a diversity of metaphors and symbols for the Divine—male and female, human and nonhuman, individual and communal, ancient and new—in the image of the God who is eternally and temporally self-communicating mystery of relation. Traditional Trinitarian terminology and imagery is that of two male figures and a dove. However, Divine Being as relation not only shifts attention from but also neutralizes such stereotypical images of the Trinity in favor of attending to the relationship among the Divine Persons. This focus on relations is consistent with the deepest meaning attributed to Trinitarian life, namely, that the Trinitarian names of Father, Son, and Spirit primarily describe intimate relationality, rather than gender or hierarchical constructs.

This emphasis on Trinitarian relationality has suggested and undergirded other analogies, images, and language for the Trinity proffered by theologians and mystics from biblical times to the twentieth-first century. Throughout Christian history, people of faith have used relational triads that are animate and inanimate, personal and impersonal. They have drawn them from the natural order and from human experience. These images and analogies have symbolized the relations of the Persons of the Trinity to one another and the relations of the Persons with the cosmos and its creatures. In fact, many of the triads have implied the relations of origin, emergence and effect demonstrated throughout this book. This history of diversity and creativity in naming the Triune God paves the way for positing novel imagery for Trinity based on the observations and experiences that reveal the Triune God in this contemporary age.

---

35. United States Conference of Catholic Bishops, *Economic Justice for All: Pastoral Letter on Catholic Social Teaching and the U.S. Economy*; available from *http://www. usccb.org/upload/economic_justice_for_all.pdf*.

Surely, some symbols of triune relation seem to transcend time, the symbols of Father, Son, and Spirit among them. Nonetheless, the mystery of God, the insatiable yearning of the human heart, and the shifting historical and cultural landscape[36] require people of faith who believe that the Word of God is living and active (Hebrews 4:12) to be open and receptive to the ways God reveals Godself in every era. And what validates this novel imagery now as then is its potential to reveal and reflect anew the profound intimacy of relation posited of the very nature of the Triune God, the mystery of relation *in se*. The following table summarizes some of the analogies, images, and names of the Triune God from the biblical narrative to the twenty-first century.

TABLE 9.1: IMAGING THE TRINITY IN TERMS OF RELATION[37]			
	Relation of Origin	Relation of Emergence	Relation of Effect
Scripture	Father	Son	Holy Spirit
Tertullian[38]	Root	Shoot (Tree)	Fruit
	Sun	Sunray	Suntan (Apex)
	Fount	River	Irrigation
	Reason	Word	Power
Augustine[39]	Knowledge	Memory	Love
	Lover	Beloved	Act of Love
Hildegard of Bingen	Brightness	Flashing Forth	Fire

Continued

---

36. See Johnson, *Quest for the Living God*, 12–13.

37. Unless otherwise noted, this summary is drawn from Johnson, "To Let the Symbol Sing Again," 309–11.

38. See Tertullian, *Apology*, Chapter XXI, *Christian Classics Ethereal Library*; available from *http://www.ccel.org/ccel/schaff/anf03.iv.iii.xxi.html* and *Against Praxeas*, Chapter XXIX, *Christian Classics Ethereal Library*, available from *http://www.ccel.org/ccel/schaff/anf03.v.ix.xxix.html*. These were also reiterated later by Augustine in *A Treatise on Faith and the Creed*, Chapter IX, *Christian Bookshelf*; available from *http://christianbookshelf.org/augustine/a_treatise_on_faith_and_the_creed_/chapter_9_of_ the_holy_spirit.htm*.

39. See Augustine, *On the Trinity*, trans. Edmund Hill (Brooklyn: New City Press, 1991), Book *XIV* (Mental analogy: 370–94) and Book *IX* (Love analogy: 271–75).

IMAGING THE TRINITY IN TERMS OF RELATION *Continued*			
Karl Barth	Revealer	Revelation	Revealedness
Fulton J. Sheen	Architect	Blueprint	Edifice
	Songwriter	Score	Song Performed
Karl Rahner	Unoriginate Origin	Word Expressed	Uniting Love
John Macquarrie	Primordial Being	Expressive Being	Unitive Being
Walter Kasper	Source of Love	Mediation of Love	Term of Love
Heribert Mühlen	I of Love	Thou of Love	We of Love
Paul Tillich	Creativity	Salvation	Transformation
Dorothy Sayers	Book Thought	Book Written	Book Read
Nicholas Lash	Eclipse	Word	Presence
Elizabeth Johnson	Mother-Sophia	Jesus-Sophia	Spirit-Sophia
Mary Catherine Hilkert	Energy	Hope	Compassion[40]
Letty Russell	Source of Life	Word of Truth	Spirit of Love[41]
Ruth C. Duck	Fountain of Life	Wellspring of Life	Living Water[42]
Gloria L. Schaab	She Who Is	Shekhinah	Sophia[43]

Some of the earliest analogies modeling the relationality of the Trinitarian Persons to one another and to the cosmos came from the theologian Tertullian who lived in the late-second to early-third centuries. He was fond of using three particular sets of images drawn from the natural world to model the Trinitarian relations: root/shoot/fruit, sun/sunray/suntan, and fount/river/irrigation. For Tertullian, these images provided a way of explaining how the Trinity of distinct persons nonetheless shared the same nature. For example, the Father is the root, who sends forth the Son as the shoot who is manifest in history, and whose effect in Christian life is the fruit of

---

40. See Mary Catherine Hilkert, "Feminist Theology: Key Religious Symbols: Christ and God," *Theological Studies* 56:2 (1995): 352.

41. See Ruth C. Duck, "The Trinity Dancing Together," *Seasons of the Spirit*; available from *http://www.graceucc.net/About_Us/trinity.htm*.

42. Ibid.

43. See Gloria L. Schaab, *The Creative Suffering of the Triune God* (New York: Oxford University Press, 2007), 169–78.

the Holy Spirit. Through this image, Tertullian demonstrated how the Trinity is all one "plant" in three distinct "parts" with its own corresponding manifestation and work.

In this simple example, Tertullian foreshadows the complex doctrinal statements to come, including the processions, the missions, and the appropriations examined in chapter 4. Somewhat surprisingly, his images also mirror the three relations drawn from the contemporary physical, natural, and social sciences used throughout this text. Each analogy corresponds quite well to the relations of origin (root, sun, fount), of emergence (shoot, sunray, river), and of effect (fruit, suntan, irrigation). Other later imagery reflecting the same relations include mystic Hildegard of Bingen's brightness (origin), flashing forth (emergence), and fire (effect); author Dorothy Sayers' Book Thought (origin), Book Written (emergence), and Book Read (effect); and Evangelical theologian Karl Barth's Revealer (origin), Revelation (emergence), and Revealedness (effect).[44] Finally, Catholic bishop Fulton Sheen added two unique Trinitarian images to the Catholic imagination; he imaged the Trinity as Architect (Father/origin), Blueprints (Son/emergence), and Edifice (Spirit/effect), as well as Songwriter (Father/origin), Score (Son/emergence), and Song Performed (Spirit/effect).[45]

The Trinitarian models of relation in this chart derive not only from the natural world but also from philosophical concepts and the scriptures. Karl Rahner's Unoriginate Origin (origin), Word Expressed (emergence), and Uniting Love (effect) reflect the thought

---

44. Through these metaphors, Barth articulates his trinitarian formulation of threefold "repetition in God" (366). Because Barth held that humans were *non capax*, or not capable of direct knowledge of God as mystery, he taught that the only way humans could come to know God was through God's own revelation of the Divine Mystery. Hence, God had to unveil the Divine Self in order to be in relation with humanity. Thus, for Barth, the Trinity results from Divine Self-Revelation in "threefold repetition," that is, God, whose Word is the Divine Self *in se*, reveals Godself "in unimpaired unity yet also in unimpaired distinction [as] Revealer, Revelation, and Revealedness" (295). The Revealer is the Father, the Origin of the Word; the Revelation is the Son, the Emergence of the Word into history; and the Spirit is Revealedness, the Effect of the Word who enables every hearer to receive and accept the revelation. See Karl Barth, *Church Dogmatics, II*, translated by G. W. Bromiley (Edinburgh: T & T Clark, 1975), 295–489.

45. Fulton J. Sheen, "Love Begins with a Dream," *CatholicTradition.org*, available from *http://www.catholictradition.org/Mary/dream.htm*.

of Augustine and Aquinas, as well as the prologue of John's Gospel (John chapter 1) and the understanding of God as Love (1 John 4:16). Theologian and philosopher John Macquarrie focuses on Aquinas's characterization of God as *Ipsum Esse*, Being Itself, to unify and distinguish the Divine Persons in terms of Being as Primordial (origin), Expressive (emergence), and Unitive (effect). Protestant theologian Paul Tillich conceptualizes the Trinitarian appropriations in his triad of the Divine as Creativity (origin), Salvation (emergence), and Transformation (effect), as does feminist theologian Letty Russell in her characterization of the Trinity as Source of Life (origin), Word of Truth (emergence), and Spirit of Love (effect).

Finally, two Trinitarian formulations ground themselves in the Hebrew and Christian biblical, theological, and mystical traditions. In her opus *She Who Is,* Catholic theologian Elizabeth Johnson mines the Wisdom literature of the Hebrew scriptures to represent the unity of the Trinity as rooted in *Divine Sophia*, the feminine-gendered Greek noun for "wisdom." Johnson then distinguishes the Divine Persons as Mother-Sophia, her beloved Child Jesus-Sophia, and their mutual love Spirit-Sophia, the "unfathomably being, self-uttering, loving" mystery Who embraces and liberates the universe.[46] In her evolutionary theology of the suffering God, the author of this book appropriates Johnson's depiction of the Divine as *She Who Is,*[47] the Jewish mystical figure of *Shekhinah*, and the Wisdom tradition's *Sophia* to construct a Trinitarian theology of the Triune God who suffers in transcendent, incarnate, and immanent relation to the cosmos and its creatures in its unfolding in time.

---

46. Johnson, "To Let the Symbol Sing," 311.

47. In her book *She Who Is: The Mystery of God in Feminist Theological Discourse,* Elizabeth Johnson reinterprets Thomas Aquinas's theological insight concerning the most appropriate name for God. In his *Summa Theologiae* (I.11), Aquinas asserted that the most proper name of God is *HE WHO IS*, based on the divine name proclaimed by God to Moses in the burning bush (Exodus 3:14). Johnson points out that in Aquinas's original text, the name is rendered "*Qui est*" or "Who is," which opens the translation to interpretation in either male or female terms. Hence, on linguistic and ultimately theological and anthropological grounds, the mystery of Being Itself is legitimately understood as She Who Is, the "sheer, exuberant, relational aliveness in the midst of the history of suffering, inexhaustible source of new being in situations of death and destruction, ground of hope for the whole created universe." See Johnson, *She Who Is*, 242–43.

Undoubtedly, some question the motivation, need, or even advisability of suggesting novel imagery for the Triune God. Nonetheless, the reasoning comes from the very nature and history of God and the God-world relation. If one holds that the nature of God as Trinity is self-communicating and that God as Trinity is living and active in intimate relation to the cosmos and its creatures in all times and all places, then it follows that God as Trinity continuously communicates to and with persons of every time and place with the aim of intimate relation. In holding this belief, then, one implicitly affirms that the God of love and freedom who offers this divine self-communication continues to seek out the most effective means and media in every age to initiate, develop, and solidify the God-world relation that flows from the relation of Divine Being Itself. Hence, God challenges this era as God challenged the ancient Israelites: "See, I am doing something new! Now it springs forth, do you not perceive it?" (Isaiah 43:19) Like the Trinity itself, "The three's [used to image Trinity] keep circling round." Nevertheless, as theologian Elizabeth Johnson observes,

> Whatever the categories used, there is reflected a livingness in God; a beyond, a with, and a within to the world and its history; a sense of God as from whom, by whom and in whom all things exist, thrive and struggle toward freedom and are gathered in.[48]

SUMMARY

The adventure through this landscape of cosmic, human, and divine relation from the mystery of God to the depth of quantum physics is drawing to an end. Perhaps readers have heard the echo of Margaret Wheatley's claim made at its beginning: "Relationships are not just interesting . . . they are *all* there is to reality. . . . None of us exists independent of our relationships with others."[49]

What more have these readers encountered along the way? Cosmic, human, and divine existence opened to reveal the relations of

---

48. Johnson, "To Let the Symbol Sing," 311.

49. Wheatley, *Leadership and the New Science*, 34 and 35.

origin, emergence, and effect that constitute them all. The intimate relations of the Persons of the Trinity manifested themselves in the enduring relations of creation, incarnation, and grace. Within an evolutionary worldview, these God-world relations were not revealed as occasional interventions disrupting the laws of nature or human events. Rather, creation, incarnation, and grace disclosed a Triune God who is intimately and ceaselessly active in the evolving history of the cosmos. On the final leg of the journey, readers uncovered the vehicle that had transported them throughout their expedition. This vehicle enabled each of them to participate in the realities being signified, gain deeper understanding of each, and yet never completely exhaust the mystery each reality contained. It was the vehicle of relation as symbol.

Has this exploration changed these travelers in any way? One hopes that those who have made this journey into the symbolic depths of relation decide to make a consciously relational life with the cosmos, with others, and with God in creation, incarnation, and grace their own. And, yet, to what end?

They may perhaps discover that, by deeply living in relation to cosmic, human, and divine life, they become a symbol of relation in the image of the Triune God. It may be that they become a symbol that points beyond themselves to the reign of God in their midst, initiated already in Christ and the Spirit, but yet to come in its fullness. It could be that they become a symbol that gives rise to thoughts of human dignity and liberation and that invites participation in a life of full flourishing. It might be that they become a symbol that functions powerfully to mold relations of healing and prophetic action for those who are marginalized and oppressed. Ultimately, it is entirely possible that those who live in relation in the image of the Triune God become a symbol that transforms human and cosmic existence through the values of compassion, justice, and right relation. Should these symbols reach critical mass, the very cosmos itself may become a symbol of the Triune God, evolving inexorably toward the coming of the reign of God through ongoing creation, incarnation, and grace. As Elizabeth Johnson states in her reflections on the relational symbol of Trinity, "For too long, this symbol has been imprisoned in misunderstanding. It is time to set it free to sing again."[50]

---

50. Johnson, "To Let the Symbol Sing," 311.

FOR FURTHER READING

Avis, Paul. *God and the Creative Imagination: Metaphor, Symbol, and Myth in Religion and Theology.* New York: Routledge, 1999.

Schaab, Gloria L. *The Creative Suffering of the Triune God.* New York: Oxford University Press, 2007.

Scott, Kieran. "Practicing the Trinity in the Local Church: The Symbol as Icon and Lure." *Review and Expositor* 99:3 (2002): 429–44.

INDEX

Note: An n following a page number indicates a footnote. Page numbers in *italics* indicate illustrations.

A

abortions, 106
accidents, 32, 34, 52, 131
Acts of the Apostles (Luke), 144–45, 153, 175
adoptionism, 125, 149, 229
Advocate (*advisor*), 143, 230
analogies and metaphors, 21, 23–24, 160–61, 164–65, 171, 183, 251. *See also* God, images of; symbols
analogy of being, 15, 17, 23–24, 133n24, 250
Ananxagoras, 35–36
"anatomy is destiny," 92n17
Anaximander, 35–36
Anselm of Canterbury, 126
ant colony example, 66
anthropic principle, 238–39, 245
Apollinarianism, 231, 233, 234
appropriations, doctrine of, 127, 146–48, 150, 156, 212, 327, 328
Aquinas, Thomas. *See also* participation; *specific works*
    analogies and, 160–61
    analogy of being and, 133n24
    creatio ex nihilo, on, 192
    dualisms and, 37, 42
    evolutionary worldview and, 24

    experience and perception, on, 19, 310
    grace, on, 268–69
    Holy Spirit, on, 154
    love, on, 133n25
    mission and procession, on, 139
    naming God, on, 13, 16–17, 328n47
    relationality and, 47–48, 156, 158
    relations of origin and, 132
    revelation through creation, on, 14–15
    substance, on, 42
    transcendence of God, on, 44n28
    Trinity and, 328
Arianism, 149, 229, 233, 234
Aristotle
    dualisms, on, 36–37, 42
    reality, on, 28, 29, 52
    relationality, on, 39
    substances, on, 31–32, 42
    Trinitarian theology and, 129
Arius the Antiochene, 124
ascetic attitude, 294
Athanasius of Alexandria, 124, 125, 231
atomic levels, 75, 272
At the Beginning of Life (Hui), 94
attraction, 302–3

Augustine of Hippo
  creatio ex nihilo, on, 192
  doctrine of appropriations and,
    148
  dualisms of substance, on, 42
  grace, on, 267–68
  hierarchy of being and, 41
  Trinity, on, 126, 131–34, 138,
    325, 328
  understanding God, on, 164
autonomy, 112–13. *See also* freedom

B

Bacon, Francis, 18
Barbour, Ian, 21, 179–81
Barth, Karl, 326, 327
Basil the Great, 40, 124, 125, 135
beaker of water example, 68
"Bearer of God," 232
beauty, 294
becoming, 38–39
begottenness, 134
being and beings. *See also* analogy
  of being; cosmos; human beings;
  ontology
  Being Itself and, 15–16, 160–61,
    175 (*See also* participation)
  Divine Matrix and, 299
  hierarchy of, 41–42, 43
  names of, 160
  nonhuman, 56
  reality and, 29–31
  relationality and, 40, 48, 49,
    51–54, 67–68, 77–78, 84,
    158, 182–83
Being in itself, 36
Being Itself. *See* God
Be-in-Relation, 27–54
Bénard phenomenon, 281
Benedict XVI, 253
Bergon, Henri, 196
Berry, Thomas, 195, 291–92

Bertalanffy, Ludwig von, 274
Bible, the. *See also specific books*
  grace and, 264–67
  images of Spirit in, 213–14
  Incarnation and, 225–29,
    246–47, 252–54
Big Bang, 21, 162, 195, 276
biological constitution, 93–95
biology, 71–72
Blamire, John, 79
bodies, 37, 42–43, 68, 89, 95–98,
  181, 230. *See also* dualisms;
  material bodies
Body of God, The (McFague), 255–56
Boethius, 89
Bohm, David, 83
Bohr, Neils, 75
Bonaventure, 192, 303
Bonting, Sjoerd L., 218
Bracken, Joseph, 159, 176, 205,
  283n64
Braden, Gregg, 283n64
Bradley, Larry, 287
brains, 20–21
*Breath of Life: Theology of the Creator
  Spirit* (Edwards), 219–22
Brierley, Michael, 178n37

C

Calvin, John, 263–64
Campbell, Donald, 280
Cappadocians, 135
care, 117
Carroll, William, 193
Carter, Brandon, 238–39
Catechism of the Catholic Church, 253,
  263, 299
categories, 32–33, 52, 70
Categories (Aristotle), 28, 34
causes, 15–16, 19, 30. *See also*
  relations of effect; whole-part
  interactions

chance, 61–64, 86, 198–99, 200–201, 207–8, 239, 272, 287n71
change, 38–39
chaos theory, 286–90
charis, 266
chemistry, 72–73
Childhood and Society (Erikson), 111n61
Christ. *See* Incarnation
Christian Faith, The (Schleiermacher), 121
Christology, 123, 240n35
Christotokos, 232
classifications, 32–33
coincidence of opposites, 244–45, 246
Colossians, Letter to (Paul), 228–29, 252
Comblin, José, 295
common story of creation, 57–58
communication, 97
communities, 114, 117, 153–54, 295, 316, 320–22
compassion, 255, 265, 297
competence, 115
complexity, 276–78
computers, 20–21, 67, 68, 301–2
consciousness. *See also* minds; personhood
  adolescents and, 116
  bodies and, 96, 97, 181
  emergence and, 65, 68, 236, 295
  evolution and, 183, 196, 236–40
  faith and, 302
  fetuses and, 94–95, 99
  God and, 134, 201–5
  grace and, 295
  Greeks on, 88
  Kant on, 37
  personhood and, 88–91, 181
  relationality and, 91, 93, 133, 330
  symbols and, 309, 313
  Trinity and, 133

Conscious Universe, The (Kafatos & Nadeau), 279
consubstantiality, 125, 241
contemplative attitude, 294
Copernicus, 18
Copleston, Frederick, 193
Corinthians, First Letter to (Paul), 252
cosmology, 29, 38, 41, 49, 53, 202, 203, 222, 301. *See also* cosmos; creation (act and immanence of God); relations of origin
cosmos (cosmic beings/nonhuman beings/nature/creation/reality). *See also* being and beings; cosmology; creation (act and immanence of God); ontology
  being and, 29–31
  creation (act of God) and, 189–223
  demise of, 274–75
  divine being and, 158–85
  evolutionary worldview and, 20–21
  God and, 24, 210, 280, 282
  grace and, 262–307, 271
  Greeks on, 30–31, 32, 35, 36
  Incarnation and, 224–61, 243, 255–56
  knowability of, 23
  language and, 20–22, 162–63, 183
  open system, as, 272–82
  quantum mechanics, relational, and, 76
  relationality and, 56–85, 156, 279
  relations of effect and, 84
  sacrament and symbol, as, 250–51
  suffering of, 247–48
  symbols and, 309
  theology and, 11–12

traditional doctrines, 28–29
Word theology and, 249–51
Council of Chalcedon, 46, 171,
230–31, 232–34, 245
Council of Constantinople, 124,
125, 231, 233
Council of Ephesus, 232, 233
Council of Nicaea, 124, 125, 230, 233
Cranach, Lucas, *311*–12
creatio continua, 203–5
creatio ex nihilo, 191–93, 203–5
creation (act and immanence of
God). *See also* cosmos; relations
of origin
contemporary theological
resonances, 215–22, 302–3
cosmos and, 189–223
deism and, 170
evolutionary worldview and, 23,
195–212, 203–7, 212
experience and, 21–22
freedom and, 302–3
God and, 12, 48, 133n24, 242
grace and self-communicating
God and, 284–86
Incarnation and, 259
informed universe and, 301
mission of, 256
nonhierarchical relationships
and, 316–17
panentheism and, 184
relationality and, 182–83,
193–95, 222–23
relation of effect, as, 147
relation of origin and, 49, 57–58,
193
revelation and, 13–16, 17, 23
Spirit and, 219
substance ontology and, 176
traditional images, revisions of,
207–11
traditional resonances and, 182,
189–93, 212–15

creativity
chance and, 201
consequences of, 202
deism and, 166
emergence and, 65–66
evolutionary worldview and, 200
pantheism and, 167
suffering and, 210–11
systems and, 276–79
Creator Spiritus (Creator Spirit), 15,
214, 217–18, 219–22
creed of Chalcedon, 233–34, 241,
245
Crick, Frances, 61
culture, 100, 102–10. *See also*
worldviews
"Culture and the Individual"
(Huxley), 102–3
Cyprian, 153
Cyril of Alexandria, 125, 232

D

Darwin, Charles, 18, 19–20, 58–61
de Chardin, Teilhard, 176, 196,
236–37
deep incarnation, 256–58
deism, 44, 165, 166, 180, 184, 197
Delio, Ilia, 302–3
Denbigh, Kenneth, 69
Dennett, Daniel C., 90–91
Descartes, René, 35, 37–38, 89
despair, 118–19
destruction, 211
Deuteronomy, Book of, 265
Devotions upon Emergent Occasions
(Donne), 39
diffusion (role confusion), 115–16
disease examples, 71
disorder, 278
dissipative structures, 198
diversity, 109–10, 207–8, 235, 236,
303, 324–29

divine being/ divinity. *See* God
divinization, 229, 263, 271
Divinum Illud Munus (Leo XIII),
　214
DNA, 61, 94, 200
Docetism, 230–31, 233, 234
doctrine of appropriations, 147–55,
　156
Dominum et vivificantem (John
　Paul II), 214–15
Donne, John, 39
double helix, 162
double movement theory, 254
double-slit experiments, *81*, *82*, *83*
doubt and shame, 112–13
"downward causation," 280–82
Do You Believe in God? (Rahner),
　294
Dreyer, Elizabeth, 294
Driesch, Hans A.E., 196
dualisms, 35–47, 53, 96, 230, 231
Duck, Ruth C., 326
Duffy, Regis, 315
dynameis, 136
dynamism, 277

E

earthquake example, 272
Eastern Christianity, 127, 135–37,
　214, 253–54, 263
　grace and, 271, 299
Easter Vigil, 151–52
Easter Vigil homily (2011)
　(Benedict XVI), 253
ecclesial writings, 214–15
ecological crisis
　attitudes toward Earth and,
　　41, 43
　contemporary theological
　　resonances, 216–18, 256,
　　294–95
　grace and, 291

nonhierarchical relationships
　and, 317
　Spirit and, 216
　traditional theological reso-
　　nances, 253
　Trinity and, 322
Economic Justice for All (U.S.
　Bishops), 323–24
economic status, 100, 108–9
Economic Trinity, 128–29, 137–38
education, 99
Edwards, Denis, 176, 177, 219–22,
　242, 258–60
effects. *See* causes; relations of effect
Eichhorn, Susan E., 276
Eigen, Manfred, 198–99
Einstein, Albert, 74, 197
electron example, 78–84
Eliot, T.S., 16
embodiment, 95–98
embodiment theology, 181
embryos, 94–95
emergence. *See* relations of
　emergence
empathy, 248, 318, 319
Empedocles, 35–36
English, Jane, 91
entropy, 274n37
environment, 98
environment *vs.* heredity, 92
Ephesians, Letter to (Paul), 229
Epictetus, 88
epistemology, 29
Epistles, 123, 153, 230, 266
Epistle to the Romans, 219
equality, 41–43. *See also* nonhierar-
　chical relationships
Erikson, Erik, 110–19
eros, 304–5
*An Essay Concerning Human Under-
　standing* (Locke), 90, 92n18
essences. *See also* ontology
　dualities and, 35

God, of, 15–16, 16–17
grace and, 271
relationality and, 51, 54, 56, 132
secondary substances and, 34
Trinity and, 125–26
Eternal, the, 294
ethical systems, 320–22
ethnicity, 99, 100, 103, 109–10
Eutychianism and Eutyches, 232,
234
Evert, Ray Franklin, 276
evil, 202, 248
evolutionary worldview (science).
See also Darwin, Charles; natural
selection; *individual scientists;*
specific sciences
Aquinas and, 24
consciousness and, 236–40
contemporary theological
resonances, 11–12, 18–24, 29
creation and, 212
creation (act and immanence
of God) and, 23, 195–212,
203–7, 212
creativity, 200
deism and, 166
emergence and, 50
freedom and, 207–11
God and, 24, 184
grace and, 282–98
hierarchy of being and, 41–42
Holy Spirit and, 217, 220
human beings and, 68–69,
235–40
Incarnation and, 235–40, 251,
260–61
language and, 18, 23–24
models and, 162
open-system universe and, 279
panentheism and, 170–71, 173,
182–83, 184, 281–82, 282–83
relationality and, 47–48, 49, 51,
53, 84–85, 182, 218–19

relations of effect and, 272
relations of emergence and,
64–65, 66–69, 84, 200
self-sufficiency and, 53
substance ontology and, 47
Trinity and, 130
experience and perception
Aristotle on, 31
electron example, 79–83
empathy and, 248
evolutionary worldview and,
19–20
grace and, 264
Kant on, 37
Locke on, 92n18
names and God and, 160–61
personhood and, 102
Plato on, 30–31
reality and, 34–35, 52
science and, 21, 74, 75, 76
symbols and, 309, 310
theology and, 19–20
Trinity and, 129–30, 137
understanding God and, 178–79
exploitation, 211
Exsultet (*hymn*), 151–52

F

faith, 302, 304
families, 99, 100–102, 117, 295
family of origin, 99, 100
Farmer, Rick, 299
Father, 148–49, 163–64, 283, 320.
See also God; Trinity
female/male dualism, 43. *See also*
gender
feminine images, 328. *See also*
gender; pregnant mother image
Fermi, Enrico, 78
Ferret, Juan, 77
fetus, 98–99
fidelity, 115

Fisher, Anthony, 95
flycatcher example, 70
Forms, 30. *See also* dualisms
freedom and free will
    chance and, 201
    consequences of, 201–2, 297
    creation and, 302–3
    Divine Matrix and, 297, 305
    ecological vulnerability and, 216
    evolutionary worldview and, 207–11
    grace and, 285–86, 297
    Information Incarnate and, 301
    love and, 181
    omnipotence and, 208–9
    Spirit and, 221
    traditional resonances and, 13–14, 206, 268
    Word theology and, 180
functional biology, 71

G

Galvin, John, 285
gays, 106–8
gender, 93, 99, 100, 105–8, 173–76, 328. *See also* pregnant mother image
genera, 34
generativity, 117–18
Genesis, Book of, 14, 190–91, 249
genetics. *See also* nature-nurture controversy
    chance and, 61–62, 64, 200
    environment and, 281, 289
    natural selection and, 61
    personhood and, 93–95, 97
    relation of effect and, 70, 72–73
    strange attractor and, 289
gnostics, 230
God (Being Itself/Being of God/ divine being/divinity). *See also* divinization; Father; immanence; matrix (cosmic/Divine); self-communicating God; transcendence of God; Trinity
    actions of, 12, 44, 145, 179–84, 203–4, 228 (*See also* creation (act and immanence of God); immanence; transcendence)
    being and, 15–16, 175 (*See also* participation)
    cosmic being and, 158–85, 24, 210, 280, 282
    creatio ex nihilo and, 192
    dualisms and, 43
    evolutionary worldview and, 24, 184
    goodness of, 161
    human beings and, 225
    images of-329, 324
    immutability and, 36, 39, 40, 43, 59, 131, 168, 180, 210, 244
    Incarnation and, 226–30, 247, 251, 259–60
    Jesus, of, 226–30, 247, 251
    knowledge of, 13–16
    logos and, 228
    metaphors for, 173–74
    metaphysics and, 30
    models of, 159, 162–64
    names of, 21, 159, 160
    open-system universe and, 280
    potentiality of, 245–46
    relationality and, 47–48, 51–52, 120–57, 137, 168–70, 239–40
    relations of emergence and, 156, 243–46
    self-sufficiency and, 40
    speaking rightly of, 13, 16–17, 23, 164–65
    terminology, inclusiveness of, 123n8
    Trinity and, 52, 134, 328
    union with the world of, 43

God for Us: The Trinity and Christian Life (LaCugna), 177
God Hides in Plain Sight (Nelson), 299
God in Creation (Moltmann), 192, 218
"God's Beloved Creation" (Johnson), 294
God's will, 297
goodness of God, 161
Gospels, 123, 150, 190, 266
grace
    contemporary theological resonances, 284–85, 292–96, 300–305
    cosmos and, 262–307
    evolutionary worldview and, 272–80, 286–92, 296–98
    evolutionary worldview and theology and, 282–98
    God and, 12
    panentheism and, 184
    relationality and, 162–63, 182–83, 264, 267–71, 305–7
    relation of effect, as, 263, 264, 265, 269, 280–82, 286–92
    self-communicating God and, 284–86
    strange attractor, as, 290–92
    traditional doctrines, 182, 263–71, 298–300
    traditional resonances, 298–300
    transcendence and, 292–96
gravity, 74
Greek philosophy, 88
"Green Face of God, The" (Wallace), 215–16
Gregersen, Niels, 256–57
Gregory of Nazianzus, 135, 136, 231
Gregory of Nyssa, 121, 135, 225
ground, 205–6
guilt, 113–14

H

Habel, Norman, 256–58
Haight, Robert, 263
Hamlet, prince of Denmark (Shakespeare), 27
Hartmann, Nicolai, 30
Haught, John, 176, 300–302
Hayes, Zachary, 249, 253
Hebrews, Letter to, 190
Hebrew scriptures, 189–90
Heisenberg, Werner, 50–51, 75
Heisenberg Principle (uncertainty), 75, 79, 180, 238
Heracleitus, 35–36, 228
heredity *vs.* environment, 92, 98. *See also* genetics
heresies, 124–25, 149. *See also specific heresies*
hesed, 266
heterosexism, 106–8
Hilary of Poitiers, 148
Hildegard of Bingen, 325, 327
Hilkert, Mary Catherine, 326
Hill, William, 137, 148
Hippolytus, 153, 230
historical periods, knowledge and, 29, 30
HIV/AIDS, 106
hnn, 266–67
Hodgson, Peter C., 303–5
Holiness of the Father, 136
Holy Spirit. *See also* Trinity
    Aquinas on, 154
    creator, as, 212–22
    divinity of, 125
    divinity of Jesus and, 229–30
    grace and, 271
    Incarnation and, 142–43, 143–45, 221
    mission of, 138, 141–46, 153
    names of, 159
    panentheistic interpretation, 212–13

personhood and, 142–46,
     152–53, 154
relations of effect and, 145,
     152–55
relations of emergence and, 156
sense perception and, 52
Trinity and, 124, 134, 215
Holy Trinity (Rublev), *311*–12
Homo sapiens, 61
hope, 211, 217–18, 242, 248, 298,
     319, 328n47
Hosea, Book of, 265
Hui, Edwin, 94, 96–98
Huineng (Buddhist Patriarch), 22
human beings. *See also* conscious-
     ness; personhood
     dualism of substances and, 42
     evolution and, 68–69, 235–40
     hierarchy of being and, 41
     Incarnation and, 225
     Jesus as, 230–32
     relationality and, 48, 86–119,
          156, 265–66
     Trinity, analogy to, 132–34
humility, 22–23, 226n6
hurricane example, 65, 67
Huxley, Aldous, 102–3
hypostasis (substance), 125–26, 127,
     135
hypostatic union, 46, 224, 232, 241

I

"I Can't Give You What I Haven't
     Got" (The Living End), 116
Ideas, 30
identities, 38–39, 90, 94, 97, 115–16
Identity: Youth and Crisis (Erikson),
     111n61
Ignatius of Antioch, 230
illiteracy, 106
immanence
     chance and, 208

creativity and, 204
defined, 45
deism and, 166
God, vulnerability of, and, 210
God and, 220–21
Holy Spirit and, 154, 212–15
logos, of, 228
Moltmann on, 218
panentheism and, 172, 178–79,
     184, 205–6
pantheism and, 167
pregnant mother image and, 175
Spirit and, 219, 221
suffering and, 211
theism and, 170
Immanent Trinity, 128, 129, 137–38
immutability, 36, 39, 40, 43, 59, 131,
     168, 180, 210, 244
impassibility, 210
Incarnation (Christ/Jesus/Son).
     See also Christology; hypostatic
     union; kenotic theology; Word
     (Logos) theology
     contemporary theological
          resonances, 254–61
     creation (act of God) and, 259
     deism and, 170
     divinity of, 121, 125, 229
     empathy and, 319
     ethical life and, 322
     evolutionary worldview and,
          235–40, 251, 260–61
     God the Matrix and, 283
     grace and self-communication
          and, 271, 284, 306
     Holy Spirit and, 142–43,
          143–45, *221*
     information and, 301
     mission and, 127, 138, 139–41,
          243
     names and, 21, 159
     nonhierarchical inclusivity and,
          315–16

oneness of God and, 124
panentheism and, 170–71, 172, 173, 178–79, 184
pantheism and, 167
personhood of, 149, 151
pregnant mother image and, 175
relationality and, 128, 182–83, 188, 229–34, 260–61
relations of effect and, 147, 149–50, 149–51
relations of emergence and, 156, 240–52
Strange Attractor and, 304–5
symbol, as, 310
traditional doctrines, 12, 182, 224–34, 242
traditional resonances of, 246–47, 252–54
Trinity and, 129, 134, 137, 280, 282
vulnerability and, 210
inclusivity, 315–17, 323
independence, 39, 113, 114. *See also* self-sufficiency
indeterminacy, 200–201
individualism, 322
individuality, 38–39, 88, 94
indulgences, 269, 270
industry, 114–15
inferiority, 114–15
Information Incarnate, 301–2
"informed universe," 301–2
initiative, 113–14
integrity, 118–19
intellect, 30–31, 36–37. *See also* consciousness; rationality (reason)
intelligent design, 197–98, 239
intelligentia sui, 133–34
intimacy, 116–17
Irenaeus of Lyons, 149n45, 191–92, 230

Isaiah, Book of, 24, 141–42, 147n42, 265
isolation, 116–17

J

Jesus. *See* Incarnation
John, Gospel of
 Holy Spirit, on, 143–44, 153
 Incarnation, on, 225, 227–29
 Jesus's actions, on, 155
 personhood of Jesus, on, 150
 self-communicating God and, 249
 Trinity and, 328
John, Letters of, 225, 230
John Paul II, 214, 253
Johnson, Elizabeth A.
 attitudes of grace, on, 294
 ecological context of, 216–18
 pregnant mother image and, 174
 speech about God, on, 13, 120–21, 313
 symbols, on, 313, 319, 329, 330
 Trinity and, 309–10, 326, 328
Judaism, 141–42, 146, 229, 240n35, 328
Judges, Book of, 214
justice, 295
Justin the Martyr, 149n45

K

Kafatos, Minas C., 279
Kant, Immanuel, 37
Kasper, Walter, 176, 177, 212, 326
Kaufmann, Stuart, 276, 277, 278–79
kenotic theology, 181, 226–27, 247–48
kinship, 316–17, 323
knowledge, 29, 30, 37, 133–34, *228*
Kochen, Simon, 76
Küppers, Bernd-Olaf, 237

L

LaCugna, Catherine, 127, 176, 177
language. *See also* symbols
    emergence and, 50, 54, 65
    evolutionary worldview and, 18,
       23–24
    Holy Spirit and, 145
    Johnson on, 13, 120–21, 313
    mystery and, 16
    Reality and, 183
    reality and, 20–22, 162–63, 183
    scientific *vs.* theological, 18,
       23–24
    social location and, 99
    Ultimate Reality and, 159–60,
       164–65
Lash, Nicholas, 326
LaViolette, Paul A., 276
law and chance, 61–64, 86, 198–99,
    207. *See also* natural law
Leadership and the New Science
    (Wheatley), 11, 76
Lee, Patrick, 95
Leo the Great, 148
Leo XIII, 214
liberation, 295–96, 319
life
    emergence of, 196–99
    meaning of, 28, 117–18
    relationship and, 11–12
linguistic theology, 180
liturgy, 214–15, 299–300
living in Trinitarian relation, 308–31
Locke, John, 90, 92n18
logos, 228–29
Logos (Word) theology, 180
Long, A.A., 89
Lorenz, Edward, 287–89
Loux, Michael J., 29
love
    chance and, 201
    charis and, 266
    cosmic matrix and, 291–92

    Erikson's stages and, 116
    God and, 13–14
    God as, 209–10, 210–11
    God's power as, 220–21
    Holy Spirit and, 153–55
    Incarnation and, 225
    self-transcendence and, 293–94
    Trinity and, 133–34
Luke, Gospel of, 163
Luther, Martin, 269–70
Lutheranism, 263, 269

M

Macedonius I of Constantinople,
    124
Macmurray, John, 101
Macquarrie, John, 326, 328
male/female dualism, 43
marginalized, the, 315–16, 322. *See
    also* poverty
Margulis, Lynn, 62
marriage, 99
Mary, mother of Jesus, 232
material bodies, 89, 91, 96, 171. *See
    also* bodies; Incarnation; minds
material substances, 53, 84, 191–92,
    196. *See also* dualisms; vitalism
material world, 203, 217, 222, 228,
    237, 250–51, 255, 295, 304
matrix (cosmic/Divine)
    being and, 299
    contemporary theological
      resonances, 302, 305
    cosmos and, 235
    Divine suffering and, 296–98,
      307
    freedom and, 305
    grace and, 262, 282–83, 285–86,
      290, 291, 293
    Incarnation and, 283
    love and, 291–92
    relationality and, 292

relations of effect and, 272, 307–8

relations of emergence and, 293

traditional theological resonances, 298–300

Matthew, Book of, 256

McFague, Sallie, 23, 161–62, 163, 176, 255–56

McKenzie, John, 266

meaning of life, 28, 117–18

memoria sui, 133–34

memory, 133

Mendel, Gregor, 61

metaphors and analogies, 21, 23–24, 161–62, 164–65, 171, 183, 251. *See also* God, images of; symbols

metaphysics, 29–30

migration of birds example, 71–72

Mills, David, 276

minds, 42–43, 45, 89. *See also* consciousness; dualisms; rationality (reason)

missions

creation (act and immanence of God), of, 256

Holy Spirit, of, 138, 141–46, 147, 153, 154, 155

Incarnation (Son) and, 139–41, 234, 243, 245

relationality and, 128

relations of emergence, as, 137–39, 156, 245

social, 322

Tertullian and, 327

Trinity and, 127

modalism, 125, 134

models, 21, 23–24, 159, 162–84. *See also specific models*

Moltmann, Jürgen, 176, 192, 218–19, 279

monophysitism, 124–25, 231, 232–33

monotheism, 123, 124, 131, 229

"Mother of Christ"/"mother of God," 232

Mühlen, Heribert, 326

mutation example, 200

"mutually illuminative interaction," 23–24

mystery

analogy and metaphor and, 133n24, 159, 162, 164–65, 183

cosmos (creation) and, 250, 282, 294

creation (act of God) and, 253, 303

God as, 13, 14

Incarnation (Christ/*Logos*/Jesus) and, 152, 226, 229, 242, 244, 250, 255, 258

panentheism and, 172, 179

paschal, 221

relationality and, 128, 324, 325

science and, 22–24, 79, 84, 197

self-revelation of God and, 327n44, 328

speaking rightly and, 16–17, 159, 164–65

symbols and, 309–10, 313

Trinity and, 122, 125, 126, 129–30, 131, 135, 137, 155

N

Nadeau, Robert, 279

names, 160

names of God, 13

"Naming a Quiet Revolution: The Panentheistic Turn in Modern Theology" (Brierley), 178n37

natural law, 20, 62–63, 196, 198, 199, 200, 207, 254, 272, 301

natural selection, 60–61, 239

natural world, 213–14, 216–18, 235–36. *See also* cosmos; ecological crisis; material world; pantheism

nature-nurture controversy, 92, 98. *See also* genetics

Nelson, Dean, 299

Neoplatonism, 123

Neo-Thomist model, 180

Nestorianism and Nestoris, 231–32, 233, 234

Newtonian physics, 73–75

Nicene Creed, 124, 125, 134, 146, 147, 148–49, 152, 214

Nicolis, Gregoire, 198, 277–78

nonhierarchical relationships, 315–17. *See also* equality

notions, 127

noumenon, 37

Nova (T.V. series), 65

Novatian, 153

O

O'Collins, Gerald, 142

oikonomia, 128

omnipotence, 208–10, 221, 248

"On Theology of the Incarnation" (Rahner), 243–44

On the Origin of Species . . . (Darwin), 19–20, 59

On the Trinity (Augustine), 126, 138

ontology, 25–26, 28, 29, 30, 38–47, 47–54, 77–78. *See also* being; being and beings; dualisms; essences; relationality (relational ontology); substances (substance ontology)

oppression, 43, 211, 323

Origen, 123

origin, relations of. *See* relations of origin

Other, the, 101, 245

ousia (essence), 125–26, 127, 135

P

Pailin, David, 167, 172

panentheism
    Christian, evolutionary and relational, as, 184
    creation and, 194–95, 205–6
    defined, 170–79, 184
    Edward's characterization of, 220n81
    evolutionary worldview and, 183, 281–82
    open-system universe and, 279, 280
    relationality and, 178
    Spirit in the cosmos and, 217
    suffering and, 219
    Trinity and, 179–83

pantheism, 45, 165, 166–67, 184

Papanikolaou, Aristotle, 271

Paraclete, 143

Parent and child model, 181

participation, 15–16, 48, 206, 250, 263, 271

particles, 42, 50–51, 57, 75, 78–79, 81, 83

Pascal, Blaise, 40

paschal mystery, 221

patriarchy, 173, 175

Paul of Samosata, 230

Paul of Tarsus, 266–67. *See also specific works*

peace, 295

Peacocke, Arthur
    creation, on, 57–58, 194
    intelligent design, on, 198
    models, on, 21
    omnipotence, on, 208
    pregnant mother image by, 174–75

principles of human knowledge of, 23
relationality, on, 87, 176–77, 194
Stent, on, 197
Pelagius, 267–68
Pentecost, 141–46, 214
peppered moth example, 63–64, 72, 281
perfection of God, 168–69, 244
perichoresis, 127, 128, 136
persona, 126
Person-body model, 181
personhood
    appropriations and, 156
    bodies and, 37
    defined, 87–91
    embodiment and, 95–98
    Holy Spirit and, 142–46, 152–53, 154
    Jesus, of, 150, 232, 233
    panentheism and, 184
    pantheism and, 167
    relationality and, 47–48, 91–92, 177, 239–40
    relations of effect and, 98–110
    relations of emergence and, 110–18
    relations of origin and, 93–98
    Son, of, 149, 151
    Trinity and, 126, 128, 148
Peter, Second Book of, 190
Phaedo (Plato), 28, 30, 36
phenomenon, 37
Philippians, Letter to (Paul), 150, 225–27
Philo of Alexandria, 228
Philosophiae Naturalis Principia Mathematica (Newton), 73
physics, 73–84
Plank, Max, 77
Plato
    dualisms of substance, on, 42
    Forms, on, 36

individuals, on, 39
ontology of, 28, 30–31, 52
stasis and, 39
Trinity and, 129, 131
pneumatology, 123
pneumatomachoi (*pneumatomachians*), 124, 125
political action, 295, 323–24
Polkinghorne, John, 201
Polycarp, 149n45
potentiality of God, 245–46
Poussaint, Alvin, 105
poverty (need/vulnerability), 108–9, 256, 265, 295–96, 323–24. *See also* marginalized, the
Power, David N., 316
pregnant mother image, 174–76, 221, 283, 320
prenatal influence, 98–99
Prigogine, Ilya, 198, 277–78
processions, 127, 128, 130–37, 134, 138–39, 156, 327
process theology, 181
productivity, 117
promise, 218
prophetic attitude, 294–95
prosōpeion (*prosōpon*) (person), 88
Protestant Reformation, 269
protopathy, 211, 317–19
Psalms, 162, 218, 266
psilanthropism, 125
psychosocial theory of personality development, 111–19

Q

qualities, 32, 34
quantum mechanics, relational (RQM), 76–84, 84–85, 130
quantum physics, 277, 279
quantum theology, 180
Quest for the Living God (Johnson), 216–18

R

race and racism, 99, 100, 103–5
radial energy, 196
Rahner, Karl
  images of Trinity of, 326, 327–28
  Incarnation, on, 243–44, 246,
    258–60
  self-communicating God, on,
    13–14, 17, 284–85
  transcendence, on, 296–97
  Trinity, on, 120, 128, 129–30,
    178
rationality (reason), 89–91, 101,
  102–3, 166, 228. *See also* intellect
Raven, Peter H., 276
reality. *See* cosmos
reason. *See* rationality
recapitulation, doctrine of, 136
relationality (relational ontology). *See also* relations of
  effect, emergence *and* origin
  basics, 25–26
  bodies and, 97
  creation and, 193–95, 219
  evolutionary worldview and,
    47–48, 49, 51, 53, 84–85, 182,
    218–19
  God and, 12, 17, 24
  individuals and, 39–40
  laws and, 62
  life and, 11–12
  mission of the Son and, 140–41
  ontology and, 25–26, 47–54,
    77–78
  open-system universe and, 279
  panentheism and, 170, 178–79
  personhood and, 47–48, 91–92,
    177, 239–40
  quantum mechanics, relational,
    and, 76
  stasis and, 39
  substance ontology and, 131–32
  symbol, as, 314–29

  traditional resonances, 47–48,
    177
  Trinity and, 128–30
relational quantum mechanics
  (RQM), 76–84, 84–85, 130
relational theology, 47–48, 181–82
relationships, human, 294
relations of effect, 53, 54. *See also*
  causes
  defined, 50–51
  deism and, 169–70
  Divine suffering and, 296–98
  doctrine of appropriations and,
    156
  emergence and, 69–70
  evolutionary worldview and, 272
  Father, of, 148–49
  Holy Spirit and, 145, 152–55
  open system of the universe and,
    280–82
  panentheism and, 184
  personhood and, 98–110
  relationality and, 54
  science and, 70–85, 87
  Son, of, 149–50
  traditional resonances, 15, 19,
    327–28
  Trinity and, 146–55
relations of emergence. *See also*
  strange attractors
  creativity and, 65–66
  defined, 50, 53–54
  evolutionary worldview and,
    64–65, 66–69, 84, 200
  freedom and, 206
  God and, 203, 243–46
  Holy Spirit and, 156
  human beings and, 86, 235–40
  Incarnation and, 240–52, 258–60
  life and, 196
  panentheism and, 184
  personhood and, 110–18
  systems and, 278

traditional resonances and, 327
Trinity and, 137–39
relations of origin
creation and, 84, 194
defined, 49, 53, 84
nonhuman beings and, 57–64
panentheism and, 184
personhood and, 93–98
processions and, 156
traditional resonances and, 327
Trinity and, 130–37
relativity (physics), 74, 77, 78
Religion and Science (Barbour),
179–81
Republic (Plato), 30
respect, 96–97
Resurrection, 248, 257–58
retirement, 118–19
revelation, 13–16, 17, 23, 137,
152–55, 218, 249–52
rhm, 266
Richard, Lucien, 208
risk, 181
Rogers, Carl, 102
role confusion (diffusion), 115–16
Romans, Letters to (Paul), 253, 270
Rublev, Andrei, *311*–12
Ruether, Rosemary Radford,
283n64
Russell, Letty, 326, 328
Russell, Robert John, 193

S

Sabellianism, 124
sacramental theology, 249–50, 254,
271, 299–300
sacred, the, 217
Sagan, Dorian, 62
sanctification, 127, 138
Sanders, Fred R., 138–39
Sayers, Dorothy, 326, 327
Schaab, Gloria, 326

Schaff, Philip, 136
Schleiermacher, Friedrich, 121
science. *See* evolutionary worldview
Scott, Kieran, 321, 322, 323–24
scriptures, 123n8. *See also* Bible, the;
specific scriptures
self-communicating God. *See also*
Word (Logos) theology
cosmos and, 17
Incarnation and, 259–60, 261,
271
missions and, 139
panentheism and, 183
Rahner on, 13–14, 17, 259,
284–86
relations of emergence and, 156
traditional resonances, 13–14,
249, 271
Trinity as, 329
self-consciousness, 133–34, 181
self-emptying theology, 181,
226–27, 247
self-knowledge, 133–34
self-love, 133–34
self-presence, 133–34
Self-Revelation, Divine, 327n44
self-sufficiency, 39–41, 52–53. *See
also* independence
self-transcendence, 202, 258–59,
263, 293–94, 298–99, 300. *See
also* transcendence of God
selves, 101–2. *See also* personhood
sexism, 106
sexuality, 97–98, 99, 322
Shakespeare, William, 27
shame and doubt, 112–13
Sheen, Fulton J., 326, 327
"Shepherd of Hermas," 229–30
She Who Is (Johnson), 328
signs, 250
Simpson, George, 236
sin and sinners, 267–69, 270, 298,
315–16

social location, 99–100
social systems, 100–102, 295
Socrates, 30
solidarity, 140, 317–20, 322
Son. *See* Incarnation
Soskice, Janet, 163
souls, 37, 38, 89. *See also* dualisms
space, 74
species, 34, 59
Sperry, Roger, 280
spiration, 134
Spirit. *See* Holy Spirit
spirit, 259. *See also* dualisms; minds;
    Spirit
stages of life (Erikson), 110–19
stagnation, 117–18
Stapp, Henry, 50–51
stasis, 38–39, 52
Stent, Gunther S., 197
Stephen, 266
Stephens, William O., 88
Stoicism, 228
Stoney, George Johnstone, 78
strange attractors, 286–92, 293, 294,
    295, 300, 303–5
St. Victor, Richard, 154
subjects, substances *vs.*, 47
subordinationism, 125, 134, 149
substances (substance ontology). *See
    also* dualisms
    Aristotle on, 31–42
    dualisms of, 35–47
    heresies and, 149
    Jesus and, 171
    ontology of, 53
    primary, 32–34, 52
    secondary, 33, 34, 52
    subjects *vs.*, 47
    theism and, 176
    Trinity and, 125–26, 131
suffering. *See also* compassion;
    marginalized, the; poverty;
    vulnerability

Divine, 209–11, 223, 247–48,
    296–98
Divine solidarity and, 140, 217,
    314, 317–20
dualisms and, 43
ethical and political systems and,
    320–21, 323–24
evolutionary theology and, 328
freedom and, 202, 305
human, 130, 179
Information Incarnate and, 302
Jesus, of, 150, 151, 257, 261, 263
Spirit, of, 216, 217, 221
Summa Contra Gentiles (*SCG*)
    (Aquinas), 15
Summa Theologica (*ST*) (Aquinas),
    14–15, 16, 19, 44n28, 47–48,
    139, 168, *192*
supervenience, 67
Swimme, Brian, 195, 291
symbols, 249–51, 254, 308–29.
    See also analogies; language;
    metaphors
sympathy, 297, 320
systems, 67–68, 76–78, 198, 237,
    272–82, 286–87

T

table fellowship, 315–16
tangential energy, 196
Tertullian, 123, 125, 325, 326–27
theism, 165, 167–70, 176, 180, 184,
    197
Theodotus of Byzantium, 229
theology. *See also individual theolo-
    gians; specific theological concepts*
    natural, 166
    relational ontology and, 47–48
    science and, 11–12, 18–24, 29
Theophilus of Antioch, 123, 191
theosis, 271
theotokos, 232

thermodynamics, laws of, 272–82
Thompson, Margie, *311*–12
Thomson, J.J., 78
Tillich, Paul, 239–40, 309, 326, 328
time, 74, 90, 139
transcendence of God. *See also*
    self-transcendence
    contemporary theological
        resonances, 283, 285, 302, 328
    creation and, 194–95, 206, 280
    creativity and, 204
    defined, 44
    Deism/Pantheism/Theism and,
        166–70
    experience and, 310
    grace and, 262, 282, 292–96, 306
    Incarnation and, 253, 255
    Jesus and, 140
    logos, of, 228
    models and, 160, 164
    mystery and, 13
    panentheism and, 170–75,
        178–79, 184, 205–6
    Plato and, 131
    pregnant mother image and, 175
    relations of effect and, 188
    suffering and, 318
    Trinity and, 129, 328
    vulnerability and, 210
transformation, 138, 295, 310, 311,
    320–24
Treatise on Man (Descartes), 89
Trinita (Thompson), *311*–12
Trinity. *See also individual persons*
    actions of, 181–83
    contemporary theological
        resonances, 121–22, 300
    creation and, 303
    ecological crisis and, 322
    ethical and political transforma-
        tion and, 320–24
    grace and, 271, 299
    Holy Spirit and, 124, 134, 215

open-system universe and, 280
panentheism and, 176–84,
    181–83
personhood and, 126, 128, 148
pregnant mother image and,
    175–76
relationality and, 41, 47–48,
    51–52, 128–30, 178–79
relations of effect and, 146–55
relations of emergence and,
    137–39, 246
relations of origin and, 130–37
self-communicating God and,
    329
Spirit and, 215
suffering and, 317–20
symbol, as, 309–10
traditional doctrines, 120–21,
    122–28, 324–29
unity of God and, 127–28
Trinity (Cranach), *311*–12
tritheism, 125, 134, 149
trust *vs.* mistrust, 112
truth, 22

U

uncertainty relation (principle), 75,
    79, 180, 238
union, 242
union of substances, 43–47, 53
Universe Is a Green Dragon, The
    (Swimme), 291
U.S. bishops, 323
utilitarianism, 322

V

violence, 211
vitalism, 196
voluntas sui, 133–34
vulnerability
    ecological crisis and, 216

God's, 181, 209–11, 221, 223, 255, 312
human, 256 (*See also* poverty)
love and, 181, 223

W

Wallace, Mark, 213–14, 215–16
Ward, Keith, 192
Washington Monument example, 168–*69*
Watson, James Dewey, 61
wave model of an electron, *80*
Wheatley, Margaret, 11, 76, 329
Whitt, Stephen, 81
whole-part interactions, 67
Winds of the Spirit (Hodgson), 303–5
Winkler, Ruthild, 198–99

wisdom, 16–17, 118–19
Wisdom of the Father, 136
women, 43, 99, 100, 105–8, 173–76, 328. *See also* pregnant mother image
Women's Learning Partnership (organization), 105
Word Day of Peace message (John Paul II), 253
Word (Logos) theology, 180, 227–29, 241, 249–52, 255–56, 303
worldviews, 165

Z

Zaner, Richard, 96
Zeno of Citium, 167
Zohar, Danah, 277